PEACE

A DREAM UNFOLDING

PEACE
A DREAM UNFOLDING

Introduction by
BERNARD LOWN, M.D. AND EVGUENI CHAZOV, M.D.

Co-Presidents
INTERNATIONAL PHYSICIANS FOR THE PREVENTION
OF NUCLEAR WAR
1985 NOBEL PEACE PRIZE LAUREATE

PENNEY KOME & PATRICK CREAN
Editors

A SOMERVILLE HOUSE BOOK PUBLISHED BY
Sierra Club Books
SAN FRANCISCO

Copyright © 1986 by Somerville House Books Ltd.
Photographs copyright © by the individuals and institutions credited on page 254.

Library of Congress Cataloging in Publication Data

Peace, a dream unfolding

1. Peace. 2. Nuclear disarmament. I. Crean, Patrick, 1949-
II. Kome, Penney. JX1952.P327 1986   327.1'72   86-42633
ISBN 0-87156-770-9   ISBN 0-87156-700-8 (pbk.)

Designed by David Wyman
Assistant Designers: Nancy Jackson and Maria Arshavsky
Project Editor: Sarah Reid
Picture Research: Cindy Deubel, Sandy Easterbrook, and Bernice Eisenstein
Text Research: Alberto Manguel, Gerald Donaldson,
Barbara Shainbaum, and Janis Alton
Typesetting by Trigraph Inc.
Set in Mergenthaler Palatino, 10/12

Printed in Canada by D. W. Friesen Ltd.

Produced by Somerville House Books Ltd.
24 Dinnick Crescent, Toronto, Ontario, Canada M4N 1L5

First Edition

Opposite title page: Keeping the Peace *by James Marsh, 1984.*

ACKNOWLEDGEMENTS

This book would not have been possible without the help of many people. The editors want to acknowledge the importance of their support. For their encouragement and advice, we wish to thank: Robert Penner, Professor Eric Fawcett, E. P. Thompson, Dr. George Ignatieff, Geoffrey Pearson, Beth Richards, Dr. Franc Joubin, Metta Spencer, Shirley Farlinger and *Peace* magazine, John Robert Colombo, David Pollock, Charis Wahl, Dr. Rosalie Bertell, Dr. Frank Sommers, Dr. Ian Hastie, Thea Jensen, Penney Hills, Julie O'Neill, Mildred and Murph Goldberger, Josette and Lowden Wingo, Rebecca and Arthur Mayeno, Kay Macpherson, Moira Armour, John McCuaig, Moe Foner, Rev. Seicho Asahi, Len Ackland, Sid Nagel, Linda Pulevski, Barbara Nagai, David Caspari, the Quaker-UN Liaison office, Toronto Friends' House, and all the organizations who co-operated with our requests for information.

For their invaluable contributions of material, we wish to thank Dr. Bernard Lown, Ruth Adams, Angela Knippenberg and the United Nations World Disarmament Campaign, Professor Delmar McCormack Smyth, Jack Overall, Mark Rogovin and the Peace Museum, Jon Lomberg, John Robertson, Joe Fisher, Setsuko Thurlow, Jim Thurlow, Dr. Tana Dineen, Margaret Atwood, Simon Dodge, Madge Strong, Nancy Erb, Lenore Young, and everybody else who passed along suggestions.

This book is the result of a team effort. Particular credit goes to designer and art director David Wyman, his assistants Nancy Jackson and Maria Arshavsky; project editor Sarah Reid; text researchers Alberto Manguel, Gerald Donaldson, Barbara Shainbaum, and Janis Alton; picture researchers Cindy Deubel, Sandy Easterbrook, and Bernice Eisenstein; and Douglas Pepper, editorial assistant. For editorial support and direction, special thanks to Danny Moses, Louise Dennys, and Malcolm Lester. One person in particular had the vision, courage, and determination to make this project a reality: Jane Somerville.

On a more personal note deep gratitude goes to Mary Crean and Bob Pond for their unflagging support, patience, and understanding over the past year during the long hours spent compiling this volume.

P.C. and P.K.

This book is dedicated

to my mother, Jane Kome Mather

P.K.

to the memory of my father, Gordon G. Crean,
and
to the memory of my father-in-law, Philip T. Kelly,
men of peace

P.C.

PEACE
A DREAM UNFOLDING

Published to celebrate
The International Year of Peace
1986

CONTENTS

Opposite: Drawing the Line in Europe *by Rafal Oblinski.*

FOREWORD

You hold in your hands a celebration of all that is finest and noblest in the human spirit, a celebration of the utmost to which human beings can aspire: bountiful peace and beauteous harmony for all living beings. People yearn for peace the same way they yearn for the other essentials of life: clean air and water, nourishing food, nurturing friendships, comfortable shelter, inspiring ideas, and happy, healthy children. Now we approach a turning point in history, where all of these essentials are threatened.

Peace is more than an absence of conflict, just as health is more than an absence of illness. In times of peace (as in times of good health), people tend to take it for granted. But when faced with its loss, we realize how precious it is, how little we understand our natural healthy functioning. Even a difficult illness may be easier to diagnose than the complex synergy of healthy, peaceful living. So, in this book, we have selected excerpts and images that document humankind's aspirations and successes.

Of course, the painful disruptions to peace are more obvious. War is unforgettable; any survivor emerges with indelible memories. Despite the more than 150 local wars since 1945, few people in the industrialized world have seen armed conflict since the Second World War. But some experts say that our international situation today amounts to a slow grinding war, a war of attrition and gradual poisoning of our minds and bodies. We have included descriptions of these low-level effects to highlight the importance of peace, and to reveal the imminent dangers which we can ignore only at our peril.

Hope can be our greatest ally in meeting the challenges of the end of the twentieth century. Anxiety and fear can only feed the paranoia that fuels the escalating nuclear tension. The threat will not go away if we ignore it; it will only grow more overwhelming. Constructive action is the best and only defence against paralyzing fear. One teacher found that all the children in her class were convinced that they would be destroyed in a nuclear war before they grew up – all the children but one. That child said confidently, "My dad is working every evening to prevent it."

Humanity's saving grace is that, in times of profound crisis, new perspectives are forged. In the midst of our trial by fire, we see again the power of individuals, ordinary and extraordinary people, to effect change. Since the industrial revolution, every generation has discovered and asserted anew its natural rights. "Justice and peace join hands," as the psalm says. We include examples of individuals' triumphs over the evils of slavery, feudalism, persecution of minorities, sexual oppression, and other obscenities, in order to show that human nature refuses to accept (for very long) such appalling cruelty.

Crisis contains the seeds of renewal. From the agony of the A-bomb victims at Hiroshima grew a world-wide awareness of the dangers of nuclear weapons, and a global conviction that they must never be used again. "Today the atomic bomb has altered profoundly the nature of the world as we know it," said Albert Einstein in 1946, "and the human race consequently finds itself in a new habitat to which it must adapt its thinking. . . . Today we must abandon competition and secure co-operation. . . . Past thinking and methods did not prevent world wars. Future thinking MUST prevent wars."

"It isn't enough to talk about peace," said Eleanor Roosevelt in 1951, "one must believe in it. And it isn't enough to believe in it. One must work at it." We document here the astonishing and unstoppable groundswell of people who have taken her words to heart, who have dedicated their every spare moment to building a new and better world beyond the possibility of war. Not surprisingly, more than half of these new crusaders are women. Partly this springs from an awareness that women and children would be the majority of casualties in modern warfare. Partly, the peace movement is a women's movement because women tend to think of the world as interconnected, whereas men tend to think of the world as competitive. As Einstein said, connections and co-operation are what we need today.

Our greatest enemies today are ignorance and indifference – not the human beings in other countries whose governments have the ability to launch their nuclear weapons. Perhaps the greatest promise of the peace movement is the way it crosses international borders and ideologies, overcoming ignorance by bringing people face to face. New ways of thinking and new ways of talking together are leading to new-found respect for our own worth. Assuming responsibility for our destinies and for our planet leads inevitably to enhanced self-respect and security.

Positive change is often invisible and its effects become apparent only in retrospect. People often ask, "But what can I do about the nuclear threat?" If everybody who reads this book takes one small step towards understanding, makes one small action for peace, we are that much closer to a better world for us all. "A bad peace is better than a good war," says the old Russian proverb. In a 1959 speech, Dwight D. Eisenhower foresaw the modern peace movement when he told world leaders that, "People want peace so much that one day governments had better get out of their way and let them have it."

P.C. and P.K.

INTRODUCTION

BY BERNARD LOWN, M.D., AND EVGUENI CHAZOV, M.D.,
CO-PRESIDENTS OF INTERNATIONAL PHYSICIANS FOR THE PREVENTION OF NUCLEAR WAR
NOBEL PEACE PRIZE LAUREATE

We live in an age of unprecedented uncertainty. Life on earth is perilously poised at the precipice of extinction. Never before has man possessed the destructive resources to commit global suicide. This fact, although widely acknowledged, is not fully comprehended. Our comprehension is defined by the boundaries of our experience and the world has never experienced the horrors of an all-out nuclear confrontation.

The twentieth century was ushered in with great excitement and hope that humankind would at last abandon the institution of war. The hope of a benevolent civilization was soon shattered in the blood-soaked trenches of the First World War. The "war to end all wars" claimed sixteen million lives and left embers which kindled an even more catastrophic conflagration.

Over the sorry course of five thousand years of endless conflicts, some limits had been set on human savagery. Moral safeguards proscribed killing unarmed civilians and health workers, poisoning drinking water, spreading infection among children and the disabled, and burning defenseless cities. But the Second World War introduced total war, unprincipled in method, unlimited in violence, and indiscriminate in victims. The ovens of Auschwitz and the atomic incineration of Hiroshima and Nagasaki inscribed a still darker chapter in the chronicle of human brutality. The prolonged agony which left fifty million dead did not provide an enduring basis for an armistice to barbarism. On the contrary, arsenals soon burgeoned with genocidal weapons equivalent to many thousands of World War Twos.

A recent authoritative study by the World Health Organization concluded that in an all-out nuclear war using only one-half of the world's nuclear stockpiles, over a billion people would be killed instantly, mainly in the United States, the Soviet Union, Europe, China, and Japan. More than a billion survivors would suffer serious injuries and radiation sickness, for which medical help would be either unavailable or unavailing. It is thus possible that almost half of all the earth's inhabitants would be killed in the immediate aftermath of a global nuclear war. Yet these grim and foreboding conclusions do not describe the full gravity of the consequences. Indeed the real situation is likely to be much worse.

Astonishingly, forty years into the atomic age, scientists are just discovering the unforeseen catastrophic global consequences of nuclear war. Nuclear explosions, particularly groundbursts, lift enormous quantities of fine soil into the atmosphere, causing what is commonly referred to as a nuclear winter. Survivors of a nuclear war would face extremes of cold; water shortages; scarcity or total lack of food and fuel; severe radiation exposure; chemical poisoning of the air, water, and food; raging epidemics; and unprecedented psychological stresses – all to be endured in a pall of pervading frigid darkness. The implications of these findings are as profound as they are disquieting. Extinction of our species cannot be excluded.

The notion is widespread that nuclear war will never happen. Common sense dictates that these weapons will never be used because they are capable of simultaneously inflicting genocide on the victim and suicide on the attacker. But the nuclear age demands different thinking. Although no national interest could justify nuclear war, sober appraisal suggests that if the present course of multiplying megatonnage continues, it will be little short of miraculous if we reach the end of the century, a mere fourteen years away, without a nuclear catastrophe. In no previous epoch were adversaries so continuously and totally mobilized for instant war. It is a statistical certainty that hair-trigger readiness cannot endure as a permanent condition. Furthermore, the unrelenting growth in nuclear arsenals, the increasing accuracy of missiles, and the continuing computerization of response systems all promote instabilities which court nuclear disaster by technical malfunction, by miscalculation, human aberration, or criminal act. The ever-decreasing time between missile launch and nuclear detonation relegates critical decision-making to computers programmed by fallible human beings.

The possession of nuclear weapons has been justified by the theory of deterrence. Such a view of human affairs has held sway throughout the ages. Unfortunately, this view has been consistently a prelude to war, not a guarantor of peace. No more untenable view of human affairs has ever gained such widespread public acceptance. In order to be effective, nuclear deterrence must operate perfectly and forever. No such expectations are possible for any human activity. The idea of inhibiting aggression by threatening to inflict unacceptable damage is jarring in its contradictions. How is one to account for an overkill capacity equivalent to more than one million Hiroshimas? A single modern submarine has close to eight times the total firepower of the Second World War. In this race the runners are no longer in control of their limbs.

This build-up is like a cancer, the cells of which multiply because they have been genetically programmed to do so. Pointing nuclear-tipped missiles at entire nations is an unprecedented act of moral depravity. The horror is obscured by its magnitude, by the sophistication of the means of slaughter, and by the language crafted to describe the attack – "delivery vehicles" promote an "exchange" in which the death of untold millions is called "collateral damage." How did we reach such a dangerous and tragic impasse? How can we justify world arms expenditures of close to $1,000 billion when forty thousand children die daily from starvation? The total cost of eradicating smallpox from this earth equalled what is spent during 150 minutes of the arms race. Providing access to sanitary water, the lack of which accounts for 80 per cent of all sickness, would require but five months of military expenditures. Technology was intended to serve human interests, to enlarge the domain of freedom against life's compelling necessities. It is clear that our technology is beginning to operate against our will and threaten our extinction.

There is an urgent need for new direction in combatting this suicidal race. It is not enough to beseech the leadership of the superpowers with specific reasonable proposals. A question needs pondering: how is it possible that a quarter of a century of negotiations, involving more than seven thousand sessions, did not result in the dismantling of a single major nuclear weapons system? In large part the absence of result relates to the very process of disarmament negotiations. They are held in secret, are snail-paced, are piecemeal, are controversial at every step, and are carried out by the wrong people.

A process of negotiation such as this has exerted adverse effects. It has fostered illusions that a serious effort was underway, that a bilateral commitment prevailed to reach agreement, that an accord would be reached expeditiously, and that nuclear overkill would be substantially reduced. Such views were tacitly or overtly encouraged by the negotiators. As people do not like to dwell on the unthinkable threat to their survival, their inherent optimism latched on to the promissory note of the negotiators, thereby diminishing their concern and involvement.

Also standing in the way of reasonable and direct negotiations for disarmament is our distorted view of the enemy. When we come around and try to face nuclear war we are entrapped in a sense of helplessness and terror with trench-like vision transforming the adversary into an implacable enemy at least ten feet tall and omnipotent.

The climate of fear and distrust leads to perceptual distortions with complex differences between diverse social systems reduced to martial combat between forces of good and evil. It has led to a state of jumbled intellectual incoherence. Any constructive utterance is deemed to be propaganda intended to dissipate the opponent's resolve. Furthermore, if it is good for them, then it is clearly bad for us. This zero-sum gibberish is part of the game-theory approach to nuclear-age strategy.

But there is a deeper reason for the dismal failure. Secret negotiations exclude what could be the critical force in disarmament negotiations – the everyday citizens who unambivalently desire peace, life, and a future. *Peace: A Dream Unfolding* documents and celebrates these everyday citizens – such as Samantha Smith and schoolgirl Katerina Lycheva who recently toured one another's countries to spread the message of world peace. As well, *Peace: A Dream Unfolding* presents the work of those celebrated individuals who have pursued humankind's enduring yet elusive passion to live in peace – artists such as Reubens and Picasso; great thinkers from Aristophanes to Freud; writers such as Tolstoi and Virginia Woolf. Their work contains lessons for us today. Without their examples and without the involvement of those whose lives are in jeopardy, nuclear disarmament negotiations will yield no substantive results.

What then are the elements of a more promising process? Simply stated, they consist of reciprocating initiatives set in motion by world public opinion. One or the other superpowers must be persuaded to launch a significant, independent, yet unilateral initiative. If this is matched, additional steps will be undertaken by each superpower.

The function of the International Physicians for the Prevention of Nuclear War (IPPNW) and other peace-related organizations is to help mold a climate of world opinion to encourage reciprocation. Instead of heightening confrontation, a competition is launched to reverse the arms race. The first step, though small, would diminish widespread resignation, passivity, and noninvolvement by millions of people. World public opinion would resume its appropriate role in compelling governments on this new course.

The IPPNW is in many ways a prototype of action for citizen groups. Doctors tend to be apolitical, involved in humane concerns in a private way, but rarely taking the step into the public forum. In spite of this tendency to prefer the private sphere of influence, over a hundred and fifty-nine thousand doctors in forty-nine countries are actively trying to influence their own governments and their patients. Interestingly, the public is beginning to listen not to the military experts but to the physicians who are the custodians of public health.

The IPPNW had its beginnings in 1966 when we by chance bumped into each other in an elevator in New Delhi. We began corresponding about medical matters and visiting each other's facilities. Although we do not agree on everything, we decided we should concentrate on the one thing we could agree on – telling the world what nuclear war would mean.

In December 1980, three American and three Soviet physicians met in Geneva, Switzerland, to lay the groundwork for IPPNW. The sense of this first meeting was tense and impatient, not because of ideological differences between us, but, paradoxically, because of our deeply shared conviction that no one knew how much time was available to avert the catastrophe; nor were there any guideposts to indicate when we had reached a point of no return. We were convinced that physicians could explain better than others that unless we change our present course, humankind belongs to the Red Book of Endangered Species. The essential principle we adopted was that controlling the nuclear arms race is an issue that must not be held hostage to any transient political difference nor to any other matters, irrespective of how vital they might seem; that we have credibility and effectiveness only if we scrupulously adhere to the province of our expertise as scientists and healers.

But let us reaffirm that public pressure and outrage toward the doomsday process is what generates and strengthens the peace initiative. Success in nuclear disarmament is not a destination, it is a journey of millions of people to assume governance over their right to survive. We must convince each generation that they are transient passengers on this planet earth. It does not belong to them. They are not free to doom generations yet unborn. They are not at liberty to erase humanity's past nor dim its future. Only life itself can lay claim to sacred continuity. The magnitude of the danger and its imminence must bring the human family together in a common pursuit of peace denied throughout this century. On the threshold of a new millennium the achievement of world peace is no longer remote. It is beckoned by the unleashing of the deepest spiritual forces imbedded in humankind when threated with extinction. The reason, the creativeness, and the courage that human beings possess foster an abiding faith that what humanity creates, humanity can and will control.

Peace: A Dream Unfolding should be read with this in mind. The brave and creative people from the past and present who have in their own way furthered the cause of world peace should be celebrated and serve as inspiration to all people. History proves that citizen involvement can accomplish what governments will not. We are living in an age where the alternative to peaceful coexistence is no existence, where peace can no longer be the preserve of politicians and generals, but must be the responsibility of everyone who treasures life.

Evgueni I. Chazov, M.D.   Bernard Lown, M.D.

THE DREAM

The first photographs of the earth taken from outer space reminded humanity of the beauties and the limitations that we all share. Ironically, the technology that renewed our sense of wonder also makes it possible to destroy utterly everything that we humans cherish. For what profiteth a people to gain such tremendous power and risk losing our bonds with one another – and with the earth?

Assuredly, those bonds do exist. Even though history books tend to read like a litany of conquest and bloodshed, overwhelmingly our kind has spent most of our short stay on this planet practising co-operation and helping one another. Wars make the history books precisely because they are drastic disruptions of our normal way of behaving – and because they're dramatic. In the same way that the male record of the world has overshadowed women's history, the record of violence has obscured the peaceful relations that truly characterize human organizations. Caught up in the anxieties and tensions of late twentieth-century life, it's important to remember that co-operation, not destruction, has gotten us this far.

For most aboriginal peoples, respect for nature animated every aspect of their daily lives. Living in harmony with their environment, dependent on one another for survival, they did perform war-like rituals (mostly as puberty rites) but abhorred wanton slaughter. Only what we call "civilization" brought us the curse of organized warfare on a mass scale.

"Love thy neighbour as thyself," is the central message of practically every major religion and every sacred Scripture. Early Christians took this literally, refusing to bear arms or take part in warfare. Philosophers, scientists, and moralists expressed the same theme, for purely practical reasons. Treating other people well is, simply, the surest route to a happy and healthy life – for the individual as well as for society. National borders may change, but this truth does not.

As nations struggled to define the rights of the state and the individual, smaller idealistic groups also set out to establish communities based on trust and neighbourly respect. While communities such as Hopedale emphasized personal responsibility to the community, uprisings such as the French Revolution stressed that the state must acknowledge that individuals also have rights. From these early dialogues and upheavals emerged the human rights that we enjoy today.

Throughout history, a few brave and far-sighted individuals have urged that a community of nations be established under one world government. Only in this century have national governments realized the merits of universal co-operation. Now that we all face a threat as devastating as the possibility of nuclear war, co-operation becomes essential for our global survival.

It takes courage to face these facts, to cry out for justice. It takes courage to try to re-organize our world to a more harmonious model. It takes courage to defy the conventions and institutions that lead inevitably to war. Yet we humans have courage aplenty, as shown by myriad examples of brave souls who refused to fight, even when threatened with death. We can all gain courage by reviewing what the best hearts and minds of our global heritage have expressed about the dream of universal peace, of trust, co-operation, and harmony.

P.C. and P.K.

Opposite: Detail of The Golden Age *by Jean Ingres, 1862.*

OUR HOME, OUR PLANET

Planet Earth

The most beautiful object I have ever seen in a photograph, in all my life, is the planet Earth seen from the distance of the moon, hanging there in space, obviously alive. Although it seems at first glance to be made up of innumerable separate species of living things, on closer examination every one of its working parts, including us, is interdependently connected to all the other working parts. It is, to put it one way, the only truly closed ecosystem any of us knows about. To put it another way, it is an organism. It came alive, I shall guess, 3.8 billion years ago today, and I wish it a happy birthday and a long life ahead, for our children and their grandchildren and theirs and theirs.

Lewis Thomas

Beyond Borders

When you go around the Earth in an hour and a half, you begin to recognize that your identity is with that whole thing. And that makes a change.

You look down there and you can't imagine how many borders and boundaries you cross, again and again and again, and you don't even see them. There you are – hundreds of people in the Mid-East killing each other over some imaginary line that you're not even aware of, that you can't see. And from where you see it, the thing is a whole, and it's so beautiful. You wish you could take one in each hand, one from each side in the various conflicts, and say, "Look. Look at it from this perspective. Look at that. What's important?"

And a little later on, your friend, again one of those same neighbors, the person next to you, goes out to the moon. And now he looks back and he sees the Earth not as something big, where he can see the beautiful details, but now he sees the Earth as a small thing out there. And the contrast between that bright blue and white Christmas tree ornament and the black sky, that infinite universe, really comes through, and the size of it, the significance of it. It is so small and so fragile and such a precious little spot in that universe that you can block it out with your thumb, and you realize that on that small spot, that little blue and white thing, is everything that means anything to you – all of history and music and poetry and art and death and birth and love, tears, joy, games, all of it on that little spot out there that you can cover with your thumb. And you realize from that perspective that you've changed, that there's something new there, that the relationship is no longer what it was.

Russell Schweickart, Astronaut

A Sense of Wonder

In the photographs of the earth from space the planet looks like a little thing that I might hold in the hollow of my hand. I can imagine it would feel warm to the touch, vibrant and sensitive. Born of stardust, this handful of matter has evolved throughout the eons of geologic time. Like a butterfly taking shape within its chrysalis, the parts have rearranged themselves, taking on new forms. Diversity has increased, and simplicity has given way to elaborately integrated complexity. Beneath the mobile membrane of cloud and air are a storehouse of splendors and a wealth of delicate detail. There are rainbows caught in waterfalls, and frost flowers etched on windowpanes, and drops of dew scattered like jewels on meadow grass, and honeycreepers singing in the jacaranda tree.

Time flows on . . . the planet continues to spin on its path through the unknown reaches of space. We cannot guess its destination or its destiny. This beautiful blue bubble of matter holds many wonders still unrealized and a mysterious future waiting to unfold.

Louise B. Young

Reclining Buddha by Nehanno Shaka.

The Way of Peace

I do my utmost to attain emptiness;
I hold firmly to stillness.
The myriad creatures all rise together
and I watch their return.
The teeming creatures
All return to their separate roots.
Returning to one's roots is known as stillness.
This is what is meant by returning to one's destiny.
Returning to one's destiny is known as the constant.
Knowledge of the constant is known as discernment.
Woe to him who wilfully innovates
While ignorant of the constant,
But should one act from knowledge of the constant,
One's action will lead to impartiality,
Impartiality to kingliness,
Kingliness to heaven,
Heaven to the way,
The way to perpetuity,
And to the end of one's days one will meet with no danger.

Lao Tzu (6th century B.C.)

The Ultimate Issue

No other generation has inherited this enormous responsibility and the privilege of saving all past and all future generations, all animals and all plants. Think of the enormous variety of delicate butterflies; think of the gorgeous birds of the earth, of the endless designs of fish in the sea; think of the beautiful and exotic flowers with their gorgeous and seductive perfumes; think of the proud lions and tigers and of the wondrous prehistoric elephants and hippopotamuses; think of what we are about to destroy.

Rapid nuclear disarmament is the ultimate issue of preventive medicine.

It is the ultimate parenting issue.

It is the ultimate Republican and ultimate Democratic issue.

It is the ultimate patriotic issue.

Above all, it is the ultimate religious issue.

We are the curators of life on earth; we hold it in the palms of our hands. Can we evolve spiritually and emotionally in time to control the overwhelming evil that our advanced and rational intellect has created? We will know the answer to this question in our lifetime. This generation will die having discovered the answer.

Helen Caldicott

Iris, Messenger of the Gods *by Auguste Rodin, 1890-1891. Iris is also the messenger of peace.*

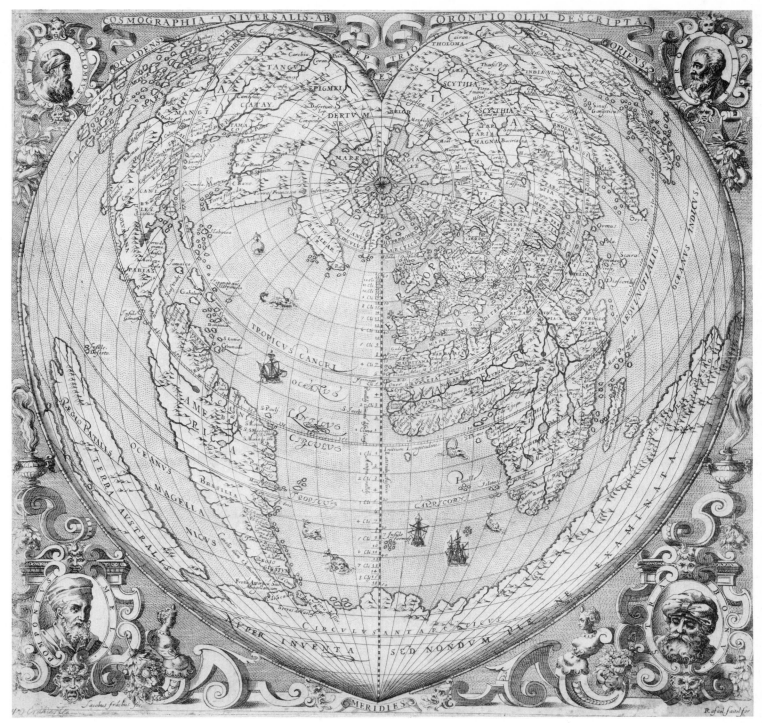

Coriform world map believed to have been engraved in Venice by Giacomo Franco in 1586-87.

The Spirit of Earth

The phrase "Sense of Earth"
    should be understood to mean
        the passionate concern for our common destiny
            which draws the thinking part of life
                    ever further onward.
In principle
    there is no feeling which has
            a firmer foundation in nature,
                or greater power.

But in fact there is also no feeling
    which awakens so belatedly,
since it can become explicit only
when our consciousness has expanded beyond the broadening,
but still far too restricted, circles of family, country and race,
            and has finally discovered
    that the only truly natural and real human Unity
                    is the Spirit of Earth.

Pierre Teilhard de Chardin (1881-1955)

Seeds of Renewal

The potential for rescue at this time of crisis is neither luck, coincidence, nor wishful thinking. Armed with a more sophisticated understanding of how change occurs, we know that the very forces that have brought us to planetary brinksmanship carry in them the seeds of renewal. The current disequilibrium – personal and social – foreshadows a new kind of society. Roles, relationships, institutions, and old ideas are being reexamined, reformulated, redesigned.

For the first time in history, humankind has come upon the control panel of change – an understanding of how transformation occurs. We are living in *the change of change,* the time in which we can intentionally align ourselves with nature for rapid remaking of ourselves and our collapsing institutions.

The [new] paradigm sees humankind embedded in nature. It promotes the autonomous individual in a decentralized society. It sees us as stewards of all our resources, inner and outer. It says that we are *not* victims, not pawns, not limited by conditions or conditioning. Heirs to evolutionary riches, we are capable of imagination, invention, and experiences we have only glimpsed.

Human nature is neither good nor bad but open to continuous transformation and transcendence. It has only to discover itself. The new perspective respects the ecology of everything: birth, death, learning, health, family, work, science, spirituality, the arts, the community, relationships, politics.

Marilyn Ferguson

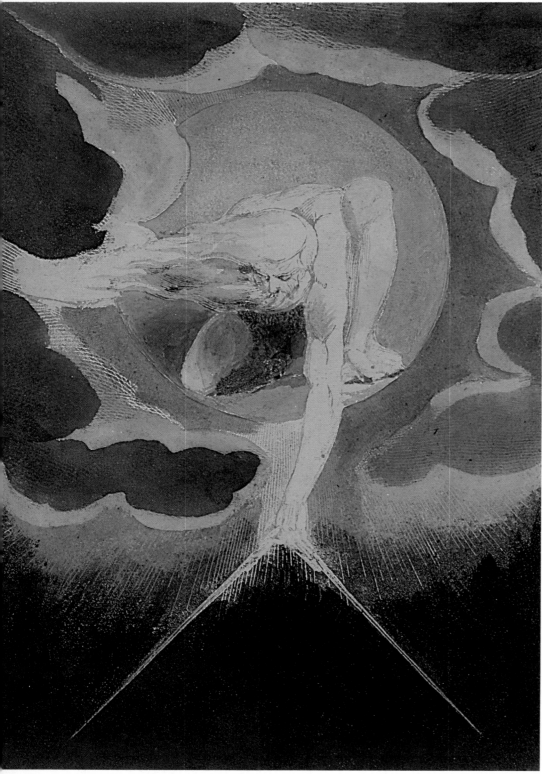

The Ancient of Days *by William Blake, 1794.*

Planet Under Threat

In the past, it was possible to destroy a village, a town, a region, even a country. Now it is the whole planet that has come under threat. This fact should fully compel everyone to face a basic moral consideration; from now on, it is only through a conscious choice and then deliberate policy that humanity can survive.

Pope John Paul II, Speech at Hiroshima

Through Conscious Choice

The conscious choice to take responsibility for the continuation of human life is further complicated by the fact that we are able to respond to it only before it happens. Since after extinction no one will be present to take responsibility, we have to take full responsibility now.

Jonathan Schell

Save Our Planet, Save Our Air *by Georgia O'Keeffe, 1971.*

To Whom We Are Beholden

What has evolved on our planet is not just life, not just grass or mice or beetles or microbes, but beings with a great intelligence, with a capacity to anticipate the future consequences of present actions, with the ability even to leave their home world and seek out life elsewhere. What a waste it would be if, after four billion years of tortuous biological evolution, the dominant organism on the planet contrived its own annihilation. No species is guaranteed its tenure on this planet. And we've been here for only about a million years, we, the first species that has devised the means for its self-destruction. I look at those other worlds, cratered, airless, cold, here and there coated with a hopeful stain of organic matter, and I remind myself what an astonishing thing has happened here. How privileged we are to live, to influence and control our future. I believe we have an obligation to fight for that life, to struggle not just for ourselves, but for all those creatures who came before us, and to whom we are beholden, and for all those who, if we are wise enough, will come after us. There is no cause more urgent, no dedication more fitting for us than to strive to eliminate the threat of nuclear war. No social convention, no political system, no economic hypothesis, no religious dogma is more important.

Carl Sagan

Part of the Whole

A human being is part of the whole, called by us the universe. A part limited in time and space. He experiences himself, his thoughts and feelings, as something separate from the rest, a kind of optical delusion of his consciousness. This delusion is a kind of prison for us, restricting us to our personal desires and to affection for a few persons nearest to us. Our task must be to free ourselves from this prison by widening our circle of compassion to embrace all living creatures.

Albert Einstein

NATURE'S WIDE DOMAIN

The Virgin Earth, *mural by Diego Rivera, 1929.*

Like to Like

Animals destitute of reason live with their own kind in a state of social amity. Elephants herd together; sheep and swine feed in flocks; cranes and crows take their flight in troops; storks have their public meetings to consult previously to their emigration, and feed their parents when unable to feed themselves; dolphins defend each other by mutual assistance; and everybody knows, that both ants and bees have respectively established by general agreement, a little friendly community.

But I need dwell no longer on animals, which, though they want reason, are evidently furnished with sense. In trees and plants one may trace the vestiges of amity and love. Many of them are barren, unless the male plant is placed on their vicinity. The vine embraces the elm, and other plants cling to the vine. So that things which have no powers of sense to perceive any thing else, seem strongly to feel the advantages of union.

But plants, though they have not powers of perception, yet, as they have life, certainly approach very nearly to those things which are endowed with sentient faculties. What then is so completely insensible as stony substance? Yet even in this, there appears to be a desire of union. Thus the lodestone attracts iron to it, and holds it fast in its embrace, when so attracted. Indeed, the attraction of cohesion, as a law of love, takes place throughout all inanimate nature.

I need not repeat, that the most savage of the savage tribes in the forest, live among each other in amity. Lions show no fierceness to the lion race. The boar does not brandish his deadly tooth against his brother boar. The lynx lives in peace with the lynx. The serpent shews no venom in his intercourse with his fellow serpent; and the loving kindness of wolf to wolf is proverbial.

Desiderius Erasmus (1465-1536)

The Lake Isle of Innisfree

I will arise and go now, and go to Innisfree,
And a small cabin build there, of clay and wattles made:
Nine bean-rows will I have there, a hive for the honeybee,
And live alone in the bee-loud glade.

And I shall have some peace there, for peace comes dropping slow,
Dropping from the veils of the morning to where the cricket sings;
There midnight's all a glimmer, and noon a purple glow,
And evening full of the linnet's wings.

I will arise and go now, for always night and day
I hear lake water lapping with low sounds by the shore;
While I stand on the roadway, or on the pavements grey,
I hear it in the deep heart's core.

W. B. Yeats (1865-1939)

Supernature

There is life on earth – one life, which embraces every animal and plant on the planet. Time has divided it up into several million parts, but each is an integral part of the whole. A rose is a rose, but it is also a robin and a rabbit. We are all of one flesh, drawn from the same crucible.

There are ninety-two chemical elements that occur in nature, but the same small selection of sixteen form the basis of all living matter. One of the sixteen, carbon, plays a central role because of its ability to form complex chains and rings that can be built into an immense number of compounds. And yet, from the thousands of possible combinations, just twenty amino acids are singled out as the units of construction for all proteins. Most significant of all, these proteins are produced in the right place at the right time by an ordered sequence of events governed by a code carried in just four molecules, called nucleotide bases. This is true whether the protein is destined to become a bacterium or a Bactrian camel. The instructions for all life are written in the same simple language.

The activities of life are governed by the second law of thermodynamics. This says that the natural state of matter is chaos and that all things tend to run down and become random and disordered. Living systems consist of highly organized matter; they create order out of disorder, but it is a constant battle against the process of disruption. Order is maintained by bringing in energy from outside to keep the system going. So biochemical systems exchange matter with their surroundings all the time, they are open, thermodynamic processes, as opposed to the closed, thermostatic structure of ordinary chemical reactions.

This is the secret of life. It means that there is a continuous communication not only between living things and their environment, but among all things living in that environment. An intricate web of interaction connects all life into one vast, self-maintaining system. Each part is related to every other part and we are all part of the whole, part of Supernature.

Lyall Watson

The Large Tuft of Grass *by Albrecht Dürer, 1513.*

"The Music of the Spheres" from Gafurius's Practica Musice, *1496.*

The Fundamental Unity

It is even possible that recognition of our environmental interdependence can do more than save us, negatively, from the final folly of war. It could, positively, give us that sense of community, of belonging and living together, without which no human society can be built up, survive, and prosper. Our links of blood and history, our sense of shared culture and achievement, our traditions, our faiths are all precious and enrich the world with the variety of scale and function required for every vital ecosystem. But we have lacked a wider rationale of unity. Our prophets have sought it. Our poets have dreamed of it. But it is only in our own day that astronomers, physicists, geologists, chemists, biologists, anthropologists, ethnologists, and archaeologists have all combined in a single witness of advanced science to tell us that, in every alphabet of our being, we do indeed belong to a single system, powered by a single energy, manifesting a fundamental unity under all its variations, depending for its survival on the balance and health of the total system.

If this vision of unity – which is not a vision only but a hard and inescapable scientific fact – can become part of the common insight of all the inhabitants of planet Earth, then we may find that, beyond all our inevitable pluralisms, we can achieve just enough unity of purpose to build a human world.

Barbara Ward and René Dubos

Landscape in Spring *by Milan Rasic, born 1931 in Zagreb, Yugoslavia.*

Making Action Possible

One way we can understand the human past is to view it as the history of our increasing consciousness both of ourselves and of the natural world of which we are a part, as the history of our increasing awareness of the self and our increasing understanding of the universe within which each self exists and has significance. We can think of the evolution of life on this planet as a process within which life itself, as evolved and manifested in human beings, has taken over the direction of its own course. In such terms, we can think of ourselves as on something like a man-made spaceship, or we can recognize that we live within a biological system and that, however

much we may probe its nature and systematize our understanding of it, however much we imitate it and improve upon it, we cannot claim credit for bringing it into existence. We can treat this Planet Earth like an expendable machine, or we can recognize that our dignity is dependent upon the respect we pay to the origins of our earthly life and upon the responsibility we take for its preservation....

Because of . . . new ways of recording and communicating, we have an opportunity to correct our mistakes, to take another breath, and, with a wider understanding of the needs of the whole world than human beings have

ever had, to begin to re-create within creation a human way of life which echoes not a few lanes and hedgerows, a few miles of reef where seashells are gathered, nor a mountaintop where a few cling to a precarious existence, but a planet whose boundaries we have come to know, whose inhabitants we have seen, and whose lives we have begun to bring into our imaginations as never before.

But what we need most are ways of thinking and acting through which we will not be overwhelmed by increasing scale, nor driven to despair or cruel indifference by the magnitudes with which we must deal. This is a central problem for us who are conscious and sentient beings, living in the midst of an evolutionary process with a beginning on this planet which we can only guess at and a future for which we must take responsibility without being able to know in what direction it may go. The importance of each daily act – rising in the morning to the day's tasks, spending an hour explaining to a sick child in a hospital how a caterpillar turns into a butterfly, sending a few dollars to relieve famine in another part of the world – have to be brought into relationship with our decisions to build more and more missiles or to consign a million tons of grain to one country instead of another. If we can see the Nigerian fishermen with their age-old nets, the Balinese farmer plowing his land for the planting of rice, and the hungry child in India, all as parts of a whole of which we are, not distant spectators, but a part; if we can see not only power-hungry manipulators, on the one hand, and oppressed and dying people, on the other, but both – and all – caught in the same moment in history, a moment when the whole future of life on the earth, and even possibly life in the galaxy, or the universe, is at stake, the very vastness of the process can ennoble the smallest hope, deflate the most grandiose dream of world dominion, and reduce species-wide guilt to human scale, making possible action by human beings on behalf of human beings.

Margaret Mead (1901-1978)

The Peaceable Kingdom *by Edward Hicks,* c. 1834.

Human Progress

One is drawn into conservation in any number of ways. A farmer becomes aware of soil erosion and soil depletion and water shortages; an angler becomes aware of water pollution and eutrophication, hydro dams, and over-fishing; a bird-watcher notices the steady disappearance of the habitats that sustain his objects of interest, and the poisoning of those natural habitats that do remain. The common factor in all of these environmental changes is man.

Something in the biosphere is drastically out of synchronization with everything else. That *something* is man. One need not be a prophet of doom, nor even a mildly conventional pessimist, to see that there are components in the biospheric life system which are dangerously out of

hand, and that time to restore the bond with nature is limited.

I have spent a lifetime in conservation affairs and have gradually but inescapably been convinced that up until the present time all we conservationists have been able to achieve is to fight a delaying action. The best we have been able to accomplish has been the temporary treatment of symptoms. We have not reached the root cause of environmental distress, which is Western industrial man.

Western civilized society appears to be indifferent toward nonhuman nature. We have seen the bison, the trumpeter swan, and the bighorn sheep fall before the gunners; we have seen the prairie dog, the black-footed ferret and the whooping crane give way

before the sod-busters; we have seen the giant baleen whales reduced to the vanishing point by international commercial greed. Most significant of all, perhaps, has been the unchanging traditional assumption that although the loss of these animals may well have been regrettable, it was inevitable and unavoidable in the context of the advancement of human progress. . . .

What is relevant is that, if for no other reason than his own survival, man must soon adopt an *ethic* toward the environment. "The environment" encompasses all nonhuman elements in the one and only home we have on Earth.

John A. Livingston

TOUCH THE EARTH

One of Nature's Children

I was born in *Nature's wide domain!* The trees were all that sheltered my infant limbs – the blue heavens all that covered me. I am one of Nature's children; I have always admired her; she shall be my glory; her features – her robes, and the wreath about her brow – the seasons – her stately oaks, and the evergreen – her hair, ringlets over the earth – all contribute to my enduring love of her; and wherever I see her, emotions of pleasure roll in my breast, and swell and burst like waves on the shores of the ocean, in prayer and praise to Him who has placed me in her hand. It is thought great to be born in palaces, surrounded with wealth – but to be born in Nature's wide domain is greater still!. . .

I remember the tall trees, and the dark woods – the swamp just by, where the little wren sang so melodiously after the going down of the sun in the west – the current of the broad river Trent – the skipping of the fish, and the noise of the rapids a little above. It was here I first saw the light; a little fallen down shelter, made of evergreens, and a few dead embers, the remains of the last fire that shed its genial warmth around, were all that marked the spot. When I last visited it, nothing but fur poles stuck in the ground, and they were leaning on account of decay. Is this dear spot, made green by the tears of memory, any less enticing and hallowed than the palaces where princes are born? I would much more glory in this birthplace, with the broad canopy of heaven above me, and the giant arms of the forest trees for my shelter, than to be born in palaces of marble, studded with pillars of gold! Nature will be Nature still, while palaces shall decay and fall in ruins. Yes, Niagara will be Niagara a thousand years hence! The rainbow, a wreath over her brow, shall continue as long as the sun, and the flowing of the river – while the work of art, however impregnable, shall in atoms fall!

George Copway (1818-1869),
Ojibwa minister and first Canadian Indian
to publish a book in English

A carved lintel at the entrance to a Maori assembly house shows a Clan Mother motif.

I Am Tied to the Earth

I suppose the first thing I must have seen was the thatched roof over my head, or closer, my mother's face bending over me. The house was the royal dwelling of the chief family of the Sousou tribe. My mother, Matara, was next in line of succession to the throne. . . .

Our tribal system was matriarchal. Grandfather sat on the throne because there was no female successor for the office in his mother's family. Ruling rights as well as property rights descended through women. I was my mother's second child. . . .

I was about six when my grandmother first made alive for me, by her telling of it, the events of the night of my birth. Grandmother told me that first time, and many times afterwards, how she had sat in an adjoining room with others of the family and waited with bowed heads while the midwives did what they could for my mother. . . .

The waiting ones heard a great roar in the distance then, the roar of a storm lashing through the jungle. A whip of lightning cracked across the black sky. A great thunder bellowed and the earth trembled. The lightning-torn clouds drenched the earth with loosened rain.

The midwife closed the door on the downpour. She smiled. It was a good sign that the clouds were delivered of rain.

There was a faint undersound beneath the din of the storm. It might have been the bleat of a baby goat caught in a drenching of rain-water from the eaves. It came again, unmistakably the whimper of a baby. The waiting ones hurried into the room where the woman lay.

"Modupe Olorun! – I thank God," the woman sighed. My name had been called – Modupe. It is the custom of our people to name children for the first significant words spoken or the first important object noticed after a birth. I was named out of my mother's gratitude. . . .

The placenta must be buried with ceremony in the compound with the witch-doctor present. As the navel cord ties an unborn child to the womb, so does the buried cord tie the child to the land, to the sacred earth of the tribe, to the Great Mother Earth. If the child ever leaves the place, he will come home again because the tug of this cord will always pull him toward his own.

When I go home I shall stand on the spot where the waiting ones stood that night in the storm and I shall speak these words: "My belly is this day reunited with the belly of my Great Mother, Earth!"

Prince Modupe

Watching the Dancers *by Edward S. Curtis.*

Lament for the Earth

The White people never cared for land or deer or bear. When we Indians kill meat, we eat it all up. When we dig roots we make little holes. When we build houses, we make little holes. When we burn grass for grasshoppers, we don't ruin things. We shake down acorns and pinenuts. We don't chop down the trees. We only use dead wood. But the White people plow up the ground, pull down the trees, kill everything. The tree says, "Don't. I am sore. Don't hurt me." But they chop it down and cut it up. The spirit of the land hates them. They blast out trees and stir it up to its depths. They saw up the trees. That hurts them. The Indians never hurt anything, but the White people destroy all. They blast rocks and scatter them on the ground. The rock says, "Don't. You are hurting me." But the White people pay no attention. When the Indians use rocks, they take little round ones for their cooking. . . . How can the spirit of the earth like the White man? . . . Everywhere the White man has touched, it is sore. . . .

Old Wintu Holy Woman (California)

Indian Peace Song

The clear sky,
The green fruitful earth is good;
But peace among men is better.

Wawan Song

Hopi Prayer

He goes to the edge of the cliff and turns his face to the rising sun and scatters the sacred corn-meal. Then he prays for all the people. He asks that we may have rain and corn and melons, and that our fields may bring us plenty. But these are not the only things he prays for. He prays that all the people may have health and long life and be happy and good in their hearts. And Hopis are not the only people he prays for. He prays for everybody in the whole world – everybody. And not people alone; Lololomai prays for all the plants. He prays for everything that has life. That is how Lololomai prays.

Chief Lololomai (*c.* 1900)

I Have Spoken

You ask me to plow the ground! Shall I take a knife and tear my mother's bosom? Then when I die she will not take me to her bosom to rest.

You ask me to dig for stone! Shall I dig under her skin for her bones? Then when I die I can not enter her body to be born again.

You ask me to cut grass and make hay and sell it, and be rich like white men! But how dare I cut off my mother's hair?

It is a bad law and my people can not obey it. I want my people to stay with me here. All the dead men will come to life again. Their spirits will come to their bodies again. We must wait here in the homes of our fathers and be ready to meet them in the bosom of our mother.

Smohalla, "The Preacher" (*c.* 1815-1890)
Columbia basin tribe

A Blackfoot travois *by Edward S. Curtis.*

29

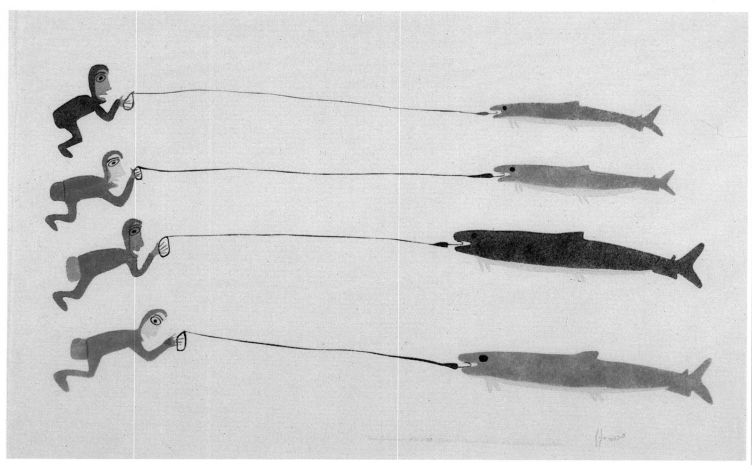

Four Fishermen *by Luke Angohadluq, 1980.*

A Change of Worlds

To us the ashes of our ancestors are sacred and their resting place is hallowed ground. You [whites] wander far from the graves of your ancestors and seemingly without regret. Your religion was written upon tables of stone by the iron finger of your God so that you could not forget. The Red Man could never comprehend nor remember it. Our religion is the traditions of our ancestors – the dreams of our old men, given them in the solemn hours of night by the Great Spirit; and the visions of our sachems, and is written in the hearts of our people.

Your dead cease to love you and the land of their nativity as soon as they pass the portals of the tomb and wander way beyond the stars. They are soon forgotten and never return. Our dead never forget the beautiful world that gave them being. They still love its verdant valleys, its murmuring rivers, its magnificent mountains, sequestered vales and verdant lined lakes and bays, and ever yearn in tender, fond affection over the lonely hearted living, and

often return from the Happy Hunting Ground to visit, guide, console and comfort them. . . .

We will not be denied the privilege without molestation of visiting at any time the tombs of our ancestors, friends and children. Every part of this soil is sacred in the estimation of my people. Every hillside, every valley, every plain and grove, has been hallowed by some sad or happy event in days long vanished. Even the rocks, which seem to be dumb and dead as they swelter in the sun along the silent shore, thrill with memories of stirring events connected with the lives of my people, and the very dust upon which you now stand responds more lovingly to their footsteps than to yours, because it is rich with the blood of our ancestors and our bare feet are conscious of the sympathetic touch. Our departed braves, fond mothers, glad, happy-hearted maidens, and even our little children who lived here and rejoiced here for a brief season, will love these somber solitudes and at

eventide they greet shadowy returning spirits. And when the last Red Man shall have perished, and the memory of my tribe shall have become a myth among the White Men, these shores will swarm with the invisible dead of my tribe, and when your children's children think of themselves alone in the field, the store, the shop, upon the highway, or in the silence of the pathless woods, they will not be alone. In all the earth there is no place dedicated to solitude. At night when the streets of your cities and villages are silent and you think them deserted, they will throng with the returning hosts that once filled them and still love this beautiful land. The White Man will never be alone.

Let him be just and deal kindly with my people, for the dead are not powerless. Dead, did I say? There is no death, only a change of worlds.

Chief Seattle (1786-1866)

The Tree of the Great Peace

I am Dekanawidah, and with the Five Nations confederate lords I plant the Tree of the Great Peace. . . . I name the tree the Tree of the Great Long Leaves. Under the shade of this Tree of the Great Peace we spread the soft white feather down of the globe thistle as seats for you, Atotarho and your cousin lords. There shall you sit and watch the council fire of the confederacy of the Five Nations. Roots have spread out from the Tree, and the name of these roots to the Great White Roots of Peace. If any man of any nation shall show a desire to obey the laws of the Great Peace, they shall trace the roots to their source, and they shall be welcomed to take shelter beneath the Tree of the Long Leaves. The smoke of the confederate council fire shall pierce the sky so that all nations may discover the central council fire of the Great Peace. I, Dekanawidah, and the confederate lords now uproot the tallest pine tree and into the cavity thereby made we cast all weapons of war. Into the depth of the earth, down into the deep underearth currents of water flowing into unknown regions; we cast all weapons of war. We bury them from sight forever and plant again the Tree.

From the Iroquois Constitution (*c.* 16th century)

The Beginning of the Wild West

We did not think of the great open plains, the beautiful rolling hills, and winding streams with tangled growth, as "wild." Only to the white man was nature a "wilderness" and only to him was the land "infested" with "wild" animals and "savage" people. To us it was tame. Earth was bountiful and we were surrounded with the blessings of the Great Mystery. Not until the hairy man from the east came and with brutal frenzy heaped injustices upon us and the families we loved was it "wild" for us. When the very animals of the forest began fleeing from his approach, then it was that for us the "Wild West" began.

Chief Luther Standing Bear of the Oglala band of Sioux (19th century)

Indian Church *by Emily Carr, 1929.*

Ruined dwellings in Canyon de Chelly, Arizona, where prehistoric Pueblo Indians found shelter for over a thousand years.

Kinship with All Creatures

The Lakota [Sioux] was a true naturist – a lover of nature. He loved the earth and all things of the earth, the attachment growing with age. The old people came literally to love the soil and they sat or reclined on the ground with a feeling of being close to a mothering power. It was good for the skin to touch the earth and the old people liked to remove their moccasins and walk with bare feet on the sacred earth. Their tipis were built upon the earth and their altars were made of earth. The birds that flew in the air came to rest upon the earth and it was the final abiding place of all things that lived and grew. The soil was soothing, strengthening, cleansing and healing.

That is why the old Indian still sits upon the earth instead of propping himself up and away from its life-giving forces. For him, to sit or lie upon the ground is to be able to think more deeply and to feel more keenly; he can see more clearly into the mysteries of life and come closer in kinship to other lives about him. . . .

Kinship with all creatures of the earth, sky and water was a real and active principle. For the animal and bird world there existed a brotherly feeling that kept the Lakota safe among them and so close did some of the Lakotas come to their feathered and furred friends that in true brotherhood they spoke a common tongue.

The old Lakota was wise. He knew that man's heart away from nature becomes hard; he knew that lack of respect for growing, living things soon led to lack of respect for humans too. So he kept his youth close to its softening influence. . . .

Chief Luther Standing Bear

Song in Favor of Peace

Let there be peace, O son – let not war prevail.
Put down thy spear and leave it as a token –
That thy posterity may behold it.
Go to thy grandparent – to Auruia,
That he may instruct thee in the korero.

Let there be no war; for a man of war can ne'er be satiated;
But let my son be instead a man of wisdom and learning,
A keeper of the traditions of his house.
Let there be no war.
Plant deeply the spirit of peace
That your rule may be known – the land of all-encompassing peace.

From the island of Rarotonga, Polynesia

Our Home

We belong to the ground
It is our power and we must stay
Close to it or maybe
We will get lost.

Narritjin Maymuru,
Australian aborigine, Yirrkala, N.T.

Right: Assiniboin placating the spirit of a slain eagle, photo by Edward S. Curtis.

THE SEEDS OF WAR

The Need to Invent Anew

The tie-up between proving oneself a man and proving this by a success in organized killing is due to a definition which many societies have made of manliness. And often, even in those societies which counted success in warfare a proof of human worth, strange turns were given to the idea, as when the plains Indians gave their highest awards to the man who touched a live enemy rather than to the man who brought in a scalp – from a dead enemy – because the latter was less risky. Warfare is just an invention known to the majority of human societies by which they permit their young men either to accumulate prestige or avenge their honor or acquire loot or wives or slaves or sago lands or cattle or appease the blood lust of their gods or the restless souls of the recently dead. It is just an invention, older and more widespread than the jury system, but none the less an invention.

Margaret Mead (1901-1978)

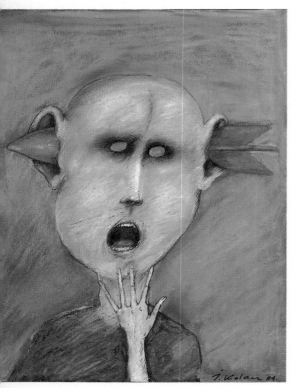

Fear of War *by Jerzy Kolacz, 1984.*

Is War Natural?

"War is a law of nature." Therefore, it is argued, we cannot get rid of it. What are the facts? They are these: conflict is certainly common in the animal kingdom. But, with very rare exceptions, conflict is between isolated individuals. "War" in the sense of conflict between armies exists among certain species of social insects. But it is significant that these insects do not make war on members of their own species, only on those of other species. Man is probably unique in making war on his own species.

Tennyson wrote of "Nature red in tooth and claw." But an animal can be bloodthirsty without being war-like. The activities of such creatures as tigers, sharks and weasels are no more war-like than those of butchers and sportsmen. The carnivores kill members of other species either for food or else, like fox-hunters and pheasant-shooters, to amuse themselves. Conflicts between individual animals of the same species are common enough. But again they are no more war-like than duels or pothouse brawls among human beings. Like human beings, animals fight mainly for love, sometimes (as with the birds that defend their "territory") for property, sometimes for social position. But they do not make war. War is quite definitely not a "law of nature."

Aldous Huxley (1894-1963)

Right: The Tower of Babel *by Pieter Brueghel, 1563.*

Four Explanations for War

All the various theories as to why groups of people go to war fall into four general categories. The first states that it is the very physical nature of man to be pugnacious and aggressive. Such a view of man holds that a warlike urge is biologically inherent in him. . . . There is no evidence in the physical makeup of man to suggest that he has been fashioned as a warlike animal. Man, in truth, is a puny creation, lacking fangs, claws, thick skin, speed, or other adaptations for combat. The whole idea of the innate belligerency of man is laid to rest by evidence that warfare is virtually absent among the most primitive of men, those whose "true" biological nature might appear to be closest to the surface. The Great Basin Shoshone, for example, never waged war, nor did most other very simple societies before the arrival of Whites.

The second explanation is an affront to logic: Men are warlike because they are warlike. Such an explanation is ridiculous. . . . Obviously, such logic is akin to explaining obesity in middle-aged males by saying that many middle-aged males are obese.

The third explanation is a psychological one, and it probably boasts the most adherents – which is understandable, for these people can bolster their case by surveys, personality tests, statistical analyses, and other impressive tools of modern scholarship. . . . All of these psychological studies, though, can explain only the motivations behind why *individuals* go to war. The real point is that although individuals slug each other in a barroom brawl or drop napalm from airplanes over Vietnam, individuals do not go to war. Only societies do that.

That leaves the fourth explanation, which states simply that the causes for war are to be found within the cultures of the contending groups. This explanation avoids confusing the issue with related problems, such as individual motivations or the kinds of warfare practised.

Peter Farb

Pro Patria

For the vast majority of mankind throughout history, the system of beliefs which they accepted, for which they were prepared to live and to die, was not of their own making or choice; it was shoved down their throats by the hazards of birth. *Pro patria mori dulce et decorum est*, whichever the *patria* into which the stork happens to drop you. Critical reasoning played, if any, only a secondary part in the process of adopting a faith, a code of ethics, a *Weltanschauung*; of becoming a fervent Christian crusader, a fervent Moslem engaged in Holy War, a Roundhead or a Cavalier. The continuous disasters in man's history are mainly due to his excessive capacity and urge to become identified with a tribe, nation, church or cause, and to espouse its credo uncritically and enthusiastically, even if its tenets are contrary to reason, devoid of self-interest and detrimental to the claims of self-preservation.

We are thus driven to the unfashionable conclusion that the trouble with our species is not an excess of *aggression*, but an excess capacity for fanatical *devotion*. Even a cursory glance at history should convince one that individual crimes committed for selfish motives play a quite insignificant part in the human tragedy, compared to the numbers massacred in unselfish loyalty to one's tribe, nation, dynasty, church, or political ideology, *ad majorem gloriam dei*. The emphasis is on unselfish. Excepting a small minority of mercenary or sadistic disposition, wars are not fought for personal gain, but out of loyalty and devotion to king, country or cause. Homicide committed for personal reasons is a statistical rarity in all cultures, including our own. Homicide for *un*selfish reasons, at the risk of one's own life, is the dominant phenomenon in history.

Arthur Koestler (1905-1984)

Naming of Parts

To-day we have naming of parts. Yesterday,
We had daily cleaning. And to-morrow morning,
We shall have what to do after firing. But to-day,
To-day we have naming of parts. Japonica
Glistens like coral in all of the neighbouring gardens,
　　　And to-day we have naming of parts.

This the lower sling swivel. And this
Is the upper sling swivel, whose use you will see,
When you are given your slings. And this is the piling swivel,
Which in your case you have not got. The branches
Hold in the gardens their silent, eloquent gestures,
　　　Which in our case we have not got.

This is the safety-catch, which is always released
With an easy flick of the thumb. And please do not let me
See anyone using his finger. You can do it quite easy
If you have any strength in your thumb. The blossoms
Are fragile and motionless, never letting anyone see
　　　Any of them using their finger.

And this you can see is the bolt. The purpose of this
Is to open the breech, as you see. We can slide it
Rapidly backwards and forwards: we call this
Easing the spring. And rapidly backwards and forwards
The early bees are assaulting and fumbling the flowers:
　　　They call it easing the Spring.

They call it easing the Spring: it is perfectly easy
If you have any strength in your thumb: like the bolt,
And the breech, and the cocking-piece, and the point of balance,
Which in our case we have not got; and the almond-blossom
Silent in all of the gardens and the bees going backwards and forwards,
　　　For to-day we have naming of parts.

Henry Reed

Aggression

We have to begin by distinguishing aggression from war-making. There is no way that life could be sustained or reproduced without some degree of aggression. But war is a particular type of *institutionalized* aggression in which social pressure is used to force individuals to kill other people they may not even hate or fear.

Note the word "force." Very few human beings have ever participated in war. Perhaps only 1 percent of the world's population have been warriors. And of those who have been engaged in battle, many found it difficult or impossible to kill other men. After World War II, General S. L. A. Marshall studied infantrymen fresh from combat with the Germans and Japanese and found that only about a quarter of all fighting soldiers had used weapons against the enemy. We are all aggressive, but we are not innately hostile. . . .

Our hope lies in the fact that war is not as old as the human race. War is not itself a need but a capacity, an institution for satisfying needs that are socially defined. There are societies today and always have been, such as the Hopi and pygmies, that do not wage war. Anthropologists argue whether hunters and gatherers engage in war. But from the point of view of a military historian they don't. They may have raiding parties for revenge, but they don't devote any real capital or energy to maintaining the capacity for war. The oldest art work we have in the caves of Lascaux and Altamira shows the use of weapons in hunting expeditions but not in war. My guess is that weapons were not specifically made in order to wage wars until the Neolithic period, about 13,000 years ago, when some people abandoned hunting and gathering and turned to agriculture. That's when you see swords and shields and the development of thick walls around cities, which people would not need for protection against animals. . . .

Ironically, industrial civilization, which began by promising mankind limitless power and security, has increased our individual sense of powerlessness and rage. With the industrial revolution no less than the agricultural revolution, we increased our control over nature at the price of subjecting the individual to greater social control. We have technological abundance only so long as we submit to the demands and disciplines of education and work. Industrial life requires us to adopt rigid timetables, suppress our emotions, and fragment our lives. We are dependent upon experts to build our houses, raise our food, cure our diseases. So urban life contains a low-level frustration, a strong feeling of incompleteness, and, for many, a sense of powerlessness and insecurity. And it is this sense of threat that we – Russians and Americans – project onto the enemy. "They" must be trying to reduce us to servitude. So each side threatens to throw a nuclear mega-tantrum.

Sue Mansfield

The Fifer by Edouard Manet, 1866.

The Hero Around Me

Water submissive and cool, the abundant sun
hot on my white back, day
of quiet pleasures, air humming
a steady soothing tune through the long hours,
ghosts slowly drifting past,
heads like broad arrows, hair coiled
about faces. Time is sliding away. . . .

I have desired many
but I wonder if I have loved one? –
remembering the cruel amusement and pleasure
of a youth called hard-hearted,
joy in a tearful eye and a frantic manner,
dismissive joy, and the day
humming and sliding away. . . .

Once heroes marched through my mind
in solid ranks, the deeds
shaped pointedly, and I knew
I could never be one of them,
though I desired it, wished for one sharp moment
in my life – thinking
of the hero as man in combat only. . . .

The day came, but not as war.
Fields of grain around me were crystal,
the sky polished, endless gold and blue,
and in the still heat a meadowlark
twisted its sculptured tune around me
once, quickly, a deft feat of superior magic,
and all time stopped, world without end,
and I was as a tree is, loathing nothing.

John Newlove

THE WAY OF PEACE

Buddha on lotus flower. Cave painting from India. 5th century A.D.

Words Go Forth

"A crane calling in the shade. Its young answers it. I have a good goblet. I will share it with you."

The Master said: The superior man abides in his room. If his words are well spoken, he meets with assent at a distance of more than a thousand miles. How much more then from near by! If the superior man abides in his room and his words are not well spoken, he meets with contradiction at a distance of more than a thousand miles. How much more then from near by! Words go forth from one's own person and exert their influence on men. Deeds are born close at hand and become visible far away. Words and deeds are the hinge and bowspring of the superior man. As hinge and bowspring move, they bring honor or disgrace. Through words and deeds the superior man moves heaven and earth. Must one not, then, be cautious?

From *The I Ching*

The Sermon on Abuse

And the Blessed One observed the ways of society and noticed how much misery came from malignity and foolish offences done only to gratify vanity and self-seeking pride.

And the Buddha said: "If a man foolishly does me wrong, I will return to him the protection of my ungrudging love; the more evil comes from him the more good shall go from me; the fragrance of goodness always comes to me, and the harmful air of evil goes to him."

A foolish man learning that the Buddha observed the principle of great love which commends the return of good for evil, came and abused him. The Buddha was silent, pitying his folly.

When the man had finished his abuse, the Buddha asked him, saying: "Son, if a man declined to accept a present made to him, to whom would it belong?" And he answered: "In that case it would belong to the man who offered it."

"My son," said the Buddha, "thou hast railed at me, but I decline to accept thy abuse, and request thee to keep it thyself. Will it not be a source of misery to thee? As the echo belongs to the sound, and the shadow to the substance, so misery will overtake the evil-doer without fail."

The abuser made no reply, and Buddha continued:

"A wicked man who reproaches a virtuous one is like one who looks up and spits at heaven; the spittle soils not the heaven, but comes back and defiles his own person.

"The slanderer is like one who flings dust at another when the wind is contrary; the dust does but return on him who threw it. The virtuous man cannot be hurt and the misery that the other would inflict comes back on himself."

The abuser went away ashamed, but he came again and took refuge in the Buddha, the Dharma, and the Sangha.

From *The Dhammapada*

Universal Love

But what is the way of universal love and mutual aid?

Motse said: It is to regard the state of others as one's own, the houses of others as one's own, the persons of others as one's self. When feudal lords love one another there will be no more war; when heads of houses love one another there will be no more mutual usurpation; when individuals love one another there will be no more mutual injury. When ruler and ruled love each other they will be gracious and loyal; when father and son love each other they will be affectionate and filial; when elder and younger brothers love each other they will be harmonious. When all the people in the world love one another, then the strong will not overpower the weak, the many will not oppress the few, the wealthy will not mock the poor, the honoured will not disdain the humble, and the cunning will not deceive the simple. And it is all due to mutual love that calamities, strifes, complaints, and hatred are prevented from arising. Therefore the benevolent exalt it.

But the gentlemen of the world would say: "So far so good. It is of course very excellent when love becomes universal. But it is only a difficult and distant ideal."

Motse said: This is simply because the gentlemen of the world do not recognize what is to the benefit of the world, or understand what is its calamity. Now, to besiege a city, to fight in the fields, or to achieve a name at the cost of death – these are what men find difficult. Yet when the superior encourages them, the multitude can do them. Besides, universal love and mutual aid is quite different from these. Whoever loves others is loved by others; whoever benefits others is benefited by others; whoever hates others is hated by others; whoever injures others is injured by others. Then, what difficulty is there with it (universal love)? Only, the ruler fails to embody it in his government and the ordinary man in his conduct.

Motse (468-401 B.C.)

Poet on a Mountain Top *by Chen Chou, Ming Dynasty (1368-1644).*

The Waters of Everlasting Life

Set thy heart on me alone, and give to me thy understanding: thou shalt in truth live in me hereafter.

But if thou art unable to rest thy mind on me, then seek to reach me by the practice of Yoga concentration.

If thou art not able to practise concentration, consecrate all thy work to me. By merely doing actions in my service thou shalt attain perfection.

And if even this thou art not able to do, then take refuge in devotion to me and surrender to me the fruit of all thy work – with the selfless devotion of a humble heart.

For concentration is better than mere practice, and meditation is better than concentration; but higher than meditation is surrender in love of the fruit of one's actions, for on surrender follows peace.

*   *   *

He whose peace is not shaken by others, and before whom other people find peace, beyond excitement and anger and fear – he is dear to me.

He who is free from vain expectations, who is pure, who is wise and knows what to do, who in inner peace watches both sides, who shakes not, who works for God and not for himself – this man loves me, and he is dear to me.

*   *   *

The man whose love is the same for his enemies or his friends, whose soul is the same in honour or disgrace, who is beyond heat or cold or pleasure or pain, who is free from the chains of attachments;

Who is balanced in blame and in praise, whose soul is silent, who is happy with whatever he has, whose home is not in this world, and who has love – this man is dear to me.

But even dearer to me are those who have faith and love, and who have me as their End Supreme: those who hear my words of Truth, and who come to the waters of Everlasting Life.

From *The Bhagavad Gita*

Noah sending the dove from the Ark. Mosaic, 12th century, Venice.

Great Is Peace

Great is peace, because peace is for the earth what yeast is for the dough. If the Holy One, blessed be he, had not given peace to the earth, it would be depopulated by the sword and by hosts of animals.

The world rests upon three things: On justice, on truth, on peace. Yet, those three are one and the same thing. For if there is justice, there is truth, and there is peace. And these three are expressed in one and the same verse: "Execute the judgment of truth and peace in your gates" (Zech. 8:16).

Wherever there is justice, there is peace, and wherever there is peace, there is justice. See how great is his reward who makes peace between men. It is written: "Thou shalt build the altar of the Lord thy God of unhewn stones" (Deut. 27:6).

If these stones which cannot hear and cannot see and cannot smell and cannot speak, because they make peace between men through the sacrifices that are offered upon them Scripture saves them from the sword and declares: "Thou shalt lift no iron tool upon them" (Deut. 27:5) – man, who can hear and see and smell and speak, how much more is this true of him, when he makes peace between his fellow-men.

*   *   *

Great is peace, for we seal all benedictions and all prayers with "peace." The recitation of "Hear, O Israel" we seal with "peace": "Spread the tabernacle of peace." The benediction of the priests is sealed with "peace": "And give thee peace" (Num. 6:26).

Thus spoke the Holy One, blessed be he, to Israel: "You have caused my house to be destroyed and my children to be banished – but ask for Jerusalem's peace and I shall forgive you." He, however, who loves peace, who pursues peace, who offers peace first, and responds to peace, the Holy One, blessed be he, will let him inherit the life of this world and the world to come, as it is written: "But the humble shall inherit the land, and delight themselves in the abundance of peace" (Ps. 37:11).

From The Talmud

Justice and Peace

Let me hear the words of the Lord:
are they not words of peace,
    peace to his people and his loyal
    servants and to all who turn and trust
    in him?
Deliverance is near to those who
    worship him, so that glory may dwell
    in our land.
Love and fidelity have come together;
justice and peace join hands.

Psalms 85:8-10

Let There Be Peace

Lord, inspiration of sacrifice! May our ears hear the good. May our eyes see the good. May we serve Him with the whole strength of our body. May we, all our life, carry out His will. May peace and peace and peace be everywhere.

Mundaka Upanishad, I.l

The Law

Hearing that he had silenced the Sadducees, the Pharisees met together; and one of their number tested him with this question: "Master, which is the greatest commandment in the Law?" He answered, "Love the Lord your God with all your heart, with all your soul, with all your mind. That is the greatest commandment. It comes first. The second is like it: Love your neighbour as yourself. Everything in the Law and the prophets hangs on these two commandments."

Matthew 22:34-41

The End of War

They shall beat their swords into ploughshares, and their spears into pruning hooks; nation shall not lift up sword against nation, neither shall they learn war any more.

Isaiah 2:4

Christic Entering Jerusalem *by Giotto, 1306.*

The Beatitudes

How blest are those who know that they are poor;
      the kingdom of Heaven is theirs.
How blest are the sorrowful;
      they shall find consolation.
How blest are those of a gentle spirit;
      they shall have the earth for their possession.
How blest are those who hunger and thirst to see right
      prevail;
      they shall be satisfied.
How blest are those who show mercy;
      mercy shall be shown to them.
How blest are those whose hearts are pure;
      they shall see God.
How blest are the peacemakers;
      God shall call them his sons.
How blest are those who have suffered persecution for the
      cause of right;
      the kingdom of Heaven is theirs.

Jesus Christ

Epicurean Ode to Aphrodite

Cause the savage works of war
to slumber and cease over land and sea.
You alone can bless mankind with tranquil
peace, since military Mars rules the savage
works of war, and he often drops
into your lap, overpowered by love's endless wound,
and looking up with shapely neck thrown back
gazes on you, goddess, and feeds his eagerness on love,
and his breath hangs on your lips as he lies there.
Goddess, bend over him with your holy body
as he lies there, pour gentle words
from your illustrious lips, ask peace and quiet for Rome.

Lucretius (99-55 B.C.)

UTOPIAN IDEALS

Flax Scutching Bee *by Linton Park, 1885.*

A New Society Is About to Be Commenced at Harmony, in Indiana

The direct object of this association is to give and secure happiness to all its members.

This object will be obtained by the adoption of a system of union and co-operation, founded on a spirit of universal charity, derived from a correct knowledge of the constitution of human nature.

The knowledge thus derived, will be found abundantly sufficient to reconcile all religious and other differences.

But, to insure success in practice, a preliminary society will be organized, and directed by those who understand the principles of this system, and who have already proved them by a partial yet extensive practice.

Into this preliminary society respectable families and individuals, with capital, and industrious and well-disposed families and individuals, without capital, will be received.

Those who possess capital and who do not wish to be employed, may partake of the benefits of this society on paying a sum annually, sufficient to recompense the society for their expenditure.

Those without capital, will be employed, according to their abilities and inclinations, in building, in agriculture, in gardening, in manufactures, in mechanical trades, in giving instruction in elementary or scientific knowledge, or in some one useful occupation, beneficial to the society.

In return for which they will be provided with the best lodging, food, and clothing, that the circumstances of the establishment will afford: they will experience every attention during sickness and in old age. All the children will be brought up together, as members of the same family, and will receive a good and superior education.

At the end of every year, a certain amount, in value, will be placed to the credit of each family, and each individual, not being a member of a family, in proportion to their expenditure, and to the services rendered by them to the society.

Anyone may leave the society at any time, and take with them, in the productions of the establishment, as much in value, as shall be placed to their credit at the annual balance immediately preceding the time when they cease to become members of the society.

During the continuance of the preliminary society, any family, or individual whose conduct may be injurious to the well-being and happiness of the association, and obstruct its progress, will be removed; but it is expected that the spirit of charity, justice, forbearance, and kindness, which will direct the whole proceedings of the society, and which will be soon diffused through all its members, will speedily render the dismissal of anyone unnecessary.

Robert Owen (1771-1858)

Community Housework

On arriving at [Oneida Community] I had some curiosity to know what were the manners and customs of the family in regard to the affairs of everyday life.

The kitchen is divided into two rooms. In the main one is a large coal stove, on which bread can be toasted, griddle-cakes baked, potatoes re-warmed, etc. Joining this main kitchen is a smaller one, on one side of which is a large zinc oven capable of baking two bushels of potatoes at once. Near this is a wood stove used for various purposes. At the end of the room and on part of one side are cupboards.

A door leads from the kitchen to the bakery, which is an institution by itself. It is supplied with large mixing-boxes, seasoning-cupboards, flour-sifters, and a zinc oven of the largest pattern, which is capable of baking sixty five-pound loaves of bread at a time, or in all three hundred pounds. Operating this bakery is the exclusive business of one man; and when necessary, he is aided by a company of young women.

At the head of the kitchen department is a man whose business it is to see that all necessary articles in the shape of provisions and table furniture, dishes, etc. are provided.

Next in order come the kitchen men. These men alternate in rising at half-past four A.M. for the purpose of building the kitchen fire and making the preparations for breakfast. They aid during the day in all the various labors of the kitchen.

The cooking department is headed by two women, one of whom is chief counsellor and manager, while the other is her assistant. These women

Amish men working together at a barn-raising.

Amish children in traditional garb peer out from the back of a horse-drawn buggy.

occupy their position usually for four weeks at a time; so that it does not become an irksome task, and gives all an opportunity to try their skill at a variety of dishes. These women make out the bill of fare, which is always ample, and in my estimation equal to any first-class hotel. They superintend all the cooking and have charge of the kitchen generally.

Next come the table waiters. These consist of young women, in age ranging from twelve to thirty. They are appointed to their position and alternated at stated periods by a committee selected by the family to attend to such matters. Waiters are in attendance at the main tables of the dining room until eight o'clock. And should you be an hour late you could still find plenty to eat on a side table.

At twelve noon the bell again rings the signal for dinner, which lasts until one o'clock in the dining room after which time you will find a table set in the back kitchen for an hour longer. At half-past five a large hand-bell is rung telling you that supper is ready; but you will be well served if you do not go until seven. Thus liberal time is given to suit all taste and business.

The dining room is capable of conveniently seating one hundred and ten persons at once. On opposite sides of the room are four oval tables, each seating eight persons. The middle of the room is occupied by two long tables; one seating twenty-six, and the other twenty persons. The rule is to fill up the farthest table on the west side of the room first, then the next, and so on, in regular order. This associates old and young, male and female, in a good and wholesome manner, and tends to diffuse a spirit of politeness and sociability not otherwise attainable.

The next thing in order is to clear the tables and wash the dishes, an operation which is provided for by itself, and is not under the supervision of the kitchen corps. Half an hour after the bell rings for any meal, part of the tables are ready to be cleared. This is performed by four women aided by one man. The women brush the refuse of the table in the pans and place dishes in piles. The man carries them to the washing-room either in his hands or in a small three-wheeled cart made for the purpose.

From the Oneida *Circular* (January 6, 1868),
New York State

The Essenes

The Essenes are totally dedicated to the worship of God.... They live without goods or property. They never make weapons or any objects which might be turned to evil purpose.... They avoid metaphysics, logic, and all philosophy except ethics which they study in the divinely given ancestral laws of the Jews. Every seventh day they keep holy and do no work but spend their time in religious assemblies seated strictly according to their rank, and listen to the exposition of their sacred books explained according to the ancient symbolical system. They study piety, holiness, justice, the sacred law, and the rules of their order, all leading to the love of God, of virtue, and of men, to which ends their lives are completely devoted. They refuse to take oaths and never lie. They believe that God is the cause only of good, never of evil. They treat all men with equal kindness and live together in a communal way. No one man owns his house. Their homes are always open to visiting members. They keep one purse and one budget. They eat together in a common meal and take their clothes from a common store. They care for the sick, the young, and the aged.

Philo of Alexandria

Fragments from the Dead Sea Scrolls, closely identified with the ascetic community of the Essenes (c. 2nd century B.C.—2nd century A.D.).

A New Society

The Jewish Village commune in Palestine owes its existence not to a doctrine but to a situation, to the needs, the stress, the demands of the situation.... This is certainly correct, but with one limitation.... What is called the ideology – I, personally, prefer the old but untarnished word "ideal" – was not just something to be added afterwards that would justify the accomplished facts. In the spirit of the members of the first Palestine communes, ideal motives joined hands with the dictates of the hour; and in the motives there was a curious mixture of memories of the Russian socialists, and the half-conscious after-effects of the Bible's teachings about social justice.... There were various dreams about the future; people saw before them a new, more comprehensive form of the family, they saw themselves as the advance guard of the Worker's Movement, as the direct instrument for the realization of Socialism, as the prototype of the new society; they had as their goal the creation of a new man and a new world.

Martin Buber

The Mormon Community

Our city now presents a lively and beautiful appearance. While it is adorned by the hand of nature in its richest dress, all hands seem engaged in adding to the comforts of the inhabitants. Numbers are employed in improving the streets and in removing every nuisance, whilst others are engaged in ploughing, digging, fencing, etc. The female part of the inhabitants are busily engaged in their flower gardens, and all around is health, peace, and happiness; and the songs of Zion are to be heard on every hand, united with those of the feathered tribe in almost every tree.

From *The Nauvoo Neighbor*, May 3, 1843, Nauvoo, Utah

Tree of Light by Hannah Cahoon, Hancock Shaker Village, 1845.

A Modern Utopia

No less than a planet will serve the purpose of a modern Utopia. Time was when a mountain valley or an island seemed to promise sufficient isolation for a polity to maintain itself intact from outward force; but the whole trend of modern thought is against the permanence of any such enclosures. A state powerful enough to keep isolated under modern conditions would be powerful enough to rule the world, would be, indeed, if not actively ruling, yet passively acquiescent in all other human organisations, and so responsible for them altogether. World-state, therefore, it must be.

*   *   *

The World State in this ideal presents itself as the sole landowner of the earth, with the local municipalities holding, as it were, feudally under it as landlords. The State or these subordinates holds all the sources of energy, and either directly or through its tenants, farmers and agents, develops these sources, and renders the energy available for the work of life. It or its tenants will produce food, and so human energy, and the exploitation of coal and electric power, and the powers of wind and wave and water will be within its right.... It will maintain order, maintain roads, maintain a cheap and efficient administration of justice, maintain cheap and rapid locomotion and be the common carrier of the planet, convey and distribute labour, control, let, or administer all natural productions, pay for and secure healthy births and a healthy and vigorous new generation, maintain the public health, coin money and sustain standards of measurement, subsidise research, and reward such commercially unprofitable undertakings as benefit the community as a whole; subsidise when needful chairs of criticism and authors and publications, and collect and distribute information. The State is for Individualities. The State is for Individuals, the law is for freedoms, the world is for experiment, experience, and change: these are the fundamental beliefs upon which a modern Utopia must go.

H. G. Wells (1866-1946)

10,000 Years Hence: A Prediction, *illustration by Hugo Gernsback which appeared in the magazine* Science and Invention, *February 1922.*

Beautiful City

The Socialist City should be beautiful, of course; it should be constructed on a definite plan, each feature having a vital relation to and complementing each other feature, thus illustrating in a concrete way the solidarity of the community; it should emphasize the fundamental principle of equal opportunity for all; and it should be the last word in the application of scientific discovery to the problems of everyday life, putting every labor saving device at the service of every citizen.

Alice Constance Austin, October 1916

VOICE OF THE PEOPLE

The seat of democracy near the Acropolis at theatre Dionysus, photograph by Costa Manos.

The Seat of Democracy

Our constitution [in Athens] is called a democracy because power is in the hands not of a minority but of the whole people. When it is a question of settling private disputes, everyone is equal before the law; when it is a question of putting one person before another in positions of public responsibility, what counts is not membership of a particular class, but the actual ability which the man possesses. No one, so long as he has it in him to be of service to the state, is kept in political obscurity because of poverty. And, just as our political life is free and open, so is our day-to-day life in our relations with each other. We do not get into a state with our next-door neighbour if he enjoys himself in his own way, nor do we give him the kind of black looks which, though they do no real harm, still do hurt people's feelings. We are free and tolerant in our private lives; but in public affairs we keep to the law. This is because it commands our deep respect.

We give our obedience to those whom we put in positions of authority, and we obey the laws themselves, especially those which are for the protection of the oppressed, and those unwritten laws which it is an acknowledged shame to break.

Pericles (*c.* 490-429 B.C.)

Rights of the People

And thereupon the said lords spiritual and temporal, and commons, pursuant to their respective letters and elections, being now assembled in a full and free representative of this nation, taking into their most serious consideration the best means for attaining the ends aforesaid; do in the first place (as their ancestors in like case have usually done) for the vindicating and asserting their ancient rights and liberties, declare:

1. That the pretended power of suspending of laws, or the execution of laws, by regal authority, without consent of parliament, is illegal.

2. That the pretended power of dispensing with laws, or the execution of laws, by regal authority, as it hath been assumed and exercised of late, is illegal.

3. That the commission for erecting the late court of commissioners for ecclesiastical causes, and all other commissions and courts of like nature are illegal and pernicious.

4. That levying money for or to the use of the crown, by pretence of prerogative, without grant of parliament, for longer time, or in other manner than the same is or shall be granted, is illegal.

5. That it is the right of the subjects to petition the King, and all commitments and prosecutions for such petitioning are illegal.

6. That the raising or keeping a standing army within the kingdom in time of peace, unless it be with consent of parliament, is against law.

7. That the subjects which are protestants, may have arms for their defence suitable to their conditions, and as allowed by law.

8. That the election of members of parliament ought to be free.

9. That the freedom of speech, and debates or proceedings in parliament, ought not to be impeached or questioned in any court or place out of parliament.

10. That excessive bail ought not to be required, nor excessive fines imposed; nor cruel and unusual punishments inflicted.

11. That jurors ought to be duly impanelled and returned, and jurors which pass upon men in trials for high treason ought to be freeholders.

12. That all grants and promises of fines and forfeitures of particular persons before conviction, are illegal and void.

13. And that for redress of all grievances, and for the amending, strengthening, and preserving of the laws, parliaments ought to be held frequently.

From the English Bill of Rights, 1689

Life, Liberty, and Happiness

We hold these truths to be self-evident: that all men are created equal; that they are endowed by their Creator with certain inalienable rights; that among these are life, liberty, and the pursuit of happiness; that to secure these rights, governments are instituted among men, deriving their just powers from the consent of the governed; that whenever any form of government becomes destructive of these ends, it is the right of the people to alter or to abolish it, and to institute new government, laying its foundation on such principles, and organizing its powers in such form, as to them shall seem most likely to effect their safety and happiness. Prudence, indeed, will dictate that governments long established should not be changed for light and transient causes; and accordingly all experience hath shown that mankind are more disposed to suffer while evils are sufferable, than to right themselves by abolishing the forms to which they are accustomed. But when a long train of abuses and usurpations, pursuing invariably the same object, evinces a design to reduce them under absolute despotism, it is their right, it is their duty to throw off such government, and to provide new guards for their future security.

American Declaration of Independence, 1776

The County Election *by George Bingham, 1852.*

Public Opinion

I am persuaded myself that the good sense of the people will always be found to be the best army. They may be led astray for a moment, but will soon correct themselves. The people are the only censors of their governors; and even their errors will tend to keep these to the true principles of their institution. To punish these errors too severely would be to suppress the only safeguard of the public liberty. The way to prevent these irregular interpositions of the people, is to give them full information of their affairs through the channel of the public papers, and to contrive that those papers should penetrate the whole mass of the people. The basis of our governments being the opinion of the people, the very first object should be to keep that right; and were it left to me to decide whether we should have a government without newspapers, or newspapers without a government, I should not hesitate a moment to prefer the latter. But I should mean that every man should receive those papers, and be capable of reading them. I am convinced that those societies (as the Indians) which live without government, enjoy in their general mass an infinitely greater degree of happiness than those who live under the European governments.

Thomas Jefferson (1743-1826), from a letter to Col. Carrington, 1787

What Is Peace?

It is the tranquillity enjoyed by a body politic, either inwardly, through the good order that reigns among its members, or outwardly, through the good understanding in which it lives with other peoples.

Hobbes claimed that men were in a state of perpetual war, one against another; the view expressed by this atrabilious philosopher seems no better founded than if he had said that the state of pain and disease is natural to man. Like physical bodies, so bodies politic may provide all too many legitimate reasons for recourse to arms, war would be much less frequent if it were waged only for genuine reasons or in case of absolute necessity: princes who love their peoples know that the most necessary war is always a disaster, and that it is worthwhile only in so far as it safeguards peace. The great Gustavus was told that his glorious victories marked him as appointed by Providence for the salvation of men; that his courage was a gift from the Almighty, and the outward sign of His favour. "Say, rather, of His anger", answered the conqueror, "if the war I am waging is a remedy, it is harder to bear than your ills".

Denis Diderot (1713-1784) from *L'Encyclopédie*

The Art of Being Free

The government of the democracy brings the notion of political rights to the level of the humblest citizens, just as the dissemination of wealth brings the notion of property within the reach of all men; to my mind, this is one of its greatest advantages. I do not say it is easy to teach men how to exercise political rights; but I maintain that, when it is possible, the effects which result from it are highly important; and I add, that, if there ever was a time at which such an attempt ought to be made, that time is now. Do you not see that religious belief is shaken, and the divine notion of right is declining? – that morality is debased, and the notion of moral right is therefore fading away? Argument is substituted for faith, and calculation for the impulses of sentiment. If, in the midst of this general disruption, you do not succeed in connecting the notion of right with that of private interest, which is the only immutable point in the human heart, what means will you have of governing the world except by fear? When I am told that the laws are weak and the people are turbulent, that passions are excited and the authority of virtue is paralyzed, and therefore no measures must be taken to increase the rights of the democracy, I reply, that, for these very reasons, some measures of the kind ought to be taken; and I believe that governments are still more interested in taking them than society at large, for governments may perish, but society cannot die....

It cannot be repeated too often, that nothing is more fertile in prodigies than the art of being free; but there is nothing more arduous than the apprenticeship of liberty. It is not so with despotism: despotism often promises to make amends for a thousand previous ills; it supports the right, it protects the oppressed, and it maintains public order. The nation is lulled by the temporary prosperity which it produces, until it is roused to a sense of its misery. Liberty, on the contrary, is generally established with difficulty in the midst of storms; it is perfected by civil discord; and its benefits cannot be appreciated until it is already old.

Alexis de Tocqueville (1805-1859)

The Oath of the Jeu de Paume *by Jean-Jacques Louis David, 1792.*

Great Are the Myths

Great are the myths....I too delight in them,
Great are Adam and Eve....I too look back and accept them;
Great the risen and fallen nations, and their poets, women, sages, inventors, rulers,
    warriors and priests.

Great is liberty! Great is equality! I am their follower,
Helmsmen of nations, choose your craft....where you sail I sail,
Yours is the muscle of life or death....yours is the perfect science....in you I have
    absolute faith.

Great is today, and beautiful,
It is good to live in this age....there never was any better.

Great are the plunges and throes and triumphs and falls of democracy,
Great the reformers with their lapses and screams,
Great the daring and venture of sailors on new explorations.

Great is the greatest nation...the nation of clusters of equal nations.

Great is the earth, and the way it became what it is,
Do you imagine it is stopped at this?....and the increase abandoned?
Understand then that it goes as far onward from this as this is from the times when
    it lay in covering waters and gases.

Great is the quality of truth in man,
The quality of truth in man supports itself through all changes,
It is inevitably in the man....He and it are in love, and never leave each other.

The truth in man is no dictum....it is vital as eyesight,
If there be any soul there is truth....if there be man or woman there is truth....If
    there be physical or moral there is truth,

If there be equilibrium or volition there is truth....if there be things at all upon the
    earth there is truth.

O truth of the earth! O truth of things! I am determined to press the whole way
    toward you,
Sound your voice! I scale mountains or dive in the sea after you.

                    *   *   *

Great is Justice; Justice is not settled by legislators and laws....it is in the soul,
It cannot be varied by statutes any more than love or pride or the attraction of
    gravity can,
It is immutable...it does not depend on majorities....majorities or what not come
    at last before the same passionless and exact tribunal.

Walt Whitman (1819-1892) from *Leaves of Grass*

The Theory of Democracy

Many people speak and write as though the beginning and end of democracy were the rule of the majority. But this is far too mechanical a view. It leaves out of account two questions of great importance, namely: (1) What should be the group of which the majority is to prevail? (2) What are the matters with which the majority has a right to interfere? Right answers to these questions are essential if nominal democracy is not to develop into a new and more stable form of tyranny; for minorities and subordinate groups have the right to live, and must not be internally subject to the malice of hostile masses.

The first question is familiar in one form, namely, that of nationality. It is recognized as contrary to the theory of democracy to combine into one State a big nation and a small one when the small nation desires to be independent. To allow votes to the citizens of the small nation is no remedy, since they can always be outvoted by the citizens of the large nation. The popularly-elected legislature, if it is to be genuinely democratic, must represent one nation; or, if more are to be represented, it must be by a federal arrangement which safeguards the smaller units. A legislature should exist for defined purposes, and should cover a larger or smaller area according to the nature of those purposes. At this moment, when an attempt is being made to create a League of Nations for certain objects, this point does not need emphasizing.

But it is not only geographical units, such as nations, that have a right, according to the true theory of democracy, to autonomy for certain purposes. Just the same principle applies to any group which has important internal concerns that affect the members of the group enormously more than they affect outsiders. The coal trade, for example, might legitimately claim autonomy. If such a demand were put forward it would be as impossible to resist on democratic grounds as the demand for autonomy on the part of the small nation. Yet it is perfectly clear that the coal trade could not induce the community to agree to such a proposal, especially if it threatened the "rights of property",

unless it were sufficiently well organised to be able to do grave injury to the community in the event of its proposal being rejected, just as no small nation except Norway, so far as my memory serves me, has ever obtained independence from a large one to which it was subject except by war or the threat of war.

The fact is that democracies, as soon as they are well established, are just as jealous of power as other forms of government. It is, therefore, necessary, if subordinate groups are to obtain their rights, that they shall have some means of bringing pressure to bear upon the Government. The Benthamite theory, upon which democracy is still defended by some doctrinaires, was that each voter would look after his own interest, and in the resultant each man's interest would receive its proportionate share of attention. But human nature is neither so rational nor so self-centred as Bentham imagined. In practice it is easier, by arousing hatred and jealousies, to induce men to vote against the interests of others than to persuade them to vote for their own interests. In the recent General Election in this country very few electors remembered their own interests at all. They voted for the man who showed the loudest zeal for hanging the Kaiser, not because they imagined they would be richer if he were hanged, but as an expression of disinterested hatred. This is one of the reasons why autonomy is important: in order that, as far as possible, no group shall have its internal concerns determined for it by those who hate it. And this result is not secured by the mere *form* of democracy; it can only be secured by careful devolution of special powers to special groups, so as to secure, as far as possible, that legislation shall be inspired by the self-interest of those concerned, not by the hostility of those not concerned.

This brings us to the second of the two questions mentioned above – a question which is, in fact, closely bound up with the first. Our second question was: What are the matters with which democracy has a right to interfere? It is now generally recognised that religion, for example, is a question

with which no Government should interfere. If a Mahometan comes to live in England we do not think it right to force him to profess Christianity. This is a comparatively recent change; three centuries ago no State recognised the right of an individual to choose his own religion. (Some other personal rights have been longer recognised: a man may choose his own wife, though in Christian countries he must not choose more than one.) When it ceased to be illegal to hold that the earth goes round the sun, it was not made illegal to believe that the sun goes round the earth. In such matters it has been found, with intense surprise, that personal liberty does not entail anarchy. Even the sternest supporters of the rule of the majority would not hold that the Archbishop of Canterbury ought to turn Buddhist if Parliament ordered him to do so. And Parliament does not, as a rule, issue orders of this kind, largely because it is known that the resistance would be formidable and that it would have support in public opinion.

In theory the formula as to legitimate interferences is simple. A democracy has a right to interfere with those of the affairs of a group which intimately concern people outside the group, but not with those which have comparatively slight effects outside the group. In practice this formula may sometimes be difficult to apply but often its application is clear. If, for example, the Welsh wish to have their elementary education conducted in Welsh, that is a matter which concerns them so much more intimately than anyone else that there can be no good reason why the rest of the United Kingdom should interfere.

Thus the theory of democracy demands a good deal more than the mere mechanical supremacy of the majority. It demands (1) division of the community into more or less autonomous groups; (2) delimitation of the powers of the autonomous groups by determining which of their concerns are so much more important to themselves than to others that others had better have no say in them.

Bertrand Russell (1872-1970)

UNIVERSAL PEACE

Prudence Brings Peace and Abundance *by Simon de Vouet, 1630.*

A Holy Resolve

Great Princes, it is you who must accomplish this holy resolve. Mankind in general and your subjects in particular will be grateful to you. No conquest could win you so much acclaim; no victory deserves so many bonfires. What greater honour can you look for than to see peace proclaimed by your authority throughout the world?

*   *   *

Now this glorious honour is not to be acquired by pillage, slaughter, and hostile actions, but by consistent government, by lawful and regulated power, in contradistinction to the kingdom of tyranny, uneasiness, and short duration.

*   *   *

How pleasant it would be to see men travel freely across frontiers and communicate with one another without any scruples whatsoever as to nation, ceremonies, or other such formalities, as if the earth were, as it is in truth, a common city for all.

*   *   *

Someone will surely say, how will it be possible to make people so different in their ways and inclinations as the Turk and the Persian, the Frenchman and the Spaniard, the Chinaman and the Tartar, the Christian and the Jew or the Muslim, agree? I believe that such differences are but political, that they cannot ignore the affinities that exist and must exist between men. Geography...does not weaken the ties of blood. It can no longer set aside the unity of nature, the true foundation of friendship and human society.

Why should I, a Frenchman, bear ill will against an Englishman or an Indian? I cannot, when I contemplate that they are men even as I, that I am like them subject to error and sin and that all nations are associated by a natural and, in consequence, indissoluble tie....

*   *   *

It depends only on the rulers to bestow by anticipation this felicity on their people. For what do we need these arms? Will we always live like brutes? If we only behaved moderately in these affairs!...Men (unless impelled by hunger or other need) quarrel for mere trifles; sometimes out of sheer wantonness they begin a campaign, not the battle of one man with another, but ten thousand against ten thousand, so that they may enjoy the spectacle of seeing the dead piled on high, streams of blood flowing on the fields. Look at two armies about to assault each other: the fierce looks, the soldiers' faces made hideous, the threats and savage shouts on every side, the roar of the cannons; now the attack and the gruesome conflict, the butchering of men, some torn limb from limb, others half dead begging aid of their companions, begging them for the death stroke to cut their wretched and fast-fading lives short. Later the slaughter extends to the weak: old men are slaughtered, children killed or captured, women raped, houses of worship profaned – only injustice is sure. This is followed by two new evils: famine and pestilence, for husbandry ends in time of war. The population has nothing to eat and must therefore eat indiscriminately good and bad meat which, instead of being nourishment, produces...diseases.

*   *   *

But we ought to aim at higher things, and take into consideration that God exists who punishes men's sins, and especially arrogance and cruelty. If these two vices were to be abandoned, wars would cease. The sword will be sheathed when we have seen the vanity of those opinions which lead us to take up arms.

Emeric Crucé (c. 1590-1648)

Detail of The Arrival of the English Ambassadors *by Vitorre Carpaccio, c. 1498, Venice.*

Settling Differences

There are three methods, by which independent nations may settle their disputed rights without coming to the decision of the sword.

The first method is that of conference. For, in the words of Cicero, "there being two methods of deciding quarrels, the one by discussion and the other by force, the former, a peculiar characteristic of man, and the latter, of the brute creation: when the first of these methods fails, men are obliged to have recourse to the latter." Mardonius, in the Polyhymnia of Herodotus, blames the Grecians, who, being united in one language, might settle their quarrels by messengers of peace, by heralds, and negotiations, rather than by war.

The other method is that of compromise, which takes place between those who have no common judge. Among innumerable instances of this kind in ancient history, we may select that given by Xenophon in his account of Cyrus, where that prince takes the king of the Indians for arbitrator between himself and the king of Assyria. The Carthaginians in their disputes with Masinissa prefer a settlement of this kind before a decision of war. Livy too informs us that the Romans themselves, in a dispute with the Samnites, made an appeal to the common allies of both.

The office of deciding wars and putting an end to the contentions of armies was assigned, according to Strabo, to the Druids of the Gauls, and upon the testimony of the same writer, it formed a part of the priestly functions amongs the Iberians.

Surely then it is a mode of terminating their disputes, balancing their powers, and settling their pretensions worthy to be adopted by Christian Kings and States. For if, in order to avoid trials before judges who were strangers to the true religion, the Jews and Christians appointed arbitrators of their own, and it was a practice recommended and enjoined by St. Paul, how much more ought such a practice to be recommended and enforced, to gain the still nobler end of preventing the calamities of war.

These and many other reasons of no less importance might be advanced for recommending to Christian powers general congresses for the adjustment of their various interests, and for compelling the refractory to submit to equitable terms of peace.

A third method of terminating disputes, without hostilities, was by lot, a practice commended by Dion Chrysostom in his speech on the interposition of fortune in directing affairs, and it was commended long before him by Solomon in the XVIII chapter of his Proverbs.

Nearly related to the last named method is that of single combat, a practice recommended under the idea that by the risque of two lives a quarrel might be decided, which would otherwise have cost the blood of thousands. In Livy we find Metius addressing Tullus in the following terms, "let us try some method of determining to whom the pre-eminence shall belong, without wasting the blood of each people." Strabo says it was the practice of the ancient Greeks, and Aeneas proposed it to Turnus, as the most equitable way of settling their pretensions.

Hugo Grotius (1583-1645)

Detail of Penn's Treaty with the Indians *by Benjamin West, 1771.*

Letter to the Delaware Indians

London, 18th of 8th Month, 1681

My Friends – There is one great God and power that hath made the world and all things therein, to whom you and I, and all people owe their being and well-being, and to whom you and I must one day give account for all that we do in the world; this great God hath written his law in our hearts, by which we are taught and commanded to love and help, and do good to one another, and not to do harm and mischief one to another. Now this great God hath been pleased to make me concerned in your parts of the world, and the king of the country where I live hath given unto me a great province, but I desire to enjoy it with your love and consent, that we may always live together as neighbours and friends, else what would the great God say to us, who hath made us not to devour and destroy one another, but live soberly and kindly together in the world? Now I would have you well observe, that I am very sensible of the unkindness and injustice that hath been too much exercised towards you by the people of these parts of the world, who sought themselves, and to make great advantages by you, rather than be examples of justice and goodness unto you, which I hear hath been matter of

trouble to you, and caused great grudgings and animosities, sometimes to the shedding of blood, which hath made the great God angry; but I am not such a man, as is well known in my own country; I have great love and regard towards you, and I desire to win and gain your love and friendship, by a kind, just, and peaceable life, and the people I send are of the same mind, and shall in all things behave themselves accordingly; and if in any thing any shall offend you or your people, you shall have a full and speedy satisfaction for the same, by an equal number of just men on both sides, that by no means you may have just occasion of being offended against them. I shall shortly come to you myself, at what time we may more largely and freely confer and discourse of these matters. In the mean time, I have sent my commissioners to treat with you about land, and a firm league of peace. Let me desire you to be kind to them and the people, and receive these presents and tokens which I have sent to you, as a testimony of my good will to you, and my resolution to live justly, peaceably, and friendly with you.

I am your loving friend,

William Penn (1644-1718)

Seven Peaceful Attitudes

1. The hatred of war inseparable from the conviction that defensive war alone can be regarded as legitimate.

2. The refusal of our soul, our conscience to worship military glory and the genius of a conqueror.

3. The profound conviction that the greatness of a reign or a government does not reside in the ability to extend the territory of the dominion.

4. A high ideal of patriotism that would stimulate in every citizen the efforts to make his own country noble, prosperous, civilized, happy and would at the same time restrain him from interfering with matters concerning the internal life of other nations.

5. The steady desire for co-operation, for a close union which would make nations ready to protest together against any unlawful action of which a member state might be found guilty.

6. The recognition of freedom of seas and rivers demanded by our sense of justice.

7. The recognition of the duty to spread the light of knowledge among men; for a cultured nation an olive branch means more than a laurel wreath.

Johann Gottfried von Herder (1744-1803)

The Divine Image

To Mercy, Pity, Peace, and Love
All pray in their distress;
And to these virtues of delight
Return their thankfulness.

For Mercy, Pity, Peace, and Love
Is God, our father dear,
And Mercy, Pity, Peace, and Love
Is Man, his child and care.

For Mercy has a human heart,
Pity a human face,
And Love, the human form divine,
And Peace, the human dress.

Then every man, of every clime,
That prays in his distress,
Prays to the human form divine,
Love, Mercy, Pity, Peace.

And all must love the human form,
In heathen, turk, or jew;
Where Mercy, Love, & Pity dwell
There God is dwelling too.

William Blake (1757-1827)

The Garden of Eden *by Erastus Salisbury Field, 1985.*

The Golden Age

Men may fail for a long time to realize their own advantage, but the time comes when they are enlightened and act accordingly. The French have adopted the English constitution, and all the peoples of Europe will adopt it gradually, as they become sufficiently enlightened to appreciate its advantages. Now the time when all the European peoples are governed by national parliaments will unquestionably be the time when a common parliament can be established without difficulties. The reasons for this proposition are so evident that it seems to me pointless to enumerate them.

But this time is still far off, and frightful wars and repeated revolutions will afflict Europe in the meantime. What is to be done to avert these new evils, the melancholy results of the disorganization in which Europe still remains? We must use our intelligence, and find means of abolishing the causes of these evils, with less delay.

I return to what I have already said. The establishment of the European parliament will be brought about without difficulty as soon as all the peoples of Europe live under a parliamentary régime. It follows that the European parliament can begin to take shape as soon as that part of the European population governed by a representative régime is superior in force to that which remains subject to arbitrary government.

*   *   *

The Golden Age of the human race is not behind us but before us; it lies in the perfection of the social order. Our ancestors never saw it; our children will one day arrive there; it is for us to clear the way.

Claude Henri de Saint-Simon (1760-1825)

The Conditions of Peace

Mere agreements may not make peace secure. It will be absolutely necessary that a force be created as a guarantor of the permanency of the settlement so much greater than the force of any nation now engaged or any alliance hitherto formed or projected that no nation, no probable combination of nations could face or withstand it. If the peace presently to be made is to endure, it must be a peace made secure by the organized major force of mankind. . . .

First of all, it must be a peace without victory. It is not pleasant to say this. I beg that I may be permitted to put my own interpretation upon it and that it may be understood that no other interpretation was in my thought. I am seeking only to face realities and to face them without soft concealments. Victory would mean peace forced upon the loser, a victor's terms imposed upon the vanquished. It would be accepted in humiliation, under duress, at an intolerable sacrifice, and would leave a sting, a resentment, a bitter memory upon which terms of peace would rest, not permanently, but only as upon quicksand. Only a peace between equals can last. Only a peace the very principle of which is equality and a common participation in a common benefit. The right state of mind, the right feeling between nations, is as necessary for a lasting peace as the just settlement of vexed questions or of racial and national allegiance.

The equality of nations, upon which peace must be founded if it is to last, must be an equality of rights; the guarantees exchanged must neither recognize nor imply a difference between big nations and small, between those that are powerful and those that are weak. Right must be based upon the common strength, not upon the individual strength, of the nations upon whose concert peace will depend. Equality of territory or of resources there of course cannot be; nor any other sort of equality not gained in the ordinary peaceful and legitimate development of the peoples themselves. But no one asks or expects anything more than an equality of rights. Mankind is looking now for freedom of life, not for equipoises of power.

And there is a deeper thing involved than even equality of right among organized nations. No peace can last, or ought to last, which does not recognize and accept the principle that governments derive all their just powers from the consent of the governed, and that no right anywhere exists to hand peoples about from sovereignty to sovereignty as if they were property. I take it for granted, for instance, if I may venture upon a single example, that statesmen everywhere are agreed that there should be a united, independent, and autonomous Poland, and that henceforth inviolable security of life, of worship, and of industrial and social development should be guaranteed to all peoples who have lived hitherto under the power of governments devoted to a faith and purpose hostile to their own.

I speak of this, not because of any desire to exalt an abstract political principle which has always been held very dear by those who have sought to build up liberty in America, but for the same reason that I have spoken of the other conditions of peace which seem to me clearly indispensable – because I wish frankly to uncover realities. Any peace which does not recognize and accept this principle will inevitably be upset. It will not rest upon the affections or the convictions of mankind. The ferment of spirit of whole populations will fight subtly and constantly against it, and all the world will sympathize. The world can be at peace only if its life is stable, and there can be no stability where the will is in rebellion, where there is not tranquility of spirit and a sense of justice, of freedom, and of right.

Woodrow Wilson (1856-1924), President of the United States, from a speech in the U.S. Senate, January 22, 1917

The Plumb-pudding in Danger *by James Gillray, February 26, 1805.*

Address to the Congrés de la Paix, 1851

A day will come when there will be no battlefields, but markets opening to commerce and minds opening to ideas. A day will come when the bullets and bombs are replaced by votes, by universal suffrage, by the venerable arbitration of a great supreme senate which will be to Europe what Parliament is to England, the Diet to Germany, and the Legislative Assembly to France. A day will come when a cannon will be a museum-piece, as instruments of torture are today. And we will be amazed to think that these things once existed! A day will come when we shall see those two immense groups, the United States of America and the United States of Europe, stretching out their hands across the sea, exchanging their products, their arts, their works of genius, clearing up the globe, making deserts fruitful, ameliorating creation under the eyes of the Creator, and joining together to reap the well-being of all. . . .

Victor Hugo (1802-1885)

The League of Nations

The committee which drafted the constitution of the League of Nations meeting in 1919 in Paris.

The High Contracting Parties,
in order to promote international
co-operation and to achieve
international peace and security

    by the acceptance of obligations not
        to resort to war,

    by the prescription of open, just and
        honourable relations between
        nations,

    by the firm establishment of the
        understandings of international
        law as the actual rule of conduct
        among Governments, and

    by the maintenance of justice and a
        scrupulous respect for all treaty
        obligations in the dealings of
        organised peoples with one
        another,

Agree to this Covenant of the League of
Nations. . . .

    Any fully self-governing State,
Dominion or Colony not named in the
Annex may become a Member of the
League if its admission is agreed to by
two-thirds of the Assembly, provided
that it shall give effective guarantees of
its sincere intention to observe its
international obligations, and shall
accept such regulations as may be
prescribed by the League in regard to its
military, naval and air forces and
armaments. . . .

    The action of the League under this
Covenant shall be effected through the
instrumentality of an Assembly and of
a Council, with a permanent
Secretariat. . . .

    The Assembly may deal at its
meetings with any matter within the
sphere of action of the League or
affecting the peace of the world.

                From the Covenant, 1920

Vision of the League of Nations, c. 1920 by Edvard Munch.

REFLECTIONS OF PEACE

Dove *by Blair Drawson, 1984.*

The Paradox of War and Peace

Yet even people with generous and understanding hearts, and peaceful instincts in their normal individual behavior, can become fighting and even savage national animals under the incitements of collective emotion. Why this happens is the core of our problem of peace and war.

That problem, why men fight who aren't necessarily fighting men, was posed for me in a new and dramatic way one Christmas Eve in London during World War Two. The air raid sirens had given their grim and accustomed warning. Almost before the last dismal moan had ended, the anti-aircraft guns began to crash. In between their bursts I could hear the deeper more menacing sound of bombs. It wasn't much of a raid, really, but one or two of the bombs seemed to fall too close to my room. I was reading in bed and, to drown out or at least to take my mind off the bombs, I reached out and turned on the radio. I was fumbling aimlessly with the dial when the room was flooded with the beauty and peace of Christmas carol music. Glorious waves of it wiped out the sound of war and conjured up visions of happier peacetime Christmases. Then the announcer spoke in German. For it was a German station and they were Germans who were singing those carols. Nazi bombs screaming through the air with their message of war and death; German music drifting through the air with its message of peace and salvation. When we resolve the paradox of those two sounds from a single national source, we will, at last, be in a good position to understand and solve the problem of peace and war.

Lester B. Pearson (1897-1972)

A Letter to Albert Einstein

Sensations which delighted our forefathers have become neutral or unbearable to us; and, if our ethical and aesthetic ideals have undergone a change, the causes of this are ultimately organic. On the psychological side two of the most important phenomena of culture are, firstly, a strengthening of the intellect, which tends to master our instinctive life, and, secondly, an introversion of the aggressive impulse, with all its consequent benefits and perils. Now war runs most emphatically counter to the psychic disposition imposed on us by the growth of culture; we are therefore bound to resent war, to find it utterly intolerable. With pacifists like us it is not merely an intellectual and affective repulsion, but a constitutional intolerance, an idiosyncrasy in its most drastic form. And it would seem that the aesthetic ignominies of warfare play almost as large a part in this repugnance as war's atrocities.

How long have we to wait before the rest of men turn pacifist? Impossible to say, and yet perhaps our hope that these two factors – man's cultural disposition and a well-founded dread of the form that future wars will take – may serve to put an end to war in the near future, is not chimerical. But by what ways or byways this will come about, we cannot guess. Meanwhile we may rest on the assurance that whatever makes for cultural development is working also against war.

With kindest regards and, should this exposé prove a disappointment to you, my sincere regrets. . . .

Sigmund Freud (1856-1939)

"If you meet a bear on a bridge, greet it softly by saying, 'my uncle,' until you have reached the other side." Turkish proverb. Detail of Turkish miniature from the 18th century.

Detail from the fresco Peace *by Ambrogio Lorenzetti.*

Lament on the Evils of the Civil War

Oh, you, knight who comes from such a battle, tell me, I pray you, what honor did you win there? Will they tell of your deeds to honor you more, that you were on the winning side that day? But may this peril, although you escaped it, be counted against your other good deeds! Because it is not proper to praise an adventure which is not blameless. Oh, would that men, since it would indeed please God, had not, on either side, the courage to bear arms!

And what will follow, in God's name? Famine, because of the wasting and ruining of things that will ensue, and the lack of cultivation, from which will spring revolts by the people who have been too often robbed, deprived and oppressed, their food taken away and stolen here and there by soldiers, subversion in the towns because of outrageous taxes which will have to be levied on the citizens and dwellers to raise the needed money, and above all, the English will obtain checkmate on the side, if Fortune agrees to it; and there will also be dissensions and mortal hatreds which will be rooted in many hearts for this reason and which will engender treason.

*   *   *

So let virtue overcome vice now! Let one way be found to bring to peace men who are loved ones by nature, and enemies by accident. Alas! Would to God that the trouble and the mobilization that is now displayed be used to seek peace instead of the opposite!...God! What joy this would be! And what high honor would it be to the kingdom forever!

Ah, Very Revered Prince, Noble Duke of Berry, do hear this, for there is nothing greater than what a human heart wants to accomplish, especially in good intent, and cannot manage to attain! And if you work constantly to that purpose, you will be called the Father of this kingdom, keeper of the crown and of the very noble lily, guardian of the high lineage, protector of noble men against death, comfort of the people, guardian of the noble ladies, widows and orphans. May the Blessed Holy Spirit, Author of all peace, give you the heart and the courage to achieve such a thing! Amen. And may He grant me, a poor voice crying in this kingdom, wanting peace and welfare for all, your servant Christine, moved by a very fair mind, the gift to see that day! Amen.

Written the 23rd day of August, in the year of grace 1410.

Christine de Pizan

How to Avoid War

If you are in your heart weary of war I will tell you how you may avoid it, and preserve a cordial and general amity.

Firm and permanent peace is not to be secured by marrying one royal family to another, nor by treaties and alliances made between such deceitful and imperfect creatures as men; for, from these very family connections, treaties, and alliances, we see wars chiefly originate. No, the fountains from which the streams of this evil flow must be cleansed. It is from the corrupt passions of the human heart that the tumults of war arise. While each king obeys the impulse of his passions, the commonwealth, the community suffers, and at the same time the poor slave to his passions is frustrated in his private and selfish purposes. Let kings then grow wise; wise for the people, not for themselves only, and let them be truly wise, in the proper sense of the word, not merely cunning, but really wise; so as to place their majesty, their felicity, their wealth, and their splendour in such things, and such only, as render them personally great, personally superior to those whom the fortune of birth has ranked, in a civil sense, below them. Let them acquire those amiable dispositions toward the commonwealth, the great body of the people, which a father feels for his family. Let a king think of himself great in proportion as his people are good; let him estimate his own happiness by the happiness of those whom he governs; let him deem himself glorious in proportion as his subjects are free; rich, if the public are rich; and flourishing if he can but keep the community flourishing, in consequence of uninterrupted peace.

Desiderius Erasmus (1465-1536)

A Step Beyond Heroism

The cause of peace is not the cause of cowardice. If peace is sought to be defended or preserved for the safety of the luxurious and the timid, it is a sham, and the peace will be base. War is better, and the peace will be broken. If peace is to be maintained, it must be by brave men, who have come up to the same height as the hero, namely, the will to carry their life in their hand, and stake it at any instant for their principle, but who have gone one step beyond the hero, and will not seek another man's life; – men who have, by their intellectual insight or else by their moral elevation, attained such a perception of their own intrinsic worth, that they do not think property or their own body a sufficient good to be saved by such dereliction of principle as treating a man like a sheep.

Ralph Waldo Emerson (1803-1882)

The Music of Peace

[Peace] is the highest and most strenuous action of the soul, but an entirely harmonious action, in which all our powers and affections are blended in a beautiful proportion, and sustain and perfect one another. It is more than silence after storms. It is as the concord of all melodious sounds....It is a conscious harmony with God and the creation..., an alliance of love with all beings, a sympathy with all that is pure and happy, a surrender of every separate will and interest, a participation of the spirit and life of the universe, an entire concord of purpose with its Infinite Original. This is peace, and the true happiness of man.

William E. Channing (1780-1842)

Right: panel from The Garden of Earthly Delights *by Hieronymus Bosch, c. 1500.*

The Peace Testimony

The Christianity which makes war impossible is a way of life which extirpates or controls the dispositions that lead to war. It eradicates the seeds of war in one's daily life. It translates the beatitudes out of the language of a printed book into the practice and spirit of a living person. It is not consistent for anyone to claim that his Christianity as a way of life stops him from war unless he is prepared to adjust his entire life – in its personal aspirations, in its relations with his fellows, in its pursuit of truth, in its economic and social bearings, in its political obligations, in its religious fellowships, in its intercourse with God – to the tremendous demands of Christ's way. If Friends are to challenge the whole world and claim the right to continue in the ways of peace while everybody else is fighting, they must reveal the fact that they are worthy of peace and that they bear in their bodies the marks of the Lord Jesus.

This fundamental religious ground... remains to-day the primary ground of the Quaker refusal to fight. Friends are as conscious as other people are of the complications of the social and political order. They are aware that perfect conditions are not to be expected at this stage of life. The Kingdom of God has obviously not yet come in all of its extensity or intensity. But they take the way of life revealed by Christ as a divinely given programme of human action and of social relationship. They do not rest their case on sporadic texts. They find themselves confronted with a Christianity, the Christianity of the Gospels, that calls for a radical transformation of man, for the creation of a new type of person and for the building of a new social order, and they take this with utmost seriousness as a thing to be ventured and tried. That it is difficult, and that it involves living, even at this imperfect stage, as though the Kingdom of God had come, and as though love were the supreme force of life, seem to them no adequate reasons against this experiment. The only way it ever can come, they believe, is to have a nucleus of people who practise it here in this very difficult present world, who have faith enough in it to make a venture and experiment of trying it, of living by it and, if need be, of dying for it. Finally, they profoundly believe that Christ's own loyalty and dedication to it, even though it cost Him life itself, has made it forever a way of sacred obligation.

From *The Peace Testimony: The Soul of Quakerism,*
1920

"*When the morning Stars sang together, and all the Sons of God shouted for joy.*"
Engraving from The Book of Job *by William Blake, 1825.*

Resist Not Evil

Ye have heard that it hath been said, An eye for an eye, and a tooth for a tooth:

But I say unto you, That ye resist not evil: but whosoever shall smite thee on thy right cheek, turn to him the other also.

And if any man will sue thee at the law, and take away thy coat, let him have thy cloak also.

And whosoever shall compel thee to go a mile, go with him twain.

Give to him that asketh thee, and from him that would borrow of thee turn not thou away.

Ye have heard that it hath been said, Thou shalt love thy neighbour, and hate thine enemy.

But I say unto you, Love your enemies, bless them that curse you, do good to them that hate you, and pray for them which despitefully use you, and persecute you:

That ye may be the children of your Father which is in heaven: for he maketh his sun to rise on the evil and on the good, and sendeth rain on the just and on the unjust.

For if ye love them which love you, what reward have ye? do not even the publicans the same?

And if ye salute your brethren only, what do ye more than others? do not even the publicans so?

Be ye therefore perfect, even as your Father which is in heaven is perfect.

Matthew 5: 38-48

Peace Starts with You

Peace is not an ideal. To me, an ideal is merely an escape, an avoidance of what *is*, a contradiction of what *is*. An ideal prevents direct action upon what *is*. To have peace, we will have to love, we will have to begin not to live an ideal life but to see things as they are and act upon them, transform them. As long as each one of us is seeking psychological security, the physiological security we need – food, clothing and shelter – is destroyed. We are seeking psychological security, which does not exist; and we seek it, if we can, through power, through position, through titles, names – all of which is destroying physical security. This is an obvious fact, if you look at it.

To bring about peace in the world, to stop all wars, there must be a revolution in the individual, in you and me. Economic revolution without this inward revolution is meaningless, for hunger is the result of the maladjustment of economic conditions produced by our psychological states – greed, envy, ill-will and possessiveness. To put an end to sorrow, to hunger, to war, there must be a psychological revolution and few of us are willing to face that. We will discuss peace, plan legislation, create new leagues, the United Nations and so on and on; but we will not win peace because we will not give up our position, our authority, our money, our properties, our stupid lives. To rely on others is utterly futile; others cannot bring us peace. No leader is going to give us peace, no government, no army, no country. What will bring peace is inward transformation which will lead to outward action. Inward transformation is not isolation, is not a withdrawal from outward action. On the contrary, there can be right action only when there is right thinking and there is no right thinking when there is no self-knowledge. Without knowing yourself, there is no peace.

To put an end to outward war, you must begin to put an end to war in yourself. Some of you will nod your heads and say, "I agree," and go outside and do exactly the same as you have been doing for the last ten or twenty years. Your agreement is merely verbal and has no significance, for the world's

A Revolution of One

When the typical reformer or revolutionist proclaims the new order, he goes on to urge men to organize, agitate, get out the vote, fight. Jesus also proclaimed The Kingdom of God [i.e., the revolution] is at hand; but immediately added in true prophetic fashion, Repent. That is to say, if we are to have a new world, we must have new men; if you want a revolution, you must be revolutionized. A world of peace will not be achieved by men who in their own souls are torn with strife and eagerness to assert themselves. In the degree that the anti-war or pacifist movement is composed of individuals who have not themselves, to use Aldous Huxley's phrase, achieved detachment, who have not undergone an inner revolution, it too will experience the same failure to achieve self-discipline, integrity, true fellowship among its own members which has afflicted other movements for social change.

A.J. Muste

The Good Samaritan *(after Delacroix) by Vincent Van Gogh, 1890.*

miseries and wars are not going to be stopped by your casual assent. They will be stopped only when you realize the danger, when you realize your responsibility, when you do not leave it to somebody else. If you realize the suffering, if you see the urgency of immediate action and do not postpone, then you will transform yourself; peace will come only when you yourself are peaceful, when you yourself are at peace with your neighbour.

Krishnamurti (1895-1985)

FOR PEACE AND JUSTICE

Harriet Tubman (far left) photographed with a group of slaves, whom she helped to freedom through the Underground Railroad.

Slavery

Never, never will we desist, till we have wiped away this scandal from the Christian name; till we have released ourselves from the load of guilt under which we at present labour; and till we have extinguished every trace of this bloody traffic, which our posterity, looking back to the history of these enlightened times, will scarcely believe to have been suffered to exist so long, a disgrace and dishonour to our country.

William Wilberforce (1805-1873),
address to British Parliament

Preach Not Moderation

During my recent tour for the purpose of exciting the minds of the people by a series of discourses on the subject of slavery, every place that I visited gave fresh evidence of the fact, that a greater revolution in public sentiment was to be effected in the free states – and *particularly in New England* – than at the south. I found contempt more bitter, opposition more active, detraction more relentless, prejudice more stubborn, and apathy more frozen, than among slave owners themselves. . . .I determined, at every hazard, to lift up the standard of emancipation in the eyes of the nation, *within sight of Bunker Hill and in the birthplace of liberty*. That standard is now unfurled; and long may it float, unhurt by the spoliations of time or the missiles of a desperate foe – yea, till every chain be broken, and every bondman set free! Let Southern oppressors tremble – let their secret abettors tremble – let their Northern apologists tremble – let all the enemies of the persecuted blacks tremble.

*   *   *

. . .I will be as harsh as truth, and as uncompromising as justice. On this subject, I do not wish to think, or speak, or write, with moderation. No! No! Tell a man whose house is on fire, to give a moderate alarm; tell him to moderately rescue his wife from the hands of the ravisher; tell the mother to gradually extricate her babe from the fire into which it has fallen; – but urge me not to use moderation in a cause like the present. I am in earnest – I will not equivocate – I will not excuse – I will not retreat a single inch – AND I WILL BE HEARD.

William Lloyd Garrison (1805-1879)

Ain't I a Woman?

The man over there says women need to be helped into carriages and lifted over ditches, and to have the best places everywhere. Nobody ever helps me into carriages or over puddles, or gives me the best place – and ain't I a woman?...I could work as much and eat as much as a man – when I could get it – and bear the lash as well. And ain't I a woman? I have born thirteen children, and seen most of 'em sold into slavery, and when I cried out with my mother's grief, none but Jesus heard me – and ain't I a woman?

Sojourner Truth, in response to a heckler,
Akron, Ohio, 1851

Virginia Woolf *by Bernice Eisenstein*.

My Country Is the Whole World

Therefore if you insist upon fighting to protect me, or "our" country, let it be understood, soberly and rationally between us, that you are fighting to gratify a sex instinct which I cannot share; to procure benefits which I have not shared and probably will not share; but not to gratify my instincts, or to protect either myself or my country. "For," the outsider will say, "in fact, as a woman, I have no country. As a woman I want no country. As a woman my country is the whole world." And if, when reason has said its say, still some obstinate emotion remains, some love of England dropped into a child's ears by the cawing of rooks in an elm tree, by the splash of waves on a beach, or by English voices murmuring nursery rhymes, this drop of pure, if irrational, emotion she will make serve her to give to England first what she desires of peace and freedom for the whole world.

Virginia Woolf (1882-1941)

Man and Woman

The history of mankind is a history of repeated injuries and usurpations on the part of man toward woman, having in direct object the establishment of an absolute tyranny over her. . . .

He has never permitted her to exercise her inalienable right to the elective franchise.

He has compelled her to submit to laws, in the formation of which she had no voice.

He has made her, if married, in the eye of the law, civilly dead. . . .

In the covenant of marriage, she is compelled to promise obedience to her husband, he becoming, to all intents and purposes, her master – the law giving him power to deprive her of her liberty, and to administer chastisement.

After depriving her of all rights as a married woman, if single, and the owner of property, he has taxed her to support a government which recognizes her only when her property can be made profitable to it.

He has endeavored, in every way that he could, to destroy her confidence in her own powers, to lessen her self-respect and to make her willing to lead a dependent and abject life.

Now, in view of this entire disfranchisement of one-half the people of this country, their social and religious degradation – in view of the unjust laws above mentioned, and because women do feel themselves aggrieved, oppressed, and fraudulently deprived of their most sacred rights, we insist that they have immediate admission to all the rights and privileges which belong to them as citizens of the United States.

Women's Rights Declaration, Seneca Falls, New York (1848)

Suffragettes celebrate California's ratification of the suffrage amendment in November 1919.

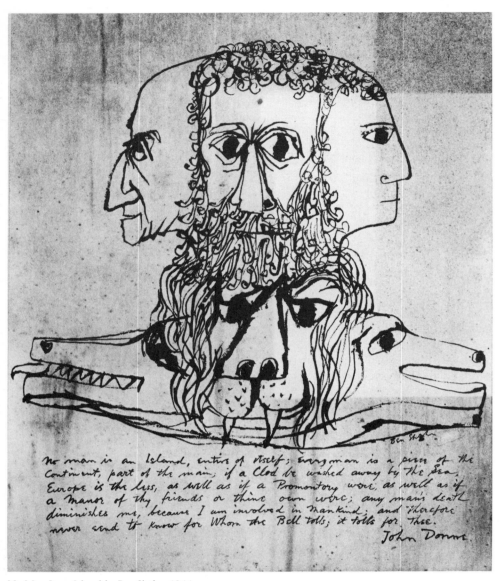

No Man Is an Island by Ben Shahn, 1966.

Evolution of Humanity

The fraternal embrace? Universal love?. . . You are right; humanity has not yet got to that point. But it does not require mutual love to give up killing. . . .

There has been talk of late of an international conference, having in view a coalition against the danger of anarchy. Never will the foolishness of the present situation have been more glaring than when these representatives of states which are living together in absolute anarchy – since they acknowledge no superior power – shall deliberate around the same table on methods of protecting themselves against five or six criminal bombs, while at the same time they will go on threatening one another with a hundred thousand legal bombs!. . .

The evolution of humanity is not a dream, it is a fact scientifically proved. Its end cannot be the premature destruction toward which it is being precipitated by the present system; its end must be the reign of law in control of force. Arms and ferocity develop in inverse ratio, – the tooth, the big stick, the sword, the musket, the explosive bomb, the electric war engine; and, on the other side, the wild beast, the savage, the warrior, the old soldier, the fighter of to-day (a so-called safeguard of peace), the humane man of the future, who, in possession of a power of boundless destructiveness, will refuse to use it.

Bertha von Suttner (1843-1914)

"No More War!"

Our watchword must be: "No more war!" What does that mean?

Not "No more world-war," leaving us free to have little private wars whenever we may want them. Not "no more war," except when, with hardly any risk to ourselves, we can crush some weaker neighbour who falls an easy victim to our power. Not "no more war," except when some matter may arise which affects what in times past we used to call our national honour.

It is none of these things; it is no more war of any kind, no more aggression, no more of the bloody and purposeless conflicts which have so long smirched the history of mankind. It is a movement to rid the politics of the nations of the world of the use of force, and the suppression of others in any form; to get rid once and for all – as we in this generation can do, if we choose – of the hideous anachronism of the institution of warfare among the different sections of the human race, whether it be between one country and another, or within the borders of any specific country.

This cause – I say it without hesitation – is the greatest of all causes at the present day. . . .

If we can raise barriers against war, if we can get rid of the burden of armaments that we are bearing, if we can slay the evil monsters of militarism that still stalk through the world, then we shall get, and get quickly, the social reforms we desire, the development of our possibilities, the progress of whatever kind we are hoping for. We shall advance irresistibly towards a new and better existence.

But if we do not get rid of war, if we do not end it altogether, if we do not reduce and limit our armaments, then we shall get no reform and no lasting progress worth having. We may be very sure that in the future, as in the past, armaments will breed counter-armaments; they will breed alliances and counter-alliances, suspicion and distrust; they will stir up fear in the hearts of the peoples, they will produce international crises, they will lead at first, perhaps, to small local wars, but in the long run, and inevitably, to a great world-war like that which we have seen in our own day and generation.

Fridtjof Nansen (1861-1930)

The Co-operative Principle

In material affairs man has for long neglected his humanity, using his strength only in the furtherance of greed. Numberless slaves are harnessed to the chariot of wealth and driven forward under the whip. The oppressed must eventually say to themselves, "It is our divided strength, concentrated in the hands of the mighty, which has given them power. By attacking the power we can break it but we cannot put it together again, and so it will be no good to us. We must, therefore, try to combine all our labour power and thereby gain economic benefits to be shared by all."

That is the co-operative principle. It is this principle which has made man great in knowledge and given a moral basis to his conduct of practical affairs. Where it is lacking, there is suffering, malice, falsity, barbarity and strife.

The clash of power against power raises conflagrations on all sides. Man is being sacrificed at the altar of individual greed. Unless stopped, this will cause the most terrible havoc in history. The rift between the mighty and the weak in the world of material affairs is the most serious danger today. Differences exist between the learned and the ignorant; but men do not raise walls of separation over the right to knowledge; the intellectual classes are not anxious to gain strength by group combination. The inordinate greed for money, however, has been raising walls to keep people apart in every country and in every home. Differences also existed between people in the past; but the walls did not reach such great heights. Greed did not overwhelm and corrupt all literature, art, politics, and domestic life. Beyond the monetary fields were other wider fields where men could unite.

It is not the rich but the poor who must rescue society from the crushing weight of great wealth. The building of an entrance gate to the heavily barred economic field must lie in their hands. . . .

That most of the advantages created in the modern age are enjoyed only by a few, while the majority are denied, is a misfortune for which society must expiate. The remedy lies not in restricting wealth or taking forcible possession of it or giving it away. The remedy is in stimulating in all people the capacity for creating new wealth; in other words, it is in expounding to the people the principles of co-operation.

Rabindranath Tagore (1861-1941)

Peace Now by Kenneth Patchen.

TO END ALL WAR

A bronze votive plaque from ancient Argos with the inscription: "A Curse upon Mars."

Wolf War God. *Anonymous, c. 1630.*

War Is Vulgar

As long as war is regarded as wicked, it will always have its fascination. When it is looked upon as vulgar, it will cease to be popular.

Oscar Wilde (1854-1900)

The Children of Peace

To those who inquire of us whence we come, or who is our founder, we reply that we are come, agreeably to the counsels of Jesus, to "cut down our hostile and insolent 'wordy' swords into ploughshares, and to convert into pruning-hooks the spears formerly employed in war." For we no longer take up "sword against nation," nor do we "learn war any more," having become children of peace, for the sake of Jesus, who is our leader, instead of those whom our fathers followed, among whom we were "strangers to the covenant," and having received a law, for which we give thanks to Him that rescued us from the error of our ways.

Origen (185-254 A.D.)

Peace Testimony of the Society of Friends

We utterly deny all outward wars and strife, and fightings with outward weapons, for any end, or under any pretence whatever; this is our testimony to the whole world. The Spirit of Christ by which we are guided is not changeable, so as once to command us from a thing as evil, and again to move unto it; and we certainly know, and testify to the world, that the Spirit of Christ, which leads us into all truth, will never move us to fight and war against any man with outward weapons, neither for the kingdom of Christ, nor for the kingdoms of the world.

From *A Declaration from the Harmless and Innocent People of God, called Quakers,*
presented to Charles II, 1660

No Quarrel

Can anything be more ridiculous than that a man should have the right to kill me because he lives on the other side of the water and because his ruler has a quarrel with mine, though I have none with him?

Why do you kill me? What: do you not live on the other side of the water? If you lived on this side, my friend, I should be an assassin, and it would be unjust to slay you in this manner. But since you live on the other side, I am a hero, and it is just.

Blaise Pascal (1623-1662)

Why?

What becomes of and what signifies to me humanity, beneficence, modesty, temperance, mildness, wisdom, and piety while half a pound of lead sent from the distance of a hundred steps pierces my body and I die at twenty years of age in inexpressible torments in the midst of five or six thousand dying men, while my eyes, which open for the last time, see the town in which I was born destroyed by fire and sword, and the last sounds that reach my ears are the cries of women and children expiring under the ruins, all for the pretended interests of a man whom I know not.

Voltaire (1694-1778)

Killed in Action *by Kathe Kollwitz, 1921.*

The Drum

I hate that drum's discordant sound,
Parading round, and round, and round:
To thoughtless youth it pleasure yields,
And lures from cities and from fields,
To sell their liberty for charms
Of tawdry lace, and glittering arms;
And when Ambition's voice commands,
To march, and fight, and fall, in foreign lands.

I hate that drum's discordant sound,
Parading round, and round, and round:
To me it talks of ravag'd plains,
And burning towns, and ruin'd swains,
And mangled limbs, and dying groans,
And widows' tears, and orphans' moans;
And all that Misery's hand bestows,
To fill the catalogue of human woes.

John Scott (1730-1783)

Detail of Rina a Garrotazos *by Francisco de Goya,* c. 1820-21.

Conscientious Objections

And it be further enacted, that the persons called Quakers, Mennonists, and Tunkers, who from certain scruples of conscience, decline bearing arms, shall not be compelled to serve in the said Militia, but every person professing that he is one of the people called Quakers, Mennonists, or Tunkers, and producing a certificate of his being a Quaker, Mennonist, or Tunker, signed by any three or more of the people (who are or shall be by them authorized to grant certificates for this or any other purpose of which a pastor, minister, or preacher shall be one) shall be excused and exempted from serving in the said Militia, and instead of such service, all and every such person and persons, that shall or may be of the people called Quakers, Mennonists, or Tunkers, shall pay to the lieutenant of the county or riding, or in his absence to the deputy lieutenant, the sum of 20 shillings per annum in time of peace, and five pounds per annum in time of actual invasion or insurrection.

Upper Canada Parliament at Niagara, Militia Act of 1793

The New England Non-Resistance Society

We register our testimony, not only against all wars, whether offensive or defensive, but all preparations of war; against every naval ship, every arsenal, every fortification; against the militia system and a standing army; against all military chieftains and soldiers; against all monuments commemorative of victory over a foreign foe, all trophies won in battle, all celebrations in honor of military or naval exploits; against all appropriations for the defence of a nation by force and arms, on the part of any legislative body; against every edict of government requiring of its subjects military service. Hence, we deem it unlawful to bear arms, or to hold a military office.

As every human government is upheld by physical strength, and its laws are enforced virtually at the point of the bayonet, we cannot hold any office which imposes upon its incumbent the obligation to compel men to do right, on pain of imprisonment or death. We therefore voluntarily exclude ourselves from every legislative and judicial body, and repudiate all human politics, worldly honors, and stations of authority. If *we* cannot occupy a seat in the legislature, or on the bench, neither can we elect *others* to act as our substitutes in any such capacity.

Non-Resistance Society, Statement of Principles, 1838

The Mask of Anarchy

Stand ye calm and resolute,
Like a forest, close and mute,
With folded arms and looks that are
Weapons of unvanquished war. . . .

And if then the tyrants dare,
Let them ride among you there,
Slash, and stab, and maim and hew –
What they like, that let them do.

With folded arms and steady eyes,
And little fear, and less surprise,
Look upon them as they slay
Till their rage has passed away.

Then they will return with shame
To the place from which they came
And the blood thus shed will speak
In hot blushes on their cheek.

Every woman in the land
Will point at them as they stand –
They will hardly dare to greet
Their acquaintance in the street.

And that slaughter to the Nation
Shall steam up like inspiration,
Eloquent, oracular,
A volcano heard afar.

Rise like Lions after slumber
In unvanquishable number –
Shake your chains to earth like dew
Which in sleep had fallen on you –
Ye are many – they are few.

Percy Bysshe Shelley (1792-1822)
inspired by the 1819 Peterloo Massacre

67

A Long Illness

There was one curious fact which I do not remember ever to have seen noticed in histories of the war [the U.S. Civil War], and that was its effect upon the nation as individuals. Men and women thought and did noble and mean things that would have been impossible to them before or after. A man cannot drink old Bourbon long and remain in his normal condition. We did not drink Bourbon, but blood. No matter how gentle or womanly we might be, we read, we talked, we thought perforce of nothing but slaughter. So many hundreds dead here, so many thousands there, were our last thoughts at night and the first in the morning. The effect was very like that produced upon a household in which there has been a long illness. There was great religious exaltation and much peevish ill temper. Under the long, nervous strain the softest women became fierce partisans, deaf to arguments or pleas for mercy. Nothing would convince some of the most intellectual women in New England that their southern sisters were not all Hecates, habitually employed in flogging their slaves; while Virginia girls believed that the wives of the men who invaded their homes were all remorseless, bloodthirsty harpies.

We no longer gave our old values to the conditions of life. Our former ideas of right and wrong were shaken to the base. The ten commandments, we began to suspect, were too old-fashioned to suit this present emergency.

I knew, for instance, of a company made up of sons and grandsons of old Scotch Covenanters. They were educated, gallant young fellows. They fought bravely, and in the field or in hospital were kind and humane to their foes. But they came home, when disbanded, with their pockets full of spoons and jewelry which they had found in farmhouses looted and burned on Sherman's march to the sea; and they gayly gave them around to their sweethearts as souvenirs of the war.

Rebecca Harding Davis (1831-1910)

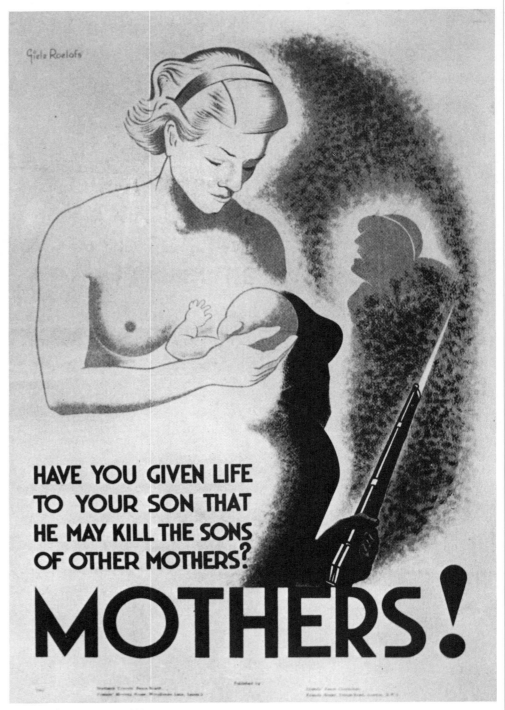

British anti-war poster, c. 1938.

Mother's Day for Peace

Arise all women who have hearts . . . say firmly: we women of one country will be too tender of those of another country to allow our sons to injure theirs. In the name of womanhood and humanity I earnestly ask that a general Congress of Women, without limit of nationality, promote the alliance of the different nationalities, the amicable settlement of international questions, the great and general interests of peace.

Julia Ward Howe (1819-1910), crusade to establish Mothers' Day, 1870

How We Rationalize War

The loud little handful – as usual – will shout for the war. The pulpit will – warily and cautiously – object – at first; the great, big, dull bulk of the nation will rub its sleepy eyes and try to make out why there should be a war, and will say, earnestly and indignantly, "It's unjust and dishonorable, and there is no necessity for it." Then the handful will shout louder. A few fair men on the other side will argue and reason against the war with speech and pen, and at first will have a hearing and be applauded; but it will not last long; those others will outshout them, and presently the anti-war audiences will thin out and lose popularity. Before long you will see this curious thing; the speakers stoned from the platform, and free speech strangled by hordes of furious men who in their secret hearts are still at one with those stoned speakers – as earlier – but do not dare say so. And now the whole nation – pulpit and all – will take up the war-cry, and shout itself hoarse, and mob any honest man who ventures to open his mouth; and presently such mouths will cease to open. Next, the statesmen will invent cheap lies, putting the blame on the nation that is attacked, and every man will be glad of those conscience-soothing falsities, and will diligently study them, and refuse to examine any refutations of them; and thus he will by and by convince himself that the war is just, and will thank God for the better sleep he enjoys after this process of grotesque self-deception.

Mark Twain (1835-1910), from *The Mysterious Stranger*, 1898

Anti-War Meeting

Then came the bombshell. Diplomatic relations with Germany broke off. . . .

Meanwhile the militarists redoubled their efforts to whip up the war spirit. Roosevelt (the fire-eating Teddy) was the star actor in a tumultuous meeting in Madison Square Garden. Thousands who couldn't get in surged round the building and listened to impromptu speeches. But there was not the undivided enthusiasm for war that the organisers had expected. There was so much opposition in every part of the vast throng that the meeting became a riot. Every interrupter was tackled in approved Fascist style and before long almost every ambulance in the city was busy carrying the wounded off to hospital. Hundreds were beaten up, and many of them seriously injured. It wasn't an easy job to get the Americans to accept war.

We decided that we must hold a counter meeting in Madison Square Garden as soon as it could be organised. The only date available was in four days. We booked the Garden, and on the advertising we could do at that short notice the place was packed, with thousands unable to get in. We resolved that it would, in fact, be a peace meeting. A large band of young Irishmen, all of them over six feet high, offered themselves as chuckers-out. I met them in an ante-room just before the meeting began. They surrounded me like a small forest of trees, and I wondered whether they could really restrain themselves, with the light of battle shining in every eye. I made an eloquent plea. I told them that we had refused to employ a single additional policeman, that we didn't want a single person in the audience injured, whatever his views. They agreed to be as gentle as lambs, and not even to tackle an interrupter unless he became a thorough nuisance. Then they were just to lift him out as gently as they could, and put him outside. Well, our meeting was a thousand times more united than the war meeting had been. But we had our hecklers. Occasionally, from the platform, I saw two of the Irish giants lifting a persistent interrupter over the heads of his neighbours, passing him from one group to another until he was outside. Not a blow was struck – not a person injured.

Lella Secor Florence, from *We Did Not Fight, 1914-1918*

The First Peace Pledge

Believing all war to be inconsistent with the spirit of Christianity, and destructive to the best interests of mankind, I do hereby pledge myself never to enlist or enter into any army or navy, or to yield any voluntary support or sanction to the preparation for or prosecution of any war, by whomsoever, for whatsoever proposed, declared, or waged. And I do hereby associate myself with all persons, of whatever country, condition, or color, who have signed, or shall hereafter sign this pledge, in a "League of Universal Brotherhood"; whose object shall be to employ all legitimate and moral means for the abolition of all war, and all spirit, and all the manifestation of war, throughout the world; for the abolition of all restrictions upon international correspondence and friendly intercourse, and of whatever else tends to make enemies of nations, or prevents their fusion into one peaceful brotherhood; for the abolition of all institutions and customs which do not recognize the image of God and a human brother in every man of whatever clime, color, or condition of humanity.

Elihu Burritt, League of Universal Brotherhood peace pledge (1847)

Great Disarmament Procession held in London showing the League of Nations section of the parade.

Objection to Military Service

Whoever I may be, whether I belong to the well-to-do dominating class or to the oppressed labouring class, the disadvantages of non-submission [to military service] are less and its advantages greater than those of submission.

If I belong to the dominating minority, the disadvantages of non-submission to the government's demands will consist in my being tried for refusing to comply and at best I shall be discharged, or (as is done with the Mennonites in Russia) I shall be obliged to serve my time at some non-military work. At worst I shall be condemned to exile or imprisonment for two or three years (I speak from examples that have occurred in Russia), or possibly to an even longer term, or to death – though the probability of such a penalty is very small.

These are the disadvantages of non-submission. But the disadvantages of submission are these: at best I shall escape being sent to kill people and shall escape being myself exposed to the danger of being maimed or killed, and shall merely be enrolled into military slavery. I shall be dressed up like a clown and domineered over by every man above me in rank from a corporal to a field-marshal. I shall be forced to contort my body as they please, and after being kept from one to five years I shall for another ten years have to hold myself in readiness to be called up at any moment to go through all these things again. In the worst case I shall, in addition to all these conditions of slavery, be sent to war, where I shall be compelled to kill men of other nations who have done me no harm, and where I may be maimed or killed or (as happened in Sevastopol and as happens in every war) sent to certain death, or (most terrible of all) be sent against my own countrymen and compelled to kill my brothers for dynastic or other reasons quite alien to me.

Such are the comparative disadvantages.

The comparative advantages of submission and non-submission are these:

For a man who submits, the advantages are that after enduring all the humiliations and performing all the cruelties demanded of him, he may if he is not killed receive a gaudy red or gold decoration for his clown's dress, and may even, if he is very fortunate, obtain command of hundreds of thousands of men as brutalized as himself, and be called field-marshal and receive a lot of money.

The advantages of a man who refuses are the preservation of his human dignity, the respect of good men, and above all the certainty that he is doing God's work and so is indubitably doing good to his fellow-man.

Such are the advantages and disadvantages on both sides for a man of the oppressing, wealthy classes. For a man of the poor working class the advantages and disadvantages are the same, but with an important addition to the disadvantages. The disadvantages for a man of the labouring classes who has not refused military service comprise also this, that by entering the military service he by his participation and apparent approval, confirms the oppression to which he himself is subject.

Leo Tolstoi (1828-1910)

War by Henri Rousseau, 1894.

The Monster, Militarism

Militarism consumes the strongest and most productive elements of each nation. Militarism swallows the largest part of the national revenue. Almost nothing is spent on education, art, literature and science compared with the amount devoted to militarism in times of peace, while in times of war everything else is set at naught; all life stagnates, all effort is curtailed; the very sweat and blood of the masses are used to feed this insatiable monster – militarism. Under such circumstances, it must become more arrogant, more aggressive, more bloated with its own importance. If for no other reason, it is out of surplus energy that militarism must act to remain alive; therefore it will seek an enemy or create one artificially. In this civilized purpose and method, militarism is sustained by the state, protected by the laws of the land, fostered by the home and the school, and glorified by public opinion. In other words, the function of militarism is to kill. It cannot live except through murder.

Emma Goldman (1869-1940)

Asleep in the Valley

A small green valley where a slow stream runs
And leaves long strands of silver on the bright
Grass; from the mountaintop stream the sun's
Rays; they fill the hollow full of light.

A soldier, very young, lies open-mouthed.
A pillow made of ferns beneath his head,
Asleep; stretched in the heavy undergrowth,
Pale in his green, warm, sun-soaked bed.

His feet among the flowers, he sleeps. His smile
Is like an infant's – gentle, without guile.
Ah, Nature, keep him warm; he may catch cold.

The humming insects don't disturb his rest;
He sleeps in sunlight, one hand on his breast,
At peace. In his side there are two red holes.

Arthur Rimbaud (1854-1891)

The Dead

These hearts were woven of human joys and cares,
    Washed marvellously with sorrow, swift to mirth.
The years had given them kindness. Dawn was theirs,
    And sunset, and the colours of the earth.
These had seen movement, and heard music; known
    Slumber and waking; loved; gone proudly friended;
Felt the quick stir of wonder; sat alone;
    Touched flowers and furs and cheeks. All this is ended.

There are waters blown by changing winds to laughter
And lit by the rich skies, all day. And after,
    Frost, with a gesture, stays the waves that dance
And wandering loveliness. He leaves a white
    Unbroken glory, a gathered radiance,
A width, a shining peace, under the night.

Rupert Brooke (1887-1915)

71

PEACEFUL COURAGE

The First Women Against War

MAGISTRATE: The war has nothing to do with money –

LYSISTRATA: Hasn't it? Why are Peisander and the other office-seekers always stirring things up? Isn't it so they can take a few more dips in the public purse? Well, as far as we're concerned they can do what they like; only they're not going to lay their hands on the money in there.

MAGISTRATE: Why, what are you going to do?

LYSISTRATA: Do? Why, we'll be in charge of it.

MAGISTRATE: *You* in charge of *our* finances?

LYSISTRATA: Well, what's so strange about that? We've been in charge of all your housekeeping finances for years.

MAGISTRATE: But that's not the same thing.

LYSISTRATA: Why not?

MAGISTRATE: Because the money here is needed for the war!

LYSISTRATA: Ah, but the war itself isn't necessary.

MAGISTRATE: Not necessary! How is the City going to be saved then?

LYSISTRATA: We'll save it for you.

MAGISTRATE: You!!!

LYSISTRATA: Us.

MAGISTRATE: This is intolerable!

LYSISTRATA: It may be, but it's what's going to happen.

MAGISTRATE: But Demeter! – I mean, it's against nature!

LYSISTRATA[*very sweetly*]: We've got to save you, after all, Sir.

MAGISTRATE: Even against my will?

LYSISTRATA: That only makes it all the more essential.

MAGISTRATE: Anyway, what business are war and peace of yours?

LYSISTRATA: I'll tell you.

* * *

LYSISTRATA: In the last war we were too modest to object to anything you men did – and in any case you wouldn't let us say a word. But don't think we approved! We knew everything that was going on. Many times we'd hear at home about some major blunder of yours, and then when you came home we'd be burning inside but we'd have to put on a smile and ask what it was you'd decided to inscribe on the pillar underneath the Peace Treaty. – And what did my husband always say? – "Shut up and mind your own business!" And I did.

STRATYLLIS: *I* wouldn't have done!

MAGISTRATE[*ignoring her – to* LYSISTRATA]: He'd have given you one if you hadn't!

LYSISTRATA: Exactly – so I kept quiet. But sure enough, next thing we knew you'd take an even sillier decision. And if I so much as said, "Darling, why are you carrying on with this silly policy?" he would glare at me and say, "Back to your weaving, woman, or you'll have a headache for a month. Go and attend to your work; let war be the care of the menfolk."

MAGISTRATE: Quite right too, by Zeus.

LYSISTRATA: Right? That we should not be allowed to make the least little suggestion to you, no matter how much you mismanage the City's affairs? And now, look, every time two people meet in the street, what do they say? "Isn't there a man in the country?" and the answer comes, "Not one." That's why we women got together and decided we were going to save Greece. What was the point of. waiting any longer, we asked ourselves. Well now, we'll make a deal. You listen to us – and we'll talk sense, not like you used to – listen to us and keep quiet, as we've had to do up to now, and we'll clear up the mess you've made.

Aristophanes, from the play *Lysistrata*, first performed in Athens, 411 B.C.

Detail of Saint Martin Lays Down His Arms *by Simone Martini, 1322-26.*

The Death of a Soldier of Peace

The Proconsul Dion said: "What are you called?"

Maximilianus answered: "But why do you want to know my name? I dare not fight, since I am a Christian."

The Proconsul Dion said: "Measure him."

But on being measured Maximilianus answered: "I cannot fight, I cannot do evil; I am a Christian."

The Proconsul Dion said: "Measure him."

And after he had been measured, the attendant read out: "He is five feet ten."

Dion said to the official: "Sign him up."

And Maximilianus cried out: "I won't, I cannot be a soldier."

Dion said: "Get into the war-service or it will cost you your life."

Maximilianus answered: "I do no war-service. . . .I do no war-service to this age, but I do war-service for my God."

The trial of Maximilianus (295 A.D.)

Heaven and Hell

A big, tough samurai once went to see a little monk. "Monk," he said, in a voice accustomed to instant obedience, "teach me about heaven and hell!"

The monk looked up at this mighty warrior and replied with utter disdain, "Teach you about heaven and hell? I couldn't teach you about anything. You're dirty. You smell. Your blade is rusty. You're a disgrace, an embarrassment to the samurai class. Get out of my sight. I can't stand you."

The samurai was furious. He shook, got all red in the face, was speechless with rage. He pulled out his sword and raised it above him, preparing to slay the monk.

"That's hell," said the monk softly.

The samurai was overwhelmed. The compassion and surrender of this little man who had offered his life to give this teaching to show him hell! He slowly put down his sword, filled with gratitude, and suddenly peaceful.

"And that's heaven," said the monk softly.

Anonymous

The Weapon of Love

BISHOP:...But the world won't leave us alone. And now this country has declared its Military Service Act. That means they will try to make us fight in their sinful war. I'm going to read to you what Menno Simons said about that four hundred years ago. [*He picks up a book and fumbles for the page*.] "I tell you the truth in Christ, those who are baptized according to the word of the Lord have no weapons except patience, love, silence and God's word. The weapons of our warfare are not weapons with which cities may be destroyed and human blood shed in torrents like water. Love is the only weapon a Christian can know, even if we be torn into a thousand pieces and if as many false witnesses rise up against us as there are spears of grass in the fields, and grains of sand on the seashore."

Anne Chislett, from the play
Quiet in the Land.

Letter to Oliver Cromwell

I, who am of the world called George Fox, do deny that the carrying or drawing of any carnal sword against any, or against thee, Oliver Cromwell, or any man. In the presence of the Lord God I declare it.

God is my witness, by whom I am moved to give this forth for the Truth's sake, from him whom the world calls George Fox: who is the son of God who is sent to stand a witness against all violence and against the works of darkness, and to turn people from the darkness to the light, and to bring them from the occasion of the war and from the occasion of the magistrate's sword, which is a terror to the evil doers who act contrary to the light of the Lord Jesus Christ, which is a praise to them that do well, a protection to them that do well and not evil. Such soldiers as are put in that place no false accusers, must be, no violence must do, but be content with their wages; and the magistrate bears not the sword in vain.

From under the occasion of that sword do I seek to bring people. My weapons are not carnal but spiritual, and "my kingdom is not of this world," therefore with a carnal weapon I do not fight, but am from those things dead; from him who is not of the world, called of the world by the name George Fox. And this I am ready to seal with my blood.

This I am moved to give forth for the Truth's sake, who a witness stand against all unrighteousness and all ungodliness, who a sufferer am for the righteous Seed's sake, waiting for the redemption of it, who a crown that is mortal seek not, for that faded away, but in the light dwell, which comprehends that crown, which light is the condemnation of all such; in which light I witness the crown is immortal, that fades not away.

From him who to all your souls is a friend, for establishing of righteousness and cleansing the land of evil doers and a witness against all wicked inventions of men and murderous plots, which answered shall be with the light in all your consciences, which makes no covenant with death, to which light in you all I speak, and am clear.

George Fox (1624-1691)

The Dutch Ten Commandments to Foil the Nazis *(which are being distributed in thousands throughout the Netherlands)*

1. Thou shalt resist the evil one with all power; thou shalt be courageous, intelligent, and stubborn.
2. Thou shalt not spread false rumour, nor accept empty phrases, but shalt speak the truth.
3. Thou shalt not extinguish thine anger, but shall master it, that thy conscience may not be blunted by adjustment to wrong causes.
4. Thou shalt renew the life of thy soul, that civilisation may find thee ready after the fires of war.
5. Thou shalt aid in building a community that offers all of good-will a fair chance, justice, peace, and truth.
6. Thou shalt not withhold thyself from common suffering, but shalt live here with a warm heart and judge thine enemy in justice.
7. Thou shalt not be passive only, but shalt turn thy soul to the permanent risk of life.
8. Thou shalt not safeguard the purity of thy soul in pernickety ways, but shalt follow thy destiny in the great order of the world, and not withhold alliance in the fulfilment thereof.
9. Thou shalt pursue light even in the darkness, for light remains light.
10. Thou shalt realise that the basis of thy life is not "must" but "may," not "law" but "mercy"; this is thy consolation, thy creed, and thy power as a Christian Netherlander.

Evening Standard, January 19, 1942

ZONGULDAK SICKNESS

BY GENEVIÈVE SERREAU

The trains rattle as they go by. Criss-crossing in all directions the territory of the night. Behind the window panes, at every window, at every door, a cluster of soldiers wearing helmets. "B" Army has a meeting set with "N" Army in a vast, deserted stretch of land, a pure, inorganic space, meticulously plotted by the general staff. In preparation for the Great Massacre. Pure and inorganic. They drag behind them their combat vehicles hooked up to the railway carriages, pieces of large artillery, a phallus pointing up towards heaven from among branches of camouflage with leaves drying and dropping off. "B" Army passes "N" Army at 200 an hour on a viaduct, with soldiers pressed against the windows. "B" rolls on northwards, "N" southwards. A failed meeting. A slight plotting error by the general staff, monstrously multiplied by time and distance. They pass each other, followed by a whitish blur of helmeted faces glued to window panes. Continuing their journey, travelling apart through the iron night. Later they would make a half-turn. Later. When they have exhausted time, speed, the purpose of the journey. When the general staff, deep in their big leather easy-chairs, have recalculated their meticulous plans.

*   *   *

Once he got over his attack, the Ancestor was placed in the small room off the dining room. They had bought him a wheelchair with a rear brake. The poor old fellow has faded away quite a bit, they would say, but he's always on the go. All you have to do is put on the brake and he'll stay where he is. In his small room, on the three walls and door, the Ancestor tacked up all of his wars. A lot of postcards, some mobilization pamphlets, medals, and a lock of hair from a Communard that he ran through with his bayonet on the barricade in the rue de Charonne. The Great War of '14—'18 occupied a place of honour: the Marne, the Chemin des Dames, Verdun, heaps of bones, trenches, the gutted cathedral at Reims, worldly women making bandages. The heaps of bones might have belonged to the next war, the one where they didn't fight, but where people died in great piles, far away from France, from starvation.

On the back of the Ossuary of Douaumont, he had secretly pasted a photograph of his son Robert, the one they called Bébert, who died of croup when he was four. Every morning, as soon as he was alone in the small room, he would grab the Ossuary, turn it over and kiss the little boy on the mouth. The photo was quite faded and worn at the spot where he placed his kiss. A stab of pain does not grow old. He looked at the warm hollow of the boy's neck where it felt so good to snuggle his face while Bébert screamed with laughter. They had invented all sorts of ways of dying up there. Little Robert had had the right to the worst of them. The sons of bitches. Comrades in the trenches, dead in the confusion of the general din, had only left behind a shovelful of sniggering bones. "Shit, I've lost my tibia," one of his pals had said just before he died. And it was true. The tibia was lying a few

metres away, there, in the mud. It had made him laugh at the time, he remembered, and he had said to himself: More than likely, I'll lose my head. And that had made him laugh, too. It had just been a matter of luck that he hadn't lost it. But, even if he had lost it, he wouldn't have known who to complain to. War was just a crazy vacation and you didn't have time to get bored, as you did in peacetime. Just as they were bored now, with a bitter taste in his mouth, dragging around his old slipper, waiting for life to amount to something, waiting for something to happen. The only thing that peace had been able to invent, underhandedly plotting its blow, was to smother Bébert, all alone in his little cot, for no reason at all.

Of course, today's wars aren't what they used to be. The most recent, the one in Kabylia, had given him, in spite of everything, a beautiful series of faces, blown to pieces in their turbans.

*   *   *

And after that, there wouldn't be any more. Not a single one. They would just meet. Once and for all. It certainly was more modern. From just about everywhere, they had taken welders, farm boys, bus drivers, gymnasts, tanners, adjusters, plumbers, sanders, garbagemen, glassworkers, miners, all strong and healthy. Quite quickly, they had all begun to look alike. That's what happens when you lose your memory. They cut across the night, their white, empty faces pressed against the window panes. Sometimes, they would stop at little lost stations, just long enough for the train to release its old pent-up breath, its piss and spit, and for the officers to have new cannons hooked up behind the old ones, which have begun to rust. Gadgets equipped with the latest technological improvements. They only take the ones that belong to them, leaving the others behind in the hangar. "B" Army's cannons bear a "B", while "N" Army's have an "N", so there can be no mistake about it.

The two convoys miss each other for months, years at a time, clanking through the night, sometimes near each other, sometimes very far apart, modernizing their weapons bit by bit. Sitting inside their leaded carriages, the officers had few problems with the troops. One morning, however, one of the "B" Convoy's soldiers started humming "Cherry Time". You see, the train had been rushing for hours through the cherry orchards, in full bloom, of Zonguldak, the province on the Black Sea, from which, it is popularly said, Caesar took back to Europe centuries ago a tree with snowy-white flowers and blood-red fruit, whose merits are still celebrated today. The soldier – a glass-blower with good lungs – had forgotten most of the words and was trying to remember them; as such he kept on without stopping, making use of his plentiful breath to keep repeating the mournful tune, from which groups of words gradually emerged. His neighbours were surprised to hear themselves humming along with him. Soon, passing from man to man, "Cherry Time" took hold of all the empty faces glued to the windows. Ravaging and reshaping them as

Illustration by Jan Lenica, 1963.

it went. Memory returned to them, like blood flowing into a frozen foot. One soldier began to vomit with nostalgia. The faces were fragmenting dangerously into individuals. The breakdown reached its height when the soldier, exhausted from all his effort, his voice cracking, remembered *And from those days on, my heart has been an open wound*, a phrase that shot with unequalled speed through the entire train, more searing than a dum-dum bullet. The officer ordered the alert. Walking through the corridor, he noted to his great surprise that one soldier had blue eyes, another hazel, and one soldier had blond hair and yet another had a wart on his left cheek. Perhaps he had fallen victim to some sort of disturbance. He thought he could see in the corner near the toilet, as thin and black as a black flag rolled around its staff, the silhouette of Louise Michel, and even, farther along, a young Lenin, his fiery eyes dancing in the snow – was it in the snow or the cherry blossoms?...That was never clear. He gave his report. The commanding officer took matters in hand. Patrols of officers were sent through the corridors of the convoy, shouting at regular intervals: Budapest..., Kolyma..., Lubjanka..., Prague..., Gulag..., Budapest..., Prague..., Kolyma....The names cracked like whips. The faces rapidly re-arranged themselves. The soldier forgot the song. Besides, they had left the cherry orchards of Zonguldak behind them and the convoy was crossing at a frenzied rate the great desert of Anatolia, white empty faces glued to the window panes under their helmets. "N" Convoy had been sighted not far from there in Uzbekistan, making its way along the shores of the Aral Sea. The long-awaited meeting might take place in the next few days. The commander jotted down the details of the incident as a lesson for future officers. He wrote on the file: "Zonguldak Sickness" and filed it under the letter *S*; but then, on further thought, put it under *Z*, which was still a pristine letter.

*   *   *

One day, a distant nephew came to visit the Ancestor, who had faded quite a bit, but who still was always on the go. A correct young man, as translucent as a half-sucked piece of candy. They brought the Ancestor out of the small room. They released the brake so he could roll for a moment around the table. Everyone noted that he had faded away a little more since the preceding visit. He hardly had anything more to say. The nephew had several university degrees and a home in the suburbs. He worked in an office and was respectful to elderly people. He said that in the future there would be no more wars, that those days were over, thank

God, at least in our beautiful country. The Ancestor pointed his index finger at the translucent young man and shouted "bang, bang." Everyone laughed. Except the Ancestor. It was a joyous scene. The Ancestor indicated that he wanted to go back to the small room.

On his second visit, the nephew with the university degrees brought the Ancestor a coloured photograph of his fiancée. As anyone could see, she was as translucent a person as the groom. He would marry her as soon as he could manage to put aside a nest-egg large enough for him to plunge into the mainstream of life. The fiancée on the photograph was wearing a light-blue dress and holding a bouquet of daisies in her hands. The nephew insisted on hanging the photograph on the wall of the small room above the Ossuary of Douaumont, which he took down. The Ancestor became exceedingly agitated on seeing the fiancée, stuck up there with a thumbtack. He waved his good hand in the air. "He'll get used to it," the nephew stated, throwing the Ossuary into the coal stove, where it curled up, blackened bones, until there was nothing left but ashes. "All these dead people," the pacifist nephew observed, "they really do have quite a demoralizing effect over time." The nephew would come back a third and final time. He noticed finger marks, fingernail scratches under the tacked-up photograph of the fiancée in the small room, almost as though the Ancestor had desperately tried to reach it. The Ancestor firmly held a (loaded) rifle from the Great War of '14 under his good arm. He aimed his cannon at his translucent nephew and fired. The nephew fell backwards. His blood, so improbable up until then, gushed out in the small room. They galloped away with the Ancestor, splattered with the blood of his victim, to the nearest insane asylum. In the hospital, the translucent nephew, unkillable and a pacifist, his chest camouflaged in metres of Velpeau bandages, waited for his wound to heal. "An Incomprehensible Drama," they would read in small bold type on the last page of the local papers.

*   *   *

They are still clattering through our nights. "B" Convoy, "N" Convoy never fail to miss each other. The general staff grow old, sinking into the dust of their big leather easy-chairs. The next generation is ready to take their place. No one any longer can recall that strange illness, the Zonguldak Sickness. Its name, however, is never spoken except with fear and trembling.

translated by G. Craig Thomas

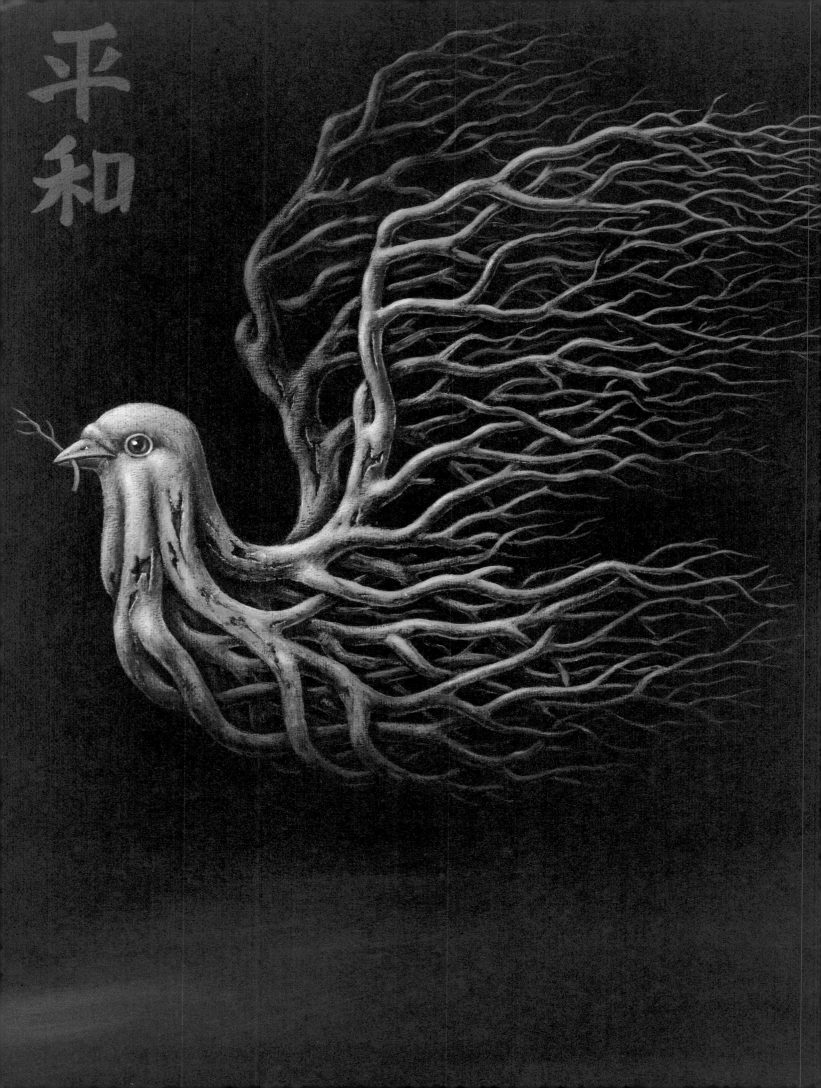

THE NIGHTMARE

The world changed forever – and not for better – in 1945, when the United States dropped the first atomic bombs on Japan, thus ushering in the nightmare of the nuclear age. As scientists learned to interpret the effects of radioactivity, slowly the public realized that the bomb was more than just another weapon, that it held the potential to extinguish all life on the planet. As our understanding grows, so does the horror. What we face now is not merely slaughter or genocide, but "omnicide," the obliteration of all humans and all living species.

Although they didn't really understand the long-term toxicity of the new weapons, the bomb's inventors warned that civilians were no longer safe, and predicted the spiralling arms race in which we are now involved. Early attempts to protect civilian populations from atomic attacks through air-raid drills and fallout shelters were soon proven laughably ineffective, as scientists accumulated information about radioactivity. Those data were gathered from observing Hiroshima and Nagasaki victims, laboratory workers, soldiers and sailors who worked with the weapons – and also people who resided near A-bomb test sites in the American southwest and the Marshall Islands.

With the onset of the Cold War, the growing mistrust and tension between east and west resulted in a race for nuclear supremacy. The arms build-up has continued, to such an absurd extent that the superpowers now have stockpiled the equivalent of fourteen tons of TNT for every man, woman, and child on the planet. There are dozens of kinds of weapons that can be delivered by various methods, including intercontinental ballistic missiles, bombers, and submarines. And all of them can be launched on the basis of human judgement and so-called computer infallibility.

Government leaders claim that these massive build-ups will deter nuclear war, that peace can only be won through strength. Ordinary people, with ordinary common sense, read the reports of numerous false missile-attack warnings each year, and somehow they don't feel very secure. In fact, the fear of nuclear holocaust has engendered psychic numbing, helplessness, and rage among children and adults in all nations.

Build-ups are justified by "demonizing" the enemy, presenting the other side as the source of all evil. But most of us realize that the real enemies today are famine, overpopulation, and pollution, and they cannot be overcome by macho posturing. Every dollar spent on arms is a dollar taken away from the hungry, the ill, and the homeless. While arms manufacturers profit, and various branches of the military compete with one another, the national and world economies edge towards bankruptcy.

Complementing the threat of nuclear war is the threat of the so-called "peaceful atom." The "peaceful atom" can be almost as expensive as the military atom, and, as the partial meltdowns at Three Mile Island and Chernobyl have shown, just as dangerous. While officials stress that they see differences between weapons and nuclear power plants, radioactivity makes no distinction between peace and war.

The nuclear story is fraught with deception and political paradoxes, including the fact that every round of arms talks has been followed by a steep increase in building weapons. Many veteran observers have said that arms talks are mainly public relations theatrics, with some notable exceptions – such as the Partial Test Ban Treaty and SALT I and II.

All leaders say that they want to make the world safe from nuclear weapons. Star Wars, for example, was suggested as a defensive system that would stop nuclear weapons in the stratosphere. However, scientists have warned that the system is so complex, as proposed, that it would be impossible to test – and if it fails, there's no second chance. Neither is there any chance to test the new theory that even a limited nuclear war would result in a "nuclear winter," when smoke from burning cities would block out the sun and lower global temperatures to year-round frost. According to this scenario, any survivors of a nuclear exchange would starve or freeze to death.

There are no second chances in this game. No matter what schemes are put forth by politicians and experts, one thing is crystal clear: no one can win in a nuclear war. We would all be losers.

P.C. and P.K.

Opposite: There is no peace after nuclear war by Rafal Olbinski.

OMNICIDE

Gotcha *by Robert Arneson, 1983.*

Omnicide: The Stark Reality of Species Death

The acceptance of the fact of one's personal death is mitigated by the experienced continuity with both the past and the future. For adults this continuity is most obviously linked with biological parenting, but it also occurs because of human memory, culture, literature and scientific endeavours. One can continue to affect history even after one's death .... Personal death is natural, although it may be premature ... or violent as happens in war.

The concept of species annihilation, on the other hand, means a relatively swift (on the scale of civilization), deliberately induced end to history, culture, science, biological reproduction and memory. It is...an act which requires a new word to describe it, namely omnicide. It is more akin to suicide or murder than to a natural death process. It is very difficult to comprehend omnicide, but it may be possible to discern the preparations for omnicide and prevent its happening.

The closest analogous human act which we can find in history on which to ground our thoughts about omnicide would be genocide, the deliberate ending of family lines. Hitler deliberately set out to annihilate all Jewish men, women and children, so that they and their offspring would disappear from history. Hitler also tried so to decimate Poland that it would be lost as a nation and culture, and its surviving people reduced to slave labour. Hitler did not declare war, however, against the earth: plants and animals, air, water and food. It was the Second Indochina War in Vietnam which first witnessed the extensive wartime use of technological power to devastate the living environment of earth....

The Jewish and Polish people condemned to death by authorities within the Third Reich were carefully "managed" and deceived, so that they would co-operate with the death plans, at least until it was too late to save themselves....It is important to examine the deliberate isolation of the Jewish people and the misrepresentation of "outside" reality as the precursor of genocide. It will give us clues for understanding omnicide in its early stages.

Dr. Rosalie Bertell

Bleeding to Death

At the present rate of "progress," and unless something is done quickly, disaster stares us in the face. Erosion, desertification and pollution have become our lot. It is a weird form of suicide, for we are bleeding our planet to death. We are led by sabre-rattling politicians who are ignorant of biology, beset by sectarian groups noted for their narrow-mindedness and intolerance, surrounded by powerful commercial interests whose only interest in nature is often to rape it.

*   *   *

By the 1990s, humankind will be exterminating one species (plant or animal) per hour, by the year 2000 one every 15 minutes. These are species that for the most part we know little or nothing about, and could well be of enormous benefit to humanity. Up to now scientists have only examined the potential of one in ten of the 250,000 species of higher plants in the world. By felling tropical forests in the senseless way that we are doing, who knows what riches we are squandering? These tropical forests, once eliminated, can never be restored. They are gone, taking with them untold numbers of foods, drugs, and other products useful to humanity. With them go innumerable birds, mammals, reptiles, and insects, many of which could be of use to us, as the humble armadillo has helped to treat leprosy....

The world is still an incredibly rich storehouse (our *only* storehouse). It can (if we live with nature and not outside it) provide all of us with all we and future generations need. But we must learn to manage it intelligently. Most of nature – if it is not destroyed or corrupted by us – is a resource that is ever renewing itself. It offers us, if managed wisely, a never-ending largesse. It is our world, but we have yet to learn to treat it with respect and gratitude. Let's hope we do so before it is altogether too late, and we find ourselves breeding like a mass of greenfly on a cinder.

Gerald Durrell

Denying Reality

Why is there so much appalling cruelty in the world? Cruelty is not just to those we call our enemies but cruelty to ourselves and the world we live in. For is it not cruel that we have created for the human race a future which could be as brief as 4 minutes but will be no longer than 150 years? A nuclear war, triggered by national pride or mere computer failure, could eradicate most of us in four minutes and the rest of us in a nuclear winter and its aftermath. Even if we avoid this, the rate at which we are despoiling the planet, cutting down the trees on which our oxygen supply depends, polluting the oceans, killing the life that exists in our rivers and lakes, disrupting the delicate network of life on earth, means that if we do not come to our senses and seek to preserve rather than destroy, then this planet will be unable to continue to support human life for much longer. Meanwhile, as our population increases so does the devastation by natural disasters, created or aggravated by the stripping of the forests and the poverty which forces more and more people to live in disaster-prone areas....

The warnings are there all the time for us to see. The planes fly overhead, the missiles are installed. Our newspapers, radio and television show us in words and pictures what cruelty we inflict on one another, either directly by killing and maiming, or indirectly by allowing such cruelty to continue. Some of us heed these warnings and try, in ways which seem puny and ineffective, to alter the course of human history so that the human race will not only continue to exist but will live with greater love and understanding. However, most of us are ignoring the warnings and go on living our lives as if all is well and life will continue forever on this bountiful planet. But denial of reality, that is, lying to yourself, is the most costly error you can ever make. Reality does not become unreal. You do. Our present world is full of people who are unreal to themselves, who do not know themselves. It is they who will destroy us all.

Dorothy Rowe

The first Hiroshima Appeals Poster, illustrated by Akira Yokoyama, designed by Yusaku Kamekura, 1983.

The Extinction of Life

Bearing in mind that the possible consequences of the detonations of thousands of megatons of nuclear explosives include the blinding of insects, birds, and beasts all over the world; the extinction of many ocean species, among them some at the base of the food chain; the temporary or permanent alteration of the climate of the globe, with the outside chance of "dramatic" and "major" alterations in the structure of the atmosphere; the pollution of the whole ecosphere with oxides of nitrogen; the incapacitation in ten minutes of unprotected people who go out into the sunlight; the blinding of people who go out into the sunlight; a significant decrease in photosynthesis in plants around the world; the scalding and killing of many crops; the increase in rates of cancer and mutation around the world, but especially in the targeted zones, and the attendant risk of global epidemics; the possible poisoning of all vertebrates by sharply increased levels of Vitamin D in their skin as a result of increased ultraviolet light; and the outright slaughter on all targeted continents of most human beings and other living things by the initial nuclear radiation, the fireballs, the thermal pulses, the blast waves, the mass fires, and the fallout from the explosions; and, considering that these consequences will all interact with one another in unguessable ways and, furthermore, are in all likelihood an incomplete list, which will be added to as our knowledge of the earth increases, one must conclude that a full-scale nuclear holocaust could lead to the extinction of mankind.

Jonathan Schell

ATOMIC BLAST EFFECTS

Nagasaki, September 13, 1945.

Nuclear Explosions

When a standard nuclear device is exploded about 50% of its potential energy is emitted as a blast wave, 35% as heat and light and 15% as radiation. (Neutron bombs are different in that they are designed to emit as much as possible of their potential energy as radiation; blast and heat are at lower levels.) Blast and heat do enormous damage over a relatively wide area, spreading out over a measurable period of seconds. The light emission is at the instant of explosion only, but it is so intense that it can cause blindness well beyond the significant reach of the blast and heat waves.

The radiation effect of nuclear weapons is slower to act and comes in two stages. At the moment of explosion there is a huge wave of radiation spreading out from the source of the explosion and weakening quite rapidly. A large dose will lead to death, but not immediately. It requires a dose of the

order of 15-20 times the lethal level to incapacitate a person and cause death the same day, but such a dose could only be received close to the centre of an explosion's effects, where blast and heat would almost certainly destroy living creatures before radiation could take its toll.

The second stage of radiation damage is fallout. Fallout consists of particles of solid matter that have been irradiated, drawn up into the atmosphere and subsequently fall, either drifting down under their own weight or washed out of the atmosphere by rain or snow. Fallout can very readily be at lethal levels – again, nowhere near sufficient to cause instant death, but ensuring a lingering death over a period of weeks or months – or it may be at lower levels that cause radiation sickness with variable consequences. Fallout is insidious by comparison with the initial wave of

radiation from the source of the explosion. Minute irradiated particles can fall on the skin and burn it; they can be inhaled and damage internal tissues; they can enter water supplies and the food chain, with adverse effects for years after an explosion. There is also little time limit on the arrival of fallout, as it can rise so high in the atmosphere that it is above cloud level and so need not be washed down for years.

The blast, heat and radiation effects of a nuclear explosion vary with the size of the weapon, the geography of the target, weather conditions and, most important of all, with the height at which it is exploded. A weapon detonated high over its target is called an air-burst; a weapon detonated on or close to the ground is called a ground-burst.

Nuclear devices can be set to explode either on the ground or at almost any height above it, up to tens of thousands of feet. Either way, the point at which a weapon hits or the point immediately below an air-burst is known as ground zero and is the point of maximum effect. In response to the massive blast potential of nuclear weapons, underground missile silos and emergency command posts have been strengthened – "hardened" in nukespeak – to withstand all but a direct hit. An air-burst could not be expected to do them significant damage: only a ground-burst on or very close to the target would be sufficient. But, as can be imagined, a nuclear explosion that blows a huge crater is not going to produce such drastic heat and radiation effects over a wide area as an air-burst; indeed, the blast too will be limited by the sides of the crater, though a local earthquake effect would do damage of a kind that would not be expected from an air-burst. Hardened targets then would be attacked with ground-bursts; softer targets such as cities and large industrial installations would be attacked with air-bursts to cause the maximum damage over the widest area.

There is another important difference between air and ground-bursts, and that is fallout. A weapon exploding on or near the ground vaporizes a large amount of material – earth, buildings and so on – which, because of the enormous heat of the fireball that any nuclear explosion causes, rises into the air. All this material is irradiated. Tons of irradiated matter has therefore to come back to earth as fallout. If the weapon is air-burst well clear of the ground however, the only solid irradiated matter is the debris of the weapon itself. Even this could cause a significant fallout problem, but a much less severe one than results from a ground-burst. An attack planner therefore has to decide which targets need a ground-burst to eliminate them, but he also has the choice of using ground-bursts on soft targets if the aim is to produce maximum fallout. A particularly unpleasant option is to attack nuclear reactors with ground-bursts, as reactor cores contain particularly long-lived radioactive isotopes; the fallout would not only be huge but especially toxic.

Michael Stephenson and Roger Hearn

The Result of an "All-Out" Nuclear War Between the U.S.A. and the U.S.S.R. (mid-1980s)

1. The population would be devastated. Over 200,000,000 men, women, and children would be killed immediately. Over 60,000,000 would be injured. Among the injured,
   - 30,000,000 would experience radiation sickness,
   - 20,000,000 would experience trauma and burns,
   - 10,000,000 would experience trauma, burns, and radiation sickness.

2. Medical resources would be incapable of coping with those injured by blast, thermal energy, and radiation.
   - 80% of physicians would die.
   - 80% of hospital beds would be destroyed.
   - Stores of blood plasma, antibiotics, and drugs would be destroyed or severely compromised.
   - Food and water would be extensively contaminated.
   - Transportation and communication facilities would be destroyed.

3. Civil defense would be unable to alter the death and devastation described above to any appreciable extent.

4. The disaster would have continuing consequences.
   - Food production would be profoundly altered.
   - Fallout would constitute a continuing problem.
   - Survivors with altered immunity, malnutrition, and unsanitary environment, and severe exposure problems would be subject to lethal enteric infections.

5. A striking increase in leukemia and other malignancies would be observed among long-term survivors. It would be most severe in those who were children at the time of exposure.

6. Profound changes would occur in weather caused by particulates and reduction of atmospheric ozone with attendant alterations in man, animal, and plant species.

7. The effect on adjacent countries is incalculable.

Summary Proceedings:
First Congress of International Physicians for the Prevention of Nuclear War

Zapping the Energy Grid

Another point of major current concern is that megaton-like bursts at altitudes above 100 kilometers would create an intense electromagnetic pulse which could result in electric fields, over a large part – or even all – of the continental United States, in excess of 25,000 volts per meter. In antennas – whether long communication lines or power lines, or even the cables associated with electronic equipment on planes or missiles – these voltages could induce currents which would destroy the transistorized circuitry on which modern versions of such systems rely for their functioning, unless they should be adequately shielded at all points against such effects.

Of particular concern are the communication links for the command and control of our missile-launching complexes as well as the guidance systems for the missiles themselves. Though of less strategic importance, the civilian alarm and confusion which would follow a widespread and extended breakdown of the U.S. power grid, with the cessation of all electric services lacking a separate power supply – communication, lighting, ventilation, pumping (of water as well as gasoline), much transportation, to say nothing of elevators – would be spectacular.

J. Carson Mark

The Effect of a Nuclear Blast

Most damage to cities from large weapons comes from the explosive blast. The blast drives air away from the site of the explosion, producing sudden changes in air pressure (called static overpressure) that can crush objects, and high winds (called dynamic pressure) that can move them suddenly or knock them down. In general, large buildings are destroyed by the overpressure, while people and objects such as trees and utility poles are destroyed by the wind.

For example, consider the effects of a one-megaton airburst on things 4 miles (6 kilometers) away. The overpressure will be in excess of 5 pounds per square inch (psi), which will exert a force of more than 180 tons on the wall of a typical two-story house. At the same place, there would be a wind of 160 mph (255 km/h). While 5 psi is not enough to crush a man, a wind of 180 mph could create fatal collisions between people and nearby objects. . . .

When a nuclear weapon is detonated on or near the surface of the earth, the blast digs out a large crater. Some of the material that used to be in the crater is deposited on the rim of the crater; the rest is carried up into the air and returns to the earth as fallout. An explosion that is farther above the earth's surface than the radius of the fireball does not dig a crater and produces negligible immediate fallout.

For the most part, blast kills people by indirect means rather than by direct pressure. While a human body can withstand up to 30 psi of simple overpressure, the winds associated with as little as 2 to 3 psi could be expected to blow people out of typical modern office buildings. Most blast deaths result from the collapse of occupied buildings, from people being blown into objects, or from buildings or smaller objects being blown onto or into people. . . .

In order to estimate the number of casualties from any given explosion, it is necessary to make assumptions about the proportion of people who will be killed or injured at any given over-pressure. . . .For example, weapons tests suggest that a typical residence will be collapsed by an overpressure of about 5 psi. People standing in such a residence have a 50 percent chance of being killed by an overpressure of 3.5 psi, but people who are lying down at the moment the blast wave hits have a 50 percent chance of surviving a 7-psi overpressure. The calculations used here assume a mean lethal overpressure of 5 to 6 psi for people in residences, meaning that more than half of those whose houses are blown down on top of them will nevertheless survive.

Office of Technology Assessment
U.S. Congress

Immediate Effects of a One-megaton Air-burst

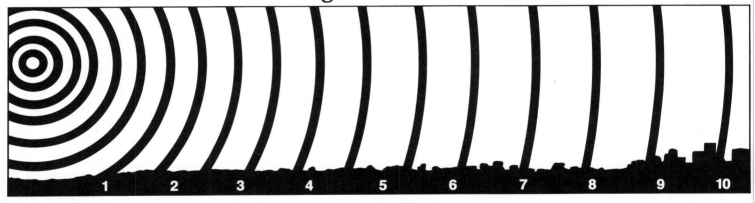

Ground zero to 1 mile
dead: 98%; injured: 2%

Blast *all buildings destroyed; 1,000 mph winds would crush any person in the open; only the best, hardened, completely self-sufficient shelters could give any worthwhile protection.*

Heat *conflagration of most combustible materials giving rise to large fires likely to combine into a firestorm; people caught in the open would melt; those in shelters would probably be baked.*

Radiation *the few people not already burned, blasted, suffocated or baked would, if exposed, receive at least twice the lethal dose; people thus affected could expect to die within 2 weeks.*

1 to 2 miles from ground zero
dead: 98%; injured 2%

Blast *reinforced buildings badly damaged, all others destroyed; 400 mph winds would hurl people in the open to their deaths, their lungs would haemorrhage and their eardrums burst.*

Heat *all survivors would be charred by the wave of heat and many corpses would be consumed in raging fires; blast and heat between them would kill almost everyone.*

Radiation *lethal for most people; perhaps 10% of irradiated people might recover with proper medical treatment if it were available, otherwise death within 3 months.*

2 to 5 miles from ground zero
dead: 50%; injured 30%

Blast *most domestic and light industrial buildings flattened, varying damage to more substantial structures; all windows blown out; people hurled off their feet by winds in excess of 130 mph, crushed by falling buildings, shredded by flying glass.*

Heat *10% of buildings gutted by fire 4-5 miles from ground zero, more towards the inner perimeter, where flesh would be fatally charred and clothing could ignite spontaneously.*

Radiation *radiation sickness almost inevitable for those not in shelters; lethal doses possible for those near inner perimeter; it is likely that many people would die unnecessarily through lack of treatment, particularly as a result of secondary infections.*

5 to 10 miles from ground zero
dead: 5%; injured 30%

Blast *many less substantial buildings flattened towards the inner perimeter, trees uprooted, widespread damage to substantial buildings; further out, all windows broken, roof tiles blown off in gale force winds; many injuries and some deaths from collapsing buildings and flying debris.*

Heat *skin charred or badly blistered to about 8 miles from ground zero, the equivalent of severe sunburn thereafter; occasional fires could be fanned by winds from 50 to 130 mph.*

Radiation *varying from survivable radiation sickness at the inner perimeter to slight discomfort at the outer.*

Michael Stephenson and Roger Hearn

HIROSHIMA AND NAGASAKI

An atomic bomb of the same type as "Little Boy," which was dropped on Hiroshima.

The Crew Said, "My God!"

It was 08:15 when we dropped our bomb and we turned the plane broadside to get the best view. Then we made as much distance from the ball of fire as we could.

We were at least ten miles away and there was a visual impact even though every man wore coloured glasses for protection. We had braced ourselves when the bomb was gone for the shock and Tibbets said "close flak" and it was just like that – a close burst of anti-aircraft fire.

The crew said, "My God," and couldn't believe what had happened.

A mountain of smoke was going up in a mushroom with the stem coming down. At the top was white smoke but up to 1,000 feet from the ground there was swirling, boiling dust. Soon afterwards small fires sprang up on the edge of the town, but the town was entirely obscured. We stayed around two or three minutes and by that time the smoke had risen to 40,000 feet. As we watched, the top of the white cloud broke off and another soon formed.

Captain Parsons of the bomber *Enola Gay*

Remains of a wrist watch found in the ruins of Hiroshima, recording the 8:15 A.M. bombing on August 6, 1945.

Zero Hour

All the dead and injured were burned beyond recognition. With houses and buildings crushed, including many emergency medical facilities, authorities are having their hands full in giving every available relief possible under the circumstances. The effect of the bomb is widespread. Those outdoors burned to death, while those indoors were killed by the indescribable pressure and heat.

Radio Tokyo

The crew of the Enola Gay, *the B-59 bomber that dropped "Little Boy."*

Nagasaki, August 9, 1945

In August, 1945, I was a freshman at Nagasaki Medical College. The ninth of August was a clear, hot, beautiful summer day. I left my lodging house, which was one and one-half miles from the hypocenter, at eight in the morning, as usual, to catch a tram car. When I got to the train stop, I found that it had been derailed in an accident. I decided to return home. I was lucky. I never made it to school that day.

At 11 A.M., I was sitting in my room with a fellow student when I heard the sound of a B-29 passing overhead. A few minutes later, the air flashed a brilliant yellow and there was a huge blast of wind.

We were terrified and ran downstairs to the toilet to hide. Later, when I came to my senses, I noticed a hole had been blown in the roof, all the glass had been shattered, and that the glass had cut my shoulder and I was bleeding. When I went outside, the sky had turned from blue to black and the black rain had started to fall. The stone walls between the houses were reduced to rubble.

After a short time, I tried to go to my medical school in Urakami, which was 1,500 feet from the hypocenter. The air dose of radiation was more than 7,000 rads at this distance. I could not complete my journey because there were fires everywhere. I met many people coming back from Urakami.

Aerial photos of Hiroshima before (left) and after (right) bombing show most dwellings and vegetation destroyed.

Their clothes were in rags, and shreds of skin hung from their bodies. They looked like ghosts with vacant stares. I cannot get rid of the sounds of crying women in the destroyed fields.

The next day I was able to enter Urakami on foot, and all that I knew had disappeared. Only the concrete and iron skeletons of the buildings remained. There were dead bodies everywhere. On each street corner we had tubs of water used for putting out fires after the air raids. In one of these small tubs, scarcely large enough for one person, was the body of a desperate man who had sought cool water. There was foam coming from his mouth, but he was not alive.

As I got nearer to school, there were black charred bodies, with the white edges of bones showing in the arms and legs. A dead horse with a bloated belly lay by the side of the road. Only the skeleton of the medical hospital remained standing. Because the school building was wood, it was completely destroyed. My classmates were in that building, attending their physiology lecture. When I arrived, some were still alive. They were unable to move their bodies. The strongest were so weak that they were slumped over on the ground. I talked with them and they thought they would be OK, but all of them would die within weeks. I cannot forget the way their eyes looked at me and their voices spoke to me, forever.

Michito Ichimaru, M.D.

Ruins of Nagasaki after the August 9, 1945, atomic blast.

I Am Alone

I spent the night in the open
and barely reached a place of refuge
to find my daddy only.
Mummy and Yu-*chan* are dead...

Next morning
daddy carried an empty box
and I took a hoe on my shoulder
as we went
into the ruins of the fires in Hiroshima.

We arrived at long last
to the stench of burning bodies
like the smell of pike mackerel.

Roof tiles litter the ground
hot with the sun.
Silently and absorbed
we search the ground.

Ah,
Mummy's bones
I take them up
and the white powder flies in the wind.
It is a feeling of utter loneliness.
We gather up the bones
placing them in the confectionery box
with a soft dry sound.
Beside mummy,
are my brother's bones,
and his flesh, not consumed yet,
lying there.

Later
all over daddy's body
with no visible wounds
spots appear.
    —"I want to eat grapes."
    —"All I have for you is cucumber."
It is the morning of September 1.
Looking vacantly into the air,
daddy said suddenly
    —"the wind is furious,
       a storm is coming...a storm."
and breathing deeply
he broke down

and moved no more.

It is less than one month
And I am alone.

No more tears come
All is vacant before me.

I sit and gaze
at the river flowing before me.

Clean and beautiful
blue sky
over Hiroshima.

Hayashi Yukiko

Injured civilians gathered on pavement west of Miyuki-bashi, August, 1945.

A Silent Flash of Light

I heard no explosion. Miles out of the city, people apparently heard a thunderous roar. But like all survivors close to the hypocentre, I heard nothing. There was just the silent flash. The moment I saw it, I tried to duck under a desk. But I had a sensation of floating. Together with the building, my body was falling....

Lying in the rubble, I couldn't move and I knew I was faced with death. Mysteriously, I never had a feeling of panic. I felt calm. After a while, I started hearing my classmates. In weak voices, they were asking for God....

My clothes were tattered and covered with blood. I had cuts and scratches all over me, but all my extremities were there. I looked around me. Even though it was morning, the sky was dark, as dark as twilight. Then I saw streams of human beings shuffling away from the centre of the city. Parts of their bodies were missing. Their eyes had been liquefied. They had blackened skin, and strips of flesh hung like ribbons from their bones. There was an awful smell in the air: the stench of burnt human flesh. I can't describe that smell, but it was a bit like broiled fish.

Setsuko Thurlow, a Hiroshima hibakusha.

The strangest thing was the silence. It is one of the most unforgettable impressions I have. You'd think that people would be panic-stricken, running, yelling. Not at Hiroshima. They moved in slow motion, like figures in a silent movie, shuffling through the dust and smoke. I heard thousands of people breathing the words, "Water, give me water." Many simply dropped to the ground and died.

Setsuko Thurlow

Crying, "Water! Water!" injured survivors flocked to throw themselves in the river, which was soon filled with corpses; by survivor Tomoe Harada.

Water

That day, the people who were hit by the A-bomb wanted water very badly. Not only was it a hot August day, but these people were ducking under blazing flames, running away for as long as they still had breath. So their mouths and throats probably became very dry. Also, they had very bad burns and injuries. But drinking water at a time like that can cause a heart attack or prevent bleeding from stopping, and thus cause death. . . .

Looking for my wife and children, I climbed up to the Shiroyama State Shrine. There in a ditch was a mother and her child. I walked closer, wondering what had happened to them. The woman told me her name and where she came from. Then she said, "Excuse me, but would you please give my child some water?" I took the water bottle hanging from my shoulder and turned it upside down and shook it. There was no water in it. Seeing this, the woman took out a small teapot. "Please fill this with water and bring it back," she said.

I was at a loss what to do. But when I looked at the mother and child who could not move, I knew I could not refuse. Taking the teapot, I ran down toward Aburagidani. I thought there should be a valley stream flowing there.

What do you think I found? There in the small area where the water was, people who had died after taking a drink were piled one on top of another. Some of their bodies were half submerged in the water. There was red blood and grease floating on the water.

I could not bring myself to fill the teapot with greasy, bloody water so I went back without any. I told the woman what had happened. She looked at me with hurt in her eyes, but said not a word. There was nothing I could do. I apologized and then quickly left as if making an escape.

The next morning I passed by there again. When I looked, I found that the mother and child had died as they lay there in the same place as the day before. Never have I felt so badly about anything I have ever done. Even water with blood and grease in it would have been good enough. Why hadn't I taken her some? To this day I cannot forgive myself.

Nagasaki Hibakusha Teachers

Eyewitness

The dead bodies lie charred, hands clutching the air. . . . A woman about thirty or so stands mindlessly not far from the hypocenter, holding a bucket. . . . As I come near, saying I belong to the military, she suddenly points at the bucket. There lies the head of a girl, 5 or 6 years old. Past shedding tears, the mother cries, "I was in my old home over the mountain. It saved me. But my husband, son and daughter were at home; now all are dead. I could not find my husband or son. Only this head, the head of my daughter I found, lying in the air-raid shelter. But her body was nowhere to be seen."

Azuma Jun,
an army reporter who covered Nagasaki

The charred body of a boy found about 700 metres south-east of the hypocentre.

Burned bodies fill a water tank beside the charred body of a woman frozen into a running posture, her baby clutched in her arms; by survivor Yamagata.

Michiko's Story

Michiko Ogino, 10 years old, was left in charge of his younger sisters when his mother went out to the fields to pick eggplants. The bomb brought the house down on them all, leaving his 2-year-old sister with her legs pinned under a crossbeam:

> Mamma was bombed at noon
> When getting eggplants in the field,
> Short, red and crisp her hair stood,
> Tender and red her skin was all over.

So Mrs. Ogino, although the clothes were burned from her body and she had received a fatal dose of radiation, could still run back from the fields to succor her children. One after another, passing sailors and neighbors heaved at the beam to release the trapped 2-year-old, failed, and, bowing with Japanese courtesy, went on their way to help others.

> Mother was looking down at my little sister. Tiny eyes looked up from below. Mother looked around, studying the way the beams were piled up. Then she got into an opening under the beam, and putting her right shoulder under a portion of it, she strained with all her might. We heard a cracking sound and the beams were lifted a little. My little sister's legs were freed.

> Peeled off was the skin
>   over her shoulder
> That once lifted the beam
>   off my sister.
> Constant blood was spurting
> From the sore flesh appearing...

Mrs. Ogino died that night.

E.P. Thompson

Nagatoshi

Nagatoshi was three years old when the A-bomb fell. Wearing nothing but a bib, he had been playing inside the house. After being thrown by the bomb blast, he scampered into the air raid shelter with three other neighborhood children. One week later, two of the neighborhood children died, one after the other. Nagatoshi worried his family because he had a fever and diarrhea for a long time, and his hair fell out. Yet, surprisingly, he got better.

Three years later, during the season when the beautiful cherry blossoms were blooming in the garden of Shiroyama Elementary School, he entered the first grade full of health and vigor. In the second grade, too, it seemed he was going to be fine, but at the beginning of winter he complained of pain in his chest. He went to see the doctor at the hospital right away. The doctor told him to stay in bed and rest for a while.

Then, in early May, when he was in third grade, Nagatoshi's body began to undergo strange changes.

He was tired and listless...

It was hard for him to climb up a slope...

He did not like any of his food...

His mother thought he was just being a difficult boy.

"You're a big boy, aren't you? Come on. Pep up! Nagatoshi, you walk like a cow. Step lively!" she scolded him.

Suddenly in the middle of May, he could not stand up. His mother became very worried and took him to the hospital. He got better in about two weeks.

Then around the beginning of July, he got a sore throat. The doctor told him it was tonsillitis. This cleared up, too, in about two weeks. But from around this time, his whole body began to swell up, and he often fainted.

At the beginning of October, he was feverish and started coughing a lot. He had stopped going to school near the end of September. On October 5, Nagatoshi's mother went to his classroom and told everyone that his illness had become worse this time.

"Sensei, you have given a lot of time to Nagatoshi. But he will no longer be able to come to school. . . . There's nothing we can do but wait for him to die."

Saying this, his mother began to cry. His teacher was taken by surprise and did not know what to say.

"Why, surely he won't die. He's just a growing boy. There has to be some chance he'll get better."

"No, Sensei. There can be no mistake about it. His blood was checked at the Atomic Bomb Casualty Commission. They say he has A-bomb disease and he'll never recover."

They now knew that Nagatoshi had A-bomb disease, and that he could not recover from it no matter how good his doctors were. Even though six years had passed since the day he was exposed to the flash of the A-bomb, the poison of it was only now coming out. Radiation lies hidden in a person's body, slowly breaking the body down.

Everyone who knew Nagatoshi prayed to God that somehow Nagatoshi would become healthy again. But his illness only got worse and worse...

In November it was cold day after day. On a day when heavy gray clouds were spread across the sky, Nagatoshi was admitted to the University Hospital. He had to go into the hospital because not only was his body totally weakened, but he had caught a cold. His high fever would not go down and it was hard for him to breathe. Even though he was in the hospital, he got pneumonia. And while his friends were having fun playing on Mt. Konpira, he died a lonely death in a hospital room.

Nagasaki Hibakusha Teachers

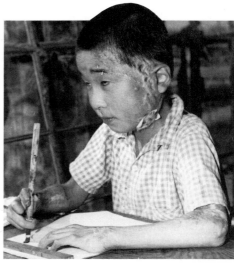

One year later, the face of this boy, blinded by the blast, shows keloid scars caused by exposure to radiation.

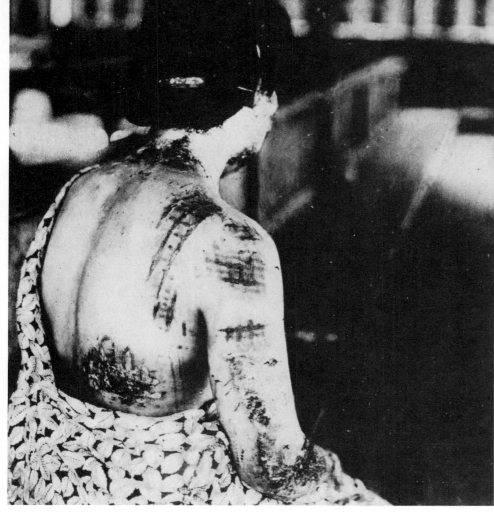

A burn victim's seared body attests to the heat of the bomb's blast.

Nuclear Injuries

Stage 1 – Early or Initial Stage
The greatest number of casualties occurred immediately after the explosion to the end of the second week; and at this stage various injurious actions of the atomic bomb explosion simultaneously led to the onset of symptoms. Approximately nine-tenths of the fatal cases died during this stage, and the majority (about 90 percent) of these injured who received medical care for several days after the explosion, complained of thermal injury.

Stage 2 – Intermittent Stage
Many moderate injuries caused by radioactivity were encountered from the beginning of the third week to the end of the eighth week; and the remaining fatal cases, or one-tenth, died. From the general course taken by the victims, stages 1 and 2 may be considered as the acute stage of atomic bomb injury.

Stage 3 – Late Stage
From the beginning of the third month to the end of the fourth, all symptoms from injury showed some improvement, although a few cases terminated in death from complications. By the end of the fourth month (early December 1945), those suffering from the disaster in both cities had recovered to a certain degree, and the course of the atomic bomb injury itself had come to a near end.

Stage 4 – Delayed Effects
After five months or more, there were various delayed effects: some – such as distortion, contracture, keloid, and so on – following recovery from thermal injury or mechanical injury; some – such as anemia – as a result of blood disorder caused by radiation injury; and some originating in disturbances of the reproductive function – such as sterility – may occur at this stage. There are, however, a few items that must be continuously examined during the following few months.

From Hiroshima and Nagasaki: The Physical, Medical and Social Effects of the Atomic Bombings

Hibakusha

Yamamoto Sumiko was 10, a fifth-grade pupil at *Yagami* elementary school, Nagasaki, at the time of the bombing. Though not strong as a young woman, Sumiko was married in 1956, rather pressed by family circumstances. A son was born two years later and a daughter in the following year. Her husband died in 1967 from illness that followed an injury at work in Osaka.

Mine Junko, her daughter, began to suffer bleeding at the nose after finishing elementary school, and died of leukaemia in April 1974.

Her son, Mine Kenichi, was a bright boy, fond of sports, and played soccer in senior high school. But in November 1974, he complained of acute pains in his knees, and next month was diagnosed as suffering from leukaemia, and hospitalized. By March next year, he showed signs of recovery and was allowed to leave the hospital. He moved up to second year. But in June he began nose bleeds at school, and the old pain returned. He completed his term examination, from July 8 through 12, and on July 13, was back in hospital. Kenichi breathed his last at two o'clock on August 6, 1975, on the thirtieth anniversary of the atomic bombing of Hiroshima.

During these 32 years since they were used, the atom bombs have continued to affect surviving *hibakusha*, the bomb victims. They suffer from cataracts, disorders of haematogenic functions, including various symptoms of anaemia, leukaemia, malignant tumors, microcephaly among children who had been exposed to radiation *in utero*, what are called "atomic bomb weakness symptoms," and abnormal chromosomes. As the *hibakusha* grow older, serious complex conditions are developing, involving both disease and poverty, making their lives much more precarious, and the succeeding generations suffer the fear that their health may be impaired at any time.

From Hiroshima/Nagasaki: A Pictorial History

THE SCIENTISTS SPEAK OUT

Early atomic scientists Enrico Fermi, John R. Dunning, and D. P. Mitchell stand in front of one of the first cyclotrons.

How Well They Meant

The concept of the atomic bomb as the final arbiter of war was recognized in 1939 with the publication of the discovery of nuclear fission. Every scientist familiar with the physics of this phenomenon understood that in theory a weapon of extraordinary power might be fashioned if the technical requirements could be mastered. To this end scientists enlisted the president's support; they formed committees to study the possibility of an atomic bomb; they lobbied the military; and they conducted experiments. But it was not until the summer of 1941, two-and-a-half years after fission was discovered in

Germany, that scientists in England thought of a way to harness the theory to practical technology. In the fall of 1941 an Anglo-American scientific partnership was initiated. Its goal was to beat the Germans in a race for the atomic bomb.

The delay literally terrified the scientists associated with the bomb project. Aware of the weapon's potential and their own desultory start, they reasoned that the Anglo-American effort lagged behind Germany's, perhaps by as much as two-and-a-half years. In their minds the atomic bomb was the *ultimate weapon*; if the Germans developed it first, the Allied

cause was lost. Arthur Compton, director of the atomic energy project at the University of Chicago, was so distressed at the slow rate of progress that, in June 1942, he urged a program for researching and developing "counter-measures" against a German atomic bomb. In July J. Robert Oppenheimer wrote despairingly that the war could be lost before answers to the immediate problems under consideration could be found. "What Is Wrong with Us?" was the heading Leo Szilard chose for a memorandum in September criticizing the rate of progress.

Martin J. Sherwin

The Fateful Decision, 1939—1945

1939

2/8: Einstein sends letter to President Roosevelt mentioning the possible construction of bombs which, exploded in a port, "might well destroy the whole port together with some surrounding territory."

A team of British scientists, led by George Thomson, studies atomic fission at Oxford, Cambridge, London and Liverpool.

1940

March: R. Peierls and O. R. Frisch inform the British Government that it is possible to construct an atomic bomb by using the isotope U-235.

1941

Spring: British atomic scientists make contact with their American counterparts through Sir John Cockroft and Ernest O. Lawrence. British scientists will collaborate in the American project.
September: Lawrence reports from Berkeley, that certain new developments now make the construction of atomic bombs a feasible project.
Autumn: President Roosevelt suggests to Churchill that British and American research teams pool their ideas. A group of British physicists arrives in the United States.
6/11: National Academy Committee submits report to Vannevar Bush, Head of the National Defense Research Committee, recommending the speedy construction of an atomic bomb.
27/11: Bush submits the recommendation to President Roosevelt.
6/12: Roosevelt votes "a few million dollars" for the project, and promises "enormous resources" in case of success.
7/12: Japanese attack on Pearl Harbour.

1942

17/6: President Roosevelt receives further report on the production of atomic bombs from plutonium or U-235, and instructs General William D. Styer, of the Military Policy Committee, to proceed with the atomic project.

June: Production of atomic bombs entrusted to U.S. Corps of Engineers.
17/9: Brigadier-General Leslie R. Groves chosen by Army to take charge of entire atomic project.
14/11: S-1 Committee meets in Washington.
19/11: Edward Teller, J. R. Oppenheimer, John H. Manley and Robert Serber submit a further "feasibility report."
2/12: Fermi succeeds in producing the first chain reaction in his laboratory in Chicago.

Albert Einstein drew public attention first to the potential and then to the hazards of atomic weapons.

1943

April: Control of entire atomic project now in hands of U.S. Army.
4/11: Experimental reactor at Clinton Labor (Oak Ridge) put into operation.
January: Work of Oppenheimer Group in Los Alamos gradually becomes central part of entire project.

1945

Secretary of War Henry Stimson asks Interim Committee whether and in what manner the bomb should be used. Oppenheimer notes that if the bomb were exploded over a city, some 20,000 people would probably be killed.
June: Lawrence, Fermi, Compton and Oppenheimer suggest the possibility of a non-military demonstration of the bomb, which would convince the Japanese of its deadly effects without actual loss of life. The idea is dropped,

since experience has shown that the Japanese will not give up their fanatical struggle until the new weapon has been demonstrated militarily. Stimson: "We see no acceptable alternative to direct military use."

Several petitions for and against the use of the atomic bomb.
Early June: The first trial bomb is built.
16/7: First successful test explosion of an American atomic bomb in Alamogordo (New Mexico) under the direction of R. Oppenheimer. Truman in Berlin (Potsdam Conference) receives the famous message: "Babies satisfactorily born."
17/7: Second telegram from Harrison at Alamogordo to Stimson in Potsdam.
24/7: Truman tells Stalin of intention to use the bomb against Japanese.
26/7: Potsdam: U.S.A., Great Britain and China call for the unconditional surrender of Japan. The alternative is utter destruction of the country.
27/7: Allies drop pamphlets on Japan calling for surrender and warning that eleven Japanese cities will be severely bombed.
28/7: Japan ignores Potsdam ultimatum. Six of the specified cities are bombed.
30/7: Thirty young scientists and technicians from Los Alamos arrive on Tinian (Marianas) to assemble the bomb, sections of which had arrived in the *Indianapolis*, a cruiser sunk by a Japanese submarine a few days later.
6/8: President Truman announces the dropping of the first atomic bomb on Hiroshima. Japan is given 48 hours to capitulate before another bomb is dropped. (The first atomic bomb hit Hiroshima at 8:15 a.m. At 8:20 a.m., those waiting at Tinian received the message: "Mission successful." Losses: 78,150 dead, 13,983 missing and 37,425 wounded. More than half the city destroyed.)
7-9/8: Millions of leaflets calling for surrender dropped over Japan.
8/8: The Soviet Union declares war on Japan with effect from midnight, 9 August.
9/8: Second atomic bomb dropped on Nagasaki at noon. Losses: 36,000 dead, 40,000 wounded, city almost completely destroyed.

Hans Dollinger

Fused sand forms a layer of glass 2,400 feet across, around a crater left by the first atomic bomb test near Alamogordo, New Mexico.

Our Greatest Worry

During 1943 and part of 1944 our greatest worry was the possibility that Germany would perfect an atomic bomb before the invasion of Europe.... In 1945, when we ceased worrying about what the Germans might do to us, we began to worry about what the government of the United States might do to other countries.

Leo Szilard

We were asked to comment on whether the bomb should be used. I think the reason we were asked for that comment was because a petition had been sent in from a very distinguished and thoughtful group of scientists: "No, it should not be used." It would be better for everything that they should not. We didn't know beans about the military situation in Japan. We didn't know whether they could be caused to surrender by other means or whether the invasion was really inevitable. But in back of our minds was the notion that the invasion was inevitable because we had been told that....

We said that we didn't think that being scientists especially qualified us as to how to answer this question of how the bombs should be used or not; opinion was divided among us as it would be among other people if they knew about it. We thought the two overriding considerations were the saving of [US] lives in the war and the effect of our actions on the stability, on our strength and the stability of the postwar world. We did say that we did not think that exploding one of these things as a firecracker over a desert was likely to be very impressive.

Robert Oppenheimer

The whole country was lighted by a searing light with an intensity many times that of the midday sun.... Thirty seconds after the explosion came, first, the air blast pressing hard against the people and things, to be followed almost immediately by the strong, sustained, awesome roar which warned of doomsday and made us feel that we puny things were blasphemous to dare tamper with the forces heretofore reserved to the Almighty. Words are inadequate tools for the job of acquainting those not present with the physical, mental, and psychological effects. It had to be witnessed to be realized.

General Farrell, at the first test site

I believe the most important question is the moral one: can we, who have always insisted on morality and human decency between nations as well as inside our own country, introduce this weapon of total annihilation into the world? The usual argument, heard in the frantic week before the President's decision and frequently since, is that we are fighting against a country which denies all the human values we cherish and that any weapon, however terrible, must be used to prevent that country and its creed from dominating the world. It is argued that it would be better for us to lose our lives than our liberty; and this I personally agree with. But I believe that this is not the question; I believe that we would lose far more than our lives in a war fought with hydrogen bombs, that we would in fact lose all our liberties and human values at the same time, and so thoroughly that we would not recover them for an unforeseeably long time.

We believe in peace based on mutual trust. Shall we achieve it by using hydrogen bombs? Shall we convince the Russians of the value of the individual by killing millions of them? If we fight a war and win it with H-bombs, what history will remember is *not* the ideals we were fighting for but the method we used to accomplish them.

Hans Bethe

Ever since the possibilities of releasing atomic energy on a vast scale came in sight, much thought has naturally been given to the question of control, but the further the exploration of the scientific problems concerned is proceeding, the clearer it becomes that no kind of customary measures will suffice for this purpose, and that the terrifying prospect of a future competition between nations about a weapon of such formidable character can only be avoided through a universal agreement in true confidence.

Neils Bohr, from his Memorandum to
President Roosevelt, July 1944

Scientists have often before been accused of providing new weapons for the mutual destruction of nations, instead of improving their well-being. It is undoubtedly true that the discovery of flying, for example, has so far brought much more misery than enjoyment and profit to humanity. However, in the past, scientists could disclaim direct responsibility for the use to which mankind had put their disinterested discoveries. We feel compelled to take a more active stand now because the success which we have achieved in the development of nuclear power is fraught with infinitely greater dangers than were all the inventions of the past. All of us, familiar with the present state of nucleonics, live with the vision before our eyes of sudden destruction visited on our own country, of a Pearl Harbour disaster repeated in thousand-fold magnification in every one of our major cities.

In the past, science has often been able to provide also new methods of protection against new weapons of aggression it made possible, but it cannot promise such efficient protection against the destructive use of nuclear power. This protection can come only from the political organization of the world. Among all the arguments calling for an efficient international organization for peace, the existence of nuclear weapons is the most compelling one. In the absence of an international authority which would make all resort to force in international conflicts impossible, nations could still be diverted from a path which must lead to total mutual destruction, by a specific international agreement barring a nuclear armaments race.

Thus, from the "optimistic" point of view – looking forward to an international agreement on the prevention of nuclear warfare – the military advantages and the saving of American lives achieved by the sudden use of atomic bombs against Japan may be outweighed by the ensuing loss of confidence and by a wave of horror and repulsion sweeping over the rest of the world and perhaps even dividing public opinion at home.

From this point of view, a demonstration of the new weapon might best be made, before the eyes of representatives of all the United Nations, on the desert or a barren island. The best possible atmosphere for the achievement of an international agreement could be achieved if America could say to the world, "You see what sort of weapon we had but did not use. We are ready to renounce its use in future if other nations join us in this renunciation and agree to the establishment of an efficient control."

J. Robert Oppenheimer led the team of Manhattan Project scientists who developed the first atomic weapon.

After such a demonstration the weapon might perhaps be used against Japan if the sanction of the United Nations (and if public opinion at home) were obtained, perhaps after a preliminary ultimatum to Japan to surrender or at least to evacuate certain regions as an alternative to their total destruction. This may sound fantastic, but in nuclear weapons we have something entirely new in order of magnitude of destructive power, and if we want to capitalize fully on the advantage their possession gives us, we must use new and imaginative methods.

The development of nuclear power not only constitutes an important addition to the technological and military power of the United States, but also creates grave political and economic problems for the future of this country.

Nuclear bombs cannot possibly remain a "secret weapon" at the exclusive disposal of this country for more than a few years. The scientific facts on which construction is based are well known to scientists of other countries. Unless an effective international control of nuclear explosives is instituted, a race for nuclear armaments is certain to ensue following the first revelation of our possession of nuclear weapons to the world. Within ten years other countries may have nuclear bombs, each of which, weighing less than a ton, could destroy an urban area of more than ten square miles. In the war to which such an armaments race is likely to lead, the United States, with its agglomeration of population and industry in comparatively few metropolitan districts, will be at a disadvantage compared to nations whose populations and industry are scattered over large areas.

We believe that these considerations make the use of nuclear bombs for an early unannounced attack against Japan inadvisable. If the United States were to be the first to release this new means of indiscriminate destruction upon mankind, she would sacrifice public support throughout the world, precipitate the race for armaments and prejudice the possibility of reaching an international agreement on the future control of such weapons.

Much more favourable conditions for the eventual achievement of such an agreement could be created if nuclear bombs were first revealed to the world by a demonstration in an appropriately selected uninhabited area.

In case chances for the establishment of an effective international control of nuclear weapons should have to be considered slight at the present time, then not only the use of these weapons against Japan, but even their early demonstration, may be contrary to the interests of this country. . . .

If the government should decide in favour of an early demonstration of nuclear weapons, it will then have the possibility of taking into account the public opinion of this country and of the other nations before deciding whether these weapons should be used against Japan. In this way, other nations may assume a share of responsibility for such a fateful decision.

Composed and signed by J. Franck, D. Hughes, L. Szilard, T. Hogness, E. Rabinowitch, G. Seaborg and C.J. Nickson from the "Franck Report," A Report to the Secretary of War, June 1945

ATOMIC VICTIMS

Just a Test *by Robert Arneson, 1984.*

Nuclear Tests (known and assumed explosions)

	U.S.	U.S.S.R.	Britain	France	China	India	Total
1984	15	27	2	7	2	0	53
1983	14	27	1	7	1	0	50
1982	18	31	1	5	0	0	55
1981	16	21	1	11	0	0	49
1980	14	21	3	11	1	0	50
1979	14	29	1	9	0	0	53
1978	12	27	2	7	3	0	51
1977	12	16	0	6	1	0	35
1976	15	17	1	4	4	0	41
1975	16	15	0	2	1	0	34
1974	7	19	1	7	1	1	36
1973	9	14	0	5	1	0	29
1972	8	22	0	3	2	0	35
1971	12	19	0	5	1	0	37
1970	30	12	0	8	1	0	51
1969	29	15	0	0	2	0	46
1968*	33	13	0	5	1	0	52
1967	28	15	0	3	2	0	46
1966	40	15	0	6	3	0	64
1965	28	9	1	4	1	0	43
1964	29	6	1	3	1	0	40
1963**	14	0	0	1	0	0	15
1945-63	331	164	23	8	0	0	526
Total	**744**	**554**	**38**	**127**	**29**	**1**	**1,493**

*In 1968, the United States, the Soviet Union and Britain signed the
Non-Proliferation Treaty that has since been ratified by 130 nations.
**August to December only. In 1963, the United States, the Soviet Union and
Britain signed the Partial Test Ban Treaty, which prohibited atmospheric
tests but allowed underground testing. France conducted atmospheric tests
through 1974 and China through 1980.

Stockholm International Peace Research Institute

A Warning

I raise my voice, together with those of others who have
lately [1956] felt it their duty to act, in speaking and writing,
as warners of the danger. My age and the sympathy that I
have gained for myself through advocating the idea of
reverence for life, permit me to hope that my appeal may
contribute to the preparing of the way for the insight so
urgently needed. . . .

Following the explosions on Bikini and Siberia, rain falling
over Japan has, from time to time, been so radioactive that the
water from it cannot be drunk. . . . And not only there; reports
of radioactive rainfall are coming from all parts of the world
where analyses have recently been made. In several places,
the water has proved to be so radioactive that it was unfit for
drinking.

Wherever radioactive rainwater is found the soil is also
radioactive – and in a higher degree. The soil is more
radioactive not only by the downpour, but also from
radioactive dust falling on it. And with the soil the vegetation
will also have become radioactive. . . .

What this storing of radioactive material implies is clearly
demonstrated by the observations made when, on one
occasion, the radioactivity of the Columbia River in North
America was analyzed. The radioactivity was caused by the
atomic plants at Hanford, which produce atomic energy for
industrial purposes, and which empty their waste water into
the river.

The radioactivity of the river water was insignificant. But
the radioactivity of the river plankton was 2,000 times higher,
that of the ducks eating the plankton 40,000 times higher,
that of the fish 15,000 times higher. In young swallows fed on
insects caught by their parents in the river, the radioactivity
was 500,000 times higher and in the egg yolks of water birds
more than 1,000,000 times higher.

From official and unofficial sources we have been assured,
time and time again, that the increase in radioactivity of the
air does not exceed the amount which the human body can
tolerate without any harmful effects. This is just evading the
problem. . . .

We are forced to regard every increase in the existing
danger through further creation of radioactive elements by
atom bomb explosions as a catastrophe for the human race, a
catastrophe that must be prevented under every
circumstance.

There can be no question of doing anything else, if only for
the reason that we cannot take the responsibility for the
consequences it might have for our descendants.

They are threatened by the greatest and most terrible
danger.

Albert Schweitzer

Fallout at Bikini

An unintended exposure of a population to the radiation from local fallout occurred in the Marshall Islands, following the Bravo test of March 1, 1954. The explosive yield of this first test of a large thermonuclear device was about 15 megatons. The detonation was near the ground, about 2 meters above a coral reef in Bikini Atoll. Some of the radioactive cloud came down unexpectedly in a long plume in an easterly direction, covering the Marshall Islands, several of which were inhabited by natives and one by U.S. personnel. An area of about 20,000 square kilometers was contaminated to such an extent that lethal doses would have been received by persons staying in the open. . . .

Two days after the test the inhabitants were evacuated. By that time some had received whole-body doses of up to 200 rads (to surface tissue), and the majority of the islanders on Rongelap Atoll had burns from beta radiation. Internal exposure from inhalation and ingestion of radioactive materials (particularly radioactive iodine) with food and water also had occurred. Some inhabitants exhibited symptoms of acute exposure (loss of appetite, nausea, and vomiting). Long-term effects (predominantly thyroid disorders) appeared later.

Almost all the children of the Rongelap Atoll had lesions of the thyroid and had to undergo surgery for the removal of thyroid nodules; later, a number of them showed symptoms of hypothyroidism. Several cases of cancer of the thyroid occurred among the female inhabitants. The population of the Rongelap Atoll islands was allowed to return in 1957, three years after the test; but more than 20 years later, in 1979, the northern islands of the atoll were still declared too radioactive to visit. . . .

The islands of the Bikini Atoll, where testing continued until 1958, remained uninhabited for many years. Vigorous decontamination measures were taken, including the removal of 5 centimeters of the topsoil, before planting new trees. In 1967, the Bikini Atoll was declared habitable, and some islanders returned. However, further geological surveys showed that the radioactivity in the soil was still too high for agriculture, and the atoll was again evacuated. By the end of 1980 some islands of the atoll were declared safe for habitation, but only if 50 percent of the food for the inhabitants was imported.

In addition to the inhabitants of the atolls, a Japanese fishing boat was showered with fallout particles from the Bravo test. The crew was exposed externally from the fallout deposited on the walls and floors of the vessel and on the surfaces of their bodies and internally from the inhaled radioactive materials.

On the first evening their eyes were affected; they suffered from excess tearing and pain in the eyeballs. After two weeks, they developed photophobia (pain on looking at light), edema of the conjunctiva (swelling of the transparent tissue layer covering the eyeball), and acute keratoconjunctivitis (inflammation of the cornea and conjunctiva). Slight opacities of the lens also occurred. Many developed liver damage, from which one died. It is claimed that another died many years later from liver damage. Because their hair and skin were highly radioactive, these men were vigorously scrubbed, and

Seriously injured crew member of the Japanese fishing boat, Fukuryu; March, 1954.

chelating agents were used to remove the contamination. All their hair, including body hair, was shaved off before they were hospitalized. Despite these efforts at decontamination, the men developed acute and long-term skin lesions.

Dr. Patricia Lindop and Joseph Rotblat

95

Early atomic tests were treated as novelties. Here, military observers lounge casually to watch a blast. Note the shorts on the man in the front row.

Downwind from the Bomb

Although America's first atomic tests were conducted in secrecy in New Mexico, after World War II the United States shifted nuclear-weapons trials to the southern Pacific Ocean. The possibility of security breaches was offset, it was reasoned, by the lessened risk to public health and safety.

With the outbreak of hostilities in Korea in June 1950 and the start of the cold war, however, the Atomic Energy Commission argued that future tests of atomic bombs must be conducted within the borders of the United States, for reasons of national security. . . . The President chose the Las Vegas-Tonopah Bombing and Gunnery Range, a Government-owned area north of Las Vegas, Nev., as the location for the nation's nuclear trials. The Nevada Proving Ground (called the Nevada Test Site, or N.T.S., after 1954) was selected because of its low population density, the "virtually uninhabitable" land downwind from the site, and favorable meteorological conditions, a reference to the prevailing winds that blew eastward away from the heavily populated Los Angeles and Las Vegas metropolitan areas.

A month later, on Jan. 27, 1951, the United States exploded its first nuclear device on American soil since the war. . . .

While it is not a heavily populated region, approximately 100,000 people lived in the three-state expanse north and east of the N.T.S. In later years, when the fallout that dusted their fields and streets had become a familiar sight,

they would refer to themselves as "the downwinders."

*   *   *

The downwinders were descendants of the Mormon pioneers who had arrived in the Southwest in the late 1840s. Although the Church of Jesus Christ of Latter-day Saints no longer completely dominated community life, these towns and villages – among them St. George, Cedar City and Parowan, Utah, and Bunkerville, Nev. – remained islands of social and political conservatism. Families were large (Utah's 1950 average family size of 8.83 people was the nation's highest) and close-knit. The downwinders were also rigid both in their anti-Communism and their support for Government policies.

*   *   *

By 1961 – ten years after the start of the atomic testing – the downwinders began to experience something new in their communities: clusters of childhood leukemia, which at the time was 90 percent fatal. During the next several years, leukemia appeared with increasing frequency in downwind families. Although the incidence of all cancers in the southwest was 20 percent lower than in the nation as a whole, the Utah Cancer Registry reported that the incidence of acute leukemia in children in the four-county area downwind of the N.T.S. between 1957 and 1974 was one-and-a-half times the national average. Between 1956 and 1964, according to the Utah Department of Health, the rate of

leukemia deaths in the same four-county region was the highest in the state. In later years, other cancers – which can take longer to develop after radiation exposure – appeared in statistically significant percentages downwind of the Nevada Test Site.

To the downwinders, the statistics represented a tragic and immediate reality. Frankie Bentley of Parowan, Utah, recalled the year 1960 vividly. "We had four teenagers die with leukemia, first ever in the Parowan area," she testified at a 1979 hearing on victims' compensation.

Elmer Pickett, a store owner from St. George, told Senator Hatch, "In my own family we have nine cancer victims, beginning with my wife who died of the disease and leukemia combined. . . . I cannot find anywhere in our family records, anywhere as far as we can go, any cancer-related deaths of any nature in our family lines. We have been a very healthy family here."

*   *   *

For the downwinders who have gone to Federal courts for compensation for their suffering, the difficult task has been to prove that the cancers and leukemia are "more likely than not" caused by exposure to radiation produced by the nuclear tests in the 1950s, the proof required by the Federal Tort Claims Act. . . .

Despite the Government's arguments, Federal District Court Judge Bruce S. Jenkins ruled in favor of 10 of the plaintiffs in 1984, awarding them approximately $2.7 million in damages. "At the core of this case is a fundamental principle, a time honored rule of law, an ethical rule, a moral tenet: The law imposes a duty on everyone to avoid acts in their nature dangerous to the lives of others," wrote Judge Jenkins in his opinion.

Howard Ball

Birth Defects Among the Navajo

Dr. Lora Shields and Dr. Alan Goodman have nearly completed a study of 13,300 Navajo live births from 1964 to 1981 in the Shiprock Uranium mining area [New Mexico]. Over six million tons of uranium ore has been taken from shallow surface outcrops from 1945-60 around Shiprock, where some 63,000 Navajo live. Medical personnel at the Shiprock hospital had noticed a high incidence of birth defects and stillbirths among Navajos born at this hospital. The Shields-Goodman study, after abstracting the 13,300 records, documented the number of birth defects identifiable at birth as two to eight times as high as nationwide, or among other Indian tribes from 1964-74. However, this rate turned decisively toward normal in 1975, paralleling or overlapping such environmental events as covering the uranium trailings piles, a steep decline in the actual mining of uranium, as well as closing an electronics plant.

Certain severe anomalies were significantly higher from 1964-74 than from 1974-81, as a percentage of total births for each period. Among these were: hydrocephaly; anencephaly, microcephaly, Down's syndrome, cleft palate/lip; club foot, and hip dysplasia. There was one case each of cebocephaly (monkeyface), osteogenesis porosa, Paget's disease, fucosidosis, and two cases of retinoblastoma.

As a result of these birth defects, there are 3,400 Navajo children in special education programs, and 2,000 other Navajo children waiting to be classified to enter such programs.

In conclusion, the role of radiation in the birth anomalies and stillbirths in the Shiprock uranium mining area cannot be established conclusively until

George and Rita Seabron at home. George served as a sailor decontaminating ships used as targets at Bikini Atoll bomb tests. He suffers from sterility, stomach problems, and debilitating back, bone, and muscle problems.

Kay Hinkle (left), widow of a navy crewman who was exposed to seventeen different nuclear tests over a four-month period, with two of her daughters, Patti and Holly, both born with spinal alignment problems. Holly (right), was also born with a vestigial left hand.

the field interviews are completed and the computer analysis is finalized. However, it would appear that the present improved birth outcomes since 1975, coincident with environmental changes noted, makes any other explanation for the fetal wastage and adverse birth outcomes difficult to support.

National Association of Radiation Survivors

DUCK AND COVER

How to "Escape" the Bomb

Children cover their heads in a 1950s air raid drill.

At the Governor's residence, Nelson Rockefeller explores a possible site for his fallout shelter, 1961.

A seven-part television series, *Survival*, was shown on NBC in 1951, reaching an estimated 12 million people. A film, *Survival Under Atomic Attack*, was made for civil defense authorities and produced under government direction with private money. Narrated by news commentator Edward R. Murrow, it circulated throughout the country with conspicuous success. A booklet with the same title told readers on the first page: "You can SURVIVE," and went on: "You can live through an atom bomb raid and you won't have to have a Geiger counter, protective clothing, or special training in order to do it. The secrets of survival are: KNOW THE BOMB'S TRUE DANGERS. KNOW THE STEPS YOU CAN TAKE TO ESCAPE THEM." The pamphlet counseled people to drop to the ground or floor, and shield themselves as much as possible.

From that advice came the civil defense slogan of the next several years: "Duck and Cover." A film by that name introduced "Bert the Turtle" to elementary school children and stressed the need to take cover from flying glass and other debris in case of a raid. A cartoon booklet, distributed to 20 million readers and widely reprinted, told the same story. For those who might have missed either movie or booklet a "Bert the Turtle" recording and a sheet music version carried the same theme.

Conveying a similar message was the "Alert America" program that began at the end of 1951. Three convoys of ten 32-foot trailers each carried portable exhibits to cities throughout the land. They contained dioramas showing the possible impact of a bomb on a typical city and scenes showing how civil defense could help....

The Interstate Highway Act of 1956, which provided easier automobile access to the suburbs, also established an expeditious means of exit from the cities in case of atomic war. While planning the road-building program, the Administration undertook to check on the readiness plans of various government agencies. A three-day "Operation Alert" in June 1955 sought to determine if officials could evacuate Washington and perform regular and emergency functions at relocation sites. The hypothetical raid involved attacks on Washington and 54 other cities, and theoretically left 8.2 million people dead, 6.5 million injured and 24 million homeless. The President and a host of other officials left Washington at the proper time for retreats outside the city, where they attempted to deal with the issues at hand. The exercise indicated the magnitude of the problems to be faced, and the kinds of coordination that had to be improved....

Yet the whole notion of evacuation suffered a real blow with the growing realization of the consequences of fallout that accompanied nuclear tests. Fallout was a little-known phenomenon before 1954. There had been a troublesome episode in May 1953 when an Atomic Energy Commission (AEC) test at the Nevada Proving Grounds dropped radioactive particles on regions more than 100 miles away, but reaction was relatively restrained. A more dramatic incident, and one which received even greater press coverage, occurred after the March 1, 1954, *Bravo* test in the Pacific, when the hydrogen blast showered fallout on inhabitants of Rongelap Atoll in the Marshall Islands, as well as on the crewmen of a Japanese fishing boat some 85 miles away. Crew members developed radiation sickness, and several months later one died. People became aware of a new atomic threat....

As interest grew, more and more firms provided readymade shelters for eager consumers. *Life* featured an "H-Bomb Hideaway" for $3,000 in 1955. A Miami firm reported numerous inquiries about shelters that sold for between $1,795 and $3,895, depending on capacity, and planned 900 franchises. By the end of 1960, OCDM [Office of Civil and Defense Mobilization] estimated that there were a million family fallout shelters nationwide.

Allan M. Winkler

Russians, Too, Joke Sadly

Russians have a way of poking fun at much in their lives that is tedious, so it's no surprise that humorists have their stock of macabre jokes about the Kremlin's elaborate civil defense program.

One concerns a worker who asks his local party secretary: "Comrade, what should we do if the Americans launch a nuclear attack?"

"Simple," the party secretary replies. "You wrap yourself in a sheet and make your way slowly to the cemetery."

"Why slowly, comrade?" the worker asks. "Simple again," the party secretary replies. "So as not to cause panic."

As the joke implies, the wide-scale effort to prepare the country to survive a nuclear war has serious credibility problems. Many Russians have apparently concluded that nothing the Kremlin has done – elaborate evacuation plans, shelters to accommodate millions, compulsory lectures on survival techniques – has significantly lowered the probability of annihilation if a nuclear conflict comes.

The program dwarfs similar undertakings elsewhere. Estimates by the Central Intelligence Agency have put the full-time civil defense establishment at more than 100,000 people. The agency calculated that a similar program in the United States would cost at least $2 billion a year.

The momentum of the program continues to carry it forward. But some Western analysts believe that it has begun to slow down under the impact of public and professional skepticism, budgetary constraints and a growing sense in the Kremlin that war is, after all, an unthinkable prospect in an era when the Soviet Union and the United States have the might to destroy each other, and many other nations as well.

John F. Burns

From When the Wind Blows *by Raymond Briggs, 1982.*

Evacuation – 1985

FEMA [Federal Emergency Management Agency] has decided that during [a] three-to-five-day preemptive period before a nuclear war, the evacuating population will remain calm, ordered, and well-behaved. This is a totally unrealistic expectation because I know that I would be in a state of total panic and doom, and there would probably be chaos throughout the land. Nevertheless, we are told to remain calm and not to forget to take our bankbooks, credit cards, insurance policies, and wills, and we must submit change-of-address cards to the post office. We must not take with us drugs or alcohol. As Dr. Herbert Abrams, professor of radiology at Harvard Medical School, has said, that is exactly what he might like to have when he is trapped in a massive traffic jam on the highway waiting to be vaporized.

Helen Caldicott

NUCLEAR BUILD-UP

The Buildup Begins

U. S. Shocked...

I believe the American people to the fullest extent consistent with the national security are entitled to be informed of all developments in the field of atomic energy. That is my reason for making public the following information.

We have evidence that within recent weeks an atomic explosion occurred in the U.S.S.R.

Ever since atomic energy was first released by man, the eventual development of this new force by other nations was to be expected. This probability has always been taken into account by us.

Nearly four years ago I pointed out that "scientific opinion appears to be practically unanimous that the essential theoretical knowledge upon which the discovery is based is already widely known. There is also substantial agreement that foreign research can come abreast of our present theoretical knowledge in time." And, in the three-nation declaration of the

Cows in Pasture with Missiles *by Robert Giusti.*

ANTI-NUCLEAR!

THE MOST DANGEROUS RACE

The Most Dangerous Race *by Noboru Matsuura, 1985.*

President of the United States and the Prime Ministers of the United Kingdom and of Canada, dated Nov. 15, 1945, it was emphasized that no single nation could, in fact, have a monopoly on atomic weapons.

This recent development emphasizes once again, if indeed such emphasis were needed, the necessity for that truly effective and enforceable international control of atomic energy which this Government and the large majority of the members of the United Nations support.

President Harry Truman, 1949

...by Russia's First A-Bomb

On Sept. 23, Mr. Truman, President of the USA, announced that according to data of the Government of the USA, during one of the recent weeks there had occurred in the USSR an atomic explosion. Simultaneously, a similar statement was made by the British and Canadian governments.

Following the publication of these statements in the American, British and Canadian press and also in the press of other countries, there appeared

numerous utterances which spread alarm among broad social circles.

In this connection, Tass is empowered to declare: In the Soviet Union, as is known, building work on a large scale is in progress; the building of hydro-electric stations, mines, canals, roads, which evoke the necessity of large-scale blasting work with the use of the latest technical means.

In so far as this blasting work has taken place and is taking place pretty frequently in various parts of the country, it is possible this might draw attention beyond the confines of the Soviet Union.

As for the production of atomic energy, Tass considers it necessary to recall that already on Nov. 6, 1947, Minister of Foreign Affairs of the USSR, V.M. Molotov, made a statement concerning the secret of the atom bomb when he declared that this secret was already long ago nonexistent.

This statement signified the Soviet Union already had discovered the secret of the atomic weapon and that it had at its disposal this weapon.

Scientific circles of the United States of America took this statement by V. M. Molotov for a bluff, considering that the Russians could not possess an atomic weapon earlier than the year 1952.

They however were mistaken, since the Soviet Union possessed the secret of the atomic weapon already in 1947.

As for the alarm that is being spread on this account by certain foreign circles, there are not the slightest grounds for alarm.

It should be pointed out that the Soviet government, despite the existence in its country of an atomic weapon, adopts and intends adopting in the future its former position in favor of the absolute prohibition of the use of the atomic weapon.

Concerning control of the atomic weapon, it has to be said that control will be essential in order to check up on fulfillment of a decision on the prohibition of production of the atomic weapon.

Tass

Action and Reaction in the Nuclear Competition

The dynamics of the nuclear arms race ensure that development of a new weapons system by one power will in a relatively brief period be followed by a comparable achievement by the other. Both powers have had "firsts." Neither has stayed ahead for long. The US generally has a technological lead of several years, but the futility of the race for short-term advantage is demonstrated by a chronology of developments to date.

atomic bomb	**US 1945** **USSR 1949**	The nuclear age began with the explosion of a US A-bomb of 12.5 kilotons (equivalent to 12,500 tons of TNT) over Hiroshima, Japan. The single bomb, which destroyed the city, introduced to the world a concentrated explosive force of unprecedented power. Within four years, the USSR conducted its first atomic test.
intercontinental bomber	**US 1948** **USSR 1955**	By 1948, the US had begun to replace the propeller planes of World War II with long-range jets. The first planes developed for strategic (intercontinental) bombing required refueling to reach another continent. In 1955, the US began deployment of the all-jet intercontinental bomber, and USSR soon followed suit.
hydrogen bomb	**US 1954** **USSR 1955**	The H-Bomb multiplied the explosive force of the A-bomb 1,000 times. The first US thermonuclear bomb had a yield equivalent to 15,000,000 tons of TNT; a year later the USSR tested a bomb in the million-ton range.
intercontinental ballistic missile (ICBM)	**USSR 1957** **US 1958**	Following intensive development by both nuclear powers, a land-based missile to carry nuclear warheads intercontinental distances was successfully flight-tested by the USSR in 1957, and by the US a year later. By 1962 both nations had ICBMs with a range of 6,000 miles, each missile able to carry a payload equivalent to 5-10,000,000 tons of TNT.
man-made satellite in orbit	**USSR 1957** **US 1958**	Sputnik I by the USSR initiated a space race which quickly took on military functions; the first US satellite was launched into orbit the following year. Well over half the superpowers' satellites have been military: for surveillance, targeting, communications, etc.
submarine-launched ballistic missile (SLBM)	**US 1960** **USSR 1968**	A nuclear-powered submarine which could fire long-range missiles from a submerged position was the third means of strategic delivery. The US produced the nuclear-powered Polaris, with missiles with a range of 1,200 nautical miles. Eight years later the USSR had comparable nuclear subs.
multiple warhead (MRV)	**US 1966** **USSR 1968**	Multiheaded missiles increased the number of targets a missile could hit. US MRV'd missiles carried three warheads, each with sixteen times the explosive force of the Hiroshima bomb. The USSR had them two years later.
anti-ballistic missile (ABM)	**USSR 1968** **US 1972**	The USSR deployed 64 defensive missiles around Moscow. The US began construction of the Safeguard system in 1969 and had one site completed when a treaty restricting ABMs was signed in 1972. Generally judged militarily ineffective, ABMs were restricted to one site in each country in 1974. Subsequently, the US site was closed.
multiple independently-targeted warhead (MIRV)	**US 1970** **USSR 1975**	Further development of multiple warheads enabled one missile to hit three to ten individually selected targets as far apart as 100 miles. USSR began to flight-test MIRVs three years after US put them in service and in 1975 began deployment.
long-range cruise missile	**US 1982** **USSR 198?**	Adaptable to launching from air, sea, and land, a new generation of missiles with a range up to 1,500 miles is in production. The cruise missile is small, relatively inexpensive, highly accurate, with the unique advantage of very low trajectory. Following the contours of the earth, and flying under radar, it will be able to destroy its target without warning. The US is reportedly 7-8 years in the lead in this technology.
neutron bomb	**US 1983** **USSR 198?**	This nuclear weapon releases its explosive energy more in the form of an invisible, penetrating bombardment of radiation rather than in heat and blast. The decision to produce and stockpile the enhanced radiation warhead in the US was announced in August 1981. The USSR promptly announced that it has the capability but had deferred a production decision.
anti-satellite weapons	**US 199?** **USSR 199?**	Because satellites play vital military roles, they have also inspired a search for weapons to destroy them. The USSR began testing intercepter satellites in 1968. Both superpowers are attempting to perfect lasers to destroy enemy satellites and nuclear missiles in event of war.

Ruth Leger Sivard—*World Military and Social Expenditures*

FIREPOWER

Overkill

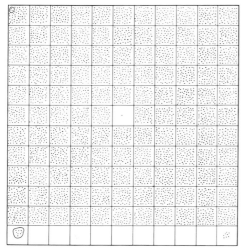

Nuclear Weapons Chart.

The chart above shows the world's current firepower as opposed to the firepower of World War II. The dot in the center square represents all the firepower of World War II: 3 megatons. The other dots represent the world's present nuclear weaponry which equals 6,000 World War IIs or 18,000 megatons. The United States and the Soviets share this firepower with approximately equal destructive capability.

The top left-hand circle enclosing 9 megatons represents the weapons on just one Poseidon submarine. This is equal to the firepower of three World War IIs and enough to destroy over 200 of the Soviets' largest cities. We have 31 such subs and 10 similar Polaris subs.

The circle in the lower left-hand square enclosing 24 megatons represents one new Trident sub with the firepower of eight World War IIs. *Enough to destroy every major city in the northern hemisphere.*

The Soviets have similar levels of destructive power.

Just two squares on this chart (300 megatons) represent enough firepower to destroy all the large and medium-size cities in the entire world. (U.S. Senate staff have reviewed this chart and found it to be an accurate representation of the nuclear weapons arsenal.)

Spectrum (March 1985)

The Nuclear Stockpile

The United States since 1945 has manufactured some 60,000 nuclear warheads in 71 types configured for 116 weapons systems costing some $750 billion. This amounts to an average production rate of about four warheads per day for 40 years. With the current rate of spending on warhead production exceeding that of the Manhattan Project, the present stockpile of some 25,000 warheads is once again on the rise.

* * *

The character of the present nuclear buildup is that huge numbers of warheads produced during the 1950s and 1960s are planned to be retired and replaced with larger numbers of new warheads. Although expenditures are at near-record highs, production rates are not. From fiscal 1984 through 1988 the stockpile will increase, under current plans, by an average of some 650 warheads per year, reaching an estimated level of over 28,000. Production rates of new warheads are in the 1,800-per-year range – five a day – with retirements at some 1,100 a year – three a day – averaging a net addition of approximately two a day.

* * *

Many warhead types have been adapted for more than one weapon system and deployed with more than one service. In 40 years the Air Force has made use of 43 warhead types, the Navy and Marine Corps 34 types, and the Army 21. Jointly, the Air Force, Navy, and Marines have deployed 29 types of bombs (18 of them thermonuclear) on 53 kinds of U.S. and Allied aircraft.

* * *

As more of the secret nuclear history is revealed, the clearer the perspective becomes with regard to current decisions and events. Bureaucratic competition and inertia have led to nuclear warheads for every conceivable military mission, arm of service, and geographic theater – all compounded by a technological momentum that overwhelmed what should have been a more sober analysis of what was enough for deterrence. The result is a gigantic nuclear weapons system – laboratories, production facilities, forces, and so on – that has become self-perpetuating, conducting its business out of public view and with little accountability.

Robert S. Norris, Thomas B. Cochran, and William M. Arkin

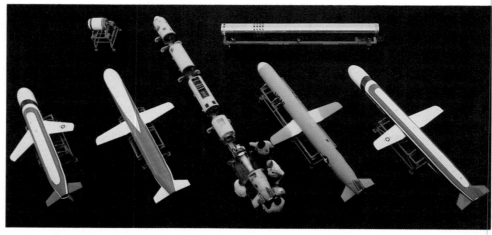

Different kinds of anti-ship cruise missiles.

The Balance of Forces

UNITED STATES		
	Delivery Systems	Warheads
ICBMs	1026	2126
SLBMs	640	5728
Bombers	297	3336
Total	1963	11,190

SOVIET UNION		
	Delivery Systems	Warheads
ICBMs	1398	6320
SLBMs	966	2246
Bombers	173	690
Total	2537	9256

Despite the great amount of information on the composition of the US and Soviet nuclear arsenals, there is no consensus as to which nation is "ahead."

Debate arises because raw numbers fail to provide sufficient answers. To be useful, the data on US and Soviet arsenals must be carefully interpreted. Differing assessments of the strategic balance can be derived as a result of how numbers are combined, which elements of the forces are emphasized, and what assumptions are made about various operational factors and scenarios. Asymmetries in the two nations' force structures and geopolitical situations also complicate assessments of the strategic balance.

*   *   *

For the most part, doctrines other than basic deterrence rest on unrealistic assumptions about nuclear war and Soviet behavior. They also tend to ignore the basic condition of the nuclear age – in a world filled with nuclear weapons, neither country is safe from devastation during a war between the superpowers without the cooperation of its adversary. Basic deterrence accepts this fact, and relies upon it to avoid war. Alternative doctrines generate force requirements far in excess of deterrence needs, and encourage misleading comparisons of forces and the belief in "inferiority" and "superiority."

In fact there is now – and has long been – an essential parity, or equality, in terms of basic deterrence.

Union of Concerned Scientists (U.S.A.)

The Effects of Nuclear War

The impact of even a "small" or "limited" nuclear attack would be enormous. Although predictions of the effects of such an attack are subject to the same uncertainties as predictions of the effects of an all-out attack, the possibilities can be bounded. OTA [US government, Office of Technological Assessment] examined the impact of a small attack on economic targets (an attack on oil refineries limited to 10 missiles), and found that while economic recovery would be possible, the economic damage and social dislocation could be immense. A review of calculations of the effects on civilian populations and economies of major counterforce attacks found that while the consequences might be endurable (since they would be on a scale with wars and epidemics that nations have endured in the past), the number of deaths might be as high as 20 million. Moreover, the uncertainties are such that no government could predict with any confidence what the results of a limited attack or counterattack would be even if there was no further escalation....

What is clear is that from the day the survivors emerged from their fallout shelters, a kind of race for survival would begin. One side of the race would be the restoration of production: production of food, of energy, of clothing, of the means to repair damaged machinery, of goods that might be used for trade with countries that had not fought in the war, and even of military weapons and supplies. The other side of the race would be consumption of goods that had survived the attack, and the wearing-out of surviving machines. If production rises to the rate of consumption before stocks are exhausted, then viability has been achieved and economic recovery has begun. If not, then each postwar year would see a lower level of economic activity than the year before, and the future of civilization itself in the nations attacked would be in doubt.

Office of Technological Assessment, U.S. Congress

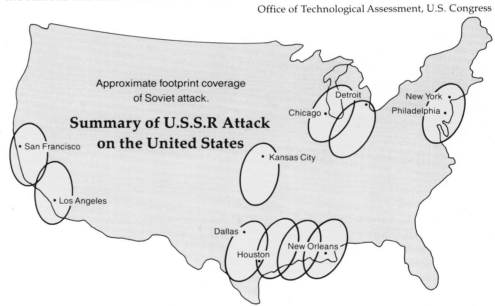

Approximate footprint coverage of Soviet attack.

Summary of U.S.S.R Attack on the United States

Footprint number	Geographic area	EMT[a]	% national refining capacity	% national storage capacity	Air burst prompt fatalities (× 1,000)
1	Texas	8	14.9	NA[b]	472
2	Indiana, Illinois, Ohio	8	8.1	NA	365
3	New Jersey, Pennsylvania, Delaware	8	7.9	NA	845
4	California	8	7.8	NA	1,252
5	Louisiana, Texas, Mississippi	8	7.5	NA	377
6	Texas	8	4.5	NA	377
7	Illinois, Indiana, Michigan	8	3.6	NA	484
8	Louisiana	8	3.6	NA	278
9	Oklahoma, Kansas	8	3.3	NA	365
10	California	8	2.5	NA	357
Totals		80	63.7	NA	5,031

[a]EMT = Equivalent megatons [b]NA = Not applicable

ACCIDENTS AND RISKS

Construction of the Berlin Wall nearly triggered a nuclear war in the 1960s. Here, in a photograph by Henri Cartier-Bresson, a child attempts to climb the Wall.

Standing at the Brink

On a number of occasions since August 1945, when we bombed Hiroshima and Nagasaki, the U. S. has stood on the brink of nuclear war.

This sort of nuclear bullying generally worked before the Soviets achieved parity, but threatening first use of nuclear weapons is now beginning to fail as a policy:

• In June 1948, Harry Truman deployed "atomic capable" B-29s to bases in Britain and Germany at the outset of the Berlin Blockade. By the end of 1948, the U. S. had effectively broken the blockade by the Soviets.

• Late in 1950, Truman warned that nuclear weapons might be used against the Chinese who surrounded U. S. troops at the Chosin Reservoir during the Korean War. The marines got out without the use of such force.

• In 1953, Dwight Eisenhower forced a settlement to the Korean War by threatening China secretly with the bomb.

• In 1954, Secretary of State John Foster Dulles *twice* offered French Prime Minister Bidault the use of American atomic weapons in the French-Indochina conflict – first, to bomb Chinese supply lines inside China; second, to relieve French forces at Dien Bien Phu. France declined.

• In 1958, Eisenhower directed the Joint Chiefs to prepare to use nuclear weapons against China if it should invade the island of Quemoy.

• In 1961, the Berlin Crisis broke out. The Berlin Wall was erected, and the U. S. threatened first use of atomic bombs if the East Germans prevented

refugees from crossing to the West.

• In 1962, John Kennedy threatened to invade Cuba and use nuclear weapons if Soviet offensive missiles, moved into that country after our Bay of Pigs invasion, were not removed.

• In 1968, the U. S. considered using nuclear weapons to save marines surrounded at Khe Sanh, Vietnam.

• On November 1, 1969, Richard Nixon sent an ultimatum to the North Vietnamese that the U. S. would use nuclear weapons if they did not settle the war. Nixon told Haldeman, "I call it the Madman Theory, Bob. I want the North Vietnamese to believe I've reached the point where I might do *anything* to stop the war."

Mother Jones Magazine

Risks of Accidental Nuclear War

Sources of Nuclear Weapons Accidents and Accidental Nuclear War

1. *Human errors within the military*. An accident can be initiated by those whose job it is to build, operate, and maintain nuclear weapons. While personnel working with nuclear weapons are screened for this special duty, an average of 5,000 service people (four percent of the total) are removed from the US nuclear weapons cadre yearly for behavior that renders them unreliable. Error can result from psychological and emotional disorders, behavioral problems including negligence and lack of motivation, and drug or alcohol abuse. Errors and unintentional mishaps in working with complex weapons technology may result from any of these factors.

2. *Human errors by those who manage and authorize the use of nuclear weapons*. The use of our nuclear weapons forces is held in check under a posture of nuclear deterrence. This theory assumes rationality at all times in our decision-makers – even under the severe stresses and time constraints of a crisis. Miscalculation, misunderstanding, hastiness, and operational rigidity may represent salient features of an international crisis, as they have in many historical instances. Just as World War I spiralled out of a local conflict, when mounting tensions and misperceptions overwhelmed the European leaders, so too, could accidental nuclear war escalate out of a smaller crisis in any part of the world.

3. *Technical malfunction within the nuclear weapons system*. Mechanical and computer errors have led to past accidents within the nuclear military sytem. A fuel leak in a Titan II missile silo, coupled with a weak propulsion system, led to an explosion which hurled the missile out of the silo. In at least two instances in the past, nuclear-tipped

Pushing the Right Buttons *by Erika Rothenberg, 1981.*

anti-aircraft missiles were actually launched by accident. A total of 32 "Broken Arrows" or major nuclear weapons accidents have been acknowledged by the US Department of Defense. It is likely that the Soviet Union experiences a similar number of mishaps.

Computer errors have led to false nuclear alerts. The North American Defense Command has reported 152 false alarms within an 18-month time span which were serious enough to warrant threat evaluations.

Factors Which Increase the Risk of Accidental Nuclear War

1. *The arms race*. The growing number of nuclear weapons built and deployed in the world, and the increasing complexity of their design, has heightened the probability of future accidents.

2. *Nuclear proliferation*. As more countries and more people gain access to nuclear weapons and nuclear materials, the likelihood of accident increases, as does the risk of nuclear terrorism and other acts of violence. As more countries join the nuclear establishment, international crises may more easily escalate into nuclear confrontations.

3. *Strategic doctrines*. The development of "first-strike weapons", which are offensive rather than defensive systems, poses serious risks of inadvertent launching. Such weapons necessitate the use of "launch-on-warning" and other hair-trigger responses to possible nuclear alerts. Nations must decide in a drastically reduced amount of time (possibly a matter of minutes) whether to launch or lose weapons of this nature.

4. *International tensions*. The political climate between nations greatly affects the way in which they view each others' actions. In an atmosphere of high tension, any act by an adversary may be interpreted as belligerent and threatening.

5. *Lack of Soviet-American dialogue*. In light of the above comments, the current lack of dialogue between the Soviet and American leaders clearly inhibits the reduction of tensions. Without open communication channels, no avenue exists for clarifying positions. Tension only mounts.

International Physicians
for the Prevention of Nuclear War

Broken Arrows and Bent Spears

1947, October – Atlantic Ocean
A retired navy pilot Lieutenant-Commander George Earl IV has claimed that he dumped radioactive waste off the densely populated Atlantic seaboard on three flights in 1947. Lieutenant-Commander Earl said he disclosed the radioactive dumping because of the U. S. Government's apparent lack of concern over the possibility of the canisters leaking.

1950, 13th February – Pacific Ocean
A B-36 which developed serious mechanical difficulties on a simulated combat mission, dropped a nuclear weapon from 8,000 ft over the Pacific Ocean before crashing. "Only the weapon's high explosive material detonated." Nothing is known of attempts to recover the nuclear weapon and presumably it is still in the ocean.

1956, 10th March – Mediterranean Sea
A B-47 carrying "two capsules of nuclear weapons material" from MacDill Air Force Base to an overseas base, disappeared in clouds. "An extensive search failed to locate any traces of the missing aircraft or crew."

1958, 11th March – South Carolina, U. S. A.
A B-47 left Hunter Air Force Base, Georgia with three other B-47s en route to an overseas base. "The aircraft accidentally jettisoned an unarmed nuclear weapon which impacted in a sparsely populated area 6½ miles east of Florence, South Carolina. The bomb's high explosive material exploded on impact."

1958, 26th November – Louisiana, U. S. A.
A B-47 caught fire on the ground. The single nuclear weapon on board was destroyed by fire. Contamination was limited to the immediate vicinity. This was the eighth and last acknowledged B-47 accident making it the most accident-prone of the nuclear-capable systems reported.

1959, 6th July – Louisiana, U. S. A.
A C-124 on a nuclear logistics movement mission crashed on take-off. The aircraft was destroyed by fire which also destroyed one weapon. Limited contamination was present over a very small area.

1961, 24th January – North Carolina, U. S. A.
A B-52 crashed during an airborne alert mission and dropped two nuclear weapons near Goldsboro, North Carolina. "A portion of one weapon containing uranium could not be recovered despite excavation in the waterlogged farmland to a depth of 50 feet. The Air Force subsequently purchased an easement requiring permission for anyone to dig there. There is no detectable radiation and no hazard in the area." The Department of Defence summary does not mention the fact that five of six interlocking safety triggers on the bomb failed. "Only a single switch," reported Dr. Ralph Lapp, head of the nuclear physics branch of the Office of Naval Research, "prevented the 24-megaton bomb from detonating and spreading fire over a wide area."

1963, April – Nuclear Submarine
Submarine disappeared on a deep test dive; 112 navy men and 17 civilians on board. No-one knows what happened but the loss underlines the implications of substandard quality control in nuclear systems, both military and civil. There are an estimated 129 nuclear attack submarines and S.S.L. submarines (those capable of launching ballistic missiles). The substandard quality of these submarines is borne out by the high number of accidents and incidents related to nuclear submarines. (Since 1963 when the first mishap was reported there have been 32 accidents and incidents involving nuclear submarines up to October, 1976.) "The dangers of nuclear submarines are incisive with horrific consequences. There are no evacuation plans for cities whose ports are used by these ships. There only needs to be one accident or malfunction while a nuclear submarine is in port and the consequences would be disastrous. Large resources are being used by the U.S. and U.S.S.R. in the development of anti-submarine warfare. When A.S.W. (Anti-Submarine Warfare) is perfected, there would be, needless to say, 'an exceedingly dangerous development with respect to world security'."

1964, 5th December – South Dakota, U. S. A.
The LGM 30B Minuteman 1 missile was on strategic alert when a "retrorocket" accidently fired during repairs. There was considerable damage but "no detonation or radioactive contamination".

1965, 5th December – Pacific Ocean
An A-4 aircraft loaded with one nuclear weapon rolled off the elevator of a U.S. aircraft carrier and fell into the sea. The pilot, aircraft and weapon were lost.

1966, 17th January – Spain
A B-52 and KC-135 collided during midair refuelling and both aircraft crashed near Palomares, Spain. The B-52 was carrying four nuclear weapons. One was recovered on the ground and one was finally found in the sea after an intensive four month search: "Two of the weapons' high explosive materials exploded on impact with the ground, releasing some radioactive materials. Approximately 1,400 tons of slightly contaminated soil and vegetation were removed to the United States for storage at an approved site." The Department of Defence has reported that the cleanup operation has cost $50 million and that the Palomares area is still being monitored for radiation today.

1968, 21st January – Greenland
A B-52 from Plattsburgh Air Force Base, New York, crashed and burnt some seven miles southwest of the runway at Thule Air Force Base, Greenland. "The Bomber carried four nuclear weapons, all of which were destroyed by fire. . . . Some 237,000 cubic feet of contaminated ice, snow and water, with crash debris, were removed to an approved storage site in the United States over the course of a four-month operation."

1968, May – Atlantic Ocean
Although this incident remains classified, the Centre for Defence Information suggests it probably refers to the nuclear powered attack submarine USS Scorpion. The Scorpion was last heard from on May 21, 1968. It sank 400-450 miles southwest of the Azores. Initial suspicion that the Soviets were somehow involved was allayed when the research ship Mizar photographed the wreckage lying at 10,000 feet on the sea floor. Ninety-nine men were lost. The nuclear weapons aboard may have been either SUBROC or ASTOR, or both.

1971, January – Charlevoix, Michigan, U. S. A.
A B-52 bomber crashed into Lake Michigan, 2 miles from a small B.W.R. reactor. An eyewitness said the plane was heading directly in line with the reactor when it crashed raising a fireball 200-600 ft in the air. "If the plane had

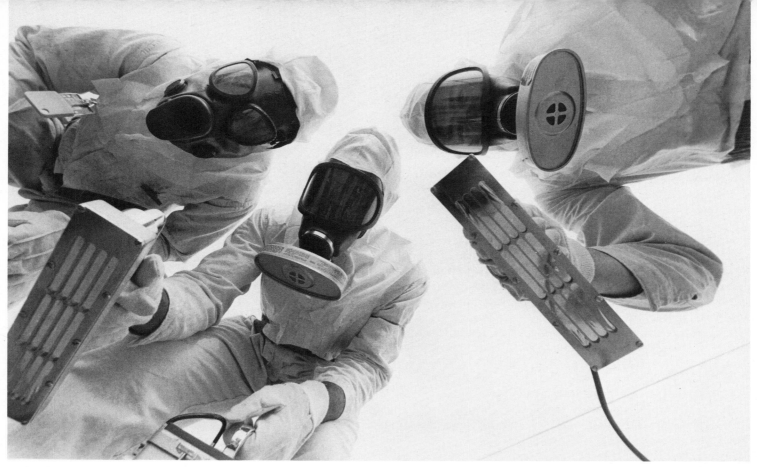
Workers in emergency garb prepare to clean up nuclear contamination.

crashed into the reactor there would have been a major public disaster. . . ." It has been speculated by the Grumman aerospace official that the plane may have flown into radioactive gases normally discharged by the reactor's effluent stack. The radioactivity could have interfered with the plane's electronic guidance systems. No report has been made to the public.

1978, 26th August—Titan 11 Nuclear Base, Kansas, U.S.A.
One man was killed and six injured when deadly fumes leaked from an intercontinental ballistic missile which was being filled with propellant. When the accident was reported gas was still leaking, forcing the evacuation of residents of Udall Rock. Reaction to the gas can range from mild to severe irritation of the eyes, ears, nose, throat and skin, to severe burns and death. The accident would have resulted in a nuclear explosion of the missile had it been carrying its nuclear warhead.

1980, 19th September – Arkansas, U. S. A.
During routine maintenance in a Titan 11 missile silo, an Air Force repairman dropped a socket wrench which punctured a fuel tank and caused an explosion. The nuclear warhead, which was hurled from the silo by the explosion, was recovered intact. Local residents were evacuated. "There was no radioactive contamination."

1981, U. S. A.
A report from the Washington-based Centre for Defence Information says that nearly all of the most toxic radioactive wastes in the United States are produced by the military and are not stored safely enough. The report also states that 99% of the most dangerous nuclear wastes come from military projects and are not subject to the storage safety standards the Government imposes on the nuclear energy industry.

1981, April—Nevada, U.S.A.
An elaborate exercise in which a helicoptor carrying three nuclear bombs crashed into the Nevada desert revealed serious problems which could occur in the case of a real mishap. More than 700 U.S. officials were involved in the exercise—the biggest simulation of "Broken Arrow", the code name for a nuclear weapons accident.

1981, 9th August—United Kingdom
An air crash 25 years ago at a United States Air Force base in eastern England could have turned the area into a nuclear 'desert' according to new details which have emerged in the U.S. The crash, in July 1956, occurred when a B-47 bombed skidded on the runway after a flight from Nebraska and burst into flames. Blazing jet fumes gushed towards a shelter housing three nuclear bombs, each containing eight tonnes of T.N.T. and a quantity of uranium, according to the new details. Had the fire ignited the T.N.T. it is possible a part of eastern England could have become a desert, while the uranium would have exposed the area to contamination.

1981, May—Tokyo, Japan
A U. S. Navy spokesman has confirmed that a U. S. guided missile cruiser based at the Yokosuka naval base near Tokyo returned to port in August 1979. The spokesman did not however confirm reports in the Japanese press that the cruiser was carrying damaged nuclear warheads. The controversy has been touched off by an assertion from the former U.S. Ambassador, Mr. Edwin Reischauer, that nuclear-armed U. S. vessels do visit Japanese ports and pass through Japanese waters, despite an official ban on the introduction of nuclear weapons into Japan's territory.

Compiled by the staff of Senator Ruth Coleman, Australia

LIFE ON THE PRECIPICE

The Nation's Number-One Health Problem

Why do we seem incapable of seeing in time the dreadful contradictions, the dilemmas of our security system?

Why is it that a man like Admiral Rickover can spend a lifetime making weapons and, on his retirement, make the stunning statement – a most welcome statement as far as I was concerned – that the United States was overspending itself on defense and creating the conditions for its own destruction, and that he wished he could have sunk most of the ships that he had spent his lifetime building?

Why is it that General Eisenhower, at the end of his career, would say something of the same sort about the crazy irrational momentum of the military-industrial complex?

Or, why is it that General MacArthur could talk so eloquently, again at the end of his career, about the madness of war, any kind of war, in the world that we had built?

* * *

We have created the situations where our own influence has been greatly reduced and threatened. It is not only the United States that has had this experience. The U.S. sent 20 billion dollars to the Shah [of Iran] – the result: a nation that considers itself an enemy of the United States. The Soviet Union sent billions to Egypt, to Sudan, to Indonesia – [and in] nation after nation, they have been thrown out and their influences undercut. The traditional notion that we can use the arms economy to buy influence in the old way, and it worked in the old days, no longer is possible. At a time when the Soviet Union is more isolated than it has been since the Second World War, the United States is now devoting its diplomatic energies to isolating itself. The web of relationships that the United States developed with other industrial nations all over the world is seriously frayed. Europe and Japan are no longer clients of the United States, but they are still being treated as such. And this failure to understand changes in the real world, the complex reality that we face, seriously undermines the

security of the American people.

* * *

The fact is that an observer from space looking down at Washington, D.C. – the city where the decisions are made to spend the trillions to counter the Russian threat, or the Nicaraguan threat, or the Libyan threat, or whatever – would be astounded by our failure to act on much less hypothetical menaces nearer home. The capital city in which I have lived for more than twenty years is in an advanced state of social dissolution. This is not an exaggeration. Large numbers of persons are ill-housed, ill-fed. More than a dozen persons have frozen to death on the streets of Washington this year. Crime is so widespread that fear stalks the city everywhere; you cannot have a middle-class conversation without talking about fear, and in the neighborhoods of the poor the shadow of crime hangs over daily life all the time. The drug trade is so pervasive that the underground economy, millions of dollars over which neither the government nor legitimate business has any control, is the only growth industry in town. The education system is in such shambles that we have seriously crippled a large part of a whole generation to deal with these incredibly complex problems that we face, as Americans and as members of the species.

* * *

The observers from space would see this situation in other cities too, and they would absolutely wonder why it is that we seem unable to deal with the far more plausible threats that face us and why we seem obsessed, transfixed by these highly implausible threats that we face, compared with the things that are really now threatening to undermine our very culture, even if we manage to avoid the nuclear war altogether. Billions of dollars are going into combatting unlikely threats with a defense and security strategy that is fundamentally, literally, incredible. I think Americans are becoming more

and more insecure because we are putting our money and our energy into combatting these remote threats instead of addressing what is really bothering us.

Richard Barnet

I think we are dealing with a shift in emphasis; adolescents have always had ample cause to criticize their elders, but they used to feel fairly certain that they could run things much better. I am not sure that the next wave of children will approach adulthood with the same confidence. In sum, children are able to live with danger, both of the acute and the anticipated uncertain sort. What has an impact on their development is their perception of the present and the future. To the extent that the present functioning of society conveys to children a picture of passive and evasive withdrawal, of fear and belligerence to other nations, and of never even trying to combat a host of evils both large and small, to that extent the effect of the nuclear peril upon us also affects the development of children. To growing children, the adult response to ultimate danger is also the ultimate test of the trustworthiness of adult society.

Sibylle Escalona

Knowledge about the needs of school-aged children and adolescents is persuasive that the role of professionals (mental health specialists, educators, clergy, etc.) is first and foremost to reassure children in the most formidable way, by actions in supporting reducing the nuclear threat, wherever they perform their role: in school or college; in church, synagogue or mosque; in clinic, agency, or mental health center; in newspaper, publisher's, or TV programmer's office, trade union, art studio, and at home; wherever, the young need to know that there are adults struggling to see that reason prevails in human affairs – strong adults, whom they can depend upon, who will give them the feeling of caring about them, adults who can serve as models, adults who care as much about the nuclear threat as their children do, and who let them know that they're afraid and that they care and that they mean to do something about it. In other words, adults who don't themselves deny the peril, who have courage enough to work to change some prevailing practices in their own organizations – a tough job to do in most, if not all, organizations – and to include the nuclear threat as an issue central to their professional activity. The role means that they help young people acquire the knowledge and skills necessary for effective participation in community affairs.

Milton Schwebel

A former assistant of mine, Michael Carey, did a study of the shelter drills of the 1950s, and he's published his first report on it, called "Psychological Fallout", in the *Bulletin of Atomic Scientists*. About five years ago, Carey interviewed people of his generation, now in their thirties, mostly about their experience in the shelter drills at that time. I've talked a lot about the absurd seriousness with which young children were told to put papers over their head to protect them from fallout, or to put their head under the desk, or to do other such life-enhancing acts. Of course, Carey found the children were too smart for that, they didn't believe it, but they didn't know what to believe, and certainly a lot of the questioning about authority since then has stemmed from that experience. In a word, Carey found that the children were overwhelmed with fear and all sorts of vivid images and dreams of annihilation which they suppressed because the culture told them to; they numbed themselves. Then, around adolescence or when kids ask questions, or through various life experiences including just ordinary experiences of loss or pain, the images would return, they didn't go away and they're in the rest of us. Those people who went through the drills are not some special group, they are a metaphor for the whole society. . . .

*   *   *

Now, just a few words about nuclear fundamentalism. Fundamentalism has

Gun/Flag *from* Tulsa, *by Larry Clark, 1971.*

a history in the Protestant faith, but to put it very simply, fundamentalism originally was a struggle to preserve fundamentals. Very easily that struggle to preserve fundamentals can lapse into a narrow demand for a single closed truth. And that's what fundamentalism often is. Certainly in the 1970s and 1980s, we see a worldwide epidemic of fundamentalism, in various forms of religious expression and some cult behavior in this country, and in political and religious forms all over the world and on all sides in the Middle East, and in ways that are indeed extremely dangerous, because of their all-or-nothing or totalistic dimension. And there are many ways in which fundamentalist cults tend to arise and then contribute to imagery of extinction, sometimes even embrace

that imagery of extinction and often put forward what I call a method of psychism. It's something like what I said about security: you try to deal with actual physical dangers by certain exercises of the mind, such as the assumption that only a particular group, like an End of the World cult, or whatever, will survive, because its members have seen the truth, and everybody else will perish. And such groups can even embrace the idea of nuclear holocaust. But certainly the worldwide epidemic of fundamentalism and its connection to nuclear weapons is something we must face, and to which we must see the all-too-visible contribution of nuclear weapons.

Robert Jay Lifton

Never So Endangered

The super-powers can destroy each
others' cities, towns, schools, children
many times over. This madness is
portrayed as "reason," but truly we are
in the hands of men whose power and
wealth have separated them from the
realities of daily life and from the
imagination.

There is fear among the people, and
that fear, created by the industrial
militarists, is used as an excuse to
accelerate the arms race. "We will
protect you . . ." they say, but we have
never been so endangered, so close to
the end of human time. We are right to
be afraid.

We women are speaking out because
life on the precipice is intolerable.

We want to know what anger is in
these men, what fear which can only be
satisfied by destruction, what coldness
of heart and ambition drives their days.

We want to know because we do not
want that dominance which is
exploitative and murderous in
international relations, and so
dangerous to women and children at
home – we do not want that sickness
transferred by the violent society
through the fathers to the sons. . . .

We want an end to the arms race. No
more bombs. No more amazing
inventions for death.

We understand that everything is
connected. With that understanding,
and by that ecological right, we oppose
the financial connections between the
war machine and the multinational
corporations and banks that thrive off
militarism. These connections are made
of gold and oil. We are made of blood
and bone and water.

We will not allow these violent games
to continue. If our stubborn voices
seem few today, we will certainly be
heard in the thousands and hundreds
of thousands in the months and years
to come.

We know that there is a healthy
sensible loving way to live and we
intend to live that way in our
neighbourhoods and on our farms here
in our country and among our sisters
and brothers in all the countries of the
world.

Women Opposing the Military-Industrial
Mentality

The Bomb *by Bush Hollyhead, 1982.*

What Should Be Said

Modern history offers no example of the cultivation by rival powers of armed force
on a huge scale that did not in the end lead to an outbreak of hostilities. And there is
no reason to believe that we are greater, or wiser, than our ancestors. It would take a
very strong voice, indeed a powerful chorus of voices, from the outside, to say to
the decision-makers of the superpowers what should be said to them:

> For the love of God, of your children, and of the civilization to which you belong, cease
> this madness. You have a duty not just to the generation of the present; you have a duty
> to civilization's past, which you threaten to render meaningless, and to its future, which
> you threaten to render nonexistent. You are mortal men. You are capable of error. You
> have no right to hold in your hands – there is no one wise enough and strong enough to
> hold in his hands – destructive powers sufficient to put an end to civilized life on a great
> portion of our planet. No one should wish to hold such powers. Thrust them from you.
> The risks you might thereby assume are not greater – could not be greater – than those
> which you are now incurring for us all.

. . . The present moment is in many respects a crucial one. Not for thirty years has
political tension reached so dangerous a point as it has attained today. Not in all this
time has there been so high a degree of misunderstanding, of suspicion, of
bewilderment, and of sheer military fear. . . . Both sides must learn to accept the fact
that only in the reduction, not in the multiplication, of existing monstrous arsenals
can the true security of any nation be found.

George Kennan

Fight Bombs with Valium

According to a report in the *Philadelphia Inquirer* May 22, the Bonn government has stockpiled two and one-half million tranquilizers with which to dose West Germans in the event of panic and injury as a result of a nuclear war or other catastrophes. An interior minister spokesman confirmed Friday that tranquilizers such as Valium were purchased with the aim of having available sufficient medicine for the mangement of the badly injured and also for people who panicked in such an emergency. Professor Erika Hickel, a specialist in medical law, described it as "madness."

Why is the German government becoming so nervous? It's because in December [1983], President Reagan is determined, despite the protests by millions of Europeans and British and lukewarm support from some heads of state, to place 464 cruise missiles and 108 first-strike missiles in Europe – in an incredible six-minute striking distance from Moscow. Hence Valium, as an antidote to nuclear war.

Ethel Taylor

Is There No Other Way?

Every gun that is made, every warship launched, every rocket fired signifies, in the final sense, a theft from those who hunger and are not fed, those who are cold and not clothed. This world in arms is not spending money alone. It is spending the sweat of its laborers, the genius of its scientists, the hopes of its children. . . . This is not a way of life, at all, in any true sense. Under the cloud of threatening war, it is humanity hanging from a cross of iron. Is there no other way the world may live?

Dwight D. Eisenhower

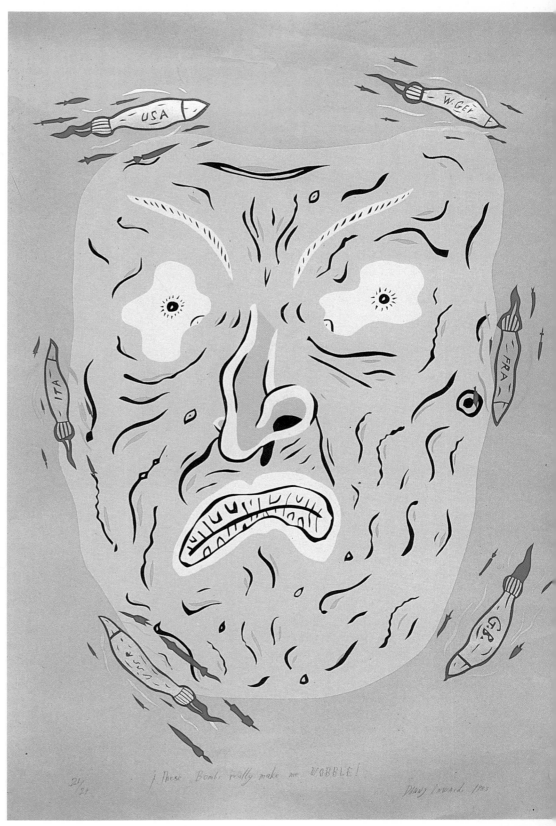

These Bombs Really Make Me Wobble *by Danny Inwards, 1983.*

DISTORTED VISION

What About the Russians?

Underlying our suspicion is a demon theory of the Soviet Union, most succinctly expressed by Richard Nixon in his book, *The Real War*, published in 1980. Nixon wrote, "It may seem melodramatic to treat the twin poles of human experience represented by the United States and the Soviet Union as the equivalent of Good and Evil, Light and Darkness, God and the Devil; yet if we allow ourselves to think of them that way, even hypothetically, it can help clarify our perspective on the world struggle." Students of the United States-Soviet relationship, like Samuel Pisar, Marshall Shulman, Ralph White and Jerome Frank, have demonstrated over and over how we use that relationship, and displace onto the Soviet Union our fears, our problems, and our failures. To recognize this fact is not to condone aggressive behavior on the part of the Soviet Union toward other nations, any more than recognition of the democratic values that our country represents requires agreement with the excesses of our policies. Former Ambassador to the Soviet Union, George Kennan, thunders with outrage like an Old Testament prophet against our dehumanization of the Soviet Union. In a speech in November 1981, he said: "I find the view of the Soviet Union that prevails today in our governmental and journalistic establishments so extreme, so subjective, so far removed from what any sober scrutiny of external reality would reveal, that it is not only ineffective but dangerous as a guide to political action. This endless series of distortions and over-simplifications, this systematic dehumanization of the leadership of another great country; this routine exaggeration of Moscow's military capabilities and of the supposed iniquity of its intentions; this monotonous misrepresentation of the nature and the attitudes of another great people and a long-suffering people at that, sorely tried by the vicissitudes of this past century; this reckless application of the

Governments in war-time whip up the war spirit with demonized images of the enemy.

double-standard to the judgment of Soviet conduct and our own; this failure to recognize, finally, the commonality of many of their problems and ours as we move inextricably into the modern technological age; these,

believe me, are not the marks of the maturity and realism one expects of the diplomacy of a great power."

John E. Mack

112

Naked and Defenceless

I object to the kind of statement given, with increasing frequency, in Parliament and in the press, of the following order:

> One new Russian SS missile, with all Europe in its sights, is installed every five days; there are already 160 of these monsters in place. . . . The Russian nuclear force threatening Europe's cities will build up to something like 2,000-3,000 warheads by the mid-1980s. Against it is a NATO plan, still on paper, to deploy Pershing II and cruise missiles – but only some 500 of them.

That is from the leading editorial of the *Sunday Times* of London for July 6, 1980. I am sorry to single out this newspaper, since it is only repeating what is said on all sides. But a paper that pretends to objectivity and authority ought to be judged by stricter standards than those which pretend only to propaganda.

What is directly false in this passage is that 160 of "these monsters" (the SS-20s) are faced only by "a NATO plan, still on paper" to introduce Pershing IIs and cruise missiles. What they and other Russian forces face are substantial long-range nuclear weapons assigned to the NATO theater: these include F-111 and Vulcan bombers, with a range of some 3,000 nautical miles; the British "independent" Polaris, which is assigned to NATO command, as well as (in Soviet perception) the French "independent" weapons; and the United States Poseidon, forty of which are also assigned to NATO command. These U. S. Poseidons each carry some ten independently targeted warheads. This is before we take into any account the U.S. carrier-based aircraft in the Mediterranean and further American strategic resources, which can be attached to any particular theater at will.

The SS-20 is based on land and the Poseidon is based at sea, and, until lately, it had been supposed, in the war-games rooms, that they traded off against each other. What has happened is not the introduction of some wholly new dimension of threat (the SS-20 came into production in 1976, the Backfire bomber in 1974) but a redefinition of the rules of the game. Our Western experts have suddenly decided to hold their hands over Poseidon, Polaris, etc., and to pretend that they do not exist. This is done as a public information exercise, aimed not at the Russians but at us, to frighten us into believing that we are naked and defended by only a plan "still on paper" against Russian "monsters."

E.P. Thompson

The Real Enemy

Through most of history, when a city was taken its inhabitants were quite likely to be killed or enslaved. The women were first raped, of course, and then killed or enslaved. Even the Bible recommends mass slaughter as a routine matter of warfare. (See Deuteronomy 20: 15-17, for instance.)

Under such circumstances, it was important to fight to the death, since one was in any case going to die, or worse, if one lost. So the people, or, at the very least, the warrior class, were constantly fed tales of violence; of heroes who fought against overwhelming odds; of Hector standing against Achilles when all his fellow Trojans had fled; of Roland fighting off hordes of Saracens and disdaining to call for help; of the Knights of the Round Table taking on all challenges.

Youngsters had to get used to violence, had to have their hearts and minds hardened to it. They had to be made to feel the glory of fighting against odds and how sweet it was to give one's life for one's tribe, or one's city, or one's nation, or one's king, or one's fatherland, or one's motherland, or one's faith, or whatever other sounds are appropriate.

And now it's over! That old-time violence that's got us in its spell must stop! We've got to get rid of violence for the simple reason that it serves no purpose anymore, but points us all in a useless direction. It would appear that human enemies are no longer the prime threat to world survival.

The new enemies we have today – overpopulation, famine, pollution, scarcity – cannot be fought by violence. There is no way to crush those enemies, or slash them, or blast them, or vaporize them.

Isaac Asimov

Sylvester Stallone as Rambo, from the movie of the same name.

The Lure of War

People are so easily led into quarrelsome attitudes by some national leaders. A fight of any kind has a hypnotic influence on most men. We men like war. We like the excitement of it, its thrill and glamor, its freedom from restraint. We like its opportunities for socially approved violence. We like its economic security and its relief from the monotony of civilian toil. We like its reward for bravery, its opportunities for travel, its companionship of men in a man's world, its intoxicating novelty.

Dr. G. H. Stevenson

Soviet child Katerina Lychera, shown during her tour of the United States in March, 1986.

Not a Knockout

There was not a word in that film that was true. Soviet people have friendly, open faces. I was frightened. I didn't know that kind of distortion was possible.

Katerina Lycheva, the 11-year-old Soviet peace emissary, after viewing *Rocky IV* in Los Angeles

ARMS RACE ECONOMICS

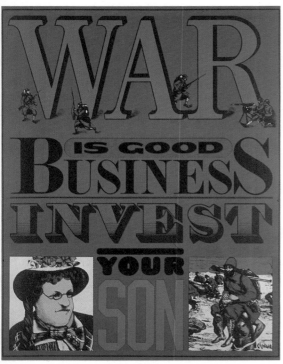

War Is Good Business *by Seymour Chwast, 1964.*

Famine in Ethiopia by Anthony Suau.

The Price of "Security"

Within the few minutes that it takes the reader to get through this portion of text, governments will devote several million dollars to military activities. Each year, we spend an average of almost $150 per world citizen on the arms race. Add all this up and the total figure reaches $750 billion a year – or 6 percent of global GNP.

Suppose that we could divert a mere 10 percent of the world's military budget into constructive activities....

In 1983 the World Bank spent $13.5 billion – barely one week of arms spending – to assist projects in developing countries. If the Bank's spending power was boosted to the equivalent of one month's spending on the arms race, we could make some real headway against the various challenges which face us. The six largest UN programmes spent $2.7 billion in 1982....The entire UN system could run for nearly two centuries on only one year's world military spending. Total support from international organizations, including the World Bank and the UN, amounted to $134 billion from 1946 to 1981 – the equivalent of little more than nine weeks of the arms race.

These figures put a fresh complexion on protests by the US, the UK, and other rich nations of the West, that they are less and less able to "afford" assistance to developing countries. The richer they become, the more they lavish on the arms race. Instead of giving the Third World tools for development, they are sold the tools for destruction. As the late Barbara Ward put it, "they ask for bread, and we give them a recoilless rifle."

*   *   *

Count out 60 seconds and 30 of the world's children will have died for lack of food and adequate health care. Count out another 60 seconds: in this short space of time, the world will have spent $1.4 million on its military. Indeed, we are currently (1984) spending $750 billion a year on the instruments of death – and, in the process, opening up a new battlefield of social neglect. Between 1945 and 1983, it is estimated that 16 million lives were lost in war. We now lose a similar number every year due to various forms of social neglect. We have got our priorities drastically wrong. The $100 billion or so now spent by developing countries on weapons is three times what it would have cost to provide essential health care, medicines, vaccinations, clean water, and sanitation for all.

From GAIA: An Atlas of Planet Management

Burden on the Taxpayer

The [1982] defense budget will take a painful bite out of the average American family's already strained budget. Individual income taxes, which provide the bulk of government revenues, must provide most of the money to finance the $1.6 trillion Reagan defense program. THIS WILL COST THE AVERAGE TAXPAYER MORE THAN $12,000.

Corporations bear the remaining tax burden to finance the Pentagon, an expense that will, of course, be passed on to consumers. The average taxpayer, as a result, could pay as much as another $5,000 over the next five years in higher prices for goods and services.

This $17,000 cost to the average taxpayer – as shocking as it is – is only a partial installment payment for the Reagan defense program. Cost overruns, program changes, sloppy Pentagon budget practices, and inflation can add hundreds of billions of dollars to the program....The $750 billion in additional funding that Pentagon planners may need to carry out the Reagan program would bring the total burden on the average taxpayer for the next five years up to more than $25,000.

Union of Concerned Scientists (U.S.A.)

The Wrong Weapons

Not only is the Administration buying weapons for the wrong reasons, but it's paying too much for them. The Pentagon's [1986] plan to spend over $2 trillion over the next five years may be more than $300 billion short of what will really be needed to fund all its programs, according to studies by Defense Department analyst Franklin Spinney and the General Accounting Office.

From the start, weapons costs are underestimated through a combination of deliberate underbidding by contractors and unrealistic projections by the Defense Department. The Pentagon's proclivity for adding complex and unnecessary high technology to its weapons adds to their price and often leads to disastrous testing results. But the weapons are produced anyway, because they develop political constituencies among military officials with careers on the line, defense contractors with profits at stake, and congressional representatives anxious to keep jobs in their districts. The Pentagon deflated opposition to the B-1 bomber, for example, by spreading contracts around to 48 states.

Once production begins, the cost overruns continue. Major military contractors such as Hughes Aircraft and General Dynamics have recently been charged with poor quality control, and possibly fraudulent overcharging for production costs, spare parts, and lobbying and public relations expenses. Even after they're deployed, complex new weapons are far costlier to fix and maintain than their predecessors. The Air Force alone will spend $1.2 trillion for repairing its weapons over the next 30 years.

The result, according to one Pentagon insider, is "a vicious cycle of rising costs, declining production rates and fewer weapons, all of which combine to produce tremendous pressure for increased defense spending....Exaggerated force requirements, inappropriate technology and high costs are symptomatic of a runaway system."

Committee for a Sane Nuclear Policy

How Much?

These are spare-parts prices for the F-16 fighter plane's radar antenna, quoted by the subcontractor, Western Electric, and subsequently by the contractor, General Dynamics. The contract was canceled after a Senate committee investigation.
The reason for cancellation, the Air Force said, was excessive costs.

Antenna pulley puller tool
Western Electric price to General Dynamics:
$6,005 each
General Dynamics price to Air Force: **$10,630 each**

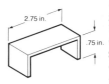

Antenna clamp alignment tool
Western Electric price to General Dynamics:
$5,618 each
General Dynamics price to Air Force: **$10,137 each**

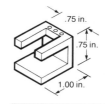

Antenna puller height gauge
Western Electric price to General Dynamics:
$6,972 each
General Dynamics price to Air Force: **$11,911 each**

Antenna hexagon wrench
Western Electric price to General Dynamics:
$5,205 each
General Dynamics price to Air Force: **$9,609 each**

Senate Committee on Governmental Affairs

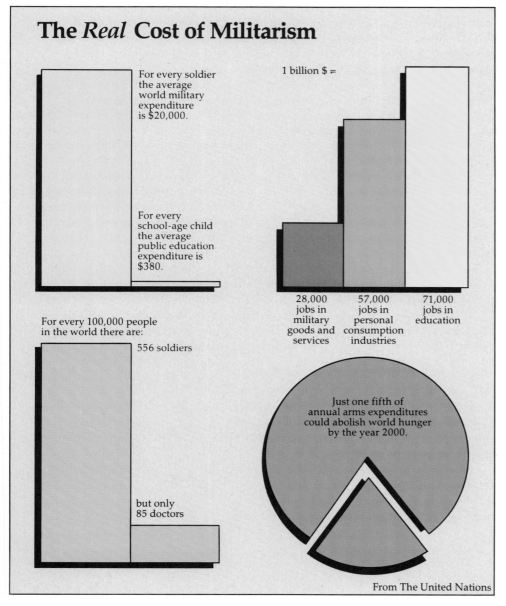

The *Real* Cost of Militarism

For every soldier the average world military expenditure is $20,000.

For every school-age child the average public education expenditure is $380.

For every 100,000 people in the world there are:

556 soldiers

but only 85 doctors

1 billion $ =

28,000 jobs in military goods and services

57,000 jobs in personal consumption industries

71,000 jobs in education

Just one fifth of annual arms expenditures could abolish world hunger by the year 2000.

From The United Nations

HAZARDS OF NUCLEAR ENERGY

A New Kind of War

The crisis we are facing is one of physical survival and moral rectitude both for ourselves and for the global community. We the people of the United States are producing extremely hazardous radioactive materials both as weapons of unbelievable destructive capability, and also for so-called peaceful uses such as generation of electricity. Nuclear generators are partly a façade for weapons research, partly a source of electricity needed to power a sophisticated weapons technology, and partly a weapon in their own right in the international economic war in which we are presently engaged. Hence right at this moment we are engaged in what I would call radiation warfare. This is a new kind of war. The war has not been legitimately declared, the soldiers are not identified as such, but the battlelines are clear. There are casualties, and the destructive capability of this new type of warfare is becoming more apparent. The victims of the war are those who are routinely exposed to its radioactive pollutants, and those random victims of its technology.

Dr. Rosalie Bertell

Truck transporting nuclear waste *by Michael O'Brien.*

The Peaceful Atom

It has been charged by some proponents of nuclear power that much of the public's attitude toward peaceful, civilian uses of nuclear power is colored by an entirely emotional identification between the civilian and military applications. In this view, production of electricity by burning nuclear fuels is an entirely benign process which shares none of the nightmarish qualities exhibited by the detonation of A-bombs.

We at Nuclear Energy Information Service disagree with this view. Apart from the very real threat to human health we see in every stage of the nuclear fuel cycle, we also believe that the spread of civilian nuclear technology carries with it the threat of more and more nations being able to build their own atomic bombs. No, we do not imagine that a nuclear reactor can blow up like an A-bomb; but we do maintain that much of the same knowledge, and certainly the same radioactive materials, that make civilian nuclear technology possible also come in handy when the goal is to build an A-bomb or develop a national weapons program. Although there may be some people who are so awed by the destructive power of nuclear weapons that they cannot conceive of anything good ever coming from anything nuclear, we base our assessment on thorough research of the facts, not blind fear.

A recap of the nuclear fuel cycle is in order at this point. The two most common fissionable materials are uranium-235 and plutonium-239. The first step in the production of either is the mining and milling of natural uranium. The latter consists of mostly uranium-238 and very little uranium-235. In order to yield sufficiently concentrated U-235 to burn in a power or research reactor or fashion into a bomb, the uranium must go through an enrichment plant. Enrichment typically reaches 3% for use in a power reactor, 90% for bomb fabrication. Research reactors can use either low or highly enriched uranium. The United States has three enrichment plants which were built for military use but now also serve the nuclear electricity-generating industry.

The U.S. government produces plutonium for its weapons program in special breeder reactors. However, the light-water reactors used to produce electricity also generate plutonium as a by-product. In either case, the plutonium results when uranium-238 (the non-fissionable isotope of uranium predominating in natural uranium) absorbs neutrons, changing into neptunium, which, in turn, changes into plutonium.

Nuclear fuel gets irradiated in a reactor until it is too poisoned with fission products and transuranics to be suitable for power generation. Similarly, A-bombs sitting on the shelf gradually lose their potency due to constant radioactive decay. Both "spent" reactor fuel and depleted bombs either have to be disposed of (stored or buried) or treated so as to recover usable uranium and/or plutonium. The latter calls for a reprocessing plant, of which the U.S. currently has none, although there are some in Europe, with others being built in Europe and South America.

In addition to the fuel cycle stages mentioned above, there is also the matter of transporting nuclear substances from one place to another. This is one of the most vulnerable aspects of the whole process because it is here that shipments can be hijacked and the materials stolen for bomb-making use. It is believed that Israel has already diverted such materials in transport twice, once from a ship, and the other time by stopping a truck.

There are also plants where fuel rods are fabricated for use in power or research reactors. The CIA thinks that enriched uranium was smuggled from such a plant in Apollo, Pennsylvania, to Israel back in the sixties. The amount is believed to be 200 pounds, enough for several atomic bombs.

Eckhard Festag

Nuclear worker in an air-supplied suit *by Michael O'Brien.*

The Perils of Peaceful Use

UNSCEAR [United Nations Scientific Committee on the Effects of Atomic Radiation] has estimated that for each gigawatt year of electricity produced by nuclear generation the public receives the equivalent of 570 person-rems (effective dose equivalent) within roughly two years and approximately 400,000 person-rems spread over millennia due to the long-lived radioactive substances released. In 1979 there were 55.48 gigawatt years of nuclear-powered electricity generated in the U.S. and Canada. Based on UNSCEAR's assumptions, the resulting dose of radiation was, from that one year, 31,624 person-rems, and mankind will receive (if it survives far into the future) another 22,192,000 person-rems due to nuclear power production in 1979 alone.

If we use UNSCEAR's estimate of 100 cancer deaths per million person-rems, we have sentenced roughly 2222 people to premature death due to cancer from that one year of nuclear power generation in North America. If we use Gofman's estimate of 3771 deaths per million person-rads we can expect 83,805 cancer deaths. Most of these deaths will be very far in the future, but a few will be among those alive today (from 3 to 120 depending on whose estimate you accept).

These figures do not account for the suffering future generations will face due to genetic damage. Two other factors should also be considered: In 1985 we are producing even more nuclear power than was produced in 1979, and in the coming years there is every reason to believe that a serious reactor accident is a real likelihood. Such an accident would have both immediate and long-lived consequences. To make matters worse the UNSCEAR estimate is based on an optimistic view of the reliability of (an as yet to be determined) long-term, high-level waste disposal technique and does not include the radiation exposures of those people employed in the various mines, mills and plants.

Nuclear industry apologists who claim there has never been a death attributable to nuclear power conveniently forget about lung cancer among uranium miners and the thousands of cancer deaths in the general population that have been predicted by even the most optimistic of scientific bodies studying the issue.

David Poch

The Flowers Report

The spread of nuclear power will inevitably facilitate the spread of the ability to make nuclear weapons and, we fear, the construction of these weapons. In reality, total agreement on a comprehensive international control system for the products of civilian nuclear power that are relevant to the construction of nuclear weapons would be possible only in a climate of general disarmament, and the prospects for this are receding rather than improving. It has been argued that the possession of these weapons by the U.S.A. and the U.S.S.R. has been a powerful force for mutual toleration, but however true this is, it would be folly to suppose that proliferation would necessarily lead to a similar balance and restraint in relations between other nations. Indeed, we see no reason to trust in the stability of any nation of any political persuasion for centuries ahead. The proliferation problem is very serious and it will not go away by refusing to acknowledge it.

*   *   *

The effects of war, even of "conventional" war, are inevitably horrifying, but if these effects could be magnified by attack on nuclear installations, then this is a major factor to consider when deciding whether, or to what extent, to use nuclear power. . . .

The unique aspect of nuclear installations is that the effects of the radioactive contamination that could be caused are so long-lasting. If nuclear power could have been developed earlier, and had it been in wide-spread use at the time of the last war, it is likely that some areas of central Europe would still be uninhabitable because of ground contamination by caesium.

Sir Brian Flowers, U.K. nuclear physicist

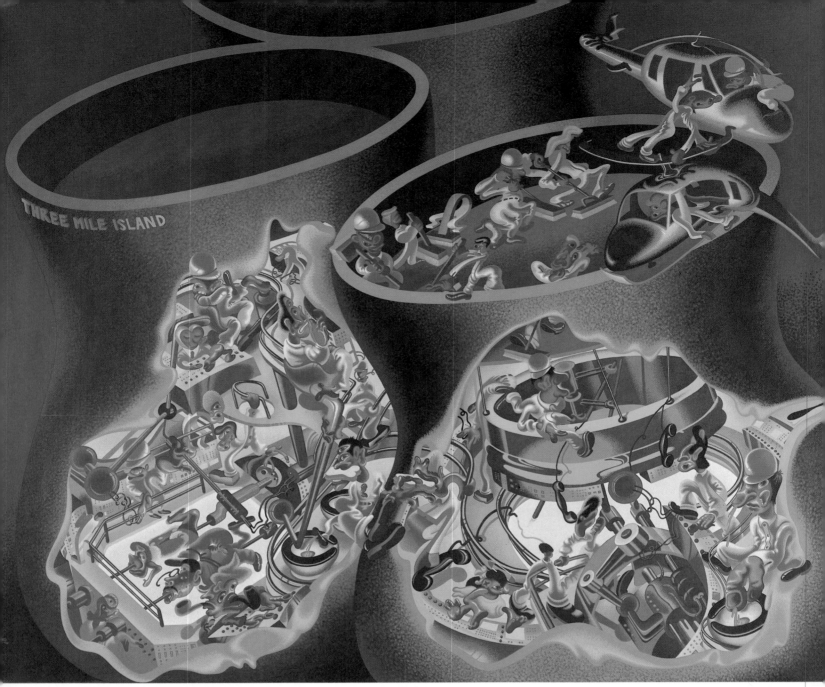

Three Mile Island *by Peter Saul, 1980.*

A Catalogue of Disasters

1957, Windscale, UK   A reactor fire led to the contamination of some 800 sq km of land. At least 20 people died from cancer.

1958, Urals, USSR   An explosion of a nuclear waste site contaminated land and probably killed hundreds of people.

1968, Detroit, USA   Part of the core of a fast breeder reactor overheated and began to melt.

1969, Colorado, USA   Spontaneous ignition in a nuclear waste pile caused a release of plutonium dust.

1972, New York, USA   A plutonium works had to be closed permanently after an explosion.

1975, Browns Ferry, USA   A workman started a fire with a candle that knocked out five emergency systems and néarly destroyed the reactor.

1976, Windscale, UK   One month after its discovery, a leak of radioactive water is reported. The size of the leak: 2 million litres.

1979, Harrisburg, USA   Operator error led to a serious core accident, destroying a $1 billion reactor.

1981, Windscale, UK   Release of iodine 131 into Cumbrian countryside. Local milk supplies contaminated.

1986, Chernobyl, USSR   World's worst nuclear accident to date. Partial core meltdown releases radioactive cloud over most of Europe.

Disaster at Kyshtym

In my article "Two decades of dissidence" I mentioned the occurrence at the end of 1957 or beginning of 1958 of a nuclear disaster in the southern Urals. I described how the disaster had resulted from a sudden explosion involving nuclear waste stored in underground shelters, not far from where the first Soviet military reactors had been built; how strong winds carried a mixture of radioactive products and soil over a large area, probably more than a thousand square miles in size; and how many villages and small towns were not evacuated on time, probably causing the deaths later of several hundred people from radiation sickness. . . .

About a month later my story was confirmed by Professor Lev Tumerman, former head of the biophysics laboratory at the Institute of Molecular Biology in Moscow, who had emigrated to Israel in 1972. Tumerman visited the area between the two Ural cities – Cheliabinsk and Sverdlovsk – in 1960. He was able to see that hundreds of square miles of land there had been so heavily contaminated by radioactive wastes that the area was forbidden territory. All the villages and small towns had been destroyed so as to make the dangerous zone uninhabitable and to prevent the evacuated people from returning. Tumerman's eye-witness evidence did not, however, convince all the experts of the truth of this disaster. Doubts remained that the story was exaggerated. . . .

There is no doubt that the Urals disaster was the biggest nuclear tragedy in peacetime that the world has known. It produced the largest radioactively contaminated ecological zone in the world. It will not be gone even a hundred years from now. When people will reinhabit this region is hard to predict. But I hope a time will come when there will be no need to keep such secrets, and that monuments will be built near Kyshtym both to the prisoners who died building this military-industrial complex and to the later victims of the Kyshtym disaster.

Dr. Zhores A. Medvedev

Dying for a Living

The world's foremost uranium producing region is northwestern New Mexico and southeastern Wyoming, which supplies about half the country's mined and milled uranium. Here, as elsewhere in the United States, much of the uranium comes from Indian land, leased to the energy industry by a pliant Bureau of Indian Affairs and local tribal councils. The mining industry is dominated by the nation's energy conglomerates – Kerr McGee (the largest single producer), Continental Oil, Anaconda, Gulf, Humble Oil, Mobil, Philips, and Exxon.

Conditions in the uranium mines of the Southwest were described by one miner to an interviewer in 1978: "They chased us in there like we were slaves. I remember that it used to be so dusty that we were always spitting up black stuff and how when we went home we all had headaches from breathing all that contamination."

A generation ago lung cancer was virtually unheard of among the Navajos. But a recent study by Dr. Gerald Buker in New Mexico found that the risk of lung cancer has increased by a factor of at least eighty-five among Navajo uranium miners.

*　　　*　　　*

The uranium ore flowing out of the western United States by the trainload enters the nuclear materials production system in the form of uranium hexafluoride gas. Four fourteen-ton cylinders of the gas, shipped from conversion plants run by Kerr McGee Corp. at Sequoyah, Oklahoma, and Allied Chemical Corp. at Metropolis, Illinois, arrive on an average day at Union Carbide's gaseous diffusion plant on the outskirts of Paducah, Kentucky. The Paducah plant is one of three huge uranium enrichment facilities owned and controlled by the Department of Energy. The others are at Oak Ridge, Tennessee (also operated by Union Carbide) and Piketon, Ohio, near Portsmouth (operated by Goodyear Atomic Corporation). The three plants employ about 11,000 workers, cost $13 billion to build, consume about 3 per cent of all the electricity in the United States, and

West German nuclear power plant; 1983.

produce all of the fission fuel for the U.S. naval and civilian nuclear power programs.

In twenty-five years of operations, the enrichment plants have brought economic growth to the Tennessee Valley, but they have also left a mounting legacy of public health and environmental problems. The most telling impact has been on the workers. One of them, Joe Harding, who worked for Union Carbide at Paducah from 1952 to 1971, gave this account of conditions:

"At the end of a day you could look back behind you and see your tracks in the uranium dust that had settled that day. You could look up at the lights and see a blue haze between you and the light. And we ate our lunch in this, every day, eight hours a day. We'd just find some place to sit down, brush away the dust, and eat lunch. Now you tell me that I didn't eat a lot of uranium during all those years."

Of the 200 or so men who began work with him in 1952, Harding kept a list of those who died of cancer, leukemia, or some unidentified ailment that may be related to radiation. It had reached fifty when he himself died of cancer, on March 1, 1980.

Nuclear Weapons Facilities Project

Long-term Storage

Although the vast domestic and military potential of nuclear energy has been a part of our daily consciousness since the first atomic bomb was dropped on Hiroshima in 1945, the equally vast problem of dealing with the tons of radioactive waste material resulting from nuclear energy is an astonishingly recent preoccupation.

*   *   *

Since Three Mile Island, some states have placed a moratorium on reactor licensing (this has not happened in Canada); presently, there are 95 reactors in operation and another 32 under construction. In Canada, 17 nuclear reactors produce 12.6 percent of the country's electricity. All of these reactors continue to produce hundreds of tons of high-level radioactive waste each year, and *none* of it is being properly stored. The safe, long-term disposal of nuclear waste is becoming one of the most urgent problems yet created by the 20th-century technology.

The principal source of high-level radioactive waste is spent reactor fuel, and its basic unit is a tiny baked pellet of uranium dioxide about the thickness of a pencil and three-quarters of an inch long. Exposure to a handful of these spent fuel pellets would wipe out a small city; each nuclear reactor contains eight million pellets.

*   *   *

A 2,000-MWe (megawatts electric) nuclear power station, such as the one in Pickering, Ontario, discharges 2,000 bundles – 30 tons – of spent fuel each year. These are currently being stored in temporary water-filled "swimming pools" located at each reactor site across North America. Each pool contains about 20 feet of constantly circulating water that cools the rods and prevents radiation remaining in the pellets – only about 30 percent of the pellets' radioactivity is used up during the fission process – from escaping into the atmosphere.

*   *   *

At present, there are 12,000 tons of spent fuel in temporary storage pools in the United States. In Canada, according to Keith Nuttall, head of Fuel Waste

Technology at the Whiteshell Nuclear Research Establishment in Pinawa, Manitoba, "about 8,800 tons of used fuel are safely and economically stored in water-filled pools at the nuclear generating stations. Pools consist of thick concrete tanks lined with either stainless steel or fibreglass and epoxy resin." These pools, however, were designed to store spent fuel for about five years, by which time, heat and radiation levels will have been reduced to transportable forms. Some of the pools in the United States have been holding radioactive waste for 30 years.

*   *   *

Spent reactor fuel is not, however, the only form of radioactive waste that is accumulating in North America. Another important source is the mining of the uranium itself. Tailings from uranium mines – heaps of slag left behind by the process of separating uranium from rock – contain "about 80 percent of the original radioactivity in uranium ore," according to a report entitled *Energy in Transition 1985-2010* published by the U.S. Committee on Nuclear and Alternative Energy Systems. The report notes that processing or milling of uranium ore removes solely uranium – and only about 93 percent of that – leaving behind other radioactive elements. These tailings are 500 times more radioactive than normal soil and exist in vast and ever-increasing quantities: the report calculated that in the United States alone, "the total quantity of tailings accumulated since 1948 totals 123 million tons." In Canada, which contains approximately 20 percent of all the uranium reserves in the Western world, there are an estimated 100 million tons of mine tailings lying about exposed to the wind and rain.

*   *   *

For an idea of how quickly these tailings can accumulate, consider the following: in 1979, according to the Ontario Ministry of Energy's annual report, Ontario Hydro contracted with three Ontario uranium mining companies. Elliot Lake would supply Ontario Hydro with 100,000 tons of uranium by the year 2020; Denison

Mines would supply an additional 63,000 tons by 2010; and Preston Mines would supply 36,000 tons by 2020. Total uranium: 199,000 tons. Total tailings: 199 million tons.

*   *   *

The first electric generating station to use nuclear energy in the United States was the Shippingport Atomic Power Station on the Ohio River, about 25 miles from Pittsburgh. Shippingport opened in 1952 and was shut down in 1982, and this summer, the plant's owner, DOE [Department of Energy], began the lengthy and expensive process of cutting it up into pieces and shipping it for storage. The 770-ton steel and concrete pressure vessel – the heart of the reactor – is being hoisted onto a barge on the Ohio River, floated downriver to Cairo, Illinois, and along the Mississippi to the Gulf of Mexico. From there, it will pass through the Panama Canal, move north along the western coast of the United States to the Columbia River and travel up the Columbia to its final burial place at Hanford, where it will be joined by truckloads of smaller atomic junk from the rest of the original station.

Scientists and engineers will be keeping a close eye on the Shippingport operation, and with good reason: there are 67 other nuclear reactors in the United States whose licences will run out by the year 2010. The low- and high-level waste from just one of these reactor sites would fill 1,000 trucks; finding burial sites for that much radioactive waste dwarfs even the huge problem of dealing with the radioactive waste that already exists. Mothballing present and projected wastes, which means simply keeping the substances cool by constantly bathing them in water until permanent sites can be built, is not feasible. As Gus Speth, chairman of the President's Council on Environmental Quality, has observed, by the turn of the century, "a volume of water in excess of Earth's total fresh water would be required to dilute the radiation of these wastes to the levels specified in the federal radiation protection standards."

Philip Norton

Nuclear Gothic: Farming After Three Mile Island

"You won't find nothing fancy in this house," says Samuel F. Conley, leading the way through a sagging screen door into his 200-year-old farm home near Yocumtown, Pennsylvania.

Conley, at 75, lives a one-room existence, heating with a venerable cast-iron coal stove, cooking over a two-burner kerosene stove, and having, as concessions to modern life, a clock radio and a single green-shaded lamp on his kitchen table.

Lest one assume that this diminutive gentleman has eschewed the larger world around him, it should be said that the pile of clutter next to the reading lamp includes current copies of *Newsweek* and *U.S. News & World Report*. And then there is Mr. Conley's Three Mile Island file, which he draws carefully from a rough-hewn bookcase.

"I've had more trouble since this danged thing blowed up last year than I ever had before," says Mr. Conley, his eyes glinting with intensity. He has just come in from burying a stillborn calf, and, with a herd of just 11, the loss is not inconsequential.

"It was a nice big bully calf. The cow couldn't have it – and she had a nice heifer last year without any trouble. Doc Weber (Veterinarian Robert Weber) said there have been a lot of them that he's had to take the calves from since this thing was built down here.

"We had trouble even before it blowed – we could tell it in our faces and eyes, more since they opened the second one. (Reactor Unit Two, which suffered the near-meltdown.) You could tell it was in the air, especially in the morning. This stuff is a whole lot worse in the morning – you can always tell in the morning when there's a lot of that stuff in the air; your eyes will burn and your face will itch and you will have more throat trouble in the morning than in the latter part of the day. Maybe the heat cuts that stuff down somehow. It works the worst in the morning when it's damp."

Mr. Conley, having farmed his 99 acres since 1932, claims to be able to sense the radioactive gases which are now known to be vented with

Farmer Joseph Conley stayed behind to take care of his cattle after sending his wife and children away following the partial meltdown at nearby Three Mile Island, March 3, 1979. He left a day after.

regularity from normally operating nuclear plants. He says his neighbours have had the same complaints, but that Metropolitan Edison disregards them.

"You can't tell them. They say, 'Oh, that don't amount to nothing.' " Mr. Conley disagrees.

"The honeybees have disappeared. I talked to different ones and if you get further over that way, they say they have some bees. But here in this basin, I talked to different ones and they say they don't see no honeybees. That's the reason I didn't have much fruit last year. I didn't know and I didn't watch it last year, but this year when my apples and pears was in blossom these warm days, I was out watching to see if there was any bees working on them. There's wasps and things working pollinating them, but there's not many and you hardly see a honeybee.

"This stuff works on clover and alfalfa some," he continues. "A lot of us was talking and our wheat is getting less. When George Weber was county agent, he said this in here was some of the best ground in the county with a good farmer on it. It was nothing for us to hit as much as 60 bushels of wheat to the acre. But in the last couple of years, you know if we got 35 – or even 30 – we was doing good.

"This stuff killed the flies in the barn the last couple of years. We didn't have near the trouble with flies with all this gas coming in here. It kills little stuff. There used to be quail here, and they disappeared.

"The toads is gone. I haven't seen a toad for a couple of years now."

Mr. Conley has also seen his brother Joe and his family leave, selling an immaculate, high production dairy farm after evacuating themselves and their animals within days of the accident.

"Joe moved right after this thing blowed up, a day or couple afterward. They had had four children before these plants opened up and the next two came premature. They came dead, ahead of time. And James Yost up here, his wife – they got married and the first one came dead, premature. Jerry Fisher's wife had one and the next one came dead, premature.

"Joe moved to Franklin County and says it wasn't long till he felt a whole lot more like working. He had stomach trouble and that left him, he said. His cows were nervous up here – they had to put kickers on them to milk them – and they aren't nervous anymore. When that stuff is in the air, nothing tastes the same and you just don't feel up to par...just don't feel like you have the gumption to go like you should have."

Putting his files away and walking out onto the porch, Samuel Conley looks into the distance and says, "My sister, she died two years ago – she lived in the second house down the road. She died of cancer and she claimed that that thing gave it to her.

"My dad, he was 92 when he was buried. I don't know if this stuff will let me live that long if I stay here. I don't know."

James Lawrence

ARMS TALKS

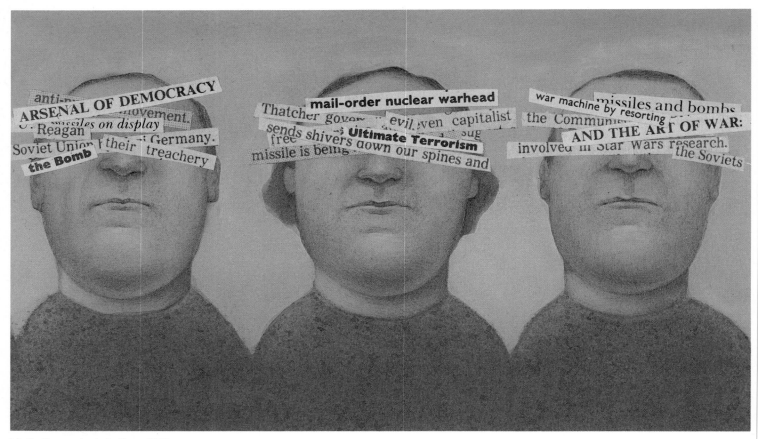

Media Barrage *by Anita Kunz, 1985.*

A Treaty a Year

In 1961 something happened that has not only been forgotten, but now seems unimaginable. Top negotiators for the United States and the Soviet Union – John J. McCloy and Vladimir Zorin – brought before the General Assembly of the United Nations a complete set of principles agreed to by both governments for General and Complete Disarmament: no more national armies, navies, or air forces; only police forces for internal security; no more stockpiles of weapons of mass destruction, nuclear or "conventional."

The General Assembly received this document with joy and at once established the Eighteen-Nation Disarmament Commission to implement it.

In retrospect we can see that the military-industrial complex looked upon this development as *the disarmament threat*, and started then what Swedish diplomat Alva Myrdal calls "the disarmament game" which

we have lived with ever since.

The first casualty was the term *disarmament*. The trouble with it is that it means something: It means fewer arms. It has been replaced in virtually all official discussions by two essentially meaningless terms: *arms control* and *arms limitation*. Of course, one can *control* arms up or down; so far it has always been up; and however far up they go, they will necessarily always be limited.

By 1963 we had the first arms control treaty: the Partial Test Ban Treaty. If that had been a Comprehensive Test Ban Treaty, we would now be living in a better and more secure world. What it did, however, was to ban testing of nuclear weapons only in the atmosphere, outer space, and under the sea; testing continued unabated underground.

*   *   *

Since then we have had ten bilateral

and seven multilateral arms agreements – on the average about one treaty a year – without even slowing the arms race.

So it is altogether a sad history of utter frustration. Far from achieving disarmament, it would by now be a signal accomplishment just to block further increase in arms. Instead we have had 19 years of almost continuous escalation of the arms race, qualitative and quantitative; 19 years of arms control treaties in which the participating nations agreed not to do what none of them had any intention of doing. One might think all that diplomatic activity a waste of time; but no – it accomplished a very useful purpose: it disarmed the disarmament movement. Always we were told, "Delicate negotiations are in progress. The negotiators know things that you don't know. Don't rock the boat."

George Wald

SALT Talks

To comply with the limits established by SALT II and the SALT I Interim Agreement, which SALT II replaced, the Soviet Union from 1972 to 1985 removed 1,007 land-based and 233 submarine-based ballistic missiles from the active force and dismantled 13 Yankee-class ballistic missile-carrying submarines as new weapons entered the force. Past Soviet military practices suggest that these missiles would not have been retired nearly as rapidly in the absence of SALT limitations. On the U.S. side, 320 land-based and 544 submarine-based missiles have been removed and 11 ballistic missile-carrying submarines have been dismantled.

*   *   *

Abandonment of the SALT II limits before a new strategic arms agreement is reached would harm U.S. security interests. By 1990 the Soviet Union could increase its total number of nuclear warheads and bomber weapons by almost 7,000, roughly twice the increase that the United States could make over the same period and 4,000 more than the Soviets could deploy under SALT II. Without SALT, the Soviet Union could significantly increase the number and improve the capabilities of its "heavy" land-based missiles, the weapons that the Reagan administration considers the most threatening. In the longer run, irrespective of which side ultimately gained a quantitative advantage, the United States would face the serious dangers and expenses of an all-out nuclear arms race.

*   *   *

An American decision to abrogate our compliance with SALT II will not give us any advantage in terms of modernization of our strategic forces. In other words, if we break out of the treaty, we do not gain something, we do not get a lead on modernizing our forces. With relatively minor exceptions, the modernization of U.S. strategic forces is possible within the limits of SALT II. The Soviets, however, have been forced to retire older arms systems as part of their modernization programs.

Senator John Chaffee

*   *   *

The second Strategic Arms Limitation Treaty (SALT II), signed by the United States and the Soviet Union in 1979 but never ratified, climaxed a decade-long series of negotiations between the United States and the Soviet Union on strategic (long-range) nuclear weaponry.

U.S. officials concluded in the 1960s that negotiated agreements to limit strategic weapons would enhance national security. Soviet leaders came to agree with their U.S. counterparts that both "defensive" anti-missile weapons and "offensive" weapons should be limited by agreement, and the SALT negotiations began in 1969.

The United States' President Ronald Reagan and President of the Union of Soviet Socialist Republics Mikhail Gorbachev at the Geneva Summit, November 1985, by Dennis Brack.

The SALT I talks ultimately produced, in 1972, two major agreements, the Anti-Ballistic Missile (ABM) Treaty and the Interim Agreement on Strategic Offensive Arms. The task of limiting offensive forces was complicated by major asymmetries between the two sides' force structures and capabilities. The SALT I negotiations addressed the problems caused by these asymmetries but failed to resolve them. The Interim Agreement was not a formal treaty, but a temporary accord meant to complement the ABM Treaty and provide a basis for mutual restraint while the two sides worked toward a SALT II treaty. The Interim Agreement was in effect a freeze, limiting each side to the number of missile launchers – land-based missile silos and submarine-based missile launch tubes – that it possessed or was constructing at the time of the agreement.

Building on the 1974 Vladivostok agreement between President Ford and General Secretary Brezhnev, the final SALT II Treaty was far wider in scope than the Interim Agreement. It mandated equal quantitative limits ("ceilings") that encompassed not only land- and submarine-based missiles but also long-range, nuclear-armed bomber aircraft. The treaty also established separate sub-limits on MIRVed missiles and cruise-missile-carrying bombers, on MIRVed missiles, and on MIRVed ICBMs. In addition, SALT II included qualitative limits, such as restrictions on the extent of MIRVing, a ban on new heavy ICBMs, a limit of one new light ICBM for each side, a ban on the Soviet SS-16 missile, and a temporary ban on cruise missiles.

Arms Control Association, Ploughshares.
(San Francisco)

Curbing the Arms Race

Formal Agreements

The historical record of official negotiations on disarmament shows limited results so far. Negotiations are a slow, tedious process. For more than three decades the major emphasis has been on nuclear weapons, but no agreement has yet been reached on the "discontinuance of all test explosions of nuclear weapons" (a pledge of the signers of the Partial Test Ban Treaty of 1963), nor on measures for the "cessation of the nuclear arms race" (a pledge of the signers of the Non-Proliferation Treaty in 1968). The last three US-USSR treaties that were signed have not been ratified, but both parties are continuing to observe them.

Nuclear Multilateral

Antarctic Treaty, 1959   30 states[1]
Bans military uses of Antarctica, including nuclear tests.

Partial Test Ban Treaty, 1963   111 states[1]
Bans nuclear weapons tests in atmosphere, outer space, and underwater.

Outer Space Treaty, 1967   81 states[1]
Bans nuclear weapons in earth orbit and stationing in outer space.

Latin American Nuclear Free Zone Treaty, 1967 25 states[1]
Bans testing, possession, deployment of nuclear weapons, and requires safeguards on facilities.

Non-Proliferation Treaty, 1968   129 states[1]
Bans transfer of nuclear weapons and technology outside of five nuclear weapons states. Commits latter to halt arms race.

Seabed Treaty, 1971   74 states[1]
Bans nuclear weapons on the seabed beyond a 12-mile coastal limit.

South Pacific Nuclear Free Zone Treaty, 1985   8 states[2]
Bans testing, manufacture, acquisition, stationing of nuclear weapons. Requests five nuclear weapons states to sign protocol banning use or threat of nuclear weapons and nuclear testing.

Other Multilateral

Geneva Protocol, 1925   118 states[1]
Bans the use in war of asphyxiating, poisonous, or other gases, and of bacteriological methods of warfare.

Biological Weapons Convention, 1972   99 states[1]
Bans the development, production, and stockpiling of biological agents and toxins; requires the destruction of stocks.

Environmental Modification Convention, 1977   45 states[1]
Bans military or other hostile use of techniques to change weather patterns, ocean currents, ozone layer, or ecological balance.

Inhumane Weapons Convention, 1981   26 states[1]
Bans use of fragmentation bombs not detectable in the human body; bans use against civilians of mines, booby traps, and incendiaries.

Nuclear Bilateral

Hot Line and Modernization Agreements, 1963   US-USSR
Establishes direct radio and wire-telegraph links between Moscow and Washington to ensure communication between heads of government in times of crisis. 1971 agreement provided for satellite communication.

Accidents Measures Agreement, 1971   US-USSR
Pledges US and USSR to improve safeguards against accidental or unauthorized use of nuclear weapons.

ABM Treaty (SALT I), 1972   US-USSR
Limits anti-ballistic missile systems to two deployment areas on each side. In Protocol of 1974, each side restricted to one deployment area.

SALT I Interim Agreement, 1972   US-USSR
Freezes the number of strategic ballistic missile launchers, and permits an increase in SLBM launchers up to an agreed level only with equivalent dismantling of older ICBM or SLBM launchers.

Prevention of Nuclear War Agreement, 1973   US-USSR
Requires consultation between the two countries if there is a danger of nuclear war.

SALT II Treaty, 1979   US-USSR[2]
Limits numbers of strategic nuclear delivery vehicles, launchers of MIRV'd missiles, bombers with long-range cruise missiles, warheads on existing ICBMs, etc. Bans testing or deploying new ICBMs.

Threshold Test Ban Treaty, 1974   US-USSR[2]
Bans underground tests having a yield above 150 kilotons.

Peaceful Nuclear Explosions Treaty, 1974   US-USSR[2]
Bans "groups explosions" with aggregate yield over 1,500 kilotons; requires on-site observers of explosions with yield over 150 kilotons.

[1] Number of accessions and ratifications, as recorded by ACDA, October 1985.
[2] Not yet ratified.

Declarations of Restraint

Action-reaction, so obviously a propelling force in the build-up of arms, can be equally effective in the reduction process. Unilateral declarations of restraint are not substitutes for formal treaties but may help to achieve them. US initiatives, particularly in the détente of the 1960s, produced results in several areas. In the 1980s, the USSR has come forward with a number of unilateral actions which could also give momentum to the disarmament process. They deserve widespread public debate and support as a means of reversing the nuclear tide.

Nuclear test moratorium, 1958-61 and 1963
At US initiative, tests were suspended by US and USSR for one year. Dissatisfied with progress on negotiations, President Eisenhower ended the moratorium but said US would not resume without notice. Premier Krushchev said USSR would not resume unless western powers did. In 1961 France conducted first test; USSR resumed testing; then US resumed. Again at US initiative in 1963, tests were suspended by US and USSR. Negotiations led to Partial Test Ban Treaty in a few months.

Reduction of military budgets, 1963-65[3]
At US initiative (but not publicly announced), US and USSR in 1963 discussed informal reciprocity on military budgets; other simple steps to disarmament. Budget restraint for two years was interrupted by Vietnam escalation.[3]

Production of biological weapons halted, 1969
US unilaterally halted production of biological and toxic weapons. Negotiations led to international Convention in 1972.

No first use of nuclear weapons, 1982

Suspension of tests on anti-satellite weapons, 1982

Six-month freeze on deployment of medium-range missiles in Europe, 1985

Five-month suspension of nuclear tests, 1985
Soviet Union's four unilateral actions above, inviting reciprocity, have had no positive US response.

[3] *World Military and Social Expenditures 1978* has summary background on this action. Cutbacks in fissionable material were also subject of reciprocity in this period.

A Comprehensive Nuclear Test Ban

A comprehensive nuclear test ban has been the goal of every American President from Eisenhower to Carter. It would serve our security and the cause of peace by restraining the technological arms race between the superpowers – a race that is every bit as dangerous as the race in number of missiles and bombers. It would reduce tension between the United States and the Soviet Union, thus opening the way to agreements on other measures to reduce the risk these weapons pose to both our nations. And it would be an important step in reducing the spread of nuclear weapons to additional nations. Not only would it demonstrate that the two superpowers were serious in their pledge to limit their arms race, but, if other nations followed our lead and signed a comprehensive ban, this ban would prevent a non-nuclear country from developing fully its own nuclear capacity.

Negotiations – so promising several years ago – have been abandoned simply to pursue elusive advantage in the nuclear arms race. Considering the array of forces already at the disposal of both nations, and given our lead in weapons technology today, continued nuclear weapons testing cannot be justified on any grounds. . . . What about the Russians? Can compliance with a CTB [Comprehensive Test Ban] Treaty be verified?

Verification of treaty compliance was once a genuine stumbling block in CTB negotiations. Today, it is an excuse for inaction. High technology has given us the eyes and ears through seismic and satellite observation to detect violations of any military significance. (See "The Verification of a Comprehensive Nuclear Test Ban," *Scientific American*, October 1982, Lynn Sykes and Jack Evernden). Incorporating these advances, the verification provisions of the draft CTB treaty of 1980 call for reciprocal placement of seismic monitoring stations (small, unmanned, but tamper-proof devices) to locate and identify underground nuclear explosions; voluntary, on-site inspection to investigate suspected violations; and exchanges of geophysical data to increase accuracy of detection. It is now possible to identify explosions down to one kiloton or less. Under a CTB treaty, any nuclear explosion is a violation, making cheating even easier to detect. Satellite reconnaissance will also be able to pick up tell-tale signs of a clandestine resumption of testing. Finally, an international panel similar to the U.S.-Soviet Standing Consultative Commission could be established to investigate and discuss alleged violations arising under the treaty.

Greenpeace and The Taskforce for a Comprehensive Test Ban of the Committee for National Security

Nuclear Battlefields

The military employs a rhetoric of piecemeal analysis and spurious geographic analogy to avoid controls of its nuclear weapons, plans, operations, and infrastructure. Defense officials issue expert statements about the feasibility or infeasibility of whatever they do or do not want to do, sprinkling in vague concepts like "strategic" to lend authority to their language. One of the most common arguments against relinquishing any option is its irreplaceability. The military insists it cannot sacrifice control of Micronesia because it needs those islands just in case it loses bases in the Philippines. Yet at the same time it argues that Philippine bases are "irreplaceable" and completely secure. . . . When the U.S. military wanted to expand its bases in Australia in the 1970s it argued such expansion was necessary because of the possibility of losing Philippine bases. . . . Secrecy prevents the public – and the Congress – from scrutinizing such arguments, from finding the incoherence beneath phrases like "strategically vital area." The military's compartmentalization of geographic jurisdictions, and competition among the armed services, prevent the military itself from having an overall view.

William Arkin and Richard Fieldhouse

STAR WARS

What Is Star Wars?

The Strategic Defense Initiative – "SDI" in bureaucratic jargon – is a long-term research and development effort aimed at developing ways to protect the United States from nuclear attack.

Today, both the United States and the Soviet Union are vulnerable to a nuclear attack. The principal threat comes from each side's intercontinental ballistic missiles (ICBMs) based on land and from submarine-launched ballistic missiles (SLBMs) carried by nuclear submarines. Both ICBMs and SLBMs are capable of reaching their targets in 30 minutes or less. . . .

The total flight time for Soviet land-based missiles aimed at the United States is about 30 minutes. An effective ballistic missile defense system would have three distinct tasks to perform during that short period: locate and track the Soviet missiles, discriminate between decoys and armed reentry vehicles, and destroy the nuclear warheads before they reach U.S. territory.

The Reagan Administration hopes to develop a missile defense system with multiple "layers" of weapons that could knock out Soviet missiles at different stages of their half-hour flight. . . .

To catch an enemy missile in its boost phase requires a defensive weapon that can destroy its target within three to five minutes of when the enemy missile was launched. Consequently, much of the current missile defense research is focused on weapons based partially or entirely in space. This basing would enable the defensive weapons to have a direct line of fire at Soviet missiles as soon as they are launched. . . .

President Reagan's SDI program anticipates the use of "directed energy weapons" to destroy Soviet missiles. Such a weapons system would generate beams of light ("laser beams") or streams of electronically-charged particles ("particle beams") to burn holes in Soviet missiles and muddle their guidance systems. . . .

To reach Soviet missiles early in flight, a beam weapon system would have to operate at least partly in space. The deployment options under consideration include basing the beam weapons on orbiting battle stations; basing beam weapons on the ground, with mirrors in orbit to reflect and aim their beams; or "popping up" (launching) the beam weapons quickly into space upon warning of a Soviet attack. . . .

There is almost universal agreement among independent scientific experts that the United States will not be able to deploy a fully effective population defense within the next two or three decades. Many experts doubt that such a defense could ever be developed. The Soviet Union has roughly 8,000 nuclear warheads on its missiles aimed at U.S. territory. Even if the United States possessed a defense system capable of intercepting 90 to 95 percent of the Soviet arsenal, this would still allow some 400 to 800 warheads to "leak" through – enough to cause enormous destruction. . . . Moreover, even if our defense were 99.9 percent effective and only eight Soviet warheads leaked through to strike eight large U.S. cities, several million people would be killed and over ten million more injured.

*   *   *

There are enormous technical obstacles to any missile defense system. Beam weapons and other exotic weaponry are still in the basic research stage, and it is not known when – or whether – such devices could be developed and deployed. The Pentagon's own chief of research has conceded that the kind of missile defense called for by President Reagan would require breakthroughs in eight separate technologies, each "equivalent to or greater than the Manhattan Project" that produced the first atomic bomb.

Common Cause, 1985

Right: Star Wars by Rene Zamic, 1985.

I Resigned from Star Wars

Early last May [1985] I was asked to "help save the world from Nuclear Conflagration." I was offered $1000 per day to serve on the U.S. Strategic Defense Initiative Organization's Panel on Computing in Support of Battle Management. The panel advises SDIO on computing technology for the "Star Wars" program. At the end of June, I decided that "Star Wars" was a fraud and resigned. This paper reports my opinions about "Star Wars." . . .

The "business ends" of SDI comprise a variety of sensors and weapons. The sensors will produce vast amounts of raw data that computers must process and analyze in order to aim and fire the weapons. Computers must detect missile firings, determine the source of the attack, and compute the attacking trajectories. Software will determine how the system discriminates between threatening warheads and objects designed to confuse it. Software is the glue that holds such systems together. Even minor errors in the software can render the system inaccurate and worthless. . . .

I have watched in amazement as SDI supporters provide statements designed to mislead the public. For example, "There could be 100,000 errors in the software and it would still work." True, but a single error caused the failure of a Venus probe!

The most misleading statement of all is made repeatedly. They argue that if each phase of a three-phase system is 90% effective, fewer than one percent of enemy missiles will get through. This argument is misleading in three ways: (1) The 90% figure is arbitrary; SDIO officials admit there is no basis for it, (2) the computation assumes that the phases are independent; that would not be true for any reasonable design, (3) using statistics assumes that the battle is a random process. It is not; it will be a battle of skills. Unless SDI is used in a U.S. first strike, the USSR will attack only if they believe they have an effective countermeasure.

David Parnas; Computer Software Expert (U.S. Navy)

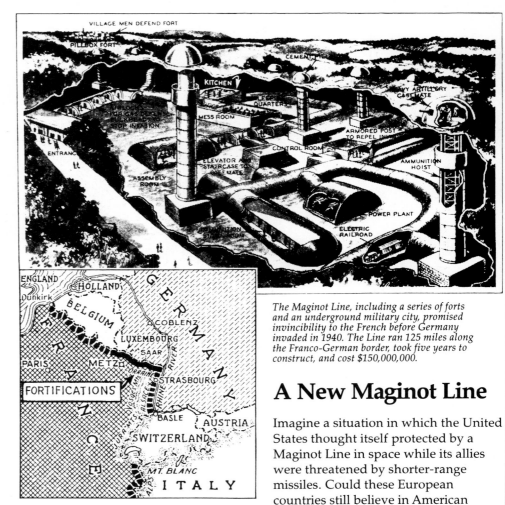

The Maginot Line, including a series of forts and an underground military city, promised invincibility to the French before Germany invaded in 1940. The Line ran 125 miles along the Franco-German border, took five years to construct, and cost $150,000,000.

A New Maginot Line

Imagine a situation in which the United States thought itself protected by a Maginot Line in space while its allies were threatened by shorter-range missiles. Could these European countries still believe in American protection?

Claude Cheysson, French Foreign Minister.

No Defense

The prospect that emerging "Star Wars" technologies, when further developed, will provide a perfect or near-perfect defense system, literally removing from the hand of the Soviet Union the ability to do socially mortal damage to the United States with nuclear weapons, is so remote that it should not serve as the basis of public expectation or national policy about ballistic missile defense.

Ashton B. Carter

No Advantage

There would be no advantage in creating a new Maginot Line of the twenty-first century, liable to be outflanked by relatively simpler and demonstrably cheaper countermeasures. . . . The implications for arms control must also be carefully considered. Would the prospect of new defenses being deployed inexorably crank up the levels of offensive nuclear systems designed to overwhelm them? History and the present state of technology suggest that this risk cannot be ignored. . . .[The ABM Treaty] represents a political and military keystone in the still shaky arch of security we have constructed with the East over the past decade and a half. But to go beyond research into defensive systems would be inconsistent with the terms of the ABM Treaty as it stands.

Sir Geoffrey Howe, British Foreign Minister

No Solution

The President and the Secretary of Defense remain convinced that this strategic revolution is at hand. Virtually all others associated with the SDI now recognize that such a leakproof defense is so far in the future, if it indeed ever proves feasible, that it offers no solution to our present dilemma.

Robert S. McNamara and Hans A. Bethe

Weapons in Space

The scenario being proposed to take war into space is the most threatening thing that faces us immediately. And I don't mean threatening in the year 2000. It is threatening now because it is the most destabilizing. It is an invitation to a preemptive first-strike by the Soviet Union because we will face them with the alternative of hitting us first and being able to damage us, or having us hit them first and their not being able to retaliate effectively.

The initial argument given for the Strategic Defense Initiative (more commonly known as Star Wars) was that this would be a total defense of the United States. It would be a defense through which no missiles would come and therefore it would make missiles useless and would make possible a total disarmament. It very rapidly became clear that this was a totally incorrect assessment of the possibility, with the technical difficulties staggering. Richard De Lauer, Undersecretary of Defense for Research and Development has said it will take eight research and development programs, each one at least the size of the Manhattan Project in order to bring the Strategic Defense Initiative into fruition. Also, the President's own committee came back with the assessment that you could not build a system that was perfect. There would in fact be a percentage of the missiles that could get through from the Soviet Union. More recent assessments have estimated that from 25% to 60% of the population could be killed by missiles that slipped through.

Vera Kistiakowsky

Star Wars Pledge Interim Returns

The scientists' pledge to refuse Star Wars work now has the signatures of 56% (388/694) of the total faculty in the nation's top 14 physics departments....In 6 of these top departments at least two thirds of the faculty have already signed this unprecedented rejection of research funds from a dangerous program. At least half the faculty in each of 23 physics departments as well as 9 other science and engineering departments have signed already. Among the departments is the nation's top math department. Over 1500 faculty and senior research staff have signed nationwide, as have 1200 graduate students and junior staff. (Departments are physics unless otherwise specified.)

Universities include:	Signed	Possible
U. of Illinois at Urbana-Champaign	53/73	73%
State U. of New York, Stonybrook	44/55	80%
Princeton	42/56	75%
Cornell	34/49	69%
U. of Pennsylvania	32/48	67%
U. of Chicago	31/44	70%
Rutgers	30/44	68%
Cal Tech	28/47	60%
Carnegie-Mellon	23/30	77%
Columbia	17/32	53%
Washington, St. Louis (chemistry)	21/24	88%
Research Centers:		
Stanford Linear Accelerator	27/50	54%
Harvard-Smithsonian Center for Astrophysics	56/115	

University of Chicago

Effects on Existing Treaties

Establishment of a legal regime governing outer space activities has been a basic object of political and military leaders, as well as of international lawyers, from the outset of the space age. As the Reagan Administration attempts in Geneva to promote its "defense-dominated" strategic relationship to the Soviet Union, it should be aware that a significant portion of this body of law is binding and relevant, both to the development of a "Star Wars" strategy, and to attempts to negotiate its implementation.

The 1967 Outer Space Treaty is central to the legal regime. Ratified by over 100 nations, including the United States, the Treaty establishes outer space as a zone to be treated differently by the international community with respect to international law than had previously been done with newly discovered territories or environments....

If deployed in space, the nuclear-pumped X-ray laser, now regarded as one of the Administration's most promising prospects, would clearly contravene Article IV of the Treaty. The X-ray laser would also run afoul of Article I of the Limited Test Ban Treaty, which prohibits nuclear tests "or any other nuclear explosion" in the atmosphere or outer space.... If X-ray laser capabilities became part of an alliance-wide defensive deterrent, they would violate Article I of the Non-Proliferation Treaty as well....

The primary purpose of the ABM Treaty is to crystallize into law the condition of mutual assured destruction (MAD) by virtually eliminating defensive weaponry from both sides' arsenals, leaving each vulnerable to assured reliation from the other. To this end, the Treaty flatly bans exactly what the president's Strategic Defense Initiative has been set up to create: a national, multi-layered, anti-ballistic-missile system for defense against incoming ballistic missiles. In fact, Article V prohibits not only deployment, but also development and testing, of "ABM systems or components which are sea-based, air-based, space-based, or mobile land-based...."

The claim most often advanced for the legality of SDI, and the one officially put forward by the Administration at the Geneva negotiations, as well as to U.S. allies, relies on the distinction between "development" of specified ABM systems or components, which is prohibited, and "research," which is not. Neither term is defined in the Treaty, but the meaning of "development" was discussed during the negotiations. In the end, the distinction was understood by the United States to have been a functional one: activities which could not be verified by national technical means would be permitted. A written submission by the executive branch to the Senate Armed Services Committee, in response to a question by Senator Henry Jackson, indicates that virtually any activity beyond the laboratory development and testing stage to the field testing stage would be prohibited. Under this interpretation, repeatedly endorsed by the Arms Control and Disarmament Agency, a number of tests and demonstrations scheduled to take place within this decade would be in violation of the treaty.

Daniel Arbess

NUCLEAR WINTER

First the Fires...

In a nuclear attack, fires would be started in and around many of the target areas either as a direct result of the thermal radiation from the fireball or indirectly from blast and shock damage. Examples of the latter would be fires started by sparks from electrical short circuits, broken gas lines and ruptured fuel storage tanks. Such fires could be numerous and could spread throughout the area of destruction and in some cases beyond, depending on the amount and type of fuel available and local meteorological conditions. These fires might generate large quantities of smoke which would be carried into the atmosphere to varying heights, depending on the meteorological conditions and the intensity of the fire.

In addition to smoke, nuclear explosions on or very near the earth's surface can produce dust that would be carried up with the rising fireball. As in the case of volcanic eruptions such as Mt. Saint Helens, a part of the dust would probably be in the form of very small particles that do not readily settle out under gravity and thus can remain suspended in the atmosphere for long periods of time. If the yield of the nuclear explosion were large enough to carry some of the dust into the stratosphere where moisture and precipitation are not present to wash it out, it could remain for months.

*   *   *

Depending upon how the atmospheric smoke and dust generated by nuclear war are ultimately characterized, the suspended particulate matter could act much like a cloud, absorbing and scattering sunlight at high altitude and reducing the amount of solar energy reaching the surface of the earth. How much and how fast the surface of the earth might cool as a result would depend on many of the yet undetermined details of the process, but if there is sufficient absorption of sunlight over a large enough area, the temperature change could be significant.

Caspar Weinberger

...Then Night Falls

1. Continuous forest fires could destroy the greater part of the planet's forests. The smoke involved would destroy the transparency of the atmosphere. A night lasting many weeks would ensue on Earth followed by a lack of oxygen in the atmosphere. As a result, this factor alone, if real, could destroy life on the planet. In less pronounced form, this factor could have important ecological, economic, and psychological consequences.

2. High-altitude wartime nuclear explosions in space (particularly the thermonuclear explosion on ABM missiles and the explosion of attacking missiles whose purpose is to disrupt enemy radar) could possibly destroy or seriously damage the ozone layer protecting Earth from the sun's ultraviolet radiation. Estimates of this danger are very imprecise – if the maximal estimates are true then this factor is sufficient to destroy life.

Andrei Sakharov

A Winter's Tale

[Following a nuclear exchange,] the upper layers of the polluted atmosphere facing the Sun will be heated more intensively than now and, as a result, the troposphere, the lower layer of the atmosphere in which temperature drops with height, will begin to disappear. The atmosphere will become superstable.....

The ocean will cool off more slowly due to its immense thermal inertia. According to estimates, ten months after, the temperature of the ocean surface will decrease on average by about 1.2 degrees Centigrade. Therefore air over its surface will cool off by "merely" several degrees which, as a matter of fact, will be sufficient for the formation of a thick fog that will stay for a long time. The enormous temperature contrast between the cooled land and the slowly cooling ocean will produce severe storms accompanied by heavy snowfall along a wide coastal area. This means that, regardless of the season, a long "nuclear winter" will set in all over the globe.

Inside the continents rainfall will be close to zero, crops will be destroyed and those domestic animals which may survive the cold spell will die of thirst because fresh water will be frozen as a rule....

Committee of Soviet Scientists for Peace

Northern Scenario

Canada is already accustomed to severe winters. Her plants and animals are very hardy, and her agriculture is fine-tuned to a short growing season. For these reasons it may be argued that a winter attack, arriving while the inland surface is already extensively frozen and snow-covered, would have less impact than one delivered in spring or summer. It might also be assumed that a direct attack on her own surface would be on a small scale by comparison with those delivered to U.S., European and Soviet targets.

*   *   *

The reduction in sunlight, and resulting cold, would kill many species of animals and plants. The severity would depend upon the season in which an attack took place – plants being most vulnerable in the summer – but would be catastrophic under any circumstances.

Despite the problems of prediction it is beyond question that if a nuclear exchange between the superpowers of the northern hemisphere takes place, the Canadian environment – irrespective of whether or not Canada receives direct hits from nuclear warheads – will be seriously affected. This might occur at levels of exchange well below those considered by the reference scenarios....

Royal Society of Canada

Down Under

The spread of the nuclear clouds from the middle latitudes of the northern hemisphere depends on the global wind systems and the heights in the atmosphere in which the debris is injected. The detonation of a 1 Mt warhead in the lower atmosphere can put debris to a height of about 20 km. The material at this height is in the stratosphere above the levels at which most rainfall is formed. The diffusing cloud travels with the global wind systems and remains in the atmosphere for months to years before being brought to the ground. Because there is an exchange of air across the equator, the cloud would spread from northern latitudes into the southern hemisphere.

Royal Society of New Zealand

Outlook for the Southern Hemisphere

Approximations were made at each stage of the complex calculations and important atmospheric processes had to be left out. The results must therefore be considered as qualitative and not as precise quantitative forecasts.

However, they have been confirmed by another more recent computer simulation carried out by a group at the National Center for Atmospheric Research (NCAR) in the United States. . . .It was used to calculate the atmospheric consequences over a few weeks of the smoke generated by a nuclear war in the middle latitudes of the northern hemisphere. The smoke was assumed to be evenly spread between latitudes 30°N and 70°N. It caused almost complete blocking of the incoming sunlight. . . .

It was found that middle latitude surface temperatures in the interiors of the continents dropped below freezing in a matter of days regardless of the season. . . .A greatly enhanced cross-equator flow was found, especially in the northern hemisphere spring. This changes the expectation of relative southern hemisphere immunity from a northern war.

U.N. General Assembly, September 17, 1985

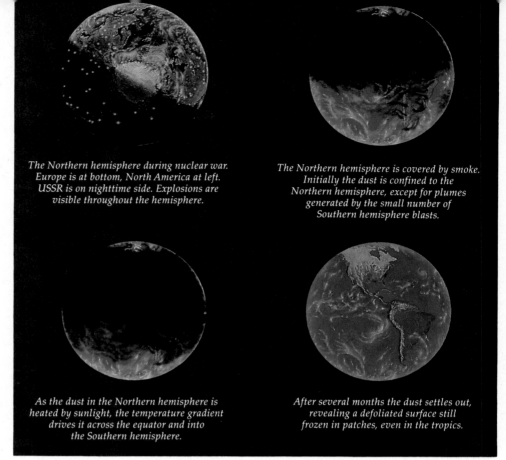

The Northern hemisphere during nuclear war. Europe is at bottom, North America at left. USSR is on nighttime side. Explosions are visible throughout the hemisphere.

The Northern hemisphere is covered by smoke. Initially the dust is confined to the Northern hemisphere, except for plumes generated by the small number of Southern hemisphere blasts.

As the dust in the Northern hemisphere is heated by sunlight, the temperature gradient drives it across the equator and into the Southern hemisphere.

After several months the dust settles out, revealing a defoliated surface still frozen in patches, even in the tropics.

Above: Best early guess of how clouds would cover the earth after a nuclear war; released with the 1983 TAPPS report; rendered by artist Jon Lomberg.

Limited War – Limited Winter?

But what if nuclear wars *can* be contained, and much less than 5000 megatons is detonated? Perhaps the greatest surprise in our work was that even small nuclear wars can have devastating climatic effects. We considered a war in which a mere 100 megatons were exploded, less than one percent of the world arsenals, and only in low-yield airbursts over cities. This scenario, we found, would ignite thousands of fires, and the smoke from these fires alone would be enough to generate an epoch of cold and dark almost as severe as in the 5000-megaton case.

Our results have been carefully scrutinized by more than 100 scientists in the United States, Europe and the Soviet Union. There are still arguments on points of detail. But the overall conclusion seems to be agreed upon: There are severe and previously unanticipated global consequences of nuclear war – sub-freezing temperatures in a twilit radioactive gloom lasting for months or longer.

Carl Sagan

The Effect on Food

The major climatic effects of nuclear war could occur in the Northern Hemisphere – where over 80 percent of the world's people live. 2.5 billion people could be at risk of starvation due to postwar crop failures and breakdown of food distribution. In countries such as the United States, U.S.S.R., and Canada, short- and long-term climatic changes could devastate agriculture. In others, such as India and China, starvation could result from low levels of stored food, reductions in food production, unavailability of important food imports, and the destruction of food distribution systems. Many farmers could no longer be able to obtain pesticides, fertilizers, imported fuel for farm machinery, or seeds.

International Council of Scientific Unions

FROM

OBASAN

BY JOY KOGAWA

"Please, Aunt Emily," I whisper as she turns aside. "Tell us."

Aunt Emily takes the letters and reads the pages, handing them back to Sensei when she is finished.

"What is written?" I ask again.

"A matter of a long time ago," Sensei says.

"What matter?"

Nakayama-sensei clears his throat. "Senso no toki – in the time of the war – your mother. Your grandmother. That there is suffering and their deep love." He reads the letters in silence once more, then begins reading aloud. The letter is addressed to Grandpa Kato. It is clear as he reads that the letters were never intended for Stephen and me. They were written by Grandma Kato.

The sound of rain beats against the windows and the roof. The rain is collecting in the eaves and pouring in a thin stream into the rain barrel at the corner near the kitchen door. Tomorrow I will fill the plastic bucket and bring the soft frothy water in – use it to water the houseplants and wash my hair.

Sensei's faltering voice is almost drowned out by the splattering gusts against the window. I stare at the gauze-curtained windows and imagine the raindrops sliding down the glass, black on black. In the sound of the howling outside, I hear other howling.

Sensei pauses as he reads. "Naomi," he says softly, "Stephen, your mother is speaking. Listen carefully to her voice."

Many of the Japanese words sound strange and the language is formal.

*   *   *

There are only two letters in the grey cardboard folder. The first is a brief and emotionless statement that Grandma Kato, her niece's daughter, and my mother are the only ones in the immediate family to have survived. The second letter is an outpouring.

I remember Grandma Kato as thin and tough, not given to melodrama or overstatement of any kind. She was unbreakable. I felt she could endure all things and would survive any catastrophe. But I did not then understand what catastrophes were possible in human affairs.

Here, the ordinary Granton rain slides down wet and clean along the glass leaving a trail on the window like the Japanese writing on the thin blue-lined paper – straight down like a bead curtain of asterisks. The rain she describes is black, oily, thick, and strange.

"In the heat of the August sun," Grandma writes, "however much the effort to forget, there is no forgetfulness. As in a dream, I can still see the maggots crawling in the sockets of my niece's eyes. Her strong intelligent young son helped me move a bonsai tree that very morning. There is no forgetfulness."

When Nakayama-sensei reaches the end of the page, he stops reading and folds the letter as if he has decided to read no more. Aunt Emily begins to speak quietly, telling of a final letter from the Canadian missionary, Miss Best.

How often, I am wondering, did Grandma and Mother waken in those years with the unthinkable memories alive in their minds, the visible evidence of horror written on their skin, in their blood, carved in every mirror they passed, felt in every step they took. As a child I was told only that Mother and Grandma Kato were safe in Tokyo, visiting Grandma Kato's ailing mother.

"Someday, surely, they will return," Obasan used to say.

The two letters that reached us in Vancouver before all communication ceased due to the war told us that Mother and Grandma Kato had arrived safely in Japan and were staying with Grandma Kato's sister and her husband in their home near the Tokyo Gas Company. My great-grandmother was then seventy-nine and was not expected to live to be eighty but, happily, she had become so well that she had returned home from the hospital and was even able on occasion to leave the house.

Nakayama-sensei opens the letter again and holds it, reading silently. Then looking over to Stephen, he says, "It is better to speak, is it not?"

"They're dead now," Stephen says.

Sensei nods.

"Please read, Sensei," I whisper.

"Yes," Aunt Emily says. "They should know."

Sensei starts again at the beginning. The letter is dated simply 1949. It was sent, Sensei says, from somewhere in Nagasaki. There was no return address.

"Though it was a time of war," Grandma writes, "what happiness that January, 1945, to hear from my niece Setsuko, in Nagasaki." Setsuko's second child was due to be born within the month. In February, just as American air raids in Tokyo were intensifying, Mother went to help her cousin in Nagasaki. The baby was born three days after she arrived. Early in March, air raids and alarms were constant day and night in Tokyo. In spite of all the dangers of travel, Grandma Kato went to Nagasaki to be with my mother and to help with the care of the new baby. The last day she spent with her mother and sister in Tokyo, she said they sat on the tatami and talked, remembering their childhood and the days they went chestnut-picking together. They parted with laughter. The following night, Grandma Kato's sister, their mother and her sister's husband died in the B-29 bombings of March 9, 1945.

From this point on, Grandma's letter becomes increasingly chaotic, the details interspersed without chronological consistency. She and my mother, she writes, were unable to talk of all the things that happened. The horror would surely die sooner, they felt, if they refused to speak. But the silence and the constancy of the nightmare had become unbearable for Grandma and she hoped that by sharing them with her husband, she could be helped to extricate herself from the grip of the past.

"If these matters are sent away in this letter, perhaps they will depart a little from our souls," she writes. "For the burden of these words, forgive me."

Mother, for her part, continued her vigil of silence. She spoke with no one about her torment. She specifically requested that Stephen and I be spared the truth.

In all my high-school days, until we heard from Sensei that her grave had been found in Tokyo, I pictured her trapped in Japan by government regulations, or by an ailing grandmother. The letters I sent to the address in Tokyo were never answered or returned. I could not know that she and Grandma Kato had gone to Nagasaki to stay with Setsuko, her husband who was a dentist, and their two children, four-year-old Tomio and the new baby, Chieko.

The baby, Grandma writes, looked so much like me that she and my mother marvelled and often caught themselves calling her Naomi. With her widow's peak, her fat cheeks and pointed chin, she had a heart-shaped face like mine. Tomio, however, was not like Stephen at all. He was a sturdy child, extremely healthy and athletic, with a strong will like his father. He was fascinated by his new baby sister, sitting and watching her for hours as she slept or nursed. He made dolls for her. He helped to dress her. He loved to hold her in the bath, feeling her fingers holding his fingers tightly. He rocked her to sleep in his arms.

The weather was hot and humid that morning of August 9. The air-raid alerts had ended. Tomio and some neighbourhood children had gone to the irrigation ditch to play and cool off as they sometimes did.

Shortly after eleven o'clock, Grandma Kato was preparing to make lunch. The baby was strapped to her back. She was bending over a bucket of water beside a large earthenware storage bin when a child in the street was heard shouting, "Look at the parachute!" A few seconds later, there was a sudden white flash, brighter than a bolt of lightning. She had no idea what could have exploded. It was as if the entire sky were swallowed up. A moment later she was hurled sideways by a blast. She had a sensation of floating tranquilly in a cool whiteness high above the earth. When she regained consciousness, she was slumped forward in a sitting position in the water bin. She gradually became aware of the moisture, an intolerable heat, blood, a mountain of debris and her niece's weak voice sounding at first distant, calling the names of her children. Then she could hear the other sounds—the far-away shouting. Around her, a thick dust made breathing difficult. Chieko was still strapped to her back, but made no sound. She was alive but unconscious.

It took Grandma a long time to claw her way out of the wreckage. When she emerged, it was into an eerie twilight formed of heavy dust and smoke that blotted out the sun. What she saw was incomprehensible. Almost all the buildings were flattened or in flames for as far as she could see. The landmarks were gone. Tall columns of fire rose through the haze and everywhere the dying and the wounded crawled, fled, stumbled like ghosts among the ruins. Voices screamed, calling the names of children, fathers, mothers, calling for help, calling for water.

Beneath some wreckage, she saw first the broken arm, then the writhing body of her niece, her head bent back, her hair singed, both her eye sockets blown out. In a weak and delirious voice, she was calling Tomio. Grandma Kato touched her niece's leg and the skin peeled off and stuck to the palm of her hand.

It isn't clear from the letter but at some point she came across Tomio, his legs pumping steadily up and down as he stood in one spot not knowing where to go. She gathered him in her arms. He was remarkably intact, his skin unburned.

She had no idea where Mother was, but with the two children, she began making her way towards the air-raid shelter. All around her people one after another collapsed and died, crying for water. One old man no longer able to keep moving lay on the ground holding up a dead baby and crying, "Save the children. Leave the old." No one took the dead child from his outstretched hands. Men, women, in many cases indistinguishable by sex, hairless, half-clothed, hobbled past. Skin hung from their bodies like tattered rags. One man held his bowels in with the stump of one hand. A child whom Grandma Kato recognized lay on the ground asking for help. She stopped and told him she would return as soon as she could. A woman she knew was begging for someone to help her lift the burning beam beneath which her children were trapped. The woman's children were friends of Tomio's. Grandma was loath to walk past, but with the two children, she could do no more and kept going. At no point does Grandma Kato mention the injuries she herself must have sustained.

Nearing the shelter, Grandma could see through the greyness that the entrance was clogged with dead bodies. She remembered then that her niece's father-in-law lived on a farm on the hillside, and she began making her way back through the burning city towards the river she would have to cross. The water, red with blood, was a raft of corpses. Farther upstream, the bridge was twisted like noodles. Eventually she came to a spot where she was able to cross and, still carrying the two children, Grandma Kato made her way up the hillside.

After wandering for some time, she found a wooden water pipe dribbling a steady stream. She held Tomio's mouth to it and allowed him to drink as much as he wished though she had heard that too much water was not good. She unstrapped the still unconscious baby from her back. Exhausted, she drank from the pipe, and gathering the two children in her arms, she looked out at the burning city and lapsed into a sleep so deep she believed she was unconscious.

When she awakened, she was in the home of her niece's relatives and the baby was being fed barley water. The little boy was nowhere.

Almost immediately, Grandma set off to look for the child. Next day she returned to the area of her niece's home and every day thereafter she looked for Mother and the lost boy, checking the lists of the dead, looking over the unclaimed corpses. She discovered that her niece's husband was among the dead.

One evening when she had given up the search for the day, she sat down beside a naked woman she'd seen earlier who was aimlessly chipping wood to make a pyre on which to cremate a dead baby. The woman was utterly disfigured. Her nose and one cheek were almost gone. Great wounds and pustules covered her entire face and body. She was completely bald. She sat in a cloud of flies and maggots wriggled among her wounds. As Grandma watched her, the woman gave her a vacant gaze, then let out a cry. It was my mother.

The little boy was never found. Mother was taken to a hospital and was expected to die, but she survived. During one night she vomited yellow fluid and passed a great deal of blood. For a long time—Grandma does not say how long—Mother wore bandages on her face. When they were removed, Mother felt her face with her fingers, then asked for a cloth mask. Thereafter she would not take off her mask from morning to night.

"At this moment," Grandma writes, "we are preparing to visit Chieko-chan in the hospital." Chieko, four years old in 1949, waited daily for their visit, standing in the hospital corridor, tubes from her wrist attached to a bottle that was hung above her. A small bald-headed girl. She was dying of leukemia.

"There may not be many more days," Grandma concludes.

After this, what could have happened? Did they leave the relatives in Nagasaki? Where and how did they survive?

When Sensei is finished reading, he folds and unfolds the letter, nodding his head slowly.

I put my hands around the teapot, feeling its round warmth against my palms. My skin feels hungry for warmth, for flesh. Grandma mentioned in her letter that she saw one woman cradling a hot-water bottle as if it were a baby.

Sensei places the letter back in the cardboard folder and closes it with the short red string around the tab.

"That there is brokenness," he says quietly. "That this world is brokenness. But within brokenness is the unbreakable name. How the whole earth groans till Love returns."

I stand up abruptly and leave the room, going into the kitchen for some more hot water. When I return, Sensei is sitting with his face in his hands.

Stephen is staring at the floor, his body hunched forward motionless. He glances up at me then looks away swiftly. I sit on a stool beside him and try to concentrate on what is being said. I can hear Aunt Emily telling us about Mother's grave. Then Nakayama-sensei stands and begins to say the Lord's Prayer under his breath. "And forgive us our trespasses – forgive us our trespasses – " he repeats, sighing deeply, "as we forgive others. . . ." He lifts his head, looking upwards. "We are powerless to forgive unless we first are forgiven. It is a high calling my friends – the calling to forgive. But no person, no people is innocent. Therefore we must forgive one another."

I am not thinking of forgiveness. The sound of Sensei's voice grows as indistinct as the hum of distant traffic. Gradually the room grows still and it is as if I am back with Uncle again, listening and listening to the silent earth and the silent sky as I have done all my life.

I close my eyes.

Mother. I am listening. Assist me to hear you.

*   *   *

Silent mother, you do not speak or write. You do not reach through the night to enter morning, but remain in the voicelessness. From the extremity of much dying, the only sound that reaches me now is the sigh of your remembered breath, a wordless word. How shall I attend that speech, Mother, how shall I trace that wave?

You are tide rushing moonward pulling back from the shore. A raft rocks on the surface bobbing in the dark. The water fills with flailing arms that beckon like seaweed on the prow. I sit on the raft begging for a tide to land me safely on the sand but you draw me to the white distance, skyward and away from this blood-drugged earth.

By the time this country opened its pale arms to you, it was too late. First, you could not, then you chose not to come. Now you are gone. Tonight, Aunt Emily has said a missionary found your name on a plaque of the dead. A Canadian maple tree grows there where your name stands. The tree utters its scarlet voice in the air. Prayers bleeding. Its rustling leaves are fingers scratching an empty sky.

There is no date on the memorial stone. There are no photographs ever again. "Do not tell Stephen and Naomi," you say. "I am praying that they may never know."

Martyr Mother, you pilot your powerful voicelessness over the ocean and across the mountain, straight as a missile to our hut on the edge of a sugar-beet field. You wish to protect us with lies, but the camouflage does not hide your cries. Beneath the hiding I am there with you. Silent Mother, lost in the abandoning, you do not share the horror. At first, stumbling and unaware of pain, you open your eyes in the red mist and sheltering a dead child, you flee through the flames. Young Mother at Nagasaki, am I not also there?

In the dark Slocan night, the bright light flares in my dreaming. I hear the screams and feel the mountain breaking. Your long black hair falls and falls into the chasm. My legs are sawn in half. The skin on your face bubbles like lava and melts from your bones. Mother, I see your face. Do not turn aside.

Maypole Mother, I dance with a long paper streamer in my hand. But the words of the May Day song are words of distress. The unknown is a hook that pierces the bone. Thongs hang down in the hot prairie air. Silence attends the long sun dance.

Grandma sits at a low table in a bombed country writing words she does not intend me to hear. "The child," she writes, "is not well." She does not declare her own state of health. The letters take months to reach Grandfather. They take years to reach me. Grandfather gives the letters to Aunt Emily. Aunt Emily sends letters to the Government. The Government makes paper airplanes out of our lives and flies us out the windows. Some people return home. Some do not. War, they all say, is war, and some people survive.

No one knows the exact day that you die. Aunt Emily writes and receives no replies. All that is left is your word, "Do not tell. . . ."

Obasan and Uncle hear your request. They give me no words from you. They hand me old photographs.

You stand on a streetcorner in Vancouver in a straight silky dress and a light black coat. On your head is a wide-brimmed hat with a feather and your black shoes have one strap and a buckle at the side. I stand leaning into you, my dress bulging over my round baby belly. My fat arm clings to your leg. Your skirt hides half my face. Your leg is a tree trunk and I am branch, vine, butterfly. I am joined to your limbs by right of birth, child of your flesh, leaf of your bough.

The tree is a dead tree in the middle of the prairies. I sit on its roots still as a stone. In my dreams, a small child sits with a wound on her knee. The wound on her knee is on the back of

Dazed survivors holding boiled rice balls, about 1.5km from the hypocentre; Nagasaki, 1945.

her skull, large and moist. A double wound. The child is forever unable to speak. The child forever fears to tell. I apply a thick bandage but nothing can soak up the seepage. I beg that the woundedness may be healed and that the limbs may learn to dance. But you stay in a black and white photograph, smiling your yasashi smile.

Gentle Mother, we were lost together in our silences. Our wordlessness was our mutual destruction.

Nakayama-sensei is still praying softly, a long long prayer. "Father, if your suffering is greater than ours, how great that suffering must be," he is saying. "How great the helplessness. How we dare not abandon the ones who suffer, lest we again abandon You." His voice rises and falls as it did when he was praying at Grandma Nakane's funeral in Slocan. "We are abandoned yet we are not abandoned. You are present in every hell. Teach us to see Love's presence in our abandonment. Teach us to forgive."

Obasan's eyes are closed and her hands are moving back and forth across the grey cardboard folder—to erase, to soothe.

I am thinking that for a child there is no presence without flesh. But perhaps it is because I am no longer a child I can know your presence though you are not here. The letters tonight are skeletons. Bones only. But the earth still stirs with dormant blooms. Love flows through the roots of the trees by our graves.

THE AWAKENING

Pro-peace activities in the 1980s have become the most widespread, constructive, and life-affirming movement of all time. The greater the challenge, the greater the joy and determination to which people can be inspired. "If you love this planet," as Helen Caldicott has said, "you are going to have to change the priorities of your life."

What would you do to avoid a nuclear war? If you said "anything," you're in good company. As you will see in the following section, the peace community welcomes new members every day. And there is a level of activity suitable for everyone. Some people support the peace movement by writing cheques to their local groups, and turning out to march in demonstrations. Some risk arrest by participating in civil disobedience, such as withholding tax money or sitting-in at weapons manufacturers; others camp outside nuclear weapons sites, trying to convert the people who work there. Then there are citizens who arrange international civilians' exchanges, meeting the "ordinary" people their governments regard as enemies. Religious people hold vigils, declare their places of worship as nuclear-free zones, and invite their communities to join them. Still other politically-minded folks spend their time writing letters or lobbying their legislators in person.

In this decade, the pacifist movement, rooted in religious and political traditions, has blossomed into a world-wide phenomenon. People from all walks of life, many of whom identify themselves as non-political, have discovered that hopeful action is better than hopeless inaction. Where national governments refused to take the initiative, people at the grass-roots level have taken the responsibility for conducting nuclear freeze referenda, or declaring their own localities to be nuclear-free zones. Where governments have declined to provide information, researchers (in the media, academic, and religious communities) have volunteered to find out and publicize the facts.

Through music, poetry, and painting, artists have declared their love of peace. Through professional organizations, doctors, lawyers, teachers, architects, computer specialists, and scientists have shown that nuclear war is illegal, immoral, irreversible, and unthinkable. Generals and admirals have come forward to say that nuclear warfare is obscene and unwinnable. Through all these voices can be heard the piping voices of children, calling for a safe, healthy, friendly world for their future.

Nine million signatures on peace petitions were delivered to the UN General Secretary in June 1982, attesting to the fervour and popularity with which people world-wide are organizing and linking up. Drawing on the strength earned and the lessons learned in past successful anti-war campaigns, present-day organizers have rallied public opinion against the financial and ethical folly of investing in weapons instead of in human welfare. With only one planet to share, one spaceship earth, people have awakened to their inherent longing to create the most beautiful world possible.

Imagining a world without weapons and without pollution, a world at peace, will be our challenge for the rest of this century. As we move into the millennium, a world government becomes more desirable and feasible. Renewal of spiritual values and research into new ways of resolving conflicts have enhanced the trend towards peaceful co-operation.

Blessed are the peacemakers, for through them, we shall have an earth for our children to inherit.

P.C. and P.K.

Opposite: One million march in New York.

ON THE MOVE FOR PEACE

Gigantic peace marches in the 1980s marked a public sense of renewed urgency about the nuclear issue. Like the marches of the 1950s and 1960s, they focused attention on peoples' concerns for the survival of their children. Unlike the anti-Vietnam marches of the 1970s, these demonstrations were peaceful, often festive. And they attracted more people than ever; in one two-month period, nearly two million people took part in European marches. One million people from around the world marched in New York on June 12, 1982.

Marchers bounce an "Earth Ball" in a 1983 West German demonstration.

Above and opposite: The awakening of millions in Europe, Japan and the United States.

The Great March Begins

In what is being called the largest public demonstration in the history of the United States, hundreds of people jammed Manhattan's East Side – from 46th to 57th Streets between Third and First Avenues – and began a colourful and orderly march to the Great Lawn in Central Park.

The 12 June [1982] event was called "to support the United Nations Special Session on Disarmament and to call for a freeze and reduction of all nuclear weapons and a transfer of military budgets to human needs."

Saturday's event, estimated to have drawn a crowd of at least 750,000, according to official police estimates, and perhaps upwards of one million, according to unofficial estimates, exceeded by several hundred thousand the crowds which gathered in Bonn last fall and in London last week.

The march was led by the Children's Walk for Life, followed by several international contingents, the giant puppets of the Bread and Puppet Theatre, and a variety of groups representing several U.S. States, labor, and ethnic groups.

A large group representing religious organizations – Catholics, Jews, Buddhists, Shintoists, Quakers, and many Protestant denominations – sang "We Shall Overcome" and carried huge banners displaying a quotation from the Bible, "Therefore, Choose Life." . . .

The demonstration was the People – their strength, which is endless as the line of marchers; their spirit, which knows no boundaries of nationality, occupation or age; their numbers, which cannot even be estimated, let alone fixed accurately. . . . Organizers of the event claimed at 3:30 P.M. that 800,000 were inside Central Park and 200,000 were still marching in. If accurate, this total of one million would make this demonstration the largest in world history . . . so far.

This enormous gathering was united by one word, which was also the only word that could characterize all the impressions of the day: Peace.

In some ways, the rally resembled the anti-war demonstrations of the sixties, but a vital difference was the lack of any violence, antagonism toward the police, or factionalism between groups. The long moratorium on popular action during the seventies seemed somehow to have matured the anti-war movement, and what emerged as the lubricant that made this diverse parade move so smoothly was humour.

Wit rather than wrath marked a surprising number of posters. Among many, I noted "Mushrooms belong on pizza." A picture of President Reagan was labeled "the flaw in the theory of evolution."

How strange that the resolution of the apparently insoluble dilemma facing the whole world should make its debut as something light-hearted, like a ray of sunlight shooting through the clouds that dominated the day's sky. The threat of a nuclear holocaust has been called a sword of Damocles hanging over everyone's head. We're all afraid of the 50,000 bombs in the world arsenal.

But fear was first the cause of the arms race before it became the result; fear perpetuates it. Fear is on the side of war, and the answer may simply be the elan that stands up to call the bogeyman's bluff; finally faced, he turns out to be old and wrinkled and helpless.

Disarmament Times

Demonstrators in New York, June 1982.

International Action Against Sea-Launched Cruise

"Disarm the oceans" was the demand on the weekend of June 14-16 [1985] when there were demonstrations in ports in at least 12 countries. June 15 was international day of action against U.S. and Soviet sea-launched Cruise Missiles. Co-ordinated by the Pacific Concerns Resource Centre and the North Atlantic Network, there were actions at many of the home ports for nuclear-armed U.S. ships and letters of protest were sent to Soviet embassies about the SS-N-21 programme.

In Honolulu, people dressed as sea creatures and a giant cockroach ("the only survivor of nuclear war") debated with a mock Reagan, Kissinger and others who favour the militarisation of the seas. Other U.S. cities saw balloon releases, civil disobedience, and a "peace armada" sailed out from San Diego to the Ballast Point Submarine Base. In Japan, the Citizens Campaign Against Deployment of Tomahawk organised a big rally, while in Australia there were actions in Sydney, Melbourne, Fremantle and Darwin. In Fremantle, while gagged and bound demonstrators held a silent vigil at the quayside, two people on a peace yacht boarded the U.S. aircraft carrier *Carl Vinson* with a letter asking questions about the ship. They were escorted off at gunpoint.

War Resisters' International Newsletter

In October 1983, demonstrations brought an estimated two million Europeans out to protest deployment of new NATO *missiles. These are marchers in London.*

The White Train

Nearly 100 people, standing in sub-freezing temperatures at 3:30 A.M in Cheyenne, Wyoming, pelted the train with flowers as it rushed by in the dark. About eight hours later, in Nampa, Idaho, seven protesters were arrested for attempting to block the train's passage. Farther up the line, in Portland, Oregon, 33 of some 175 protesters were booked for blocking the tracks – and stopping the train – for two-and-a-half hours. And in Bangor, Washington, 250 demonstrators welcomed the train to its last stop with signs of protest, singing, and prayers. Nine people, including two priests and a nun, were arrested for kneeling on the tracks in front of the Trident submarine base.

These were just a few of the demonstrations that dogged the latest journey of the train that carries nuclear warheads from the Pantex plant in Amarillo, Texas, where they are assembled, to nuclear weapons installations across the country. With cars painted white to keep their cargo cool, the so-called "white train" moved unchallenged through U.S. cities and towns for two decades. It wasn't until December 8, 1982, that the train was stripped of its anonymity by Jim and Shelley Douglass, founders of the Ground Zero Center for Nonviolent Action in Poulsbo, Washington. Their house, perched alongside the tracks, sits just 200 feet from the gate of the Trident submarine base.

On that December day, the Douglasses, who had recently moved into their house, got a tip about the white train from a reporter. "We went outside, and there it was," says Shelley Douglass. "It was horrifying – as if something from *Star Wars* had landed in our yard." With its turreted, armored cars, the train is an unnerving sight. "Imagine this eerie white thing emerging from the darkness and plowing right by you," says Nat Pierce, one of the seven arrested in Idaho. "It's like a Bergman movie."

Since that first spotting, the "tracks campaign" has grown to embrace 300 communities (called the Agape Community) across the country. "We have an extensive phone chain of people who are willing to jump out of bed at 2 A.M. to witness the train's passage," says Kate Boyers in Salt Lake City, Utah. Members of the network are responsible for calling ahead to activists in towns down the line, so that a chain of demonstrations and vigils is forged along the tracks.

Nuclear Times

Another glimpse of the 1983 European marches; this one in Ulm, West Germany.

The Nordic Peace March, 1982

Why should three hundred people, most of them women, spend the best part of their summer holiday marching 3,000 miles, from Stockholm to Minsk?

The answer goes back to last summer, when a group of Scandinavian women had the idea for a Peace March from Copenhagen to Paris. Critics then said: "Why are you marching in the West? You should be going to Moscow." This was the start of Peace March '82, organised by Women for Peace from Scandinavia, a three-week-long journey by foot, boat and train from Stockholm to Minsk.

This was an historical occasion. The first time the slogans "No to Nuclear Weapons in Europe, East and West," "No to Nuclear Weapons in the World" and "Yes, to Disarmament and Peace" would be carried by West Europeans in Russia.

"The main idea behind the march," said Eva Nordland, one of the chief organisers, "is that we are marching against the suicide weapons to raise the consciousness in ourselves and everyone else of the need to fight against destruction. We are *not* against NATO *or* the Warsaw Pact."

This message was not a difficult one to put across to the Russian people. During the marches through Leningrad, Moscow and Minsk many women watching cried. The memory of twenty million dead in World War II is still very close to their hearts and there is a real fear of another war – and of the United States.

Altogether the march left a cobweb of impressions. Spontaneous meetings with Russian people in Leningrad. Short marches and tight security in Moscow. Much singing and dancing in Minsk, all accompanied by a tight schedule of sightseeing and factory visits.

There were frustrations but the march was a success as it held out a hand of friendship with no strings attached. Above all, it showed once again the leading role women are playing in the struggle for peace and disarmament.

Danielle Grünberg

Feminists march in Italy, bearing the banner of the Comiso peace camp.

The Peace Ribbon

The idea came to Justine Merritt, a former high school teacher from Denver, following a religious retreat three years ago. Deeply troubled that the threat of nuclear war cast a long shadow over the future for her seven grandchildren, Merritt had a brainstorm. Why not wrap a huge embroidered ribbon around the Pentagon? "It will be just like tying a ribbon around your finger," Merritt told herself. "It will serve as a gentle reminder that we love the earth and its people."

Though she had no money to finance the project (indeed she is impoverished and lives in a bare, two-room walk-up apartment), Merritt was undeterred. She quickly sent a note to people on her Christmas mailing list asking each of them to make a yard-long tapestry for the Pentagon Ribbon based on a universal theme: "What I cannot bear to think of as lost in a nuclear war." In addition everyone was asked to dig out their own Christmas lists and to encourage all their friends to participate as well. Within months a sizable army of volunteers had been mustered. Then miraculously the numbers of would-be artists and just-plain-folks inspired by Merritt's simple plea for peace continued to grow and grow at an exponential rate. . . .

While giving voice to a political message of hope rather than anger, the event also unveiled perhaps the most ambitious needlework project ever seen. Many of the Pentagon Ribbon's individual panels (most measure 36 by 18 inches) have been embroidered; others have been silk-screened, tie-dyed, painted, quilted or appliquéd. Home, family, pets and friends are recurrent subjects of the artwork, as is the word "peace," which appears in several languages. One panel which features a huge cockroach with rhinestone eyes and corduroy wings poses the question: "Will they be the only survivors?"

David Grogan and David Chandler

Demonstration co-ordinator Jennifer Weiss and her sleeping son, ready to wrap the Peace Ribbon around the Pentagon.

THE PACIFIST CONSCIENCE

The Law of Love

The law of love will work, just as the law of gravitation will work, whether we accept it or not. Just as the scientist will work wonders out of various applications of the law of nature, even so a man who applies the law of love with scientific precision can work greater wonders. For the force of nonviolence is infinitely more wonderful and subtle than the material forces of nature, like, for instance, electricity. The men who discovered for us the law of love were greater scientists than any of our modern scientists. Only our explorations have not gone far enough and so it is not possible for everyone to see all its workings. Such, at any rate, is the hallucination, if it is one, under which I am laboring. The more I work at this law the more I feel the delight in life, the delight in the scheme of this universe. It gives me a peace and a meaning of the mysteries of nature that I have no power to describe.

Mahatma Gandhi (1869-1948)

A South African Resister

Whatever I was doing in my life I wanted to reflect my Christianity. In considering the issue of military service, which is obligatory in South Africa for men, I had to consider it in the light of Christian faith. Just in seeing who Jesus Christ is, someone absolutely gentle and caring and life-giving, you come to ask a simple question: Would he, if he received military call-up papers, go and do military service? My conclusion was that he wouldn't. . . .

I object to *all* military training. The only way a soldier can be effective is to deny the humanity of his opponent: he is a terrorist, a fascist, a nazi, a communist, a racist – whatever word in a given context that makes him better dead than alive. An object. You cannot

Mahatma Gandhi in a portrait taken after his release from prison in 1931.

afford to think of that person as a husband, father, brother, uncle. You consciously repress any sense of connection, and in de-humanizing the other, you lessen your own humanity as well. Military training relies on this process of repression, seeks to obliterate individual identity and to introduce unquestioning obedience without consideration of generally accepted moral values of not killing or desecrating another person.

Richard Steele

Resisters in America's History

Historians have long emphasized the importance of wars in United States history, yet war resistance has been virtually unmentioned, not only in our public schools but even in colleges and universities. Despite the omission of such material in the traditional accounts of our national past, war resistance has a history. . . .

None of the wars in which we have participated has received the support of all Americans. Three of them – the War of 1812, the Mexican War and the Vietnam War – aroused widespread and open dissent which eventually influenced some members of Congress. . . .Moreover, many of the anti-war actions used during the Vietnam era had their counterparts in the past. . . .

John Woolman, for example, was one of a number of Friends who refused to pay taxes levied for the Indian Wars in 1757, although the majority of Quakers paid the tax without qualms. Woolman's own comment summarized the problem: "To refuse the active payment of a Tax which our Society generally paid was exceedingly disagreeable," he wrote, "but to do a thing contrary to my Conscience appeared yet more dreadfull. . . ."

The best known selective conscientious objector in the Mexican War, and probably in all our history, was Henry David Thoreau. Since Thoreau viewed slavery as an unmitigated evil he rejected the war and refused to pay the tax levied to support it. His one night in Concord jail was probably the most influential single night of imprisonment in modern history. Out of it came the famous essay "Civil Disobedience" which profoundly influenced such men as Tolstoy, Gandhi and Martin Luther King, Jr. His essay is an impassioned plea for moral commitment in the face of injustice, and a justification for opposing the state when law and conscience conflict. "There will never be a really free and enlightened State," he said, "until the State comes to recognize the individual as a higher and independent power, from which all its own power and authority are derived, and treats him accordingly." As for the punishment which might befall those who accepted

Thoreau's challenge he wrote, "Under a government which imprisons any unjustly, the true place for a just man is also a prison. . . ."

The Oneida and Hopedale communities also had strong anti-war overtones. Along with traditional marriage and private property, John Humphrey Noyes, founder and guiding spirit of the Oneida Community, rejected war. Noyes and his followers were Christian Perfectionists, practicing what they called Bible Communism in their model for the perfect society. Oneida lasted from 1848 until 1878, and all of its male members refused to fight during the Civil War. A collision between the Oneida communitarians and the government was avoided because of a confusion of official records specifying the draft district in which they were located. Hopedale's founder, Adin Ballou, was a leading spirit in the New England Non-Resistance Society and author of an important work, *Christian Non-Resistance*. A working model for a society without war was also a part of the vision of other utopian communists in the nineteenth century. . . .

One of the reforms which war resisters have recently emphasized is the elimination of conscription from our national life. This, too, is an aspect of contemporary war resistance with a long history. In the early years of the Republic many Americans feared a national standing army as a potential handmaiden of tyranny. Nevertheless, provision for such an army was included in the United States Constitution, but the reference was to a volunteer, not a conscript army, and in practice it was a very small affair. The idea of conscription was anathema to most Americans.

Although the Civil War draft was more an inducement to volunteering than a well-devised structure for raising an army of conscripts, reaction to it was swift and extreme. Draft riots broke out in various cities, the most serious in New York where for three days in July of 1863 a mob battled the police, attacked Black people and burned homes and other buildings, including an orphanage for Black youth. Before order returned to the city more than a

thousand had been killed or wounded in the riots. These disturbances illustrate the deep and traditional dislike that Americans of the mid-nineteenth century had for the idea of conscription, even when it was applied during the most serious crisis in our national history. . . .

Draft resistance was frequently motivated by conscience and carried out on an individual basis. During the war in Vietnam, however, such resistance was organized, characterized by such actions as public draft card burnings and support actions for those arrested for refusal to be drafted. Those actions were sometimes viewed as part of an ambitious program for change referred to as The Movement. Although the idea of a movement was fuzzily defined and virtually non-existent in any formal sense, it did serve to provide a sense of identity for the objectors of that time. It was an extension of the peace movement concept. The fact is that since the early 19th century there have been American organizations dedicated specifically to the abolition of war, although the members of such groups frequently were involved in other reform movements as well.

Larry Gara

A 1972 demonstration protesting the Vietnam War.

Probably the first recorded successful anti-war campaign was the Greek women's protest, led by Lysistrata, as recounted in the play by Aristophanes, first performed in Athens in 411 B.C. Here, an illustration by Norman Lindsay, circa 1926.

Not Killing Is a Crime?

Because it was a Federal jail, West Street held few murderers. The only killers were men convicted of some Federal offense in addition. A famous inmate was Louis Lepke, then sought by New York authorities for the chair at Sing Sing. In West Street he was well liked because he was friendly with other inmates and told nothing to the authorities. That is what counts in jail. What a man was sentenced for is almost immaterial. Unless an inmate talks about his case you do not question him.

Next to Lepke's cell at one time was a young [conscientious objector] from Iowa, Lowell Naeve. He tried to explain to Lepke what a [conscientious objector] was, but the gangster had trouble understanding. "You mean they put you in here for *not* killing?" Lepke finally exclaimed – and he laughed and laughed.

James Peck

Aldous Huxley to Leonard Woolf

Dear Leonard,

Thank you for the pamphlet. I think you mis-state the pacifist position. The pacifist doesn't behave like an ostrich and say he will "have nothing to do with evil". He examines the evil and asks what is the best way of dealing with it. To this question experience gives a clear answer: the worst way of dealing with one evil is to do another evil, or to threaten another evil. Making threats of war doesn't prevent people from making aggressions—merely stimulates them to build up their own armaments. And the results of war are always identical, however good the intentions of the war makers and however "collective" their actions: people are slaughtered and a passionate sense of wrong and desire for vengeance are created in the survivors—feelings which make yet further wars inevitable. What you say of albatrosses is profoundly true. All evil acts have their consequences. Acts of generous reparation can neutralize the effects of evil acts—witness our policy in S. Africa after the Boer War. What the pacifist suggests is the eminently reasonable course of using intelligent generosity to begin with—rather than waiting to use it till the evil act has been committed. In the present circumstances this policy expresses itself in the pacifist proposal to call a conference at which the dissatisfied powers [would] be asked to express their grievances. An honest attempt on the part of the satisfied to find out how many of these grievances [could] be met and in what way might have a chance of securing peace. Banding together in military alliances for protective security will certainly not achieve this end. The other, pacifist way may not succeed; but on the other hand it might. And if it succeeded only partially, the international atmosphere [would] be cleared and a chance given for the reconstruction of the League on a more satisfactory basis.

Yours
Aldous H.

A Choice of Utopias

What with the general fear of a war now being prepared by all nations and the specific fear of murderous ideologies, who can deny that we live in a state of terror? We live in terror because persuasion is no longer possible; because man has been wholly submerged in History; because he can no longer tap that part of his nature, as real as the historical part, which he recaptures in contemplating the beauty of nature and of human faces; because we live in a world of abstractions, of bureaus and machines, of absolute ideas and of crude messianism. We suffocate among people who think they are absolutely right, whether in their machines or in their ideas. And for all who can live only in an atmosphere of human dialogue and sociability, this silence is the end of the world. . . .

To come to terms, one must understand what fear means: what it implies and what it rejects. It implies and rejects the same fact: a world where murder is legitimate, and where human life is considered trifling. This is the great political question of our times, and before dealing with other issues, one must take a position on it. Before anything can be done, two questions must be put: "Do you or do you not, directly or indirectly, want to be killed or assaulted? Do you or do you not, directly or indirectly, want to kill or assault?" All who say No to both these questions are automatically committed to a series of consequences which must modify their way of posing the problem. . . .

Let us, then, admit that our refusal to legitimize murder forces us to reconsider our whole idea of Utopia. This much seems clear: Utopia is whatever is in contradiction with reality. From this standpoint, it would be completely Utopian to wish that men should no longer kill each other. That would be absolute Utopia. But a much sounder Utopia is that which insists that murder be no longer legitimized. Indeed, the Marxian and the capitalist ideologies, both based on the idea of progress, both certain that the application of their principles must inevitably bring about a harmonious society, are Utopian to a much greater degree. Furthermore, they are both at the moment costing us dearly.

We may therefore conclude, practically, that in the next few years the struggle will be not between the forces of Utopia and the forces of reality, but between the different Utopias which are attempting to be born into reality. It will be simply a matter of choosing the least costly among them. I am convinced that we can no longer reasonably hope to save everything, but that we can at least propose to save our skins, so that *a* future, if not *the* future, remains a possibility. . . .

We know today that there are no more islands, that frontiers are just lines on a map. We know that in a steadily accelerating world, where the Atlantic is crossed in less than a day and Moscow speaks to Washington in a few minutes, we are forced into fraternity—or complicity. The forties have taught us that an injury done a student in Prague strikes down simultaneously a worker in Clichy, that blood shed on the banks of a Central European river brings a Texas farmer to spill his own blood in the Ardennes, which he sees for the first time. There is no suffering, no torture anywhere in the world which does not affect our everyday lives. . . .

To conclude: all I ask is that, in the midst of a murderous world, we agree to reflect on murder and to make a choice. After that, we can distinguish those who accept the consequences of being murderers themselves or the accomplices of murderers, and those who refuse to do so with all their force and being. Since this terrible dividing line does actually exist, it will be a gain if it be clearly marked. Over the expanse of five continents throughout the coming years an endless struggle is going to be pursued between violence and friendly persuasion, a struggle in which, granted, the former has a thousand times the chances of success than that of the latter. But I have always held that, if he who bases his hopes on human nature is a fool, he who gives up in the face of circumstances is a coward. And henceforth, the only honorable course will be to stake everything on a formidable gamble: that words are more powerful than munitions.

Albert Camus (1913-1960)

Conscientious Objector

I shall die, but that is all that I shall do for Death.
I hear him leading his horse out of the stall; I hear the clatter on the barn-floor.
He is in haste; he has business in Cuba, business in the Balkans, many
     calls to make this morning.
But I will not hold the bridle while he cinches the girth.
And he may mount by himself: I will not give him a leg up.

Though he flick my shoulders with his whip, I will not tell him which
     way the fox ran.
With his hoof on my breast, I will not tell him where the black boy
     hides in the swamp.
I shall die, but that is all that I shall do for Death; I am not on his pay-roll.

I will not tell him the whereabouts of my friends nor of my enemies
     either.
Though he promise me much, I will not map him the route to any man's door.
Am I a spy in the land of the living, that I should deliver men to Death?
Brother, the password and the plans of our city are safe with me; never through me
Shall you be overcome.

Edna St. Vincent Millay (1892-1950)

CIVIL DISOBEDIENCE

The Most Glorious State

The authority of government, even such as I am willing to submit to – for I will cheerfully obey those who know and can do better than I, and in many things even those who neither know nor can do so well – is still an impure one: to be strictly just, it must have the sanction and consent of the governed. It can have no pure right over my person and property but what I concede to it. The progress from an absolute to a limited monarchy, from a limited monarchy to a democracy, is a progress toward a true respect for the individual. Even the Chinese philosopher was wise enough to regard the individual as the basis of the empire. Is a democracy, such as we know it, the last improvement possible in government? Is it not possible to take a step further towards recognizing and organizing the rights of man? There will never be a really free and enlightened State, until the State comes to recognize the individual as a higher and independent power, from which all its own power and authority are derived, and treats him accordingly. I please myself with imagining a State at last which can afford to be just to all men, and to treat the individual with respect as a neighbor; which even would not think it inconsistent with its own repose, if a few were to live aloof from it, not meddling with it, nor embraced by it, who fulfilled all the duties of neighbors and fellow-men. A State which bore this kind of fruit, and suffered it to drop off as fast as it ripened, would prepare the way for a still more perfect and glorious State, which also I have imagined, but not yet anywhere seen.

Henry David Thoreau (1817-1862)

Mike Nolan sits atop an American nuclear submarine to protest its being stationed at the Holy Loch, Scotland; March 1961.

When and How to Disobey

Any movement which seeks to stop the arms race and achieve disarmament must be prepared to incorporate a variety of tactics. Civil disobedience is one such tactic. But more important, civil disobedience will *dramatize* our firm commitment to disarmament. A movement serious about making fundamental change must be willing to take risks. But the minor risks involved in our arrest and possible imprisonment are far less than the risks involved in allowing the arms race to continue. To paraphrase Daniel Ellsberg, "Wouldn't you go to jail if it would help end war?"

There have been thousands of international disarmament meetings. We have made countless appeals, sent petitions, gone to rallies, walked on marches, spoken at meetings, participated in pickets and boycotts, written letters to newspaper editors – for decades. Yet, not one single bomb has been dismantled (without several more "improved" ones to take its place). . . .

We must go beyond appeals to reason. The time has come to raise the stakes of our struggle against the arms race, and to accelerate pressure on those who continue to justify the existence of *any* nuclear weapons. We will no longer passively accept any more excuses, justifications, distortion, or lies. We seek to disrupt "diplomacy as usual" through mass nonviolent direct action. In this way the governments cannot ignore our presence and our demands.

*   *   *

Civil disobedience is not always warranted or appropriate. What follows are four instances of when civil disobedience is appropriate: 1) in an escalating sequence of a campaign when other less drastic measures have been exhausted; 2) a personal "witness" to an injustice, such as Thoreau's tax resistance or Rosa Parks' violation of the bus segregation law; 3) confronting a sudden injustice or wrong, such as the 1970 invasion of Cambodia; 4) dramatizing a national or international issue (*e.g.*, the escalating arms race) to arouse public concern.

Many people misunderstand nonviolence as everything which is not violent and as basically passive. Most movement people are able to see beyond this, but fall into the misconception of nonviolence being simply a set of tactics.

To maximize effectiveness nonviolence must involve a spirit and an attitude which transcends concepts of vindication, enemy, and harassment. Nonviolence is dependent on reason, imagination, and discipline. Winning should not be in terms of victory by one side over another, but victory over injustice. . . .

In his book *The Politics of Nonviolent Action*, Gene Sharp has categorized 198 methods of nonviolent action, which can be broken into three main types:
1) protest and persuasion (e.g., leaflets, pickets, vigils, marches, teach-ins)
2) noncooperation
   —social (e.g., social boycott, student strike, suspension of social activities)
   —economic (e.g., strikes, tax resistance, boycotts)
   —political (e.g., boycott of elections, civil disobedience of bad laws, draft resistance)
3) intervention (e.g., sit-ins, occupations, alternative economic institutions, civil disobedience of neutral laws, obstruction).

Civil Disobedience Campaign Handbook

Action Is Eloquence

My friend Bill Huntington and I are planning to sail a small vessel westward into the Pacific H-bomb test area. By April [1958] we expect to reach nuclear testing grounds at Eniwetok. We will remain there as long as the tests of H-bombs continue. With us will be two other volunteers.

Why? Because it is the way I can say to my government, to the British government, and to the Kremlin: "Stop! Stop this madness before it is too late. For God's sake, turn back!"

I am going because, as Shakespeare said, "Action is eloquence." Without some such direct action, ordinary citizens lack the power any longer to be seen or heard by their government.

I am going because it is time to *do something* about peace, not just *talk* about peace.

I am going because, like all men, in my heart I know that *all* nuclear explosions are monstrous, evil, unworthy of human beings.

I am going because war is no longer a feudal jousting match; it is an unthinkable catastrophe for all men.

I am going because it is now the little children, and, most of all, the as yet unborn who are the front line troops. It is my duty to stand between them and this horrible danger.

I am going because it is cowardly and degrading for me to stand by any longer, to consent, and thus to collaborate in atrocities.

I am going because I cannot say that the end justifies the means. A Quaker, William Penn, said, "A good end cannot sanctify evil means; nor must we ever do evil that good may come of it." A Communist, Milovan Djilas, says, "As soon as means which would ensure an end are shown to be evil, the end will show itself as unrealizable."

I am going because, as Gandhi said, "God sits in the man opposite me; therefore to injure him is to injure God himself."

I am going to witness to the deep inward truth we all know, "Force can subdue, but love gains."

I am going because however mistaken, unrighteous, and unrepentant governments may seem, I still believe all men are really good at heart, and that my act will speak to them.

I am going in the hope of helping change the hearts and minds of men in government. If necessary I am willing to give my life to help change a policy of fear, force, and destruction to one of trust, kindness, and help.

I am going in order to say, "Quit this waste, this arms race. Turn instead to a disarmament race. Stop competing for evil, compete for good."

I am going because I have to – if I am to call myself a human being.

When you see something horrible happening, your instinct is to do something about it. You can freeze in fearful apathy or you can even talk yourself into saying that it isn't horrible. I can't do that. I have to act. This is too horrible. We know it. Let's all act.

Albert Bigelow, captain, The Golden Rule

Brave Men Do Not Hide

Friday – April 28th [1961] – is the day for the "Civil Defense Alert." At 4 P.M. in the afternoon the sirens will whine. The law says every citizen in New York must hide in doorways, basements or subway stations during this drill. Civil Defense officials tell us that if we hide we can survive an atomic bomb.

This is not true. Our best scientists have warned us that if a hydrogen bomb falls on New York City there will be nothing left. Even those in the deepest basements will be destroyed by blast, by radiation, and by fire. **There is no defense and no shelter against the bomb**.

It is easy, when the sirens whine, to run down into a basement or cower in a doorway. But that will not protect your child. It will not save your family. Brave men do not hide from danger. They face the danger openly and fight against it. The greatest danger now is war. The real defense against hydrogen bombs is peace.

The men who plan Civil Defense are good men but they threaten the safety of America because they are trying to convince us we can survive another war. **We cannot survive another war**. We will find our safety in disarmament, not in basements. We appeal to the Civil Defense Officials to stop playing children's games. We appeal to them to act like grown men and to speak the truth to the citizens of New York. And we appeal to you to think carefully before you take "shelter" on Friday, April 28th.

Many of us handing out this leaflet will not hide when the sirens whine this Friday. We will gather quietly in City Hall Park and we will remain there until the police come and order us to take shelter. Last year one thousand persons gathered in City Hall Park to silently protest the madness of "Civil Defense."

When the sirens blow,
1. Some of us will distribute this leaflet in "shelters" during the air-raid drill.
2. Others will sit openly in City Hall Park knowing we are as safe there as anywhere in the city. When the police formally order us to take shelter we will do so under protest.
3. There will be many of us who will refuse to take shelter at all, even under police order.

We know that "Civil Defense" cannot defend us. We know the real job is peace – finding ways to defend freedom without using hydrogen bombs. For the hydrogen bombs can destroy all men and all freedom. On that issue we shall not run, we shall not hide. We shall stand quietly together in City Hall Park. We invite you to stand there with us.

Leaflet from the
Civil Defense Protest Committee

"It's an American Thing to Do"

Arrested for civil disobedience, anti-nuclear demonstrators are released from prison in Santa Rita, California; June 1983.

Offering daisies to policemen or chanting prayers for peace, more than 1,600 nonviolent demonstrators for disarmament were arrested in midtown Manhattan yesterday as they tried to block the entrances of the United Nations missions of five countries that have atomic weapons.

In an assembly-line operation that began at 7:30 A.M., the police carried the unresisting demonstrators to rented city buses to be booked for disorderly conduct. Some who had been arrested in the morning were back later in the day, encouraging their friends or sitting down again for another arrest.

The Police Department, which had 3,000 extra officers at the demonstration sites, said the total booked was a record for a civil disobedience campaign in the city. . . .

The demonstrations, rehearsed beforehand by the participants and prepared for by the police, were a continuation of Saturday's protest, which brought more than 500,000 people to midtown Manhattan and Central Park for a disarmament march and rally. The planners, the June 14 Civil Disobedience Campaign, were an outgrowth of the June 12 Committee that organized the rally. Both embrace religious, peace and community groups.

"I think the time has come, especially for religious people, to consider breaking the human law in favour of a higher law," said the Rev. Paul Mayer, a teacher at New York Theological Seminary, who was arrested outside the Soviet Mission. "I think we're following a good tradition – Gandhi, King, Jesus, Thoreau. It's an American thing to do. . . ."

Most of those arrested were given summonses returnable at a later date. Such cases are usually adjourned without penalty when the defendant appears, although technically the maximum penalty is 15 days in jail or a $250 fine. The police said 134 of those arrested refused to identify themselves and were fingerprinted and arraigned, with most then getting conditional discharges. More than 20 people who refused to be fingerprinted were ordered held. . . .

The main body of demonstrators began assembling near the missions before 7 A.M., greeting one another in the overcast dawn. The organizers had divided them into "affinity groups" of a dozen or so and the groups had had a four-hour training course in nonviolence.

In the training, participants were asked to pretend to be policemen to feel what it was like. The organizers had also had several meetings last week with the police to discuss procedures.

The affinity groups gathered at selected sites, arms around each other's shoulders. Some prayed, some discussed tactics or synchronized watches. The police had erected lines of barricades around the missions, and the masses of extra forces, many in slickers and helmets, were lined up in rows. Buses, rented from the Transit Authority for $250 each for the day, were in rows, and there were piles of stretchers to carry off those unwilling to walk. . . .

All except James D. Peck, a veteran of nearly 50 years of peace and civil-rights activism, refused to walk to the waiting bus and were carried on stretchers. Mr. Peck, who is 67 years old, said it was his 59th arrest; he walked off with his fingers in a V for peace. . . .

The mood was generally good-humored. On one corner, an affinity group sang "We Shall Overcome" while a squad of policemen waiting in one of the buses sang "God Bless America."

Paul L. Montgomery

The Peace Tax Fund

Dear Friends in Conscience:

Over the past six years, the Peace Tax Fund concept has moved from being the dream of a small group of people in Victoria, to a dynamic concept which is gathering strength across Canada, as it has in many other countries. In 1982, our new Constitution guaranteed certain rights and freedoms. For the first time, freedom of conscience was guaranteed.

We understand this to mean that every person has the right to live according to conscience. It means, for those who object to killing on religious or other ethical grounds, a legal alternative should be provided to supporting war, in the military or through taxes.

We have moved from concept to principle in law. But Parliament has left it to the courts to interpret the guarantees in practice. And the cost of taking one test case all the way to the Supreme Court, if necessary, is estimated at $255,000. It is a lot of money, but only a fraction of our military-related spending, which will amount to some $12 billion in 1984-85.

Already, in 1982 and 1983, more than 200 taxpayers from coast to coast have directed their military-related taxes to a trust account, to be held until an official peace fund or equivalent is established. This will only happen if we are able to carry the test case forward, successfully.

For this reason, we ask you to give as generously as you can, to help secure your freedom of conscience in practice. You will then be able to direct your taxes to peace education, research, removing the causes of war and building a more peaceful world, instead of contributing to the possible extinction of life on earth.

Help Conscience Canada Inc. to secure a legal alternative to paying for war.

Help to make your right a reality.

Yours for peace,
Edith Adamson, Coordinator

Love's Power

You may well ask, "Why direct action? Why sit-ins, marches, etc.? Isn't negotiation a better path?" You are exactly right in your call for negotiation. Indeed, this is the purpose of direct action. Nonviolent direct action seeks to create such a crisis and establish such creative tension that a community that has constantly refused to negotiate is forced to confront the issue. It seeks so to dramatize the issue that it can no longer be ignored. I just referred to the creation of tension as a part of the work of the nonviolent resister. This may sound rather shocking. But I must confess that I am not afraid of the word tension. I have earnestly worked and preached against violent tension, but there is a type of constructive nonviolent tension that is necessary for growth. Just as Socrates felt that it was necessary to create a tension in the mind so that individuals could rise from the bondage of myths and halftruths to the unfettered realm of creative analysis and objective appraisal, we must see the need of having nonviolent gadflies to create the kind of tension in society that will help men to rise from the dark depths of prejudice and racism to the majestic heights of understanding and brotherhood. So the purpose of the direct action is to create a situation so crisis-packed that it will inevitably open the door to negotiation.

*   *   *

To our most bitter opponents we say: "We shall match your capacity to inflict suffering by our capacity to endure suffering. We shall meet your physical force with soul force. Do to us what you will, and we shall continue to love you. We cannot in all good conscience obey your unjust laws, because noncooperation with evil is as much a moral obligation as is cooperation with good. Throw us in jail, and we shall still love you. Bomb our homes and threaten our children, and we shall still love you. Send your hooded perpetrators of violence into our community at the midnight hour and beat us and leave us half dead, and we shall still love you. But be ye assured that we will wear you down by our capacity to suffer. One day we shall win freedom, but not only for ourselves. We shall so appeal to your heart and conscience that we shall win *you* in the process, and our victory will be a double victory."

Martin Luther King (1929-1968)

Dr. Martin Luther King leads a civil rights march in Selma, Alabama in 1965.

PEACEFUL SIEGE

Peace Camps: A Worldwide Phenomenon

On August 27, 1981, a group of English and Welsh women and children marched 125 miles from Cardiff, Wales, to the U.S. air force base at Greenham Common, England, where Cruise missiles – NATO's new nuclear weapons – were due to be deployed. The women then refused to leave the grounds outside the entrance to the base, pitched their tents, and vowed to stay until the deployment plan was scrapped. That was the start of the first "women's peace camp."

Other protesters have "camped" to make their point – one of the most memorable was Resurrection City, in Washington, D.C., erected by civil rights activists in the 1960s. And in 1980, several hundred women and men in Gorleben, West Germany, set up an "environmental" camp on the proposed site of a nuclear waste recycling factory, staying until plans for the factory were abandoned.

What distinguishes Greenham from Gorleben, however, is the focus on militarism from a woman's point of view, and an analysis of the common effect of a military-based economy on women's lives worldwide.

Greenham Common

Since 1979, the U.S. air force base at Greenham Common has been scheduled to receive some 96 Cruise missiles, part of a NATO force. Since 1981, women have lived outside the base entrance, and conducted a series of direct protest actions: the takeover of a guard sentry box inside the base and subsequent arrest; a sit-in at Parliament that forced an open debate of the Cruise issue; various "raids" of the base, one that publicly exposed nuclear missile silos previously hidden and denied by the U.S. military. On December 12, 1982, 30,000 women, men, and children from all over Western Europe linked arms to completely "embrace" the base; many women participated in a mass civil disobedience the next day.

Despite continuous legal battles with local British authorities, the Greenham protest has endured. Perhaps the best indicator of its success is the public's opinion: a national poll in January, 1983 showed that more than 60 percent of Britons opposed deployment of Cruise and Pershing missiles; some credited their view to the actions of the Greenham women. . . .

Comiso

On March 6 of 1983, 100 women, some from a collective in Catania (in southeastern Sicily), others from Western Europe and the United States, began a sit-in protest for peace at the Magliocco airport, where 112 Cruise missiles are due to arrive starting this month [August, 1983]. Two days later, 600 other women marched to the U.S. military base in Sigonella, where some 1,500 U.S. technicians and soldiers work. Many women were brutally arrested and 13 were jailed for a week; 12 Western European women were expelled from the country without trial. Later, police destroyed the tents at one of the camps. Undaunted, protesters (both men and women) continue to camp at Comiso, pursuing their cause in the courts, on the streets, and at the base. In early August, police clashed with protesters at a mass demonstration, injuring 70 people, including four members of the Italian Parliament.

Seneca

The Women's Encampment for a Future of Peace and Justice is located on 53 acres of farmland in upstate Romulus, New York, and borders on the Seneca Army Depot, a storage site for the neutron bomb, and a trans-shipment point for Pershing II missiles. More than 500 women, most from the northeastern U.S., participated in the opening of the camp on July 4 [1983], and during the summer protests continued with candlelight vigils, leafletting, sleep-ins at the depot gates, blockades, and several sit-ins at the depot. On August 1, more than 3,000 women demonstrated to protest deployment; more than 250 scaled the depot fence in a mass civil disobedience. First offenders were "banned and barred" from reentering the depot; second offenders were tried and fined for trespassing. From 15 to 20 women were at the camp on a regular basis through October.

Puget Sound

More than 500 women gathered at the Puget Sound Women's Peace Camp in Kent, Washington, on June 18 [1983] to protest activities at the Boeing Space Center. Currently, 40 Cruise missiles a month are built, and Boeing hopes to complete 1,829 Cruise missiles by late 1985. Despite initial opposition, city authorities agreed to rent city property near the center for the campsite.

Elsewhere

Other women's and mixed peace camps have taken place outside of West Berlin (for two weeks), in Scotland, Northern Germany, Norway, and Sweden. Recently [summer, 1983], women organized a peace camp outside the Davis Monthan Air Force Base in Tucson, Arizona, where battalions are training to accompany Cruise missiles to Europe. Women are also camping at Clam Lake in Madison, Wisconsin, to protest the Navy's Extra Low Frequency (ELF) Project (a new communications system), and at the Savannah River Plutonium Production Plant in Aikens, South Carolina.

While stopping deployment is at the heart of the peace camps, the development of the camps themselves and of the concept of a women's community based on a philosophy of feminism and peace are also important. Church- and peace-group women, radical lesbians, women of color, mothers and grandmothers from all countries and cultures – for each woman, the camp represents her concerns and lifestyle. Quoting Virginia Woolf, a statement from Puget Sound sums it up: "As a woman, I have no country; as a woman, my country is the world."

Anne-Christine D'Adesky

The Clash at Comiso

Women from Italy, Holland, Denmark, Switzerland, West Germany, Britain, Ireland, and the U.S.A. gathered in Comiso [Italy], to celebrate International Women's day and to express their determined opposition to the increasing militarisation of our continent and to the deployment of Cruise missiles. The events began on 6th March [1983] with a march against sexual violence through the streets of the town and although there was limited support from the women of Comiso, a great many Sicilian women from nearby towns were present. . . .

The following day local women joined debates about how to break down the even greater wall of silence created around issues concerning the construction of the missile base. The morning after these debates, on March 8th, 70 women symbolically blockaded the entrance to the base, spinning a web of wool and singing in Sicilian, Italian, English, German and Dutch. Having gained strength from this action, the same women joined by coachloads from other Sicilian towns, marched through the streets of Comiso that afternoon. The Comiso women were singing and calling to others standing on the pavement or watching from windows and balconies. Many joined us along the march and when we arrived in the main square our number had increased to about 700.

Later that evening a local woman told us, "After these few days together we women of Comiso feel much stronger and better able to convince other women to join us." Nearly all the women participated as individuals and felt personally involved, "We are all beginning to realize that we just cannot delegate such important matters – we have a responsibility for our own lives and those of our children." "We can't leave our future to the mercy of the warmongers." Many women had to go back to their home towns but we arranged to meet again at Easter. The air was full of optimism and we all felt a new energy growing within ourselves. The women who could stay on planned to blockade the future cruise base the following morning. Throughout the previous day there had been a massive police presence but they

had not intervened at all; this was not the case on the morning of the 9th. They brutally attacked the women, pulling their hair out at its roots, dragging them by their feet and twisting their arms to prevent them from returning to block the road again.

The women were not to be so easily defeated. Two days later a group of women returned to the base to blockade the entrance yet again. This time the police were even more violent despite the fact that no woman had, during any of the actions, reacted violently or abused the police verbally. The Italian-speaking women asked them not to be violent and explained why they were taking this action. They met with replies such as "Go back to where you belong!" and "What about the Russians?"

Each time there was a long queue of traffic waiting to enter the base the women were dragged and thrown violently from the road and police prevented them from returning by twisting their wrists and placing their feet on them. Once the traffic had gone into the base the women returned to block the entrance.

This was repeated five times during which Katherine Barker of Greenham Common Peace Camp had her wrist broken. The women were finally formally advised they were to be arrested and immediately grabbed and pushed into a police van.

A German woman who was acting as a legal observer and had been writing down details was pushed off her bicycle and taken to the van. Another woman who'd been photographing the incident was also grabbed and two men who were standing at the side of the road were arrested and taken along with the women to the prison in the nearby town of Ragusa.

The account that follows is by Tommes Breiding who stayed behind at the camp after the women were arrested.

After midday a big crowd of polizia came back. They took away all the signs and information boards from beside the road. Then they left to return later at 4:15, among them many carabinieri, and they forced us to pack up our belongings. At the same time

they started to throw all the things together into a pile. Then they bulldozed the houses and tents we had built. The bulldozer had come from inside the base from where it was used for construction of the base. The land we were on was private and they destroyed our Peace Camp illegally as we had verbal permission to be there.

The carabinieri and polizia had their fun destroying the bamboo tents and burning them down. We could not move our things away quickly enough because at the time there were only three of us in the camp.

There was only one car there, belonging to two visitors from West Germany, but they were questioned there at length, so they could not help us. Then the polizia started to burn some of the collected things, even one space mat although I was protesting. Eight tents and all the sleeping bags they took away. When it got dark all that was left were two burnt patches on the ground. I suggest that this violent action of the polizia will strengthen the resignation of most of the inhabitants of Comiso and Sicily, and their belief that they can do nothing against Cruise Missiles.

Martine Grice and Tommes Breiding

A feminist at a Rome peace march calls for an "explosion of love."

153

Scenes from the Greenham Common Peace Camp: top, demonstrating at the missile-site gate; above, holding vigil at the fence.

"Down Among the Wimmin'"

On one side of the camp [Greenham Common] at Green Gate was the fire, a clever arrangement of grill over dugout, covered with blackened kettles and enormous cooking pots. Tea and coffee were in constant preparation, and boxes and bins nearby stored the rest of the kitchen – odd mugs and cutlery and plates, vegetables and granola and biscuits (all encampments are vegetarian). Someone was nonchalantly mixing batter in a saucepan, wiping the smoke from her eyes; another cooked tortillas in a vast skillet; another somehow cleaned dishes in icy water; a fourth chopped rhubarb and grapefruit for the evening sweet. Around the fire, logs or boards on rocks and one old wicker chair supported a full circle of women – of every age but mostly young, big-boned and strong. Hair was short ("Fearful dearth of shampooing facilities," as one put it), lots cut boyishly with tails down the back, some colored outlandish shades of pink and green. Everyone seemed healthy and grubby, and when you sat for a quarter-hour your hands became coated with grime, fingernails black, just from picking up a kettle or adding wood to the flames.

Nobody was "in charge." The one who took over at any given moment was the one doing the work – getting the meal, pouring the coffee, organizing the night watch which would wake the others should a cruise launcher and convoy take to the road. Volunteers were easy to come by, even for the 4 A.M. shift. There was a warmth and camaraderie among them, the kind you'd expect from front-line troops in a constant state of risk. It was often hard to realize that is what they are. Given their "invisibility," it was even harder to understand the degree of support they continue to receive from behind the scenes: abundant contributions of food, wood, clothing and generous checks, arriving daily from people throughout Britain and abroad.

At Green Gate, U.S. Army personnel flashed their passes to go in and out, and police cars crept along, checking out the license plates of the campers' parked cars. Beyond the road was a lovely encampment under the trees of an old wood. Sunlight shone spots on tents dotted around and on a couple of "benders" – plastic sheeting draped on branches, a Greenham invention to bypass a law forbidding dwellings on the Common. A washstand with a mirror was attached to a tree, and two dozen toothbrushes stood in a mug beside the basin. Plastic jugs of water rested on ground soft from decades of embedded woodland debris. The base's generators roared in the distance, and you could hear the barking from the kennels where the Alsatians are kept; at night, spotlights penetrated the trees at intervals, and the women were always watched. Otherwise, you might think it a holiday camping ground of great charm.

Off to one side was the "sanctuary," a small hollow owned by a friendly local where the women store their things away from the threat of eviction. Nearby was the "shit pit," boards over a hole in the ground, a heap of freshly dug earth for cover and, in it, a child's spade. No smell at all. Everything extremely neat and well organized, with a respect for nature given scant attention on the other side of the fence.

Divided by barbed wire, a world created by powerless women and another made by powerful men: anyone walking by the fence might have a thought about which they would like to live in. Over there, new rolls of razor wire were constantly being unwound; bunkers, barracks and missile silos were being built in the mud where the trees had been torn up. Over here, patches of flowers had been planted. In a clearing near a fire, a cardboard box with a bit of blanket inside and a matching tent slung from a branch above was labeled "Igon's Bender"; a huge black-and-white cat was usually to be seen within, peering out at what was going on. Over there, a soldier sat in a tower under corrugated iron, doing something similar, a bright orange spotlight beside him and a crackling radio set to send and receive reports of female mischief. . . .

On Bank Holiday Monday there was large-scale activity among the women, and charabancs of supporters arrived from across the country at Orange Gate with kites and pots of paint. Meetings were scheduled at distant clearings in the bushes to avoid being overheard by directional microphones, and while kites flew and got caught in the wire, women mixed paint and dressed in plastic bags. At 3 P.M.

Women decorate the fence at Greenham with ribbons, candles, and balloons to protest against the installation of cruise missiles.

hundreds of them emerged from the wood and converged on the gate, long called "Orange" by them but just "L" by the authorities. Within minutes they made the gate worthy of their name for it, sloshing every conceivable shade of orange on the posts and wire as the police and soldiers inside gazed on bemused. Women held other women on their shoulders to reach the highest bits, others clapped and sang while up and down the road rainbows of color suddenly decorated the hideous fence, and on the road itself slogans, doves and peace signs appeared as far as the eye could see. It looked like the road to Oz. Police, too late, arrived in vans and seized the leftover paint and brushes, hurling them over the barbed wire, making unintentional bright splotches of color inside the base. . . .

"They really ought to get out of here," said one woman who has come every weekend for more than two years, leaving her three children with her husband in Derbyshire. "And we're not moving until they do. We don't mind how long it takes. The newspapers may ignore us, but we're still here and the base knows we're still here. We've got too much commitment to give up now. I used to think of life as something merely nasty, British and short. It's nasty here all right, and not even particularly British, but for my children's sake I've got to do what I can to see that it isn't short."

Sally Belfcage

155

Japanese woman prays, remembering the fortieth anniversary of Hiroshima.

War Against Old Women

It was in winter – 6 December 1981 – that I first met the Shibokusa women. They had come to the teeming megalopolis of Tokyo in order to address a Japanese women's peace rally, close to the anniversary of the bombing of Pearl Harbor 41 years earlier. . . .

Their land, which was at the north foot of Mount Fuji, was being used by the Japanese self-defence force (Japan is not supposed to have an army as such, and her constitution is pledged to peace) for military exercises. Some of the women in the area had . . . established a resistance movement to protest against this. By now I was well and truly hooked: my mind's eye leapt out of the city to the foot of the mountain. I resolved to get up there and talk to those women.

Sumiko Shimizu, secretary general of the Japan Women's Council, liaised for me with the *Shibokusa Hahano Kai* (Shibokusa Mothers' Committee) to which the women belonged, and made a date to visit them a week later. She accompanied Yumiko (my interpreter) and me herself, and during the two-hour bus journey between Tokyo and Mount Fuji, she explained a good deal of the background of the Shibokusa women's story. They came, she said, from a rural Japanese community in which women were not so long ago (and perhaps still) treated little better than cattle, sitting on the ground while their menfolk occupied the *tatami* mat, eating the leftovers after the men had been fed, giving birth in the straw. And yet these women had become the leading lights of the Japanese peace movement, which at that time had not yet reached its new peak (resulting in nearly half a million people demonstrating in Tokyo six months later). The courageous example of the Shibokusa women, said Mrs Shimizu, was crucial at a time when Japan was showing signs of re-militarisation, increasing its arms budget and deleting references to war crimes from the history books. . . .

A taxi took us outside the town and down a dirt track through some woods, the mountain lying ahead of us. We soon came to the perimeter of the military base; right next to the gate leading into it, there was a cottage enclosed in a small compound. It was from here, said Mrs Shimizu, that the Shibokusa women co-ordinated their resistance activities. They took it in turn – in shifts of two – to maintain a presence in the cottage. That day I met four of them, two of whom had stayed on from the previous shift. One of them, Mie Amano, acted as spokeswoman, the other three, including their leader Kimie Watanabe, occasionally adding a few words of their own. Mie Amano's behaviour was quite unlike the traditional image of cautious, formal Japanese womanhood. Her hands, which like those of her companions were worn and leathery from manual labour, were constantly moving as she spoke.

As we walked into the compound where the cottage stood, I saw that the thatch on the roof had been covered with shiny sheets of corrugated metal. Mie Amano, noticing our enquiring glances, told us that rightwing groups had started harassing the women, gathering outside the cottage with taunts and cries of "go home you old witches", throwing stones and burning brands. The women, afraid that the thatch would catch fire, had been forced to cover it. Other precautions were in evidence as well – bits of barbed wire on the walls of the compound, and even two young lads from the village who had been brought in to protect the women should the need arise. These women had obviously touched a raw nerve somewhere, I thought, as I stepped into the tiny cottage and removed my shoes. They could hardly be dismissed as insignificant. . . .

But the Shibokusa women's main activity is disrupting military exercises. In groups of up to ten, they make their way into the exercise area (there are a host of routes, they say, the secret of which they keep to themselves), crawling around the undergrowth and popping up in the middle of the firing. They plant scarecrows to decoy the troops. Sometimes they'll build a fire and sit round it singing and clapping their hands, totally ignoring officials who try to move them on. They are frequently arrested and taken to the police station.

"They are quite gentle with us, because they are afraid of provoking us – they hate it when we start screaming! The police have realised that though we are physically easier to arrest than men, we're more trouble afterwards. Men put up a fight, but once it's over, they just give everything away. We never give our name, age or anything. We just say that we're so old we can't remember when we were born or who we are. . . ."

I asked Mie Amano what they hoped to achieve in the long run. She answered that it now went much deeper than the desire to get their land back. "As we carried on with our campaign, we realised that the whole phenomenon of militarism is violence against the land, wherever it takes place. So we are really a part of the wider anti-war movement. You see, Mount Fuji is the symbol of Japan. If they are preparing war on her flanks, how can they say Japan desires peace?"

Leonie Caldecott

Right: Name Any City *by Francesc Torres, 1985.*

UNFORGETTABLE FIRE

The Day You First Heard the News

Where were you when you first heard about the atomic bomb? My guess is that most Americans over the age of 50 can answer that question instantly.

Aug. 6, 1945 was one of those days that stick in the brain. The most trivial details of such days can often be recalled decades later, simply because they are associated with the moment one first heard a piece of shocking or frightening news.

I must confess that the radio newscasts of that distant August afternoon have blurred a bit in my mind. But the newspaper memory remains starkly vivid. I can visualize just where the afternoon edition of *The Dayton Daily News* was lying in our kitchen when my eye caught the riveting headline. I can recall reading it aloud to my parents, mispronouncing the strange new word "A-tome" because I had never heard anyone say it before.

Other people, older than I, were also deeply shocked by President Harry S. Truman's announcement. It was a moment that, even then, struck many as a radical turning point in human history, and a surprising number felt impelled to put pen to paper and record their feelings and reactions.

In New York City, Norman Cousins, editor of *The Saturday Review of Literature*, spent the night of Aug. 6 composing an impassioned essay, "Modern Man Is Obsolete." The atomic bomb had made nationalism outmoded and dangerous, he argued; only a world government could save mankind.

In Charlotte, N.C., a country-music singer, Fred Kirby, also spent a sleepless night after hearing the news. The next day, he wrote "Atomic Power," a song evoking grim images of divine judgement and apocalyptic destruction. It caught on immediately and, for several weeks early in 1946, was on Billboard's list of top country favorites.

At his summer cottage in Kennebunk, Maine, the Rev. John Haynes Holmes of New York City's Community Church was enjoying the ocean view when he heard the report. "Everything else seemed suddenly to

become insignificant," he wrote a few days later. "I seemed to grow cold, as though I had been transported to the waste spaces of the moon. The summer beauty seemed to vanish, and the waves of the sea to be pounding upon the shores of an empty world. . . .For I knew that the final crisis in human history had come. What that atomic bomb had done to Japan, it could do to us."

In Pelham Manor, N.Y., Patricia E. Munk had just returned from the hospital, having given birth to her second son, when the word arrived. "Since then," she wrote in a letter six days later, "I have hardly been able to smile, the future seems so utterly grim for our two little boys. Most of the time I have been in tears or near tears, and fleeting but torturing regrets that I have brought children into the world to face such a dreadful thing as this have shivered through me. It seems that it will be for them all their lives like living on a keg of dynamite which may go off at any moment."

The atomic bomb announcement elicited very little celebration. A few newspapers published gloating editorials and cartoons; a radio comedian joked about Japan's "atomic ache." Another said the bomb "made Hiroshima look like Ebbetts Field after a game between the Giants and the Dodgers." For most Americans, however, the news brought not joy but profound apprehension.

The *St. Louis Post-Dispatch* warned on Aug. 7 that science may have "signed the mammalian world's death warrant, and deeded an earth in ruins to the ants." The next day, *The Milwaukee Journal* published a map of Milwaukee overlaid with concentric circles showing the pattern of destruction in Hiroshima.

The more highly placed the observer, it seemed, the deeper the uneasiness. Washington D.C., a reporter wrote, was "pervaded by a sense of oppression." "For all we know," intoned the radio announcer H. V. Kaltenborn in his broadcast on the evening of Aug. 6, "We have created a Frankenstein! We

must assume that with the passage of only a little time, an improved form of the new weapon we used today can be turned against us."

This primal fear of extinction cut across all political and ideological lines, from the staunchly conservative *Chicago Tribune*, which wrote of an atomic war that would leave the earth "a barren waste, in which the survivors of the race will hide in caves or live among ruins," to the liberal *New Republic*, which on Aug. 20 offered an almost identical vision of a conflict that would "obliterate all the great cities of the belligerents, bring industry and technology to a grinding halt," and leave only "scattered remnants of humanity living on the periphery of civilization."

From our contemporary perspective, perhaps, such cataclysmic imagery seems so familiar as to be almost trite – if visions of universal destruction can ever become trite. But it is sobering to realize how quickly these dark visions surfaced. Within hours of President Truman's announcement, and years before the world's nuclear arsenals made such a holocaust likely or even possible, the prospect of global annihilation already filled the nation's consciousness. In the earliest moments of the nuclear era, the fear that would come to haunt millions of people not yet born in 1945 had already found urgent expression.

In most cases, our memories of even the highest moments of public drama are eventually filed away: They become a reassuring part of our general stock of recollections, to be brought out and nostalgically relived from time to time. But Aug. 6, 1945, is different. After 40 years, it still has not receded into that safe and static realm we call "the past".

H.V. Kaltenborn's Frankenstein still roams; *The Post-Dispatch's* kingdom of the ants still waits in the wings. The stab of fear we felt when we read that first newspaper headline or heard that first radio bulletin may have receded from the center of our awareness, but it remains with us still.

Paul Boyer

The International Shadow Project

When the first atomic bomb exploded over Hiroshima forty years ago, human beings who were within three hundred metres of Ground Zero were instantly vaporized by the searing heat, leaving behind only their shadows.

The remnants of these innocent victims provide the image and theme of The Shadow Project, a solemn memorial with a single purpose: to help people understand and imagine the disappearance of life through nuclear war.

The silent, anonymous shadows scattered throughout the city are representations of a sight which, if a bomb had been detonated, would be seen by no one. Unlike the shadows left by a nuclear holocaust, the images painted on the streets are non-permanent.

As artists and responsible human beings, the participants in The International Shadow Project want to make the dangers of nuclear annihilation vivid. We have attempted to provide images that will awaken all of us to the immeasurable threat to human life proposed by our nuclear arsenals. Those who view the human shadows are encouraged to identify personally with victims of nuclear destruction. We need to draw the connection between the present arms build-up and the inevitability of the same sort of nuclear holocaust that occurred at Hiroshima and Nagasaki. It is our hope, indeed it is our expectation, that people, seeing what is left after nuclear war, will take actions together to preserve life on earth and avert our collective disintegration.

The International Shadow Project 1985 Handbook

The Shadow Project saw human shadows painted about city streets to remind citizens of the power of the atomic bomb. Photo by John Roper.

Shadows of a Summer Night

Between the hours of midnight and 6 A.M. on August 6, 1985, many things happened that could have happened otherwise. But in the cold light of morning these things seemed fated to be so. . . . Among much else, small bands of people in New York and other cities traveled from block to block, sticking vinyl cutout figures down on sidewalks and fixing imprints of them with faint applications of white paint.

Some figures represented people. Others depicted animals. These were intended to suggest one of the many striking visual effects of the atomic explosion over Hiroshima, where the blast fixed people's very shadows on walls. Come morning, thousands, or perhaps millions, of people rushing to work would see the painted shadows and think about Hiroshima, atomic weapons, and death.

Brainchild of Alan Gussow and Donna Grund Slepack, the Shadow Project dates back to 1982, and now occurs, when it does, simultaneously around the world. This year there were shadow painters in New Zealand, Hungary, Nigeria, Brazil, "most of Western Europe and even in remote Mauritius!" This is an impressive organizational feat, akin to the Live Aid festival. . . .

The Shadow Project workers used an impermanent latex paint that would fade off in a couple of weeks. . . . I witnessed only a few shadow paintings, in the World Trade Center vicinity. A dog caught by the fireball. A bunch of people crawling in the street. Just before midnight, my colleagues and I, members of the dreaded press, stopped for a drink in a glittery fun-filled Tribeca restaurant. . . .

I tried to imagine the effects of an atomic explosion on the restaurant: the shadows of pendant smoked hams and dangling mozzarella baubles forever embedded in the particolored ceramic tiles. Irradiated beakers of blue margaritas dripping senselessly amid the wreckage. The dentures of busty socialites and dashing European auto salesmen gleaming amid the charred ultramarine Formica. Not a pretty picture. Where once there was laughter and bright voices, all would be rubble and hardy cockroaches. . . .

After the calming drink we pushed off towards Wall Street and the Shadow Project. Surely this would center one's thoughts on the reality of nuclear weapons.

Several shadows had been painted by the time we got near the Trade Center. The outlines were slapped down with rollers, in milky-thin applications. The resulting figures looked puzzlingly crude, less than human size, with weirdly proportioned limbs and unnaturally tapered extremities. A legend had been stenciled here and there: "Hiroshima 1945, New York 19??"

Gary Indiana

Families gather to contribute origami cranes at the monument to Sadako, on the fortieth anniversary of the atomic bombing of Hiroshima.

Song of the Cranes

For ever more, for ever more
For ever and ever, for ever and ever
Only tears of joy shall we cry
For ever and ever, for ever and ever
The roots of trees grow deep hold tight
For ever and ever, for ever and ever
We sing out, we cry out
All nature is one
For ever and ever, for ever and ever
Peace on earth, peace on earth
This is our hope, this is our prayer
Peace on earth, peace on earth
This is our hope, this is our prayer
For ever and ever, for ever and ever
With faith and love we cannot fail
For ever and ever, for ever and ever
Truth is marching in
For ever and ever, for ever and ever
Filled with love that comes from above
For ever and ever, for ever and ever
Truth is marching in.

                    Children's Peace Opera

A Thousand Cranes

Children and many others in Japan believe that a crane lives a thousand years. If one folds a thousand paper cranes and keeps them at his side, they will protect him from illness. After the atomic bomb had fallen on Hiroshima that August 6, 1945, and the people lay dying, as if by prearrangement sympathizers all over the country began sending thousands of folded paper cranes to relatives and friends, and strangers in the hospitals.

The children of Hiroshima, who had neither toys or immunity to the radiation sickness which was taking the lives of their parents, also folded cranes. It was a lot for a child to ask of a thousand paper cranes, that they should match the power of one uranium bomb. The city officials have estimated that almost 200,000 people died from the bomb, many children among them. And now seventeen years later when I visited Hiroshima, I found children were still dying from atomic radiation effects, and still folding paper cranes.

There is hardly a child in Japan who doesn't know the name of Sadako Sasaki. In the fall of 1954 she was a healthy young girl of twelve, the fastest runner in her class in the Noborimachi Primary School. One day while she was playing in the schoolyard she fainted, and just a few weeks later she was in the A-bomb hospital with the dread diagnosis: acute leukemia. But Sadako wasn't hurt in the bombing, her mother tearfully protested. She was just two years old at the time and a mile from where the bomb fell. She had been hurled to the top of a chest by the blast, it was true, but that was nine years ago. Why should Sadako have to suffer now?

Sadako was very brave in the hospital. "I don't want to die," she wrote solemnly in her diary, but she managed to laugh and sing when her classmates came to visit

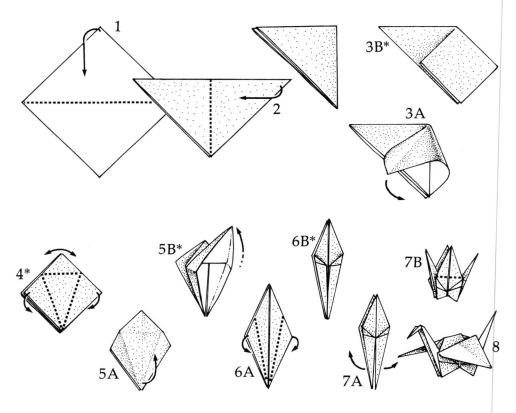

*Repeat this on the reverse side.
5A – Pull up gently maintaining fold.
8 – Blow air into hole on the bottom to flatten the crane.

                    How To Make a Paper Crane *by Dave Mazierski*

Symbol of Hope

her. And she folded paper cranes. However, Sadako did not have the strength or time to reach 1,000 cranes. In October of 1955, when she had made only 964, she died. Her grieving friends added the missing cranes and placed the 1,000 with her in her coffin.

And then, as if the children of Hiroshima spontaneously and at the same moment realized that the death of Sadako symbolized the deaths of all children killed by the bomb, they rose up together to do something about it. They would raise funds for a monument to Sadako and place it in the middle of the Peace Park. It would stand in this City of Peace as a reminder to all who saw it what the bomb had done to the first children who had ever experienced it and what it might do to others in the years to come.

With the zeal of crusaders, they wrote to children all over Japan asking them to send their allowances to help them in their cause. They managed to raise what to their elders in that struggling city was a miraculous sum of money, seven million yen (twenty thousand dollars), and commissioned a distinguished sculptor to design their memorial.

It is a powerful monument. On top of an oval granite pedestal which symbolizes Mt. Horai, that fabled mountain of paradise, a young girl stands holding in her outstretched hands a golden folded crane. Just below her on the mountain a young boy and a girl reach out their arms to the sky. Within the pedestal hang colorful leis, each a thousand cranes, that people from all over the country have placed there as an offering; and on the base are inscribed the words: "This is our cry, this is our prayer: peace in the world."

Betty Jean Lifton

I am often invited these days to speak to groups of people who want to learn more about the effects of the world's first atomic war. But what I prefer doing is working with children. I go around to the schools and I show the children how to make paper cranes, like the ones that fly in Hiroshima's Peace Memorial Park. The pretty, colored origami crane is a symbol of peace not only for the children of Japan but for people all around the world. I find that children love making these cranes every bit as much as they do playing with toy weapons of war. I believe that how people start out, when young, determines where they will end up, when older. So instead of arguing with the grownups, who think that nuclear weapons are necessary, I devote my time to the children, showing them that the world *can* be a beautiful place.

Kinuko Laskey, Vancouver Founder of the
Canadian Society of Atomic Bomb Survivors

One thousand origami cranes, folded by Tina Koyama of Project Ploughshares, Seattle.

Gathered at the River

for Beatrice Hawley and John Jagel

As if the trees were not indifferent...

A breeze flutters the candles but the
    trees give off
a sense of listening, of hush.

The dust of August on their leaves.
But it grows dark. Their dark green
is something known about, not seen.

But summer twilight takes away
only color, not form. The tree-forms,
massive trunks and the great domed
    heads,
leaning in towards us, are visible,

a half-circle of attention.

They listen because the war
we speak of, the human war with
    ourselves,

the war against earth
against nature,
is a war against them.

The words are spoken
of those who survived a while,
living shadowgraphs, eyes fixed forever
on witnessed horror,

who survived to give
testimony, that no-one
may plead ignorance.
Contra naturam. The trees,
the trees are not indifferent.

We intone together, *Never again*,

we stand in a circle,
singing, speaking, making vows,

remembering the dead
of Hiroshima,
of Nagasaki.

We are holding candles: we kneel to set
    them
afloat on the dark river
as they do
there in Hiroshima. We are invoking

saints and prophets,
heroes and heroines of justice and
    peace,
to be with us, to help us
stop the torment of our evil dreams...

Windthreatened flames bob on the
current...

They don't get far from shore. But none
    capsizes
even in the swell of a boat's wake.
The waxy paper cups sheltering them
catch fire. But still the candles
sail their gold downstream.

And still the trees ponder our strange
    doings, as if
well aware that if we fail,
we fail also for them:
if our resolves and prayers are weak
    and fail

there will be nothing left of their slow
    and innocent wisdom,

no roots,
no bole nor branch,

no memory
of shade,
of leaf,

no pollen.

Denise Levertov

No More Hibakusha

We want no one else ever to suffer the hell we have
experienced. "Make no more Hibakusha [nuclear victims]" is
our appeal, for which we give our lives. It is not until our
wish becomes a reality that the Hibakusha will be able to live
as a foundation of peace, and the dead will rest in peace. The
Hibakusha cannot agree to the existence of nuclear weapons
either for "national security" or "deterrence". To accept the
"nuclear umbrella" is to accept nuclear weapons as a
necessary evil. The Hibakusha will live on and keep
protesting until all nuclear arms are abolished. Fulfilling this
mission is the real heritage we can pass onto coming
generations.

Nuclear Victims' Demand

Now, 40 years later, there are nearly 400,000 "Hibakusha," or
nuclear victims, in Japan, most of whom have suffered and
are still suffering from delayed after effects, including atomic
"bura-bura" diseases, a physical condition of deep lassitude
and enervation. The Hibakusha are not free from fear that
nuclear radiation will have genetic effects on offspring. For
that reason quite a number of atomic bomb victims gave up
the idea of marriage or decided not to have children.

Mobilization for Survival

Right: Brightly coloured candle boxes, each bearing the name of a Hiroshima victim, are launched on the river every anniversary of the bombing.

NUCLEAR FREE

The Definition

Nuclear free zone: Any well-defined geographical area, regardless of size, in which no nuclear weapons shall be produced, transported, stored, processed, disposed of or detonated. Neither shall any facility, equipment, supply or substance for their production, transportation, storage, processing, disposal or detonation be permitted within its borders.

The Possibilities

The concept may catch the imagination of more and more cities, states and countries until we have reduced the number of nuclearized zones to just two, Moscow and Washington, D.C. Perhaps then they will get the message.

Carl Eggers

The Beginning

This effort can begin by *declaring our own church, synagogue, diocese, religious school, hospital or home a Nuclear Free Zone*. Besides the valuable process of dialogue, disagreement and education which such a decision entails, it can help to change the self image of a congregation from a static building to a dynamic, spiritual center for transforming your community and the world. Many religious properties are designated civil defense shelters – thus contributing to the myth that a nuclear war can be survived or won. The transformation of such a shelter into a Nuclear Free Zone can be an important step in redefining a religious institution's role in a community. Each religious Nuclear Free Zone is distinct. Its resolution depends on the local reality and levels of concern.

Your local congregation can exert its influence on local government to have your community declared a Nuclear Free Zone. This can involve a congregation working to halt nuclear research at a local university, close a uranium mine or convert a local weapons facility into a mass transit equipment plant. Such a campaign can help us to move beyond what we don't want – nuclear facilities and arms production – to what we do want – communities that provide for our social needs, economic survival and a decent quality of life for everyone. As we press local institutions to stop using local resources for destructive purposes, we can demand that they be used to meet our area's human needs.

Such a Nuclear Free Zone campaign will help a local religious community to look at its own locale with more searching, critical and even prophetic eyes.

Religious Task Force/Mobilization for Survival

Nuclear Free Zones in the World

5 Nuclear Free Zone Treaties
The number of countries that have signed and ratified the treaty is given in parentheses. Antarctic Treaty, 1959 (26 states, including USA and USSR); Outer Space Treaty, 1967 (83 states, including USA and USSR); Latin American Treaty, 1967 (also known as the Treaty of Tlatelolco; 24 states, including USA and USSR); International Seabed, 1971 (73 states, including USA and USSR); South Pacific, 1985 (8 states with 5 pending, not yet signed by USA or USSR).

17 Nuclear Free Zone Countries
Countries that either explicitly or implicitly prohibit nuclear weapons by law or as part of their constitution. (?) means NFZ law may not be enforced.)

Australia	Federated States of Micronesia	The Seychelles
Faeroe Islands	(Ponape, Kosrae, Truk, and Yap)	The Solomons
Greenland (?)	New Zealand	Spain
Iceland (?)	The Northern Marianas (?)	Sri Lanka
Japan (?)	Republic of Palau	Sweden
Malta	Papua New Guinea	Vanuata

2,840 Nuclear Free Zone Communities in 17 Countries
Declared by cities, counties, and towns. The grass-roots NFZ movement is spreading quickly throughout the world, and many of the figures given below may be out of date.

Argentina   1
Australia (over 56% of the population)   96
Belgium   281
Canada (includes all of Manitoba)   65
Denmark   9
Great Britain (over 60% of the population, including all of Wales)   160
Greece   1
Ireland (over 50% of the population)   117
Italy   170
Japan (first NFZ declared in 1958; 240 declared in 1984)   638
Netherlands   400
New Zealand (over 65% of the population)   100
Norway   107
Portugal   86
W. Germany   154
Spain (over 60% of the population)   350
United States of America (39 are legally-binding)   105

The New Abolitionist

Legal Argument

Of the legal arguments raised against the legality of Nuclear Free Zone laws, the most frequent is the assertion that such laws are preempted by the exclusive power of federal government to provide for the national defense.

Our legal analysis, however, indicates that where Nuclear Free Zone laws are drafted carefully so as to articulate a range of purely local reasons for the adoption of the legislation [*e.g.,* to promote sound economic development by relying on a non-military economy that is not subject to the whims of Congress], the law should not be found unconstitutional.

The U.S. Supreme Court's recent decisions in *Pacific Gas and Electric v. State Energy Resources Conservation & Development Commission* (1983) and *Silkwood v. Kerr-McGee Corporation* (1984) provide strong support for our argument that, absent the clearest expression of intent by the Congress, mere inconsistency with national policy does not invalidate a local or state law adopted pursuant to the jurisdiction's traditional police power authority. Unless Congress passes legislation specifically designed to preempt local Nuclear Free Zone laws, such local laws should be upheld.

Lawyers' Committee on Nuclear Policy Newsletter

New Zealand

In the first major test of New Zealand's Nuclear Free Zone policy, Prime Minister David Lange has stood firm against the United States. The Reagan administration had requested permission to send a Navy destroyer, the USS *Buchanan*, on a port-of-call visit to New Zealand (as part of annual ANZUS Treaty exercises scheduled for March [1985] involving Australia, New Zealand, and USA). As usual, however, the U.S. refused to confirm or deny whether the ship would carry nuclear weapons, and so, on February 4th (after months of U.S. pressure and two days of direct negotiations) Prime Minister Lange denied the request: "If we don't know whether or not they are nuclear-armed or not they can't come. This is going to be our continuing policy. This is not anti-American, it is not anti-alliance, it is anti-nuclear." The Reagan Administration obviously saw things differently, however, and the next day, together with Australia, it cancelled the ANZUS exercises altogether. Charging the "anti-nuclear movements seek to diminish defense cooperation," the State Department warned: "We would hope that our response to New Zealand would signal that the course these movements advocate would not be cost-free..." Lange called the cancellation of the exercise "an utterly unexpected consequence" but stressed that New Zealand would not be intimidated by such actions, and that his government had no intention of backing down on its NFZ policies.

The New Abolitionist

Population of U.S. Nuclear Free Zone Cities and Counties 1981-1984

Year   Population

'81 | 92,053

'82 | 111,003

'83 ■ 626,061

'84 ■■■■■■■■■■■■■■■■■■■■■■■■■■■■ 9,907,449

Denmark

Århus, a major port and the second largest city in Denmark, was declared a Nuclear Free Zone on 23 October 1985 after a three-year campaign initiated by the local Women for Peace. The declaration was signed by a majority of the town council over the objections of the Lord Mayor, who claims Nuclear Free Zones should be a matter of foreign – not local – policy. Århus and many other Danish towns, however, are also refusing to do business with firms involved in South Africa, and this too is considered a matter of foreign policy. Several members of the Århus council are now pressing for a binding NFZ policy to prohibit visits of U.S. warships unless they first certify that they are not carrying nuclear weapons. (Major demonstrations have been held recently in Århus and several other Danish cities, as well as in Oslo, Norway and Kiel, West Germany, protesting port visits of the USS *Iowa*.)

The New Abolitionist

Wales

Wales, the first country to officially declare itself a nuclear free zone, will celebrate the third anniversary of the declaration on 23 February [1985]. A major peace march and rally will take place in Cardiff, the Welsh capital, which will also include protest against WINTEX '85, NATO's Command Post Exercise.

At the rally, civil leaders and representatives of the Japanese and European embassies will be presented with a new peace scroll signed by all eight nuclear free county councils and 200 peace groups in Wales. Five thousand anniversary peace cards from Nuclear Free Wales will be sent to the United Nations and its member states and to people all over the world, containing a verse by the distinguished Welsh poet, R. S. Thomas:

> They are far off now; let it not be
> through war they are brought near.
> Their languages are different.
> Let them learn it is peace in the hand
> is the translation of peace in the mind.

The New Abolitionist

Poster in the Save Life On Earth International Exhibition by Caye Huss, Sweden.

Japan

The Debate on Japan's Three Non-Nuclear Principles (not to possess, manufacture or allow nuclear weapons to be brought into the country) began in the Diet in 1968. They were considered in conjunction with the return of Okinawa and were finally adopted as a resolution in November, 1971. At that time, weapons armed with nuclear warheads were openly deployed at U.S. bases in Okinawa. However, the question of whether or not it would be returned to Japan free of nuclear weapons was an issue of great concern. After the experience of Hiroshima and Nagasaki, it was difficult for the Japanese people to bear the idea of U.S. nuclear bases on Japanese territory.

According to one survey of public opinion, 70-80 per cent of the Japanese public believe that the clause of the Three Non-Nuclear Principles prohibiting the bringing of nuclear weapons into the country is not being upheld. Strictly speaking, from the standpoint of the Three Non-Nuclear Principles, the Japanese government should check as to whether warships and aircraft entering Japan are carrying nuclear weapons, and entry should be barred to those which, in fact, are.

According to "A Newsletter for a Nuclear-Free Japan and Pacific-Asia", as of December 5th, 1984, 5 prefectures, 8 wards, 155 cities, 119 towns and 12 villages in Japan [10 percent of the national total] had made nuclear-free zone declarations. . . .

The Japanese nuclear-free zone movement had its impetus with the movement in western Europe, particularly the U.K. (the first nuclear-free zone [post 1958] was declared in a resolution by the Manchester City Council on November 5th, 1980). . . .

A characteristic common to all of the Japanese nuclear-free zone declarations is that they call on the government to strictly enforce the Three Non-Nuclear Principles.

Hideaki Nagai

Norway

Approximately a fourth of Norway's 430 municipal councils and 11 of its 19 county councils have adopted Nuclear Free Zone resolutions asking the Norwegian Parliament to prohibit the use of nuclear weapons on or from Norwegian territory and to support the establishment of a Nordic Nuclear-Weapon-Free Zone. At the initiative of *Nej Til Atomvapen* (No to Nuclear Weapons), several municipal councils along the coast have ruled that military vessels capable of carrying nuclear weapons will not be given permission to enter their ports unless they receive assurances that no nuclear weapons are on board. The first such law was adopted in Horten (a Navy shipyard about 90 kilometers south of Oslo) on 22 April 1985, and, as of early June, it had been copied by seven other communities along the north coast: Kvaefjord, Torsken, Nordreisa, Gratangen, Dyroy, and Ibestad.

The New Abolitionist

The United States

From the Boston Tea Party and the abolitionists' boycott of slave products to the Nestle boycott and current demands for divestment from South Africa, there is a long history of economic resistance in the U.S. Just as we have succeeded as consumers and investors in forcing many U.S. businesses out of South Africa, the potential exists to force corporations out of the nuclear arms race. . . .

Several communities are already taking action: Takoma Park, Maryland, and Hoboken, New Jersey, have barred nuclear weapons industries from bidding on city contracts; Amherst, Massachusetts, has adopted a socially responsible investment policy mandating the withdrawal of public investments from companies with nuclear weapons contracts or business in South Africa; and, in Chicago, thirteen religious congregations sold off $1.8 million in stocks and bonds of nuclear weapons contractors. A citizens' group in Madison, Wisconsin, is holding vigils and leafletting outside local banks that invest heavily in the nuclear weapons industry, and in Ann Arbor, Michigan, a coalition of local peace groups led by the Gray Panthers is putting together a "Socially Responsible Buyer's Guide" and urging individuals, organizations, and local businesses not to purchase products or services from companies that produce nuclear weapons.

The New Abolitionist

Australia

Australian Prime Minister Robert Hawke was forced in early February [1985] to acknowledge – and within less than a week to cancel a secret defense agreement with the U.S. providing Australian support for flight testing of the MX-missile in the S. Pacific. News of the agreement provoked a storm of protest in Australia and a near-revolt in his own Labor Party, which places the highest priority on nuclear arms control. (Like neighboring Prime Minister Lange of New Zealand, Hawke was elected on a Nuclear Free Zone platform but, unlike Lange, he gave in immediately to U.S. pressure and abandoned his party's pledge to ban nuclear-powered or armed ships.)

That Hawke reversed himself so quickly on the MX (and at such an embarrassing moment – just 2 days before he was scheduled to meet with President Reagan to discuss sanctions against New Zealand) testifies to the growing strength of the anti-nuclear movement in Australia. Despite the U.S. furor over New Zealand, however, no one in the Reagan Administration has suggested sanctions against Australia, and American officials have gone out of their way to downplay the significance of the cancelled Australian agreement.

The New Abolitionist

Iceland

Iceland has banned all vessels carrying nuclear arms, including those of fellow NATO members, from the island nation's territorial waters, Foreign Minister Geir Hallgrimmsson said today [April 18, 1985].

"Our position is clear. No nuclear deployment of any sort may be made in or around Iceland. We do not want these weapons here," he said.

The minister was elaborating on a statement he made to Parliament... outlining the government's antinuclear policy.

UPI

The Arctic

All intercontinental ballistic missiles (ICBM's) – the U.S. Minuteman and M-X, the Soviet SS-9's, SS-18's and others – will pass over the Arctic in the event of a superpower nuclear war. The more important and more numerous types of Soviet submarine-launched ballistic missiles (SLBM's), carried aboard Delta class submarines, will be launched from Barents Sea and will cross the Arctic on their way to North American targets. Many of the U.S. SLBM's, especially the longer range Trident missiles, will cross the Arctic. U.S. B-52 bombers, accompanied by flocks of tanker aircraft, will mostly use Arctic routes, as will any Soviet Bear or Backfire bombers which attempt to bomb the U.S.

We have seen that in time of war, a quite large proportion of the nuclear weapons being used by the superpowers against each other will be crossing the Arctic, and the U.S. in particular has a large proportion of its strategic warning systems located in the Arctic. During a nuclear war, or when one is threatening, there will be a strong temptation for each side to attempt to destroy the warning systems of the other. ...

All this means that a significant number of nuclear explosions would take place in the Arctic. Probably all the warning systems described above would be attacked, as well as other installations which would contribute to a nuclear war. ...

A feasible Arctic nuclear free zone

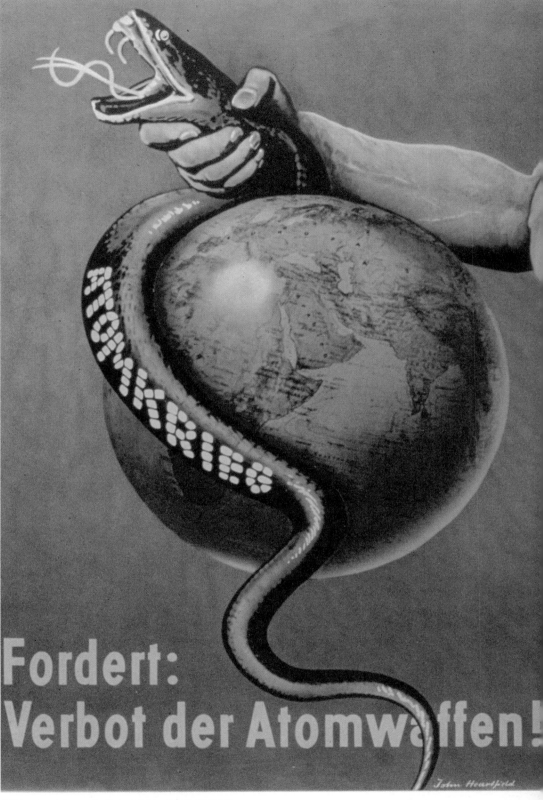

A German poster protesting against nuclear weapons.

has been outlined by Hannah Newcombe, of the Peace Research Institute at Dundas, Ontario as including all the area north of 60 degrees north. Within this area, all nuclear weapons and installations that aid in the use of nuclear weapons are to be banned while the strategic warning systems are to be put under international control.

Owen Wilkes

HANDS AROUND THE GLOBE

Multilingual signs carried by demonstrators marking the fortieth anniversary of the dropping of the atomic bomb on Hiroshima.

Public Opinion On the Move

In the past few years, there has been an enormous growth of a world-wide movement for nuclear disarmament. Because of technological advances in nuclear weapons systems, every nation-state is now vulnerable to immediate attack and potential destruction. . . .

Perhaps nowhere else is the escalation of the nuclear arms race more blatant than in Europe. In response, a genuinely popular movement of majority proportions has emerged to demand a nuclear weapons-free Europe—East and West. The recent demonstrations in the fall of 1981 in London, Bonn, Rome, Bucharest, Paris, Berlin and Amsterdam, testify to the political diversity and strength of this majority mass movement. In turn, the nuclear disarmament movement has kindled similar developments elsewhere on other continents.

The mass movement for the abolition of nuclear weapons in Japan has also experienced a new resurgence. Even the governing political parties there have joined in the popular campaign for nuclear disarmament. Mass organizations in Japan are now embarked on competitive petition campaigns to secure more than fifty million signatures that call for the banning of nuclear weapons. In Japan, the political campaign for nuclear disarmament is without doubt a majority mass movement.

The occasion of the United Nations Special Session on Disarmament (UN SSD-II) provides an historic opportunity to mobilize public opinion the world over in support of a comprehensive disarmament program. In this respect, Non-Governmental Organizations (NGO's) can now play a critical role in influencing the internal legislative process of the UN SSD-II as well as mobilizing world public opinion through a variety of mass events parallel to the work of the UN SSD-II.

International Liaison Office:
Riverside Church, New York City

Japan's Outspoken Peace Movement

Two major organizations have helped to coordinate Japan's national movement: Gensuikin and Gensuikyo. Both sponsor annual World Conferences each August in commemoration of the Hiroshima/Nagasaki bombings. The conferences draw tens of thousands of people from the U.S., Europe, Asia, and the Pacific. The Hibakusha play a vital role throughout the movement, sharing the agony of personal experience, and expressing their commitment to peace in the Atomic Victims Demand "NO MORE HIBAKUSHA." At a local level, a growing number (currently over 100) of assembly bodies from cities, towns and villages have issued declarations against nuclear arms, banning military actions and exercises in local communities, or declaring their municipalities nuclear free zones.

The Japanese peace movement developed around the experiences of atomic bomb victims from Hiroshima/Nagasaki and Pacific island testing sites. Impelled by the universal suffering of Japan's 400,000 Hibakusha, the network has grown into a powerful political force, supported by a greater percentage of the population than any other peace movement in the world. Peace and antinuclear activists focus on both national and international

Japanese students protest against the arrival of a U.S. aircraft carrier which they believe carries nuclear weapons; Yokosuka, Japan; June 1981.

policymaking, as they work to uphold Japan's Three Non-Nuclear Principles – no production, possession, or introduction of nuclear weapons into Japan. Efforts include resisting overtures from the U.S. to involve Japan in nuclear and conventional war

strategies, raising sufficient Government aid programs for the Hibakusha, and calling on "humanity to implement a total prohibition and elimination of nuclear weapons."

Mobilization for Survival

The Soviet Peace Movement

The international Peace March Stockholm-Moscow-Minsk organised by several women's organisations of Norway, Sweden, Denmark and Finland jointly with the Soviet Peace Committee and the Soviet Women's Committee (the March covered the Soviet section of the route in July-August 1982) was a new landmark in the development of cooperation between the Soviet peace movement and anti-war movements in various countries. The Peace March Moscow-Kiev-Vienna (via Budapest and Bratislava) that followed, drew participants from anti-war movements of 30 countries. Over 700,000 Soviet people took part in meetings,

demonstrations and rallies together with the participants in the March in Moscow, Leningrad, Kiev, Minsk, Uzhgorod, Kalinin and Smolensk and voiced their support for the March slogans.

The International Moscow-Washington Bike for Peace – '83, held from July 6 to August 8, 1983, became an important joint anti-war action of peace supporters of both West and East. Representatives of anti-war organisations of the USSR, USA, Finland, Sweden and Norway took part in the event. Travelling over the territory of the USSR, Finland, Sweden, Norway and the USA the Bike for Peace – '83 participants covered a total

of 2,340 kilometres and collected over 70 signatures of representatives of various government bodies and public figures in these countries for the Appeal to the United Nations Organisation and the Peoples of the World. The Appeal contains a strong protest against the nuclear arms race and calls on governments and peoples to take measures to curb the arms race. The Appeal with signatures affixed to it was handed in New York to the Secretary-General of the United Nations who highly appraised the Bike for Peace – '83 which was held within the framework of the World Disarmament Campaign.

Soviet Peace Committee

Make the First Strike a Knock on the Door

About 800 cities and towns across the United States have mailed "community portraits" to selected cities in the Soviet Union, hoping to help thaw frosty relations between the two superpowers.

The Portland-based Ground Zero Pairing Project is coordinating the effort, aimed at lessening the chances of a nuclear war. "Make the first strike a knock on the door" is its slogan.

Packages were mailed this week to Soviet communities selected for geography, population and economic characteristics similar to the cities sending the "portraits," said Earl Molander, executive director of the project.

Each city's portrait contains items intended to show the Soviets what the American community is like, Molander said. They include demographic data, photos and books describing the city, and messages from residents, including children.

"I'm sure many people are thinking 'My, what a naive exercise,'" said Freda Tarbell, a member of the Ground Zero chapter in Erie, Pa., which sent information and photographs to Poltava in the Ukraine. Poltava is the site of Peter the Great's 1709 victory over Charles XII of Sweden, a battle that established Russia as a European power.

"But," she added, "we don't believe this is an exercise in naivete at all. We feel the governments have not been effective in handling the nuclear issue at all, so perhaps we can approach it on another plane."

In Tucson, Ariz., which sent letters and information to its Russian master city, Novokuinetsk, organizer Roger Hagglund said, "It's about time we recognize each other as brothers and sisters."

"We believe that if we can establish extensive community-to-community communication and exchange, we will have made a major contribution to reducing the polarization between the United States and Soviet Union that seems to be the trend these days," Molander said.

He said he has contacted a Soviet official in Washington, whom he described as "supportive" of the idea. But organizers remain unsure how the packages will be received by the mayors and councils of the Soviet cities.

Molander said he was told it will be up to each Soviet city to decide if and how it will respond to the Americans' request for similar information in reply.

He plans to travel to Washington...with a sample of the portrait materials to show Soviet Embassy officials.

Response by Americans has been encouraging, he said, attracting a diverse mix of people who do not necessarily "see this as an activity that implies a strong position one way or the other on nuclear war issues."

The hope is that the "first strike" will lead to more sister-city relationships, Molander said. "The 'second strike' will be real people trying to establish person-to-person contact..." he added.

The Ground Zero Pairing Project grew out of Ground Zero Week in April 1982, when seminars were held across the country on the effects of a nuclear attack. Ground Zero's headquarters is in Washington, where it disseminates information on the effects of nuclear war.

Organizers say a little more than 1,100 American cities and towns have agreed to participate in the pairing project, of which about 800 sent their portraits this week. The rest will be mailed during the next few months.

Most of the cities have between 25,000 and 100,000 residents, Molander said. Larger ones include Tucson, New Orleans, Denver and Portland—which has sent its package to Khabaroviz in the Soviet Far East.

Associated Press

Target Seattle Project

Declaration for Peace and Prevention of Nuclear War.

The Sister Cites Tashkent and Seattle in the name of their citizens, express their deep concern about the continuing buildup of nuclear weapons.

The main task of all people is to prevent a new war, to achieve the prohibition of production and use of all types of weapons of mass annihilation, and to advocate peace in the whole world.

Our Sister Cities reject the use of space and atomic weapons as a means of settling differences, and consider that the mere existence of nuclear weapons is a serious threat to the future of all humanity.

Only the mutual efforts of all peoples of the world will prevent nuclear catastrophe and help establish lasting peace on earth.

We call on all United States and Soviet citizens to unite to strengthen peace, reverse the arms race, and diminish nuclear weapons stockpiles; and to direct their efforts toward the improvement of the international climate. On the eve of the Summit Conference in Geneva, we appeal to our national leaders to exercise their greatest efforts to conclude this meeting for the well-being of our nations and the whole world.

We believe that the bright future of mankind is in our hands, and we shall devote all our strength to building a world where conflict between nations is resolved without the mass violence of war.

Chairman, Executive Committee
of the Tashkent City Soviet
of People's Deputies

Charles Royer, Mayor,
City of Seattle

September 27, 1985

Right: Peace Bike '83 participants cycled from Moscow to Washington, collecting signatures on a peace petition; here, cyclists pass through the settlement of Valdai, in the Novgorod region of the U.S.S.R.

Founder, Alden Bell, holds Target Seattle sign.

Stop Shooting! Start Writing!

Personal peace treaties are an idea that originated in East Germany. Individuals in East and West Europe make a commitment to each other, for instance that they won't use violence against each other or against each other's country. They are a form of detente from below.

These treaties aim at more personal contact between people east and west; for example:
This peace treaty opens the door to constructive collaboration, without paying attention to existing boundaries, to help stop the danger of war.

As a treaty partner, we principally reject:
—the abuse of power
—discrimination against races and minority groups
—the glorification and practice of violence
Our efforts should aim at:
—respecting people in their different way of life, opinions and culture
—breaking down enemy-images
—explaining to friends and other people the necessity of solving conflicts without violence
—taking part in political life
Even if this treaty is not acknowledged by authorities, it is binding for the signatories and asks them to abide by it. This peace treaty should not be taken to imply anything about the religious, political and ideological beliefs of the signatories.

If you want to make a personal peace treaty, contact Groningen Vredeswinkel (peace shop) telling them your name, address, gender, whether you're a soldier, a CO, someone active or not active in the peace movement, and your occupation. . . . Then say what kind of person you wish to make a treaty with. The Vredeswinkel is keeping a register of personal peace treaties. All names are confidential and they advise parties to a personal peace treaty not to publish it without permission of their partner.

Contact: Vredeswinkel, PO Box 1667, 970 BR Groningen, Netherlands.

War Resisters' International Newsletter

A Venerable League

Since its founding in 1915, the Women's International League for Peace and Freedom has united countless women working for Peace and Freedom. Two of its founders, Americans Jane Addams and Emily Greene Balch, were awarded Nobel Peace Prizes for their work. WILPF has a worldwide network with sections in 26 countries on five continents and an international office in Geneva. The U.S. section alone has more than 100 branches. As an international organ-ization with official representation in the U.N., we are committed to the United Nations as a strong force for settling disputes among nations.

Throughout its unique history, WILPF has affirmed that peace and freedom are inseparable, two sides of the same coin. WILPF continues to be a multi-issue, multi-racial organization emphasizing the connections between war and poverty, racism and economic exploitation and sexism and violence. WILPF stands for the equality of all people in a world free of racism and sexism; the building of a constructive peace through world disarmament; changing U.S. government priorities to meet human needs.

The Women's International
League for Peace and Freedom

Jane Addams, founder of the Women's International League for Peace and Freedom.

USSR Group to Establish Trust

We wanted to organize a genuine peace movement, not one that is on paper. There are no formal differences between our goals [and the gov't].

We started our group by announcing that the government was too burdened by its own political interests to solve the problem of disarmament. It's not that we're accusing the politicians of anything necessarily. Maybe it looks that way – but we perceive ourselves as attempting to help them, to encourage them to solve the issues. In our view, we thought that this was the only real way to press for disarmament. In other words, it has to come from the people and not just the government.

Mikhail Ostrovsky,
founding member

People to People

The main objective of the non-governmental group is to foster trust through more people-to-people contacts. They have proposed a number of ideas that the government Soviet Peace Committee has adopted - such as exchanging children's drawings between East and West, and including Soviet Baptists in the delegations that are sent abroad. They were the source of the idea for a peace march between Moscow and Washington, which actually took place.

Above all, they support all sorts of cultural exchanges and visits - anything that would enable people to know one another personally. They are especially keen on the idea of having children go for extended visits to live with families in the other bloc. They encourage the Soviet Peace Committee to make Western visitors more visible.

Metta Spencer

The Voice of Women

We 350 women of the world community, from 33 countries, meeting at the Women's International Peace Conference in Halifax, Canada, June 5-9, 1985, affirm the overwhelming need and desperate urgency for peace, which we believe is both the process we live and the goal for which we work.

At this conference, women from diverse racial, cultural, ethnic and political backgrounds representing different sides of conflict areas, came together as a living example of women negotiating peace. . . .

Although women's voices have not been heard and women have not participated equally in peace negotiations or in formulation of the institutions and the cultural fabric in which we live, we are more than half the world's population; we do have power, and we are shaping it for peaceful living.

We reject a world order based on domination, exploitation, patriarchy, racism and sexism. We demand a new order based on justice and the equitable distribution of the world's resources.

We condemn militarism. Militarism is an addiction that distorts human development, causing world-wide poverty, starvation, pollution, repression, torture and death. Feeding this habit robs all the world's children and future generations of their inheritance.

We all live in the shadow of the threat of nuclear war. We demand an end to research, testing, development, and deployment of all weapons of mass destruction, to the militarization of space and to all forms of violence. As a first step, we call for a comprehensive test ban treaty. . . .

We will continue to communicate and join with women all over the world in our struggle for peace. As a result of this conference, we are developing a world-wide women's peace network. . . .

We will not compromise our commitment to the survival and healing of this planet.

We affirm the right of every human being to live with dignity, equality, justice and joy.

Women's International Peace Conference

Bridges for Peace

U.S.–U.S.S.R. Bridges for Peace is a coalition of civic, church, and peace groups working together to build understanding between the US and USSR. We believe this is one way to reduce the threat of nuclear war, and thereby to free resources devoted to the arms race for meeting the urgent needs of global development.

From its conception, as the idea of a Norwich, Vermont church group in 1981, the "Bridges" project has rapidly expanded its program of U.S.–U.S.S.R. citizen exchange...to date 50 Soviet citizens have been hosted by the "Bridges" network in the course of the five completed exchanges. In the six U.S. visits, 75 different persons have taken part.

"Bridges" has also begun to sponsor tours to the U.S.S.R., as a supplement to our exchange program. In August and October of 1985, 30 U.S. citizens travelled to the Soviet Union on our first two tours...

The nuclear arms race now threatens the survival of the human race. Distorted and untrue views of the U.S.S.R. (and corresponding ones of the U.S.) help fuel that arms race. To break out of the cycle of fear and suspicion, both sides need to catch a new vision of each other and the future.

These are the problems that U.S. – U.S.S.R. Bridges for Peace will seek to address. We will work with church, educational and civic organizations in both countries to establish ongoing cooperation among groups committed to building understanding and overcoming enemy images. Today, on both sides, there are profound misunderstandings of the motives, history, culture and goals of the other country. A lack of direct communication between citizen leaders in the two countries compounds the long history of mutual fear and recrimination.

Specifically, U.S.–U.S.S.R. Bridges for Peace will begin what we hope will become an ongoing series of exchange visits between citizen leaders of both countries....The focuses of these exchange visits are conferences, seminars and discussions held in churches, universities and other forums. The dialogue achieved at those

Youthful emissaries for peace, Samantha Smith (above) traveled to the Soviet Union in 1983; her Russian counterpart, Katerina Lycheva (below), visited the U.S. in 1986.

meetings in turn will be shared with large segments of the public via print and broadcast media. Public lectures, publications, and audio and video cassettes will extend the dialogue to church and civic groups nationally.

*   *   *

Thus, U.S.–U.S.S.R. Bridges for Peace sees itself as helping to call into existence a trans-national network of organizations whose goal is to break the spell which seems to hover over U.S.–U.S.S.R. relations.

U.S.–U.S.S.R. Bridges for Peace

LISTEN TO THE CHILDREN

Painting from the children's film, Bombs Will Make the Rainbow Break. *The film is a documentary of the Children's Campaign for Nuclear Disarmament, a movement organized by and for children to protest the nuclear arms race.*

Declaration of the Rights of the Child

In this nuclear age, the continuance of the human race is threatened. We who give life must unite to ensure all children a future. War must be abolished. Military-Industrial domination of the world must be ended. Resources must be channeled quickly into filling desperate human needs. The capacity for life and growth must be nurtured and cherished as humanity's only real resource.

To this end we declare that every child, whatever their race or nationality, has the inalienable right to a life free from the threat of nuclear war, protection and shelter, pure air and water, nourishing food, free relationship with other children, access to the most current and relevant knowledge, and the best of medical care.

For each young child we claim the right to explore, to experiment; to climb a mountain, fish a stream; to sail, to fly, to dream; to laugh, to dance, to sing, to read, to write, to create, to learn; to respect and to be respected; to know the joy of belonging to the human race and of finding their unique place in life.

For older children we claim the right to participate freely in forming the future, and to pursue the paths they feel will lead to greater awareness of the world's oneness; the right to heed their conscience in refusing to participate in war. Institutions which deny, distort, or inhibit these rights must be restructured.

We dedicate our lives and commit our strength to the task of achieving the rights of all children. We ask women everywhere to join us now, if we are to build a humane society in time to preserve the human race.

Taimi Halonen,
International Year of the Child, 1979

174

How Does One Explain the Bomb to a Child of Three?

This letter, I somewhat embarrassingly admit, is being written at the instigation of my 3¹/₂-year-old daughter. I am a jaded, tired and retired anti-war activist from the 1960s-70s. She's a child still new to this earth, whose initial response to the "painted people" on the streets of Toronto on Aug. 6 was one of preschool artistic delight, especially since many of the stenciled figures looked to be not-too-distant relatives of her own developing schema of human form.

"Why are these painted people lying on the streets, Mama?" she asked. Well, while her figure drawings are a painstaking striving for human form, these figures represented the painful, forcible expulsion from human form wreaked on man by man. How could I explain the Bomb?

I tried; I, the mother who birthed her into this world from my own body, told her of war in that same world, of a bomb that dropped from the skies, horribly killed and could with intense heat and radiation coldly record humans in the agony of their disappearance, poisoning the earth and those on it left alive. These shadows, I said, were to remind us of the historic tragedy, to remind us not to allow its recurrence.

The Bomb was difficult enough to comprehend. Where in the categories of man, beast and thing did it occur, or was it itself a mutant hybrid of that trinity? No, no, sweetheart, the shadows are not to remind the Bomb but us, us, mankind, of the catastrophe that lurks like an everpresent nightmare in the unconscious, just waiting for us to lessen our watchfulness and wakefulness to the genuine outcome of nuclear war. It is people, governments, who drop the Bomb. It does not fall by itself. Man makes it. Man deploys it.

All of this was said in 3-year-old language, of course, and with a concerned, caring tone of voice that tried its best to smooth and soothe her, and thus my, growing anxiety. To no avail.

Endless reassurances that yes, the air-planes over Toronto only carry passengers, that it is unlikely the Bomb would be dropped here, everything said while the Mother crossed a maximum of toes and fingers and crossed-her-heart-hope-not-to-die.

Those 3-year-old bluest of eyes brimmed with tears. "Mama, how long will those shadows stay on the sidewalks?" "Until the first rain, Brie. It will wash the paint away." Her strong young voice trembled. "But I don't want the rain to wash them away!" "Why, Brie?" Her anxiety peaked. "Because then the people will forget again and the Bombs will come!"

From me, numerous endless hugs, desperate silly-sounding murmurs of "Don't worry about it," a tentative "The people won't forget." And then came her responsible 3-year-old question that shamed me into at least this small action of letter writing, that roused the sleeping activist to at least a sitting position: "What can we do, Mama, to remind the people so they won't forget?"

I told her reassuringly of peace marches, sit-ins, letter writing and lobbying governments – reassuringly because I am after all, her present security, her Mama – while inside, I, over 30, am 3 again and there wells up in me the compelling one-word-fits-all question of that tender age, augmented by overtones of angst 30 and 4 years strong: WHY? WHY? WHY?

I would like to tell her the species is wise, but I cannot. I would like to tell her the species is ultimately compassionate. . . .

"I want a bomb, Mama," she said. "Why do you want a bomb, Brie?" "Because I want to kill war."

Elizabeth Anthony

The Children of War

The Children of War Tour was an unprecedented achievement in youth peace leadership development and ultimately a witness to the inconquerable and universally held affirmation of hope over despair. It brought together 38 teenagers from 14 war-torn countries for a 54 city tour to U.S. schools, churches, synagogues and community centers. These young people spoke honestly and with great courage about the realities of growing up amidst constant warfare, violence and oppression. They asked for partners in their mission of conquering doom and cynicism and they encouraged students and adults alike to involve themselves in a positive and active crusade for worldwide peace and justice. . . .

The Children of War Tour marked the beginning of an international youth peace and justice program being developed by the Religious Task Force (RTF) of the Mobilization for Survival. The roots of the program are grounded in a deep respect for the courage and vision of young people living in circumstances of war and injustice and the belief that these youth can be role models for American youth, many of whom are experiencing a growing sense of fear, powerlessness and cynicism in the face of the nuclear threat. Through this forum for youth-to-youth exchange encompassing a variety of cultures and war experiences, young people can develop their own bonds of friendship and empowerment with the greatest effectiveness.

The message I would like to give the world leaders is that nuclear war isn't going to kill us tomorrow – it's killing us today. Many young people turn to drugs or alcohol as an escape because they figure "what's the use, my life probably won't go on long enough for me to have a career or a family." That's a killing attitude. We've got to urge our leaders to take some responsibility for the despair the younger generation feels and to do something about it. When I see the commitment of my friends here from the war zones, they are giving me a reason to get involved. They are teaching me that you can survive, and that it is important to keep trying, and never give up.

Anna Elise Price,
Children of War Tour

East Meets West

A painting from Bombs Will Make the Rainbow Break.

How do Soviet children feel about the threat of nuclear war?...Psychiatrists Eric Chivian of the Massachusetts Institute of Technology, John Mack of Harvard University and Jeremy Waletzky of George Washington University went to the Soviet Union to find out.

They gave a questionnaire to 300 youths between the ages of 10 and 15 at two Pioneer camps. (Pioneers are similar to American Scouts.) The three researchers wanted to find out how much Soviet children knew about nuclear war and whether they thought nuclear war was likely or survivable. The questions asked were similar to those used in a study of more than 900 California students.

Chivian, Mack and Waletzky had been warned before they went that Soviet youths would not know anything about nuclear war. But they found the opposite to be true. Soviet children were very aware of what the consequences of a nuclear war would be. "The entire Earth will become a wasteland. All buildings will be destroyed....All living things will perish—no grass, no trees, no greenery," said a 13-year-old.

According to Mack, most Americans believe that the Soviet Union is preparing its population for civil defense. But, he says, "The Soviet children didn't believe in civil defense. The whole notion that the Soviet Union is telling people that nuclear war is survivable is wrong."...

Said one boy, "You couldn't survive a nuclear strike. The nuclear radioactivity remains for a very long time. Even if a person goes underground, no matter

The Children's Summit

A Soviet rock group played yesterday [December 1985] in Moscow while a young audience in Minneapolis, joining in on a satellite television "space bridge" clapped and sang along in a prayer for world peace.

"Talking to each other we can create the world of peace we dream about," said singer John Denver, who was host for the U.S. side of the international production.

Young singers and actors from the United States and the Soviet Union sang duets and asked each other questions about their countries while taping the hour-long program, a "children's summit" dedicated to the late Samantha Smith. The Maine teen-ager who visited the Soviet Union as an unofficial peace envoy in 1983 was killed in a plane crash in August.

"She embodied the young of America that we want to be good neighbors with," said the Soviet host, Vladimir Pozner. Denver called Smith "a young lady whose sparkling personality lit up both our countries. Samantha Smith is not with us now, but it is our dream to keep alive her dream of peace."...

Seventeen U.S. teen-agers, who visited the Soviet Union last July to present the play Peace Child, performed with the Minnetonka Children's Choir at the Minneapolis Children's Theatre, while Soviet youngsters performed simultaneously in Moscow. The two groups—15,000 kilometres apart—were linked by a satellite that allowed them to see and hear each other on television. Translators helped the two sides talk to each other.

In one segment, a U.S. boy and a Soviet girl performed a scene from *Peace Child*, which calls for an end to the nuclear arms race. The performers' images were superimposed on a TV screen, and they appeared to clasp hands.

A U.S. girl and a Soviet boy also sang a duet in a tribute to Reverend Martin Luther King Jr., the slain civil rights leader, and a Soviet rock group, the Stas Namin, played while the U.S. audience sang in Russian and clapped.

In a question-and-answer session, the children asked each other about life in their countries.

"Do you go on dates, and when you do, do you have chaperones?" was one U.S. question.

"We have lots of opportunities. We go to the theatre. We have lots of fun," was the answer.

The program will be shown on WCCO TV, a commercial station, here tomorrow night and transmitted to 180 stations in the Public Broadcasting System by satellite Thursday. Gosterleradio, the Soviet state television, will show it to an estimated 100 million viewers, organizers said.

Associated Press

how much he wants to live, he wouldn't.

The Soviet youths were pessimistic about the chances of surviving a nuclear war: Only 3 percent thought that they and their families would survive one, compared to 16 percent of the American students. But Soviet children were more optimistic than Americans about avoiding a nuclear war.

Only 12 percent of the Soviet children thought that nuclear war would occur in their lifetimes, as compared to 38 percent of the American youths polled. And an overwhelming 93 percent of the Soviet youths thought that a nuclear war was avoidable; only 65 percent of the American students thought so.

Chivian explains that Soviet children are "very active in trying to prevent nuclear war. They sign petitions to send to NATO, they belong to International Friendship Clubs. The message they get is that their activities are helpful, and this gives them a sense of hope. American kids aren't as involved, and there is more despair."

At the end of the interview, the researchers asked the Soviet youths if they had any messages for American children. One said, "I'd like to wish that they'd struggle and fight against nuclear war." Another added, "We are the same type of people as they. We also want peace."

Elizabeth Stark

The Tunnel of Peace

Should I come across
  the tunnel of Peace –
I shall go down and cut out
  its most precious delicacy,
And spread it among human beings
    everywhere,
  for Peace to rule over land and sea.
Nations inimical, then, the sons of the
    same race,
Who were always meeting only in
    battle,
  now will mutually embrace,
And conciliated, at last each other
bless,
Looking up and weeping with joy
  as one another they address.
Then will they go to the sacred river,
  the river of Peace,
Their weapons break there
  and their guns to the deep release.
They will melt down their planes
  and into ploughshares beat their
    swords.
To fulfill the worthy Isaiah's admirable
    words.
Then will our lives be relieved
  of disappointment and despair,
Our afflictions and grief disappear;
From every spot and habitation, all
    hatreds gone,
Buried our fears, with a past we shall
    not mourn.
Come then, come to the Tree-of-Peace,
Let us shake each other's hands
  extended in Peace,
So that we may live lives of joy
  and happiness to come—
Come then, come together, come!

Ghassan Sarsour,
Age 13½, Kfar Kassem (Arab village)

War photographer Eugene Smith was injured in battle. It was thought he would never again use a camera. After many operations, he did manage to take photographs. This, his first, is full of hope.

What About the Children?

In one town, a group of children prepared their own statement on disarmament. They sent 12,000 copies of the statement to other children, urging them to write to their political leaders. The statement points out:

"Every day the threat of nuclear war becomes greater. Our leaders are making decisions that affect us, as children, more than anyone else. We believe that the only way all the people, all the children, will be safe from a nuclear holocaust is for the United States and the Soviet Union to stop building nuclear bombs and take apart the ones that are already built."

These children have expressed a powerful determination to live as free human beings and not as hostages to the threat of nuclear annihilation.

Parents and Teachers for
Social Responsibility

Italian children demonstrate with their peace banner.

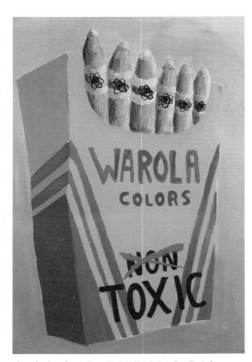

A painting from Bombs Will Make the Rainbow Break.

Young Voices

If I could ask the Pope one question I would ask if I could travel with him on his peace trips so I could meet other children in other countries and I could show them we are all alike and want to live happily together in this world.

Geoffrey O'Brien, age 7

The Paint-Box

I had a paint-box—
Each color glowing with delight;
I had a paint-box with colors
Warm and cool and bright.
I had no red for wounds and blood,
I had no black for an orphaned child,
I had no white for the face of the dead.
I had no yellow for burning sands.
I had orange for joy and life.
I had green for buds and blooms,
I had blue for clear bright skies.
I had pink for dreams and rest.
I sat down
and painted
Peace.

Tali Shurek, age 13, Beer Sheva

If everybody in the world says that they want peace how can we still have nuclear bombs? Somebody in the world must be lying.

Joan G
Age 10
Brooklyn

Dear God:
Please talk to the people. They don't know what they are doing.

The animals understand.

Cynthia K
Age 10
Boston

Grownups can't be trusted with guns and bombs.

Cynthia G
Age 8
Milwaukee

178

A Soviet child's plea for peace.

An anonymous child's drawing, likely from the Soviet Union.

Dear President Reagan,

I really want peace on earth and you can help me and all of these other children who are writing to you, to make peace.

I think you are really acting stupid twards the whole situation with Russia, like two babies, really, like two babies who are fighting, one has five rocks to throw at the other, but the other one only has four, so he get two more rocks so he has one more. Then the one that has five gets two more so he has one more again, they could go into the thousands. And what if one dropped a rock by accident and it fell on the other babies foot? then the other one would throw a rock back and they could throw all their rocks at each other instead of making up and saying sorry to each other.

This is just what will happen here, except that instead of two people getting hurt, everyone in the whole world will die, in a third world war. So please try to stop the competition. Please care, that's the least you can do.

Tanya Birenbaum, age 11

The world of the Twenty-first century

People in the Twenty-first century will be clever and kind. Now there are many animals which disappear, and people must take care of them. But animals like tasty, green grass and so we must make the air clean. There will be no hunters who like to kill

LEARNING THROUGH PLAY

Television violence.

Toys Teach the Children

The MX for a more lethal weapon. Then *Rambo* for a model of brutality. Finally the *Rambo* doll to teach our children the practice of violence. War toys prepare children for war and other kinds of violence. If that is not what you want, don't buy those toys.

Dr. Benjamin Spock

Hug O'War

I will not play at tug o'war,
I'd rather play at hug o'war,
Where everyone hugs
Instead of tugs,
Where everyone giggles
And rolls on the rug,
Where everyone kisses,
And everyone grins,
And everyone cuddles,
And everyone wins.

Shel Silverstein

War Toys

Almost like Defence White Papers (the Government's plans for the coming year) – children's arsenals of war toys tend to be re-appraised and restocked with the latest imitations of instruments of death that their parents favour. Ironically this happens during the season of "good-will."

While thousands of children are dying of hunger others are being acclimatised to the very ways of the world which make so many of these deaths inevitable.

But the issue of war toys is not a seasonal one nor is it simply to do with children or war toys. Playing with war toys does not turn youngsters into "lean mean killers" but it is not a neutral activity either. . . .

War toys help to "legitimise" and "make natural" a most unnatural and barbaric activity. Campaigning "against" war toys is not only a personal but a social responsibility. By buying war toys and by not discouraging children from playing with them, we are in a small but far from insignificant way supporting a view of the world where war – the arbitrary killing of strangers – is seen as "natural" and inevitable. Futhermore, by perpetuating such a view we are sowing the seeds of future wars. . . .

A great deal of energy goes into "teaching" children how to cross roads safely so that they don't get hurt or killed. Should not at least as much energy go into teaching children to beware of dangerous politicians, governments and the military who have acquired awesome destructive power and if not stopped soon are likely to make any war so far seem like child's play?

Peace Pledge Union

Right: Learn *by Francesc Torres.*

A painting from Bombs Will Make the Rainbow Break.

Video Games and Star Wars

Millions of people don't need to meditate along with Jonathan Schell to know that the world might end. To them, especially if they are young, the world has ended many times over. Indeed, at this very instant thousands are at Ground Zero, watching the world and themselves explode. . . . To them, the world is ending, not with a bang or a whimper, but with a zap. They are playing video games.

Video games in their present form would be inconceivable if the world did not have the means to blow itself to pieces. Not only because it is the same computer technology which spawned real missiles with warheads and mock missiles with psychedelic flares on a screen. Nor because the games in the machine imitate the strategy, the targeting, the jargon, of the "war games" played in real rooms by real adults in uniform. (*Newsweek* even reported that the Pentagon has been using versions of them as training devices.)

Video games are. . .part of a general process of what is now being called psychic numbing – as if this numbing had not been around much longer than nuclear weapons. It is not a *consequence* of that sort of armament but its *cause*. Those who play video games, and leave their sensitivity and ethics aside when they deal with fictitious extinction on the blithe screen, when they militarize their free time, do so in the same society which contemplates mass murder as deterrence, corpses as statistics, 40 million dead as victory, permanent escalation as peace. Their remoteness from what their fingers are pressing, their failure to seriously imagine what might be happening at the other end, is just a minor product and prolongation of the general remoteness of a system that has lost its capacity for caring about, or even believing in the reality of, other human beings. Video games are anesthetics because we live in a dehumanized society, where suffering has been made invisible by indifference, where the pain of others is simply not real.

Ariel Dorfman

Using Play Positively

Play is an ideal medium for positive social learning because it is natural, active, and highly motivating for most children. Games constantly involve people in the processes of acting, reacting, feeling, and experiencing. They can be a beautiful way to bring people together. However, if you distort children's play by rewarding excessive competition, physical aggression against others, cheating, and unfair play, you distort children's lives.

In cooperative sports, we are actually going back to an ancient form to help more children blossom into happy and fully functioning human beings. Cooperative play and games began thousands of years ago, when tribal peoples gathered to celebrate life.

The concept behind cooperative games is simple: People play with one another rather than against one another; they play to overcome challenges, not to overcome other people; and they are freed by the very structure of the games to enjoy the play experience itself. . . .

One of the things we hope to teach the children of the future is to become more receptive to *sharing* both human and material resources (for example, ideas, talents, concerns, feelings, respect, possessions, equipment, time, space, and responsibility). Our studies assessing the social impact of well-designed cooperative-games programs have consistently shown an increase in cooperative behavior in games, in free play, and in the classroom for children involved in these programs. The change does not occur overnight; but over a period of several months, the children seem to become more considerate and caring human beings.

The distinctive feature of cooperative games that separates them from all other games, old and new, is their structural makeup. For example, in the traditional game King of the Mountain, the rules dictate that one person be king while all others are to be shoved down the mountain. The game has competitive structure in that it demands that players act against one another and excludes all but one from attaining the object of the game. In the cooperative version, People of the Mountain, the structural demands of the game are completely reversed. The objective is to get as many people as possible to the top of the mountain, and children play together to accomplish it. This frees them from the pressure to compete, eliminates the need for destructive behavior, and by its very design encourages helpful and fun-filled interaction. . . .

Do you see children playing games that involve hitting and sometimes hurting one another with their bodies, fists, forearms, helmets, or even rolled-up newspapers or padded sticks? If so, someone is teaching them that pushing, shoving, hitting, and perhaps even hurting is OK and that other people's feelings don't count.

Hitting "sports," war games, war toys, and other types of actual or ritualized violence teach similar lessons. By promoting physical aggression or requiring it in the rules of a game, you teach children that it is perfectly acceptable to hit, push, shove, and otherwise mistreat other human beings.

Why in the world do we want to encourage young children to act out the hurting or killing of others in war simulations, shoot-outs, and so on? Why organize children into competitive games or leagues that by their very rules necessitate pushing, shoving, or hitting (for example, boxing, tackle football, full-contact hockey)?

There is not a single shred of evidence to support the position that aggressive tendencies are reduced "harmlessly" by engaging in physical aggression against others. Through physical activity children release energy and may become fatigued. However, if physical aggression is promoted in the process, the likelihood of that child's engaging in destructive dehumanizing behavior is increased. Children in peaceful societies are not nurtured on games of aggression or destruction. . . .

Cooperation is directly related to communication, cohesiveness, trust, and the development of positive social-interaction skills. Through cooperative ventures, children learn to share, to empathize with others, to be concerned with others' feelings, and to work to get along better. The players in the game must help one another by working together as a unit – each player being a necessary part of that unit, with a contribution to make – and leaving no one out of the action to sit around waiting for a chance to play. . . .

I went to a movie with my eight-month-old daughter sleeping in my arms and was refused entry at the door. The law was read to me. She must be eighteen years old to get in (even if sound asleep). "Them's the rules." I went back another day and noted that the film had a few nude dancing scenes. It is interesting that she would have been admitted to a theater across the street that was showing a film filled with war and killing (general admission). I never could figure that out.

Terry Orlick, *The Cooperative Sports and Games Book*

No War Toys, *Poster.*

FREEZE

A Bold Call

The Soviets are certainly not "superior" to the United States in any meaningful way today. If they were, we would see them using that superiority, rather than indicating concern over the technological superiority of the U.S. and its ability to leap ahead in technology in the coming years. . . .

What we need today is a bold move to halt the arms race, as a clear indication of resolution to reduce the nuclear terror to which all our populations are subjected. . . . This is the basis for the call for a mutual and verifiable freeze on the testing, production and deployment of nuclear weapons and their delivery systems. . . .

We can protect the United States better by convincing the Soviet Union not to develop new weapons systems than by developing the defensive systems to shoot them down if they are used against us.

William Colby, former CIA director

Demonstrator supporting the nuclear freeze; 1983.

Call to Halt the Nuclear Arms Race

To improve national and international security, the United States and the Soviet Union should stop the nuclear arms race. Specifically, they should adopt a mutual freeze on the testing, production and deployment of nuclear weapons and of missiles and new aircraft designed primarily to deliver nuclear weapons. This is an essential, verifiable first step toward lessening the risk of nuclear war and reducing the nuclear arsenals.

The horror of a nuclear holocaust is universally acknowledged. Today, the United States and the Soviet Union possess 50,000 nuclear weapons. In half an hour, a fraction of these weapons can destroy all cities in the northern hemisphere. Yet over the next decade, the U.S.A. and U.S.S.R. plan to build over 20,000 more nuclear warheads, along with a new generation of nuclear missiles and aircraft.

The weapon programs of the next decade, if not stopped, will pull the nuclear tripwire tighter. Counterforce and other "nuclear warfighting" systems will improve the ability of the U.S.A. and U.S.S.R. to attack the opponent's nuclear forces and other military targets. This will increase the pressure on both sides to use their nuclear weapons in a crisis, rather than risk losing them in a first strike.

Such developments will increase hairtrigger readiness for a massive nuclear exchange at a time when economic difficulties, political dissension, revolution and competition for energy supplies may be rising worldwide. At the same time, more countries may acquire nuclear weapons. Unless we change this combination of trends, the danger of nuclear war will be greater in the late 1980s and 1990s than ever before.

Rather than permit this dangerous future to evolve, the United States and the Soviet Union should stop the nuclear arms race.

A freeze on nuclear missiles and aircraft can be verified by existing national means. A total freeze can be verified more easily than the complex SALT I and II agreements. The freeze on warhead production could be verified by the Safeguards of the International Atomic Energy Agency. Stopping the production of nuclear weapons and weapon-grade material and applying the Safeguards to U.S. and Soviet nuclear programs would increase the incentive of other countries to adhere to the Nonproliferation Treaty, renouncing acquisition of their own nuclear weapons, and to accept the same Safeguards.

A freeze would hold constant the existing nuclear parity between the United States and the Soviet Union. By precluding production of counterforce weaponry on either side, it would eliminate excuses for further arming on both sides. Later, following the immediate adoption of the freeze, its terms should be negotiated into the more durable form of a treaty.

A nuclear weapons freeze, accompanied by government-aided conversion of nuclear industries, would save at least $100 billion in U.S. and Soviet military spending (at today's prices) in 1981-1990. This would reduce inflation. The savings could be applied to balance the budget, reduce taxes, improve services, subsidize renewable energy, or increase aid to poverty-stricken third world regions. By shifting personnel to more labor-intensive civilian jobs, a nuclear weapons freeze would also raise employment.

Stopping the U.S.-Soviet nuclear arms race is the single most useful step that can be taken now to reduce the likelihood of nuclear war and to prevent the spread of nuclear weapons to more countries. This step is a necessary prelude to creating international conditions in which:
— further steps can be taken toward a stable, peaceful international order;
— the threat of first use of nuclear weaponry can be ended;
— the freeze can be extended to other nations; and
— the nuclear arsenals on all sides can be drastically reduced or eliminated, making the world truly safe from nuclear destruction.

Nuclear Weapons Freeze Campaign (U.S.)

Galileo is startled by the change in earth's surface *by Honoré Daumier; 1867.*

Yes, Verification Works

Crucial to the Freeze strategy is the fact that it does not require us to trust the Soviet Union. It does not require either of the superpowers to trust each other. It is workable under a high level of distrust. The reason is that neither side can cheat without being discovered by the other.

*　　　*　　　*

It is widely believed that the Soviet Union, with its ability to suppress free inquiry and to operate in secrecy, could easily cheat on any agreement to limit nuclear weapons. The U.S., by contrast, is an open book. The Soviets would cheat readily while the U.S. could not get away with cheating at all. This view, with many variations, is widely held, but it is seriously mistaken.

The U.S. possesses a remarkable array of equipment which enables it to monitor Soviet nuclear weapon systems with a high degree of confidence. The fact is that the Soviet Union could not cheat in any significant way without being caught.

*　　　*　　　*

With this astounding array of detection equipment, each type supplementing and supporting the others, the U.S. misses very little that the Soviet Union does with its nuclear weapons. Not every move can be detected. But that is not necessary. The principle of "adequate verification" was accepted by Nixon and Brezhnev in 1973.

*　　　*　　　*

Existing nuclear arms control treaties have created difficulties for verification because they have allowed limited numbers of some weapons to be deployed, but not others. The Freeze, allowing no new nuclear weapons, would greatly simplify verification. It is far easier to tell from satellite photos that a weapons factory is completely shut down than it is to distinguish whether its activity is permissible or not.

George H. Crowell

Why the Freeze?

The nuclear freeze is the most prominent proposal to halt and then reverse the nuclear arms race. After decades of arms talks mired in technicalities and political cowardice, the freeze promises a simple means to a mutually agreed upon deceleration of the arms race. It would require the superpowers to agree to stop the production, testing and deployment of new nuclear weapons and their delivery vehicles to pave the way for cutbacks in present arsenals.

Project Ploughshares (Canada)

Supporting the Freeze

Among the prominent endorsers of the Freeze proposal are such statesmen and arms control experts as: George Ball, former Under Secretary of State; Warren Christopher, former Deputy Secretary of State; Clark Clifford, former Secretary of Defense; William Colby, former Director of the CIA; Major General William Fairbourn, U.S.M.C. (Ret.); William Foster, former Deputy Secretary of Defense; Admiral Noel Gayler, former Director National Security Agency; Averell Harriman, former Governor of New York and Ambassador to the U.S.S.R.; George Kennan, former Ambassador to U.S.S.R; Admiral Gene LaRocque; Paul Warnke, former Director Arms Control and Disarmament Agency; Thomas Watson, former Chairman IBM and Ambassador to the U.S.S.R.; and Jerome Wiesner, former President M.I.T.

Among the many religious leaders endorsing the Freeze are 140 of the 280 active Roman Catholic Bishops. Over 78 organizations have endorsed it, including: The National Council of Churches, the Union of American Hebrew Congregations, the YWCA of USA, the Conference of Black Mayors, the United Methodist Church and the United Presbyterian Church.

The Norwich Peace Center (U.S.)

THE PEACEFUL MUSE

American Dream #1, Everything is Coming up Roses *by W. Buchanan.*

A Poem for Now

A poem can be many things
in miniature:
a short story
about people
a photograph
a surreal landscape

It can be
a wild experiment
with music and sound
a small sermon
a prophetic warning
(*all a poet can do
is to warn* – Owen said)

Above all
a poem records speech:
the way it was said
between humans   animals   birds
a poem is an archive for our times

That is why NOW today
a poem must cry out
against war!

Dorothy Livesay

The Responsibility of the Artist

I have to speak about how I feel as a writer. I don't like calling myself "an artist," but I guess I am, and would join my tribal sisters and brothers in many ways. I believe that as a writer...an artist, if you will...I have a responsibility, a moral responsibility, to work against the nuclear arms race, to work for a recognition on the part of governments and military leaders that nuclear weapons must never be used and must systematically be reduced. Throughout human history, artists have affirmed and celebrated life. Whether we work in words, in music, in painting, in film, in bronze or stone or whatever our medium may be, the artist affirms the value of life itself and of our only home, the planet Earth. Art mirrors and ponders the pain and joy of our experience as human beings. In many parts of the world, and over many centuries, artists have risked and even given their own lives to portray the society around them as they perceived it, and to speak out against injustices. Since the most ancient times,

artists have passed on to succeeding generations the tales, the histories, the songs, the sagas, the skills of their trade. Can we conceive of a world in which there would be no succeeding generations? A world in which all the powerful works of the human imagination would be destroyed, would never again be seen or listened to or experienced? We must conceive that this is now a possibility, and one not too far in our uncertain future, either. We must not, as artists, or so I feel, stand by and passively allow this to happen. The death of the individual is the end which we will all one day meet, but in the knowledge that our children and their children will live, that *someone's* children will go on. . . . The individual is the leaf on the tree. The leaves fall but the tree endures. New leaves are born. This concept has been the mainstay of our species from time immemorial. Now the tree itself is threatened. All art is a product of the human imagination. It is, deeply, an honouring of the past, a perception of the present in one way or

another, and a looking towards the future. . . . Artists, the real ones, the committed ones, have always sought, sometimes in ways prophetic and beyond their own times, to clarify and proclaim and enhance life, not to obscure and demean and destroy it. Even the so-called literature of despair is not really that at all. Despair is total silence, total withdrawal. Art, by its very nature of necessary expression, is an act of faith, an acknowledgement of the profound mystery at the core of life. As a writer, therefore, I feel I have a responsibility. Not to write pamphlets, not to write didactic fiction. That would be, in many ways, a betrayal of how I feel about my work. But my responsibility seems to me to be to write as truthfully as I can, about human individuals and their dilemmas, to honour them as living, suffering, and sometimes joyful people. My responsibility also must extend into my life as a citizen of my own land and ultimately of the world.

Margaret Laurence

The Peace Museum

It's certainly not your typical Establishment museum ensconced in neoclassical trappings. Its home is a lavender-and-peach storefront at 364 West Erie Street [in Chicago]. Its expanding permanent collection includes a four-leaf clover picked more than 35 years ago by a Hiroshima survivor, an abundance of antiwar buttons, and a Fritz Eichenberg lithograph of a dove swooping down on a hawk. But as the world's first and only peace museum, its *raison d'être* is as unique as its exhibits.

"What we're trying to do here is to explore issues of war and peace through the visual, literary, and performing arts," says the museum's co-founder and director, Mark Rogovin. "Our purpose is to grab people on an emotional level, to raise their consciousness to the urgency of the nuclear question and the many other issues involved in building peace." And it appears that Rogovin, his staff of seven, and a veritable "peace army" of 40 volunteers are doing just that. In the 19 months since the museum opened, nearly 75,000 people have viewed eight art exhibitions and attended a variety of films, lectures, concerts, and festivals, all intended, according to Rogovin, "to communicate the horrors of war and/or express the visions and dreams of peace."

Judith Neisser

Poster by Takashi Ishida; Toho Gakuen Junior College Thirteenth Graphic Design Course Graduation Work; 1981.

Imagine There's a Future

Can art be political? Can it avoid being political? Whether the political views of artists ultimately make a difference may be less germane than the inevitability that their opinions appear in their art. And, it seems, quite a few artists are concerned about the threat of nuclear war. "Imagine There's a Future," an arts festival mourning and commemorating the 40th anniversary of the bombing of Hiroshima and Nagasaki, starts tomorrow in Los Angeles.

Artists in the areas of theatre, film, music and the visual arts are taking their cues from John Lennon, whose song "Imagine" is the anthem of a generation. "Imagine There's a Future" was initiated by the Hollywood Women's Coalition, an organization of executive women from the entertainment industry, and by the Interfaith Center to Reverse the Arms Race. They have coordinated protests, performances and events around the Hiroshima anniversary date of Aug. 6. Beginning tomorrow, however, nine galleries in Los Angeles will offer art exhibitions addressing the nuclear issue. Significantly, the art selected for these shows focuses not on the looming mushroom cloud of the past, but on the possibility of a future without the threat of nuclear war.

According to Linda Lopez, one of the coordinators of the visual arts exhibitions, the goal is "to apply as artists our best creative thinking toward envisioning a future free of nuclear threat."

Hunter Drohojowska

Griefkit

Good evening. My name is Veronica Mandel, and I've come to talk to you tonight about the psychiatric effects of nuclear war, or what can be done for mental health after the Bomb has dropped.

American psychiatrist Robert Jay Lifton has identified one of the major problem areas as "psychic numbing:" a profound blandness, insensitivity, and inability to experience grief—or indeed to feel anything at all. This will be detrimental to our continued development as whole human beings inside the bomb shelter, and may seriously limit our capacity to form co-operating groups in the new world outside.

The natural mourning process, which could alleviate the severer symptoms of "psychic numbing," will be inhibited in many cases, or made very difficult, by the absence of bodies to bury – through vaporization, incineration, or other forms of corporeal annihilation. It is hard to bury a shadow on the wall. Another problem with nuclear devastation is its scale. Try to imagine one hundred million dead. Try it. And of those of us left, how many will be therapists? On a more individual level, it is unlikely that we will survive together with anyone close to us, or even be anywhere near our loved ones at the moment of impact. In the aftermath, the process of grieving and saying goodbye to those we have lost may assume supreme importance.

It is vital—and I use the word in its original sense of "essential to life"—that we are all prepared, in the event of nuclear attack, to be our own therapists. There are self-help books now available: *Good Life, Good Death*, by Dr. Christian Barnard; *Positive Thinking at a Time Like This*, by Norman Vincent Peale; *How To Be Awake And Alive*, by Mildren Newman and Bernard Berkowitz. These are no longer enough. Researching into more appropriate ways to meet an imminent need, psychologists have devised a "griefkit" to keep always by you in a safe, accessible place. It is very simple, consisting of ordinary household items:
— a box, with a well-fitting lid—clearly marked with your name
— a cushion or pillow
— photographs of the people you love
— a safety pin
— some kitty litter.
In the coming emergency, we believe that grief and mourning must have their place: the dead, as well as the living, need space. To this end there will be racks made available for griefboxes in every government shelter, but it is up to the individual to be responsible for his or her own kit. So, when the warning sounds, be sure to bring yours with you. Your future sanity could depend upon it.

Now, how to use your griefkit: Place the pillow directly in front of you. Take the photographs one by one and name them, give them a name, their name: Grandad, Suzy and Michelle, Bill, Jimmy, Anita.

Visualize them. See them smile. Hear them breathe. Now, take a safety pin and pin your loved ones to the griefpillow. Say to yourself: "This is me. I am here and I am alive. These are the people I love. They had their own individual existence, and now they are dead." Take the pillow and hold it to you for a moment. (Pause) Now, bury them: place the pillow in the griefbox, take some kitty litter, a handful should be enough, and sprinkle it over the ones you love, repeating:
"Death is random, death is not fair, death is random, death is not fair, death is random . . ."

When you are ready to say goodbye, close the lid firmly and put your box away handily should the need arise.

Remember, when the nuclear warning is given, if you bring nothing else, bring this. It may mean the difference to your emotional well-being, after the Bomb has dropped. Thank you.

Kate Lushington

Peace Mission

The Brigandeer-General ceremoniously receives three ladies who have been selected to deposit with him a petition for peace, bearing the signatures of ten zillion women. These three sumptuously clothed ladies represent respectively: the first, the second and the third worlds. The Brigandeer-General thanks them courteously, shakes each gloved hand and holds it a bit too long, and with a cursory glance at his Aide-de-Camp, indicates that the moment has come to show the ladies to the door. He places the petition on the mirror-polished grain of his vast mahogany desk; sensuously, he riffles its pages. He is comforted by it, this voluminous petition. It assures him that, after the holocaust, there will be at least someone to whom he can turn for moments of solace and cosiness. After the dust and the debris, after the disease and the radiation plagues have swept death along before them, after the dead have been gathered and are being disposed of, he will be guaranteed at least one thankful forgiving cuddle with one of the ten zillion who so crave peace.

Greta Hofman Nemiroff

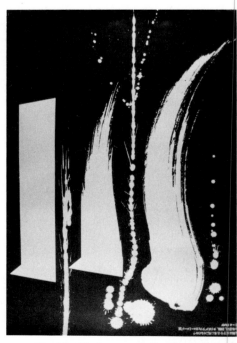

Can Mankind pass on Letters to the Future?
by Yoji Yamamoto, 1980.

The Face of Peace *by Pablo Picasso, 1944-1945.*

Them and Us

...His expression immediately stern, he presses his lips tightly together. "Isobel, you have to understand. The Russians are not entirely rational. They're quite different from us. Taking over the world is, after all, part of their ideology."

Them. Us. Yes, this is his way of thinking. She has heard it before.

"Look dear, nobody is for nuclear weapons. But when you live under a political system that guarantees your freedom, you have to be prepared to fight to preserve it. Do you think for one minute you could have a conversation like this in Russia?"

She shakes her head. "That's not the point. Russia's not the enemy. Don't you see, Dad? The bomb is the enemy. It's the enemy of every living thing!"

She hears herself talking on. *Treaties. SALT II not ratified by the U.S. Pershing and cruise missiles. Computer accidents. Nuclear war.*

But she can tell he is not really listening. He is counting numbers, missiles, thinking whatever you think to pretend objectivity. He is a scientist, he is good at that.

"Don't be so glum, Isobel. And don't believe all that *Day After* nonsense either. There'll be survivors. There always have been. A few people will go without work for awhile. A few will go hungry. But life will go on."

The fear rises in her. The fear of him, of people like him—"the enemy"—even as she tries to grasp the inherent contradiction in that, tries to make herself understand, *it's not so much what you say but how you say it; forget politics, this is a human issue; one human being caring about the next....*

"Dad, that's not what matters to me, don't you see?"

She looks down at the table, fumbling with the napkin. But what is she doing now—crying? She dabs her

eyes quickly with the napkin. She never meant this to happen.

Immediately he is concerned. "I'm sorry, dear. I didn't mean to upset you."

Sorry. Upset. The words startle her.

"You shouldn't take my opinion so seriously. We have to learn to live with our differences. Isobel?" He squeezes one of her hands affectionately, pausing. "I probably won't live to see a nuclear war in my life."

"But I might," she says.

"Yes, that is possible. But hopefully, Isobel, there won't be a nuclear war. Hopefully each side will be too scared to do it."

She suddenly remembers her father's foot heavy on the gas pedal, and her, the frightened twelve year old beside him, watching as the car skidded down the icy winter road....

Irene Mock, from *Neapolitan*

Big Bang on the Big Screen

Now spanning two generations, atomic movies are the longest-running genre in postwar Hollywood. A proposal for a film series, the following countdown is also a sentimental journey recalling fallout highlights.

10...*Notorious* inaugurated the genre in 1946, its title less descriptive of the movie than of Alfred Hitchcock's FBI file upon its release. A World War II romantic suspenser in which a CIA agent (Cary Grant) blackmails a German émigré (Ingrid Bergman) into investigating the Nazi underground in South America, *Notorious*'s "McGuffin" leads us to an Axis stockpile of uranium hidden in the villain's (Claude Rains) wine cellar.

9...Also in 1946: *Gilda*, a romantic look at cynicism which shares *Notorious*'s Buenos Aires locale and its contorted love/hate triangle. Its sinister plot revolves around an entrepreneur's (George Macready) efforts to establish a tungsten cartel, and the way Macready's eyes glint nefariously when he says "tungsten," licking his lips, you know it has something to do with the Ultimate Weapon.

8...In a little-seen but pleasant 1949 Warners musical, *My Dream Is Yours*, Doris Day enthusiastically scats a breath-stopping ditty, "Tic-Tic-Tic,"

From the T.V. film: **The Day After.**

that makes "Mame" sound like a lullabye. Playing a would-be swing vocalist auditioning for "Cuddles" Szakall (acting the part of a frankfurter mogul who might hire her for his company's radio hour), Day snaps her fingers and jitterbugs to what must be the only upbeat song about the bomb – the power of the blast, the glory of the geiger counter and all that.

7...In order not to offend the French Communist Party, Sam Fuller's *Pickup on South Street* (1953) was retitled *Porte de la Drouge*, and reedited to tell a story about drug smugglers rather than the Tale of Two Larcenies – what happens when Soviet agents in Manhatten try to pass microfilm of the bomb formula and get foiled by a petty grifter (Richard Widmark) who's just picking pockets.

6...Although a comedy, *The 5000 Fingers of Dr. T.* (also 1953) written by Dr. Seuss himself (under his real name, Ted Geisel), crystallized the twin fears of the American kid: piano practice and the bomb.

5..."The Big Whatsit" is how Mike Hammer (Ralph Meeker) refers to the bomb in *Kiss Me, Deadly* (1955), a demoniacally funny riff on the Mickey Spillane novel....In A.I. Bezzarides's astonishingly literate screenplay, quoting from Christina Rossetti and Robert Oppenheimer, director Robert Aldrich captures echt L.A.: hucksters trying to cash in other people's chips in the casino of a city that Aldrich frames like Dick Tracy Meets Tinseltown.

4...I was seven when I first saw *On the Beach* (1959), based on Nevil Shute's novel about survivors of nuclear war living the last days on earth in Australia. In it Fred Astaire plays Julian Osborn, a nuclear physicist who, when people begin succumbing to radiation sickness, closes himself off in his garage and starts his Ferrari....

3...An esoteric but equally compelling assessment of life after atomic wartime is Alain Resnais and Marguerite Duras's *Hiroshima, Mon Amour* (also 1959) in which a thirtyish Frenchwoman (Emmanuelle Riva) plays an actress starring as a nurse in a movie "about peace" when she meets handsome Hiroshima architect (Eiji Okada) and they have an affair.

2...*Shock Corridor* (1965), a volatile Sam Fuller movie which begins with a Euripides epigram, "Those whom the gods wish to destroy they first make insane," is about the transvaluation of the American Dream—into American Madness....The germane character is Dr. Boden, a composite Edward Teller and Robert Oppenheimer, who "went insane working on nuclear fission." In his rare moments of lucidity Boden tells the reporter he went nuts from living "with a two-week notice to quit living....I got fed up with men taking daily hammer-and-sickle-coated pills of venom."...Such viewpoints, Fuller suggests, get a man committed.

1...In that manifesto of amoral superiority, *Dr. Strangelove, (Or, How I Learned To Stop Worrying and Love the Bomb)*, General Jack D. Ripper (Sterling Hayden) personifies the American Cold Warrior – a bonkers air force commander who, worried that the Soviet "Doomsday Device" (bigger than a breadbox, bigger than an H-bomb) is about to sap his vital fluids, dispatches a fleet of B-52 bombers to destroy Russia, despite the fact that President Mucketymuck (Peter Sellers) hasn't authorized it.

0...An antidote to *Strangelove*'s amorality, *Fail-Safe* shows how even America's moral superiority can be eroded by paranoia when the president (Henry Fonda) has to be responsible for the unplanned American annihilation of Moscow.

Carrie Rickey

Poster for the movie Dr. Strangelove.

Politics

The superpowers have the privilege of being able to destroy our planet several times in rapid succession, and yet there are still those who try to score political points by declaring that one or other of them is lagging dangerously behind the other in potential for obliteration.

Peter Ustinov

Escalation

I think we're closer to nuclear war now than we've ever been...even closer than during the Bay of Pigs crisis. We are not achieving anything by a buildup of weapons that we cannot possibly use. We all know rationally that the first country that sets off a weapon is guilty of genocide, because it's not possible to use just one nuclear weapon. There would have to be escalation, and every scientist, every physicist, has told us that if this happens, the world as we know it will be destroyed.

Joanne Woodward

SING OUT FOR PEACE

The Peace Anthem

Folk singer Pete Seeger stepped to the microphone at the Washington Monument last week to sing the John Lennon-Yoko Ono song "Give Peace a Chance." A handful of the quarter of a million peace marchers joined in. Soon the entire assemblage was chanting the plaintive hymn – "All we are saying /Is give peace a chance" – over and over. The peace movement had found an anthem.

Newsweek

Peace Will Guide

When the moon is in the seventh house
And Jupiter aligns with Mars,

Then peace will guide the planets,
and love will steer the stars;

This is the dawning of the Age of Aquarius,
The Age of Aquarius.

Rado & Ragni

May There Always Be Sunshine

Bright blue the sky, sunshining high
That was the little boy's picture:
He drew it for you
Wrote on it, too
Just to make clear what he drew:

May there always be sunshine!
May there always be blue skies
May there always be Mommy!
May there always be me! May there
always be me!

My little friend, kind little friend,
this is the dream of the people;
Hearts old and young never have done breathing the
hope you have sung.

Soldier, do hear,
Hear what we fear:
War would make all of us losers.
Peace is our prize;
Millions of eyes
Anxiously gaze at the skies.

Gone be all war!
We want no more!
Let us stand up for our children.
Sing, everyone,
Peace must be won,
Dark clouds must not hide the sun.

Soviet Children's Peace Song

John Lennon gives the peace salute in front of the Statue of Liberty.

Imagine

Imagine there's no heaven
it's easy if you try
no hell below us
above us only sky

Imagine all the people
living for today – ah

Imagine there's no countries
it isn't hard to do
nothing to kill or die for
and no religion too

Imagine all the people
living life in peace
you may say I'm a dreamer
but I'm not the only one
I hope some day you'll join us
and the world will be as one (live as one)

Imagine no possessions
I wonder if you can
no need for greed or hunger
a brotherhood of man

Imagine all the people
sharing all the world

John Lennon

I Am Singing

There're songs to make you smile
There're songs to make you sad
But with a happy song to sing
It never seems as bad
To me came this melody
So I've tried to put in words how I feel
Tomorrow will be for you and me

I am singing of tomorrow
I am singing of love
I am singing someday love will reign
Throughout this world of ours
I am singing of love from my heart

Let's all sing someday sweet love will reign
Throughout this world of ours
Let's start singing
Of love from our hearts
Let's start singing
Of love from our hearts

Stevie Wonder

Russians

In Europe and America, there's a growing feeling of hysteria
Conditioned to respond to all the threats
In the rhetorical speeches of the Soviets.
Mr. Krushchev said We will bury you.
I don't subscribe to that point of view.
It would be such an ignorant thing to do
If the Russians love their children too.

How can I save my little boy
From Oppenheimer's deadly toy?
There is no monopoly of common sense
On either side of the political fence.
We share the same biology
Regardless of ideology
Believe me when I say to you
I hope the Russians love their children too.

There is no historical precedent
To put the words in the mouth of the president
There's no such thing as a winnable war
It's a lie we don't believe anymore.
Mr Reagan says we will protect you
I don't subscribe to that point of view.
Believe me when I say to you
I hope the Russians love their children too.

We share the same biology
Regardless of ideology
What might save us, me and you
Is that the Russians love their children too.

Sting

Andorra

I want to go to Andorra, Andorra, Andorra
I want to go to Andorra, it's the land that I adore
They spent $4.90 on armaments and their defence
Did you ever hear of such confidence—Andorra hip hoorah!

In the mountains of the Pyrenees, there's an independent
    state
It's population 5000 souls and I think they're simply great
170 square miles big and it's mighty plain to see
They spent less than $5 on armaments and this I've got to see.

They're governed by a council – all gentle souls and wise
Spent less than $5 on armaments and the rest on cakes and
    pies
They didn't invest in a Pershing, or a cruise to sweep the
    skies,
They bought some blanks for their cap pistols to shoot on
    their 1st of July

I wandered on down by the Pentagon, this newspaper
    clipping in hand
I hollered I want to see the ones who say they're defending
    the land
I said "Look what they've done in Andorra – they put us all to
    shame
The least is first, the biggest is last – let's get there just the
    same."

The generals said "My dear boy, you don't understand
We need these things to feel secure in our great and wealthy
    land."
I said "If security's what you need, I'll buy a couch for you –
A head-shrinker's cheaper and quicker, and a damned sight
    safer too."

Pete Seeger

Last Night I Had The Strangest Dream

Last night I had the strangest dream I'd ever had before.
I dreamed the world had all agreed to put an end to war.
I dreamed I saw a mighty room the room was full of men,
And the paper they were signing said they's never fight again.
And when the paper was all signed, and a
    million copies made,
They all joined hands and bowed their heads and grateful
    prayers were prayed.
And the people in the streets were dancing round and round,
While swords and guns and uniforms were scattered on the
    ground.

Ed McCurdy

THE PROFESSIONAL CONSCIENCE

A Call to Professionals

The Professionals' Coalition for Nuclear Arms Control is a lobbying coalition of professionals concerned about stopping the nuclear arms race. Based in Washington, D.C., the Professionals' Coalition offers up-to-date information on arms control legislation. We maintain a legislative alert network to inform supporters by mail or telephone of upcoming arms control votes in the Congress. We publish a quarterly newsletter, an annual Voting Record of arms control votes in Congress and a Citizen Lobbyist Skills Manual.

Most important, the Professionals' Coalition provides our supporters with practical and timely advice about when and how to lobby their Members of Congress.

We help professionals stay well-informed, cogent and persuasive on arms control issues. They are well prepared when they talk with peers or politicians. In short, the Professionals' Coalition helps professionals use their special expertise to promote effective arms control legislation.

- Lawyers are working to ensure carefully defined arms control agreements with a strong impact on international law and treaties.

- Scientists are bringing their knowledge of nuclear technology and the feasibility of proposed weapons systems.

- Physicians are documenting the medical consequences of nuclear war, as well as the human costs of the arms race.

- Architects, Designers and Planners, trained in creative problem-solving, are contributing their vision of a better quality of life, less threatened by the financial demands and destructive potential of today's nuclear weapons.

- Other Professionals are needed and welcome to become part of this hard-hitting and effective lobbying network.

Professionals' Coalition for
Nuclear Arms Control

The Legality of Nuclear Weapons

The Lawyers Committee on Nuclear Policy is one of a number of organizations that organizes people through their professions by appealing to shared values and expertise.

It is the position of the Lawyers Committee that *nuclear weapons are illegal and ought to be abolished.* Our organizing is with lawyers, students, scholars, and other members of the legal community to build that recognition, and to build expertise within the legal community to make those arguments in the pages of scholarly publications, in courts, to legislators, to neighbors, to each other.

We have done that in our work with a group of women from Greenham Common Women's Peace Camp in Great Britain, whom we represent in a suit against the present administration. They are co-plaintiffs, with several members of Congress claiming that the deployment of cruise missiles in that country is illegal, violates international law, and violates the Constitution. It's not just immoral, which is bad enough. It's not just horribly dangerous, which is bad enough. It is illegal and the courts and all of us have an obligation to do something about that.

Anne Simon,
Lawyers Committee on Nuclear Policy

Writers and Publishers

On the subject of the arms race more than any other, we in publishing have a responsibility to try to change attitudes, not just follow them. We have a duty to educate ourselves and the public about the danger we are in and the most promising directions out of it.

And there are other ways in which writers and publishers can speak out. A little over two years ago, we and some of our book industry colleagues founded the Writers and Publishers Alliance for Nuclear Disarmament (WPA), to give the publishing industry a group through which to work against escalation of the arms race, much as the Freedom-to-Read Committee of the Association of American Publishers gives us an organization through which to work against censorship. . . . We have organized several conferences on the arms race, in conjunction with a magazine group known as the Editors' Organizing Committee. With the EOC we cosponsor the annual Olive Branch Awards, which recognize outstanding magazine articles on the arms race.

The Writers and Publishers Alliance is doing what we best know how to do—spreading the word—about the most important issue of our time.

Peter Matson and Bob Bender,
co-founders of the WPA.

STOP THE
NUCLEAR WEAPONS
核兵器廃絶

Stop the nuclear weapons *poster.*

Falkland War *by Ralph Steadman.*

Peace in the Media

It really mystifies me that the same media which take such immense pride in their ability to fearlessly cover every bloody aspect of a war—and serve us a side order of entrails with our nightly dinner—are reduced to quivering blobs of indecision at the prospect of how to handle a walk for peace.

I mean, war is straight-ahead stuff. Pure jock, if you will.

That's why war correspondents and sportswriters are considered the Macho Men of any major metropolitan daily.

They both cover the home team. They both cheer from the press box (some openly, some through closed lips). And there's always lots of action.

But peace?

Who ever heard of a peace correspondent? He'd probably stand there in front of the camera with a disarming smile and talk about peace and love and motherhood and God and all those other highly controversial subjects; which are considered journalistically unsound in some quarters.

War-talk is manly, front-page stuff.

Peace-talk is sissy and suspect.

Maybe that's why more than 50 U.S. journalists are assigned to cover the Pentagon, while not one major news organization in North America has made peace and disarmament a regular beat.

Missile rattling has become the phallic symbol of the 80s.

Forget about the fact that the world is sitting on the nuclear equivalent of one million Hiroshima bombs. We want the baseball box scores!

But as Richard Pollak put it in. . .*The Nation*:

"If we're all crisped in a missile exchange, it won't matter how many hits Pete Rose got yesterday, or whether showers are expected tomorrow."

John Robertson

195

Physicians for Social Responsibility

The medical profession cannot remain quiet in the face of the increasing diversion of scarce resources to the military compared to the meager efforts devoted to combatting global poverty, malnutrition and disease. . . .We are already living in the rubble of World War III.

Perhaps the signal acomplishment of IPPNW [International Physicians for the Prevention of Nuclear War] has been the broad-based, free-flowing dialogue between physicians of the two contending power blocs. We heed Einstein's words, "Peace cannot be kept by force. It can only be achieved by understanding." In a world riven with confrontation and strife, the IPPNW has become a model for cooperation among physicans from East and West, from North and South. Paranoid fantasies of a dehumanized adversary cannot withstand the common pursuit of healing and preventing illness. Our success in forging such cooperation derives largely from an insistant avoidance of linkage with problems that have embittered relations between the great powers. We have resisted being sidetracked to other issues, no matter how morally lofty. Combatting the nuclear threat has been our exclusive preoccupation, since we are dedicated to the proposition that to insure the conditions of life, we must prevent the conditions of death. Ultimately, we believe people must come to terms with the fact that the struggle is not between different national destinies, between opposing ideologies, but rather between catastrophe and survival. All nations share a linked destiny; nuclear weapons are their shared enemy.

The physicians' movement is contributing to a positive world outlook, rejecting the view that human life is merely the molecular unwinding of a dismal biologic clock. For the physician, whose role is to affirm life, optimism is a medical imperative. Even when the outcome is doubtful, a patient's hopeful attitude promotes well-being and frequently leads to recovery. Pessimism degrades the quality of life and jeopardizes the tomorrows yet to come. An affirmative world view is essential if we are to shape a more promising future.

Physicians For Social Responsibility

University Women for Peace

The American Association of University Women is the oldest and largest national organization for the educational advancement of women. We have 190,000 members in 50 states, the District of Columbia and two U.S. territories. . . .While our struggle for equal rights is often considered an issue separate from the broader question of the arms race, our members have grown increasingly aware of the impact of the arms race on the daily lives of American women. Our own leaders were aware of this connection as early as 1946 when AAUW General Director Helen Dwight Reed wrote:

> It is difficult for Americans to fully realize that the shrinking world involves a threat to our individual lives, and that our security as a nation is no longer something that the U.S. can assure by military strength alone. . . .Only through sincere and effective international cooperation can the world be kept at peace.

Our members know that the arms race is a women's issue, but the stakes in 1982 are qualitatively different. Like all members of the human race, American women live in dread of a nuclear war and its disasterous consequences. In the U.S., as in other nations, the unprecedented build-up of nuclear and conventional weapons robs society of resources for peaceful development. It robs societies of funding for education, for child care, for health benefits, for research, and for agriculture. . . .

Women in the U.S., and in our Association, now realize the direct connection between arms spending and their own well being. They are also painfully aware that women and children are the principal victims of poverty wherever it exists and that monies spent on arms are not available to help people in need.

American Association of University Women

Scientists for Peace

The Union of Concerned Scientists (UCS) is an independent nonprofit organization of scientists and other citizens concerned about the impact of advanced technology on society. UCS's efforts focus on nuclear arms control, nuclear power safety, and national energy policy. Formed in 1969 as an informal group of MIT faculty and students, UCS today is a nationally respected advocate of arms control and safe energy policy.

UCS directly affects policy debates by conducting independent research, sponsoring and participating in conferences and panels, testifying at congressional and regulatory hearings, and other educational activities. We make a unique contribution to public debate because of the scientific and technical expertise we offer.

Union of Concerned Scientists

The Sorcerer's Apprentice

The jargon and style of military planners today is not significantly different from that of their counterparts in business, which is not surprising, given the close relationship between the military and large American corporations. Just as American business forecasters talk incessantly of the important role of "information" in maintaining a competitive economy, military planners speak of information as the key to prevailing in any conflict. Some even speak of future conflict as "a war of information," which certainly sounds less threatening than talk of casualties and destruction. Consider the following passage from a paper called "Application of Artificial Intelligence to Tactical Operations," by Major Timothy Campen and Don E. Gordon of HRB-Singer, Inc.:

> More information will be collected for the battle than ever before. Both opponents will be confronted with handling unsurpassed quantities of information to use for operational planning and intelligence. The force that can get the information needed the most and use it the best will have an advantage far more critical than numerical superiority of combat forces.

There is a similarity in this passage with advertisements for business computer systems that promise small companies the competitive advantages of larger companies without the expense of more capital and personnel. This "doing more with less" spirit is now a fundamental part of American Army planning, despite the enormous defense budgets. The managerial revolution in American business has finally penetrated the American military. Thus it is not surprising to find that a new buzz word in military planning is the oxymoron "battle management." . . .

If the experience in Vietnam is repeated, future wars using high tech battle management systems are likely to produce a level of firepower and corresponding destruction that will dwarf that of any previous conflict. Battle management systems will be explicitly designed, according to Campen and Gordon, to allow commanders to "see and engage the enemy at maximum effective range." It is not hard to imagine the next war looking much like a video game to many of its "combatants." In fact, the U.S. Army self-consciously reversed a policy some years ago that kept coin-operated video games to a minimum on Army bases, when it discovered that the games were useful in improving soldiers' hand-eye coordination and in adjusting them to the task of destroying fast moving electronic representations of targets. Even back in the Vietnam years, two *Washington Monthly* reporters, Paul Dickson and John Rothchild, suggested that high tech war

> eliminates a constant problem of Vietnam and other wars—that some men must go and fight while others watch on television. With the truly automated system, everybody, including the soldiers, will watch the war on televisions—the only difference between the Army and the American Legion being the placement of the viewing screen. . . .

The idea that people might be sent off to kill, and be sent off to their deaths, because of the decisions of a machine is also a concentrated form of modern barbarism. There is no known way to hold a machine responsible for its actions. Machines given the capacity to kill are capable of murder, probably of even more senseless murder than humans, because machines would have no motive whatsoever. But they are incapable of remorse, suffering, guilt or a sense of responsibility, and thus incapable of being punished. There has not yet to my knowledge been a demon in the world's entire history that was capable of murder but incapable of being punished. But we are on the path to building such a demon, and the consequences of such an historical act would be as profound, and probably as irreversible, as the development of nuclear weapons.

Thus the momentum of the Strategic Computing Initiative, which includes research and development on an autonomous vehicle, or combat robot, as well as the Airland Battle Management system and its seaborne counterpart, must be opposed with all vigor. The SCI has all the features of a tragic analogue to the story of the Sorcerer's Apprentice, an apprentice that would come back to torment us in a time of greatest need.

Gary Chapman,
Computer Professionals for Social Responsibility

Peace mural on Chicago street. Photo by René Burri; Sept. 1981.

A Declaration from Murikka

We, adult educators from 21 countries, gathered at the annual meeting in Finland held at the Murikka Folk High School, Teisko, Finland (theme of the 1983 meeting: Preparation for Peace):

aware that our profession is dedicated to life-long learning in a world which spends 650 billion U.S. dollars a year on arms and in which 900 million adults are illiterate,

and concerned that our efforts to seek "the full development of the human personality and the strengthening of respect for fundamental liberties" (from the U.N. Universal Declaration of Human Rights) are increasingly threatened by the technology and practice of repression throughout the world, and by the prevailing international economic order,

therefore call on all adult educators numbering today several million, to join with us in a global effort to help stop the arms race and to urge that substantial resources now spent on weapons be used instead to:

1) promote adult literacy and learning for international understanding,

2) meet basic human needs, such as primary health care and the elimination of poverty and unemployment,

3) create the conditions for guaranteeing and enforcing basic rights and freedoms in all countries, as a specific example, examined at the Murikka meeting, to support the efforts of National Liberation Movements in Southern Africa recognized by the Organization of African Unity to Achieve Self-Determination and National Independence,

4) help to create an awareness of existing unjust economic relations in the world and to support United Nations' efforts towards the establishment of a new international economic order.

Conference participants 18th June 1983

Military Recruiting in the High Schools: Creating a Dialogue

ESR is continuing the efforts begun by the Philadelphia and Metro New York ESR chapters. Surveys of public high schools in cities across the country are underway to determine the nature and extent of military recruitment on campuses. The project will conclude with recommendations of appropriate educational guidelines to assure accurate and balanced presentations of military service and its alternatives. The Military Recruiting in the Schools packet has been completed and mailed to every chapter.

From the ESR National Board

Peace in the Classroom

Over the last three years, Chicago ESR [Educators for Social Responsibility] has written two curriculum packets, sponsored conferences, spoken at meetings, and conducted in services. But our newest and proudest achievement has been a fifteen week course taught under the auspices of the Chicago Board of Education to seventeen Chicago public elementary and high school teachers. This feat didn't come easily, but the net result of our efforts seems really to have paid off.

Now we have a core of teachers with some training, who can go back to the classroom and try out these ideas. In addition, each of them can and has passed on information to others.

With our teacher training program, we now hope to bring some of our ideas directly to the teachers in the schools. We have hired a half-time staff person to make contacts and present workshops in the schools. Probably, we will start with those schools in which the participants in our course teach. And—after a few revisions—we hope to offer the course again.

Paula Baron

Building the Future

Architects, Designers, and Planners for Social Responsibility (ADPSR) welcomes the opportunity to communicate with design professionals bound by one very fundamental concern – to build shelters of beauty and strength. Before we build again, we must first fathom the weakness in our shelters when fortressed by nuclear arms. As we mount our campaign against environmental issues which threaten the quality of life for present and future generations, ADPSR continues to seek out interested designers, architects and planners to join with us in addressing the current economic and social deterioration of our cities and built environment and the issue of nuclear disarmament. We invite you to join us.

Architects, Designers and Planners for Social Responsibility

The Challenge for Social Science

It is no joke to say that the behavior of people in national governments currently poses a threat not just to human civilization, but to human survival. Nor to say that to assure our survival and civilization, national governments must be dissuaded by a deep transformation of political culture and international law from having the ability to visit catastrophes on the human race, and, indeed, the entire biosphere, as scientists now predict would result from even a less-than-full nuclear war.

Social scientists can help prevent nuclear war by studying and participating in that transformation. The psychological and other factors that have caused leaders and most citizens to avoid facing this transformation must be impartially exposed and constructively overcome.

The World Constitution and
Parliament Association

Psychology's Task

The question that keeps coming up, in letter after letter and in every face-to-face encounter is, Is there anything I can *do*, right *now*, to help stop the drift toward nuclear war?

And on one level, at least, the answer is a simply and resounding *Yes*! Literally thousands of organizations are springing up, in every community, and they need able and committed people. These are groups lobbying for the freeze at the village, county, and state level; urging serious negotiations on their U.S. representative and senators; advocating local resistance to illusory civil defense programs; voting nuclear weapons and facilities out of their community; keeping the issue, in general, alive before the public. . . .

But these are all things nearly any relatively informed person can do. Is there something else, something special, that we as psychologists can be involved with?

Again, the answer is *Yes of course*, but the territory is less explored and will require some innovation. Here are a few ideas that have been suggested:

Nuclear family *by Don Carr, 1982.*

- First of all, join or establish a local group of psychologists concerned with issues of nuclear disarmament.

- Affiliate with a national organization like PsySR, individually and as a group.

- Set up study groups to discuss alternatives to present policies. Bring in technical experts. Release the proceedings to the media.

- Do the same thing in a public forum, or on radio and television.

- Study the *psychological* aspects of the arms race, and write and speak on this issue.

- Volunteer as a facilitator for other groups working on disarmament, either for their internal process or for public panels sponsored by them.

Psychologists for Social Responsibility

ON GUARD FOR PEACE

No More War *by James Grashaw, winner of the* Avant Garde *"No More War" poster contest, November 1968.*

Beyond Victory

The hydrogen bomb is not the answer to the Western peoples' dream of full and final insurance of their security. It is not a "cure-all" for the dangers that beset them. While it has increased their striking power it has sharpened their anxiety and deepened their sense of insecurity.

The atomic bomb in 1945 looked to the responsible statesmen of the West an easy and simple way of assuring a swift and complete victory – and subsequent world peace. Their thought, Sir Winston Churchill says, was that "to bring the war to an end, to give peace to the world, to lay healing hands upon its tortured peoples by a manifestation of overwhelming power at the cost of a few explosions, seemed after all our toils and perils, a miracle of deliverance." But the anxious state of the peoples of the free world today is a manifestation that the directing minds failed to think *through* the problem – of attaining peace through such a victory.

Captain Sir Basil Liddell Hart (1895-1970)

War

War is at best barbarism. . .
Its glory is all moonshine. It is only those who have neither fired a shot nor heard the shrieks and groans of the wounded who cry aloud for blood, more vengeance, more desolation. War is hell.

William Tecumseh Sherman (1820-1891)

No Security

Stimulated by the need for offensive weapons in this second world war, science has unlocked new secrets of mass destruction in the atom bomb and in other deadly weapons. Because those secrets have unmistakably revolution-ized the character of war itself, they have also confounded the problem of how we shall keep the peace.

The discovery and stockpiling of these new weapons can give no nation a lasting assurance of safety. The capacities of science are not only unlimited, but they are also available to the many nations throughout the earth.

In this new age of science, the technology of offense will always be superior to the weapons of defense. Science has, therefore, unwittingly allied itself on the side of aggressors. New weapons with their potential capacity for knock-out blows offer an invitation to attack.

We can be reasonably certain that we shall find no adequate security against long-range rocket bombardment in the creation of buffer states and in the acquisition of island bases. We have finished the last great war where natural barriers can serve as effective defenses.

We shall find no adequate security in the development of new weapons; science will forever be devising superior ones.

We shall find no permanent and adequate assurances of safety in the longtime maintenance of huge national armies and navies.

General Omar Bradley (1893-1981)

Russian soldiers shake hands with U.S. officers and enlisted men when they meet at Orabow, Germany; May 3, 1945.

Vested Interests

In the councils of government, we must guard against the acquisition of unwarranted influence, whether sought or unsought, by the military-industrial complex. The potential for the disastrous rise of misplaced power exists and will persist. . . . We must also be alert to the equal and opposite danger that public policy could itself become the captive of a scientific-technological elite.

I think you know that I believe we must be strong militarily, but beyond a certain point military strength can become a national weakness. The trouble with collecting military strength beyond our needs is that it tends to become a substitute for all the other things involved in true national security.

It fosters the notion that national security is automatically tied to the amount of money we spend on arms. What we overlook is that we may be spending our money on the wrong things. When we get into over-spending we get into misspending and inefficiencies.

I don't want to see us subsidize fraud and incompetence. I don't want people who have a financial stake in crisis and tensions to have a voice in national policy.

Dwight D. Eisenhower, (1890-1969)
from farewell presidential address, 1961

The Need to Reconcile

Let there be no illusions about space weapons: They are not for Star Wars but for nuclear war on Earth. Space weapons combined with offensive nuclear missiles, such as MX, Pershing II and Trident II, destroy the opponent's second-strike capability, thus making possible a first-strike. A first-strike capability leads with certainty to war. We resolutely demand: Let us not continue the insanity of the arms race by extending it into space. Let us instead unite our creative energies in the struggle against hunger and poverty and for the reconciliation of humanity!

Retired NATO Generals
for Peace and Disarmament

No Winners

Now, electronics and other processes of science have raised the destructive potential to encompass millions. And with relentless hands we work feverishly in dark laboratories to find the means to destroy all at one blow.

But this very triumph of scientific annihilation – this very success of invention – has destroyed the possibility of war's being a medium for the practical settlement of international differences. The enormous destruction to both sides of closely matched opponents makes it impossible for even the winner to translate it into anything but his own disaster.

Global war has become a Frankenstein to destroy both sides. No longer is it a weapon of adventure – the shortcut to international power. If you lose, you are annihilated. If you win, you stand only to lose. No longer does it possess even the chance of the winner of a duel. It contains now only the germs of double suicide.

General Douglas MacArthur (1880-1964)

Nuclear Nonsense

As a military man who has given half a century of active service I say in all sincerity that the nuclear arms race has no military purpose. Wars cannot be fought with nuclear weapons. Their existence only adds to our perils because of the illusions which they have generated.

There are powerful voices around the world who still give credence to the old Roman concept – if you desire peace, prepare for war. This is absolute nuclear nonsense and I repeat – it is a disastrous misconception to believe that by increasing the total uncertainty one increases one's own certainty.

Lord Mountbatten (1900-1979)

Affordable by Kim MacConnel, 1981.

Reduce the Fear

Frankly, I think people at both ends of the political spectrum expect too much from arms control. They tend to think the negotiations will somehow make all our problems go away. But in my judgment, the arms control process itself is almost as important as any agreement. For even if both sides scrapped 5,000 nuclear weapons tomorrow, the world would be no safer if tensions between the two countries remained the same. What these negotiations do is establish some degree of mutual confidence.

There must be some way to break through the tremendous suspicions and fears that are to a large extent the driving forces in superpower relations. One way to begin would be to establish a regular dialogue between American and Soviet military leaders—who, from my experience, tend to be more moderate than many of the political people on either side. When SALT II was signed in 1979 I accompanied President Carter to Vienna and met with Marshal Ogarkov. It sounds incredible, but that was the first time the two most senior military officers of the two countries had conferred since General Marshall met with Marshal Zhukov after World War II. In that one meeting we were able to clear up some misrepresentations and suspicions. I think a regular dialogue would go a long way toward reducing the fear that drives both nations.

General David Jones, U.S. Army

War: An Unintelligent Option

For 50 years I've dedicated my intellect and my energies to preparing for wars, fighting in wars and analyzing wars. I'm here to tell you tonight that war is a very dumb way to settle differences between nations. And nuclear war is utterly insane.

*　　　*　　　*

So pervasive have nuclear weapons become in our military today that they are now the conventional weapons. We've nuclearized our army divisions, our air wings, and 80 percent of U.S. Navy warships routinely carry nuclear weapons. When you see a warship off your coast, if it's a U.S. Navy warship, you've got an 80 percent chance that it is floating around with nuclear weapons.

When I had command of a guided missile cruiser, the *Providence*, in 1964, we used to ride up and down your coast with nuclear weapons. We were one of the first to get them on surface ships, and when I had command nobody told me I couldn't use them. Nobody said I had to get a message from anybody to use them. They were my main battery. They were, in fact, the only weapons that I had to shoot down a Soviet or any other enemy missile or aircraft that were any good. As a matter of fact, while I'm mentioning that, the only way that we could destroy a Soviet submarine today is with a nuclear weapon. The only way the Soviets can destroy one of our submarines today is with a nuclear weapon. The old fashioned depth charges are gone. We have nuclearized our military forces.

We've got them, you'll say, but we're never going to use them. Well, the United States and the Soviet Union are both planning, training, arming and practicing for nuclear war everyday.

Okay, you say, but are we going to have a nuclear war? Yes, we are. We are going to have a nuclear war if we stay on this course. We and the Soviet Union are on a collision course. They're trying to expand. We're trying to control them. We don't like their economic system. They're anti-God. We don't like their political system. We don't like anything about them.

Our Secretary of Defense has identified the Soviet Union as the enemy. Our President says the Soviet Union is an evil empire and ought to be relegated to the ash heap of history. Our Vice-President says we can fight and win a nuclear war. We're dramatically increasing the number of nuclear weapons we have. You and I are building five nuclear weapons a day. In a ten year period, we're building 17,000 new nuclear weapons. . . .

I was giving a talk at one of our major war colleges a couple of years ago to colonels, captains, generals and admirals, and I said, "Look, fellows, we're all professionals. You know, I know, there's no way to fight and win a nuclear war, right?" I finished my lecture, and a colonel gets up and says, "Admiral, you're right. We don't know how to fight and win a nuclear war. But it's our job to *find* a way to win a nuclear war!" That's what's driving the arms race. I said, "Colonel, I understand where you're coming from. Sure, you and I didn't join this outfit to fight a war to a draw. We didn't join this outfit to lose a war, but you ought to level with the American public. Tell them you don't know how to win a nuclear war, and stop trying to fool them by suggesting that if they'll give you thousands of more nuclear weapons and billions of more dollars that you can find a way to win a nuclear war. There isn't a way. That's the dangerous part of Mr. Reagan's Space Defense Initiative."

You hear a lot of people, even in the military, talk about controlling a nuclear war. "We're gonna use a few nukes, and they'll use a few nukes. We're gonna control it." That is just *crazy*. Once you start exploding nuclear weapons, the lid is off.

*　　　*　　　*

There is one thing in this country that is different from other countries, and that is simply this: You can call the White House. You can't call the Kremlin; you can't call the Blue House in Korea; but you can call the White House. And I want to suggest that you do that on any weekday from 9 to 5. I call every week. When you call, they'll answer: "White House, Executive Office," and you say, "I'd like to speak to the Comment Section, please." Then say, "I want to tell Mr. Reagan to please not buy more nuclear weapons." And the lady will say, "yes, thank you, anything else?" Say that you'll call him next week about something else. I know about this because my wife, Lili, was a volunteer in the White House under Mr. Carter. They do keep records. Here's the telephone number, and you don't even have to write it down. Just call Washington, area code 202, then 4-5-6 (everybody can remember 4,5,6), and then the others are 76-39. You see, I'm 76, and Lili's 39. Now give the President a call; it's a very exciting and wonderful experience in participatory democracy because after you've called the White House a couple of times, you'll want to start calling everybody else, and that's good. The more people you call, the better off we're going to be.

Admiral Gene LaRoque, U.S. Navy (Ret'd)

BREAD OR BOMBS

Scrapped B-52 bombers lie in Tucson, Arizona, field for 20 days so that USSR satellites can verify their destruction, in accordance with the SALT agreement.

Buying Insecurity

Military consumption has increased spectacularly over time, as fleets and armies in Europe and elsewhere become more expensive and more destructive. World military expenditure is more than twelve times as great in real terms as it was fifty years ago; it is more than twenty-eight times as great as it was in 1908.

Yet such expenditure has failed in its objective of buying "security." The process of military spending yields decreasing returns to increasing "inputs" of money. Even the richest military powers buy something less than security with their immense resources: military forces which may be useless in real crises; military equipment which may be matched by an enemy who emulates their military exertions. In many developing countries, the price of military "security" is increased human misery....

Since the colonial wars of the 1750s or before, rapid increases in military spending have been associated with rising prices. The "peacetime" wars since 1945 were times of inflation in Western countries. In 1950-51, the year of sharply increased weapons procurement for the Korean War, the increase in the consumer price index in the U.S. went from less than one per cent a year to 7.9 per cent, and in Britain from 2.8 per cent to 9.7 per cent....

It is possible, too, that military involvement may alter the character of a country's scientific institutions, even when it provides extra resources for scientific work. Military science requires qualities – secrecy and the isolation of scientists – which are not necessarily favourable to civilian research, or to the civilian diffusion of discoveries. The most spectacular applications of American research in military electronics have come not in the U.S. but in a country – Japan – with a different and impeccably civilian organization of science, technology, and commercial innovation; whose military industry is about the size of its toy industry; and which, with an economy over half the size of that of the U.S., spends less than one hundredth as much public money on military research....

The import and export of weapons have become an essential feature of international trade in the last ten years. This commerce is likely to have serious economic costs for arms-importing developing countries. It has evident benefits for exporting countries. But in the long term it may not be in the economic self-interest of either group, or of the world economy as a whole....

Military spending is a charge on the economic future of all countries, the richest and the poorest, those who import and those who export arms, the East and the West. Its economic consequences are in certain respects similar in the most diverse countries. Everywhere, it demands resources which are already scarce and which are becoming yet more scarce in the early 1980s.

United Nations report, 1982
Common Security

Trolleys that Don't Run on Time

What is to be done about the military economy which operates as a deadly detractor, for competence of every kind, in civilian economy? Let me give you an example – the case of Boeing Vertol. It's a division of the Boeing company located outside Philadelphia that has specialized in military helicopters. In the early 1970s, someone had an idea – they should try to compete for design of a trolley car called the light rail vehicle, and for subway cars. They did that – they won the competition, they got contracts from Boston and from San Francisco and from other cities and they proceeded to manufacture and deliver trolley cars. Five years later, they were out of the trolley car business and a recent visit to the plant disclosed not a trace of any of that activity.

Why couldn't they make a trolley car? Why wasn't it a satisfactory business? Trolley cars are being bought in the U.S. but they are all being imported. There isn't a single trolley car factory in the U.S. What happened? Why couldn't they make a competent trolley car? The reason is they went into the enterprise and made it a further application of aerospace technology. So, concurrency was the practice and they went from the drawing board right into production and, lo and behold, as the trolleys were produced and put on

the rails, things happened. There were little glitches and defects in design. Those were, of course, corrected in the further cars that were produced and a team of technicians was sent up to Boston and the company stood by its warranty to the full letter of the word and then some. They wanted to protect the good name of Boeing. They put an engineering staff to work on this, of which one member had some railroad experience, and the others as described to me were full of confidence, the excess of which is called arrogance. Judging, as they did, that if we could design an aircraft to fly with the speed of sound, we can certainly design a vehicle to roll wheels on rails at 50 m.p.h. Famous last words!

In order to develop that competence, they would have had to either send a team of their people abroad to work in firms that were producing competent vehicles of that class, or hire a team of instructors from such firms to teach them how to do it on their premises. But that was out of the question, unthinkable. So they did no occupational conversion of the engineers, no re-training to civilian competence, no re-training of the management to civilian competence, no re-orientation of the blue collar workers to what was required in the making of a

trolley car, and they produced vehicles that finally wouldn't run. They broke down so frequently that they were a disaster in civilian service.

Now if you look at some of the data you might discover that they had, say, half the trolley cars in repair at a given moment. Why that's no different than, say, half of the F-15 airplanes being in repair at a given moment, which in fact has been the average record in a recent year. What's the difference? Well the difference is dramatic and clear. When the F-15s are in repair, it happens behind barb wire fences, either inside the United States, usually in remote locations, abroad, or on similar aircraft on aircraft carriers. Now when the trolley cars go out of service suddenly, there is no transportation into town. People can't get to work and when it happens more than once, the newspapers take notice.

So competence in producing the civilian product has importance that is not to be matched in the case of the military; or, to put it differently, unreliability in a civilian product is unbearable, where comparable unreliability is bearable in a military product. That's the point.

Seymour Melman

Who Pays?

A balanced budget has been the Reagan Administration's prescription for curing the ills of the economy, although this goal has proven elusive in the face of massive tax cuts for the wealthy and for corporations, which decrease government revenue. Nevertheless, Reagan is committed to spending at least $1.6 trillion on the military in the next five years and at the same time keeping a lid on overall government spending.

So who is bearing the brunt of this balancing act?

It is the poor (those people living below the government-defined poverty level of $8,414 a year for a non-farm family of four) and the disadvantaged...and that means women. Seventy-five percent of poor people are women. One in three female-headed households lives in poverty, compared to one in 18 male-headed households. Women 65 and over are the poorest of the poor, many living on $2,800 or less a year.

Minority women, because of the combined effects of racial and sexual discrimination, form a disproportionate share of the poor. Two-thirds of all poor Black families are headed by women. Almost half of all families headed by Black and Hispanic women live in poverty.

Council for a Livable World

Peace marcher stresses need for bread, not bombs.

Bringing Star Wars Down to Earth

The dream scenario goes as follows:

Each superpower independently and cleverly decides that the only sane objective is to lower the opponent's military threat, rather than racing endlessly to keep ahead of him. . . .

Together the U.S. and U.S.S.R. announce that $100 billion a year will be made available for an unprecedented human development program, to which other nations are asked to contribute in proportion to their military expenditures. Global response is immediate and wildly enthusiastic. A World Peace Corps is formed. . . .

They also agree on the immediate objective: a direct attack on poverty, to bring help to the very poorest first. Planning is left to an international board of dedicated specialists. Meanwhile, the traditional international development agencies will continue their efforts on structural adjustments and long-term development programs.

As the governing board of wise men and women meet to determine priorities, the mails are flooded with world-wide expressions of support and a growing list of unmet needs with initial annual price tags. A random sampling shows the scope of poverty and neglect awaiting attention.

Growing long-term unemployment, now common in industrialized as well as poorer countries, has serious psychological effects on society. Skills and motivation decline. Visible projects, clinics, housing, schools, generate employment and community pride. Highly publicized development programs in some slum and squatter areas could stimulate public action in others.

Community projects for job creation . . . . $18 billion

Hunger is the enemy faced daily by hundreds of millions of people throughout the world. Children are the major victims. Those who survive malnutrition in early life are mentally and physically handicapped. As a supplement to emergency food aid, nutrients such as iron, Vitamin A, and iodine, should be provided to fortify staple foods.

Nutrients to supplement staple foods . . . . $2 billion

In rural areas of the Third World, the majority of the population does not yet have access to health services even of the most basic kind. A crash program for training of bare-foot doctors and medical auxiliaries, and provision of small health posts is essential for improving health care outreach.

Community-based health service . . . . $10 billion

In the coming decade the increase in the world's school-age population will center in the Third World, where only half the children of school-age are now attending school. Even to maintain present enrollment ratios, 100 million new school places will be needed by 1995. Training and construction programs should target areas of greatest deficiencies.

New schools and teacher training . . . . $12 billion

The earth's forests are shrinking at an alarming rate, the result of rapid population increases in regions dependent on wood for fuel, and urban and industrial spread. Deforestation represents a fuel crisis in developing countries, and also leads to soil erosion and desertification. A widespread tree-planting program is needed.

A major increase in tree planting . . . . $3 billion

Young people constitute 40 percent of the unemployed in many areas. By the end of the century the youth population is expected to exceed 700 million in the Third World where unemployment is acute and chronic. Training and apprenticeship programs emphasizing new skills must be expanded.

Training programs for young people . . . . $5 billion

Subsistence agriculture, the major employer of the labor force in the Third World, is also the key to eliminating food shortages. Planning and assistance must include women, who are the major food growers in many areas, and include sufficient acreage to support a family. Technical aid, irrigation, pest control, fertilizers, are essential for increasing yields.

Development of small farm holdings . . . . $15 billion

Unsafe water and inadequate sanitation account for three-fourths of illnesses in poor countries. Over half the population lacks an adequate supply of safe water; even larger numbers are without sanitation facilities. Water taps and sewage systems could sharply reduce the incidence of diseases like malaria, and add 10 years to low life expectancies.

Safe water and sanitation for all . . . . $20 billion

Industrialization has neglected labor-intensive, light-capital manufacturing which could increase employment and improve living conditions especially among poorest families. There is a universal need for such low-cost technology as simple stoves, small biomass plants, hand-powered grinders for grain.

Labor-intensive, low-cost technology . . . . $4 billion

Repeated child-bearing, short birth intervals, and pregnancy at an early or late age, all pose high risks to the health of women and their children. Programs for family planning, food supplements in pregnancy, prenatal and perinatal care are limited especially in South Asia and Africa where mortality is highest and population growth most rapid.

Health-care network for women . . . . $6 billion

Street people are increasing in numbers in cities throughout the world. Estimates for Latin America alone indicate that there may be as many as 40 million street children, many abandoned, most suffering from malnutrition. Community-support programs are needed for housing, health care, and education.

Community care for street people . . . . $2 billion

The lag in basic educational opportunities for women is evident in an increasing gap between male and female literacy. The problem requires specifically targeted programs for deprived groups, particularly in rural areas. Young school graduates should be trained to help in these programs.

Literacy drive emphasizing skills for women . . . $3 billion

Ruth Leger Sivard, from *World Military and Social Expenditures, 1985*

Untitled painting by Cathie Felstead.

Weighing the Costs

- Over 100 million people around the world are paid by the various war ministries. *This is a working population almost as large as that of Europe.*

- The number of governments under military rule has, between 1960 and 1979, trebled.

- Wars around the world continue erupting *(there have been over 150 wars fought since 1945)* and the major industrialised countries continue to make profits from the sale of arms to the warring countries.

- Where people escape being killed by bombs or bullets, they may not escape the famine and disease which often follows war. *Over 100 million people have died from wars this century.*

- In countries not directly involved in war, people, in various ways, are being deprived as resources, both human and material, are being absorbed by military activities. *In Britain it costs some £60,000 to train a fully qualified surgeon, it also costs £1,700,000 to train a fully qualified fighter pilot.*

Peace Pledge Union

On average it costs about the same:

- to arm and train one soldier as it does to educate 80 children

- to build one modern bomber as it did to wipe out smallpox over a 10-year period

- to launch the latest nuclear-missile submarine as it does to build 450,000 homes

Council on Economic Priorities

GRASSROOT LINKS

Everyone Makes A Difference

There are times when each of us is frustrated. What can one person do? The power of the Pentagon seems so great, the money of the corporations so limitless, the CIA so massive. And it is necessary for our sanity to remember our limits. None of us alone can change the world – which is the reason we join organizations, find strength in community. But we must also keep two things in mind. *First*, every majority began as a minority of one. Every revolution was once a lost cause. Societies never change until many join together—but the change always begins with one person. *Second*, no one knows when the addition of one more voice, one more body, one more action suddenly changes a situation totally, in the same way that one more degree of heat causes water to boil. It is around a particle of dust that rain drops form – in our case, political "rain drops" that can become a flood for justice, and disarmament.

Be informed. Read up on crisis areas such as Central America, the Euromissiles, the Middle East, the link between high military spending and high unemployment and inflation. . . . *Facts* are one of our strongest allies.

Write the editor of your paper. People read the letters column. Write a short, factual letter on a current issue and send it in.

Call-in radio shows. Do you listen to the "Call-in" shows? So do millions of others. Why not call in? Be brief, be courteous, but be heard.

Talk with friends. You aren't the only one in your community worried about where things are going. Have some friends by and see if they would be interested in starting a group to study issues together. An informal group of citizens thoughtfully meeting together can be the basis for changing the thinking of a whole town.

War Resisters League

Design by Shigeo Fukuda.

More Peace Activities

- Help your children put on a backyard play or neighborhood "fair" which has as its theme the prevention of nuclear war.

- Get friends and neighbors to contribute money to rent a billboard somewhere amidst the rush-hour traffic and place a statement of your views on it. Even better, change the statement at regular intervals to keep motorists looking for the latest message.

- Call or write to an advertising agency and ask them to consider donating some of their resources toward educating the public about these issues.

- Run marathons and other road races while wearing a T-shirt bearing a message concerning the arms race.

- Design and build a homecoming float that bears a message against nuclear war. Get it into the halftime show on a nationally televised football game.

- Donate or raise the money to duplicate particularly good essays, articles on the topic, and distribute these to school classes, church groups, etc.

The Nuclear War Study Group, Harvard Medical School

Let Them Know

Your representative's vote on the MX missile system, arms limitation agreements, military budgets, and other matters is strongly affected by local public opinion. How many times has each of us said: "I've been meaning to write my representative, but I just can't seem to get around to it." Perhaps you're making too big a project of it. Keep a stack of postcards ready, and jot down your opinions whenever an item in the news gets you riled up. . . .

If you have a particularly strong opinion about an issue, and want more than a pro or con vote, then write a personal letter. Don't wait until you can compose the perfect letter. One Congressman commented that he pays more attention to the sincere letter legibly handwritten on scrap paper than to all the form letters he receives. Your own common sense will tell you what to write but if you'd like a few tips to help you get started, try these:

1) Start with a positive comment, perhaps commending your representative's openness to citizen opinion.

2) Show you know something about your representative's stand on military issues by mentioning a recent speech, vote, or newspaper comment. (If you don't know how he or she stands on the issue, ask.)

3) Relate a personal story about the way nuclear war concerns or frightens your family, or has an economic impact on you. Don't hesitate to take a moral or religious stand, or to relate a conversation, a nightmare, a personal insight, or your reaction to a TV program or a film.

4) Focus on a specific issue—a proposed new weapon system, the new Pentagon budget, a treaty or other bill. State your own position clearly, and ask your representative to do likewise. Don't feel you have to be an expert.

5) Suggest to your representative where he or she can turn for accurate, expert information, independent of the Pentagon and military contractors.

6) Ask your representative if he or she would be willing to meet with you.

7) Tell your representative that you are deeply concerned about nuclear war and hope for a personal reply rather than a form letter.

8) Save all the rest of your ideas for the next letter – don't try to cover more than one issue at a time!

9) Put a legible return address and phone number on your letter. Envelopes may get thrown away.

What Not To Do

Many groups attempt to start from scratch to create a new community organization. They rent a room, make posters and leaflets, and urge people to interrupt their routine to come to a meeting and join the group. They are discouraged when only a handful of people show up.

Don't try to organize your community! It is already organized. It's organized into Rotary and Lions Clubs. It's organized into Y's, schools, labor unions, religious bodies, and Chambers of Commerce. There are also political parties, world affairs groups, environmentalists, consumers, and government units. Plug in!

Center for Defense Information

Grassroots in motion; 100,000 demonstrators took part in the great "March for Democracy and National Reconstruction" in Buenos Aires; December 16, 1982.

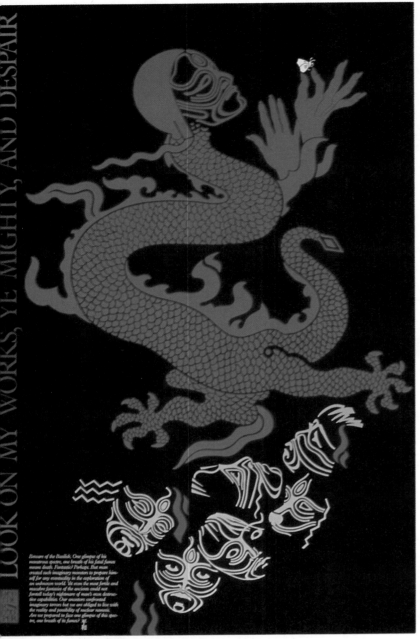

Look on My Works Ye Mighty and Despair *by Heather Cooper.*

A Personal Statement

Beware of the Basilisk. One glimpse of his monstrous spectre, one breath of his fatal fumes means death. Fantastic? Perhaps. But man created such imaginary monsters to prepare himself for any eventuality in the exploration of an unknown world. Yet even the most fertile and macabre fantasies of the ancients could not foretell today's nightmare of man's own destructive capabilities. Our ancestors confronted imaginary terrors but we are obliged to live with the reality and possibility of nuclear nemesis. Are we prepared to face one glimpse of this spectre, one breath of its fumes?

                                        From poster above

You Are Cordially Invited...

This is one possible way to present a Coffee Party for Peace.

1) Introduce yourself; then introduce those attending to one another. (An alternative is to go around and have people introduce themselves and state briefly why they are there.)

2) Tell why you decided to have the Coffee Party, what motivated you to contact Peace Links, why you want to do something to prevent nuclear war.

3) Provide basic facts – talk about one or two points you feel particularly concerned about. (Contact the Peace Links office and let us know how many information packets you need.)

4) Allow time for mutual sharing – go around the table and have everyone express feelings, fears and hopes, any suggestions for action, etc.

5) Provide a way for those gathered to "do something" about their concerns.

The Coffee party format can be modified for presentations for local mainstream groups, for women's groups, or for your place of worship.

                                        Peace Links

Ten Steps You Can Take For Peace

1) Write to the President, your Representative and Senators.

2) Set up a meeting with your Representative and/or Senators at the local district office or attend a Candidates' Night.

3) Call the White House Public Comment Number: (202) 456-7639.

4) Write a letter-to-the-editor expressing your opinion about the arms race (especially appropriate when there has been national news coverage on the issue).

5) Invite 5 friends to your house to discuss the issue and how you can work together in your community to help prevent nuclear war.

6) Talk to local school leaders about beginning peace studies and global awareness programs in the schools.

7) Present "Peace Panels" to local mainstream groups such as the League of Women Voters, the Rotary Club, and local churches or synagogues.

8) Show a film to a club or organization you belong to, or at your place of worship.

9) Start a Peace Links group to involve other community members in ongoing activities to prevent nuclear war.

10) Vote "Peace" every chance you get.

                                        Peace Links

I CALL HEAVEN AND EARTH TO WITNESS AGAINST YOU THIS DAY, THAT I HAVE SET BEFORE YOU LIFE AND DEATH, BLESSING AND CURSE;

AS FAR AS IT DEPENDS ON YOU LIVE AT PEACE WITH EVERYONE

THEREFORE CHOOSE LIFE, THAT YOU AND YOUR DESCENDANTS MAY LIVE. DEUTERONOMY 30:19 AND ROMANS 12:18

As far as it depends by calligrapher Timothy Botts.

Brainstorming

One of the best ways we have found to come up with ideas about community-based actions is to "brainstorm" as a group all our fantasies and imaginings of what we would like to have happen locally. Letting the creative side of our brain run wild and not judging any of the ideas while that is happening is not only productive but also a lot of fun. From those "brainstorms" we then pick up on those ideas which appeal the most. And then we think about what is possible.

We want to share with you some possibilities for community-based organizing which are a result of our brainstorming and experience.

Vigils. . . on November 13 (Karen Silkwood's Memorial), August 6 (Hiroshima Day), August 9 (Nagasaki Day), March 28 (Three Mile Island) or an on-going vigil until nuclear power and arms are discontinued. One of the comments we have heard most often after holding a vigil is that townspeople are at first startled, and when they recognize a familiar face in the group holding the vigil it is much harder to ignore the issue.

Pickets. . . in front of the office of a local utility on the day electric bills are due or when the utility comes out with offensive advertisements for nuclear power generation. . . .

Research. . .the percentage of electricity that is generated by nuclear power for local use and what sources are available locally for a change-over to safe, economic and renewable energy. This can be time-consuming, but it can produce some interesting and valuable information. We discovered that a local hydroelectric plant, owned by a utility, generated electricity which was transmitted hundreds of miles away and that several other hydro sites had been phased out in anticipation of nuclear construction in Seabrook. When a tabloid was put together with this information along with proposals for community control of energy resources, thousands of people in the area became more aware of the fallacy in the utility's claim that "we need Seabrook." The possibility of community ownership rather than corporate control of local energy resources developed into a concrete issue for many in the area.

Propose Town/City Ordinances. . . that ban nuclear construction, transportation of nuclear materials, nuclear waste storage or mining and milling uranium within the town/city limits. Over 35 towns in Vermont have accomplished all four proposals by either requesting the selectwomen and selectmen to list the ban with the articles voted on during town meeting or, if they refused, obtaining the necessary signatures on a petition to insure the inclusion of the article at town meeting. Ways to make sure the ban is passed by the voters in the town are to print a fact sheet about the reasons for needing a ban, write letters to the editor of the local newspaper, and be prepared to talk about the issue at town meeting day. One of the many satisfying results of this approach, besides the education potential and the success of locally restricting nuclear development, is the connections that are made with other people who feel similarly. At our town meeting, where we had an article proposing a ban on uranium mining and milling, people we had not met before spoke out in support of the article.

From *a Handbook for Women on the Nuclear Morality*

WE THE UNDERSIGNED

An Open Letter to the Canadian Government on Cruise Missile Testing

A Gallup Poll taken last month [January 1983] indicated that 52% of all Canadians don't want Cruise missiles tested in Canada. Last November, 70 to 80% who voted in the municipal referenda voted "Yes" for disarmament. Clearly, there is no public mandate for such testing.

Despite these results, your government recently signed an agreement to allow United States weapons tests in Canada. We understand you are considering a further agreement to allow Cruise missile tests in Alberta and Saskatchewan.

We are opposed to testing the Cruise missile, for nuclear weapons do not provide security. Their existence is a threat to the continuation of life on earth. Testing the Cruise missile will contribute to a dramatic escalation of the arms race and will make verifiable arms control agreements extremely difficult. It will also weaken Canada's ability to play its traditional constructive international role for peace.

We therefore urge you to refuse to allow the testing of Cruise missiles in Canada, and to press for productive negotiations towards disarmament. We encourage you to initiate a full national debate that will allow all Canadians to decide the role they wish Canada to play in ending the arms race and building a durable peace. For humanity's sake, please act now!

Project Ploughshares

A Statement from the Emergency Committee of Atomic Scientists, 1947

- Atomic bombs can now be made cheaply and in large numbers. They will become more destructive.

- There is no military defense against atomic bombs, and none is to be expected.

- Other nations can rediscover our secret processes by themselves.

- Preparedness against atomic war is futile and, if attempted, will ruin the structure of our social order.

- If war breaks out, atomic bombs will be used, and they will surely destroy our civilization.

- There is no solution to this problem except international control of atomic energy and, ultimately, the elimination of war.

Duty Is Universal

It has become vitally important for scientists all over the world to warn all men of the new dimensions of the approaching danger, which threatens the health not only of those men now alive, but also of future generations of mankind. . . .

Collective and individual statements asking for immediate cessation of test explosions of atomic weapons have been recently made [1957] by the Scientific Council of Japan, 2,200 American scientists, 256 English scientists, 230 French scientists, 18 prominent German physicists, by many scientists in China, Czechoslovakia, India, Sweden, and other countries. . . .

In such a tense time, full of danger of a general destructive war, scientists cannot remain aside. Their duty is to add their voices to the requests for the cessation of the atomic tests.

The danger which hangs over mankind because of the possibility of using atomic energy for war purposes, is common to all countries, independent of their political and economic systems. We believe, therefore, that scientists of all countries should show their common concern with the dangers which threaten mankind, and combine their efforts in the fight for immediate prohibition of atomic weapons and of its tests and the prevention of wars.

We Soviet scientists express our full readiness for common effort with scientists of any other country, to discuss any proposals directed toward the prevention of atomic war, the creation of secure peace, and tranquility for all mankind.

A. Nesmejanow (President of the Academy of Sciences); N. Semenov (Secretary, Division of Chemistry – Nobel Prize in Chemistry, 1956)

Bulletin of *Atomic Scientists* (November 1957)

More than 120,000 signatures on petitions collected in the USSR by 16 young construction workers who undertook a "supermarathon of peace" of 6,000 kilometres on their vacation.

Women of the World

We are women in five European countries where the deployment of new American and Soviet weapons has begun. We are women from different cultures, from Eastern and Western, Northern and Southern Europe, some of us involved in the church, others not, some of us feminists, pacifists, and members of many other human rights and environmental movements.

Despite our differences, we are united by the will for self-determination, to struggle against the culture of militarism in the world, against uniforms and violence, against our children being educated as soldiers, and against the senseless waste of resources. We demand the right of determination for all individuals and peoples. We want to...change existing social structures. That is why we also challenge conventional gender roles and why we ask them to do the same.

The freedom to determine one's own fate also means freedom from exploitation and violence: in our thoughts and actions, at our places of work, in our relationship to nature in the relationships between men and women, between generations, between states, between East and West and between North and South in global terms....There can be no realistic peace perspective without respect for human rights.

The deployment of new nuclear weapons in our countries has limited our freedom and increased or fears....We are conscious of being both perpetrators and victims of systems of violence. In both roles, we are not the ones who have made the decisions. We reject both roles. Nor are we reassured by the fact that representatives of both superpowers are about to negotiate over our heads again in Geneva....Instead of this, we choose the way of self-determined initiatives from below. This road does not go via the militarization of society, which is why we reject any involvement in the preparations for war; nor does it traverse missile ramps or the destruction of nature and interpersonal relationships.

We do not want a peace which oppresses us, nor a war which will annihilate us. Forty years after Auschwitz and Hiroshima, forty years after the bloc confrontation began, we want now, at last, to begin collectively getting to know and understand each other better and meeting one another beyond the wall which divides not merely the borders of our countries but all too often our hearts and minds as well.

We have begun detente from below. Join us!

Signed by women from the United Kingdom (women's peace groups and Labour Party parliamentarians), German Democratic Republic (independent peace groups), Federal Republic of Germany (women for peace and parliamentarians of the Greens), Italy (women for peace and many parliamentarians), and Czechoslovakia (women of Charter 77) 1985.

Listen Real Loud Fall, 1985.

Appeal by American Scientists to Ban Space Weapons

The development of antisatellite weapons and space-based missile defenses would increase the risk of nuclear war and stimulate a dangerous competition in offensive nuclear arms. An arms race in space poses a great threat to the national security of the United States.

Outer space must remain free of any weapons. It should be preserved as an arena for non-threatening uses: peaceful cooperation, exploration, and scientific discovery among all nations.

We call upon the United States and the Soviet Union to negotiate a total ban on the testing and deployment of weapons in space. To create a constructive environment for the negotiations, both nations should join in a moratorium on further tests of antisatellite weapons. The Soviet Union should bring the Krasnoyarsk radar into conformity with the ABM Treaty, or dismantle it.

We ask the United States and the Soviet Union to reaffirm their commitment to the 1972 ABM Treaty, which prohibits the development, testing, and deployment of space-based ABM systems. We support the continuance of a program of research on ABM technologies in strict conformity with the provisions of the 1972 ABM Treaty.

Union of Concerned Scientists

FROM PROTEST TO VICTORY

Defeating the Junta

We struggle by rendering operative the force of love in the battle for liberation. Active nonviolence is a response, a step forward (whether the world realizes it or not) that is based on the gospel. Nonviolence is a way of answering evil and injustice with truth and hate with love. For truth and love are the weapons of the spirit in the face of repression. Nonviolence is not passivity or conformism. It is a spirit, and a method. It is a spirit of prophecy, for it denounces all sundering of a community of brothers and sisters and proclaims that this community can only be rebuilt through love. And it is a method – an organized set of ruptures in the civil order so as to disturb the system responsible for the injustices we see around us. . . . Here we see the power of the dispossessed, the weapon of the poor. The struggle, then, will be the people's struggle. Here is no elitist contest, no partisan struggle. The means will include boycotts, strikes, noncooperation, civil disobedience, hunger strikes, and many other actions.

Adolfo Perez Esquivel
Argentinian human rights activist
(1980 Nobel Peace Prize winner)

San Francisco to Moscow for Peace

During the Polaris Action, CNVA [Committee for Non Violent Action] demonstrators were often told to take their ideas about peace to the Russians, and so Brad Lyttle, Scott Herrick, Julius Jacobs, and others took up the challenge. On December 1, 1960, eleven pacifists left San Francisco on a walk that would take them across the United States and Europe to Moscow. After ten months and 6000 miles of walking, a combined group of American and European peace walkers reached Moscow and demonstrated in Red Square for Peace and disarmament. Few projects, however, made so many friends for the American peace movement or made the demand for an end to nuclear bomb tests so public.

From *The Power of the People*

The Lessons of Vietnam

The world now demands a maturity of America that we may not be able to achieve. It demands that we admit that we have been wrong from the beginning of our adventure in Vietnam, that we have been detrimental to the life of her people.

In order to atone for our sins and errors in Vietnam, we should take the initiative in bringing the war to a halt. I would like to suggest five concrete things that our government should do immediately to begin the long and difficult process of extricating ourselves from this nightmare.

1) End all bombing in North and South Vietnam.

2) Declare a unilateral cease-fire in the hope that such action will create the atmosphere for negotiation.

3) Take immediate steps to prevent other battlegrounds in Southeast Asia by curtailing our military build-up in Thailand and our interference in Laos.

4) Realistically accept the fact that the National Liberation Front has substantial support in South Vietnam and must thereby play a role in any meaningful negotiations and in any future Vietnam government.

5) Set a date on which we will remove all foreign troops from Vietnam in accordance with the 1954 Geneva Agreement.

Part of our ongoing commitment might well express itself in an offer to grant asylum to any Vietnamese who fears for his life under a new regime which included the NLF. Then we must make what reparations we can for the damage we have done. We must provide the medical aid that is badly needed, in this country if necessary.

Meanwhile, we in the churches and synagogues have a continuing task while we urge our government to disengage itself from a disgraceful commitment. We must be prepared to match actions with words by seeking out every creative means of protest possible.

In 1957 a sensitive American official overseas said that it seemed to him that our nation was on the wrong side of a world revolution. During the past ten years we have seen emerge a pattern of suppression which now has justified the presense of U.S. military "advisors" in Venezuela. The need to maintain social stability for our investments accounts for the counterrevolutionary action of American forces in Guatemala. It tells why American helicopters are being used against guerrillas in Colombia and why American napalm and green beret forces have already been active against rebels in Peru. With such activity in mind, the words of John F. Kennedy come back to haunt us. Five years ago he said, "Those who make peaceful revolution impossible will make violent revolution inevitable."

Increasingly, by choice or by accident, this is the role our nation has taken – by refusing to give up the privileges and the pleasures that come from the immense profits of overseas investment.

I am convinced that if we are to get on the right side of the world revolution, we as a nation must undergo a radical revolution of values. When machines and computers, profit and property rights are considered more important than people, the giant triplets of racism, materialism, and militarism are incapable of being conquered.

Martin Luther King (1929-1968)

BILLY JOE BENNETT · WILLIAM G BENNETT · CHARLES F BIG
LLINS · JAMES L DANIEL · JAMES R DUNCAN · JERRALD L ED
RNER · JON J GIORGIANNI · ROY L GREENSAGE · WILLIAM
N · MICHAEL J HOLSTIUS · JOHN T HOLTMAN · LLOYD R H
N · ARTHUR W REINHARDT · ALLAN G KALFAS · JAMES L KE
H · WILLIE J LIGHTFORD · BRUCE B LIVINGSTON · JAMES E
ARTIN · ALAN L MATTHEWS · LARRY A MERRILL · KYNARD
RKLE · WAYNE I McDANIEL · WILLIAM J McGEE IV · HOLLIS
REEVES · PERCY JULIAN · SANFORD SHROUT Jr · RONALD W
OMPSON · NICHOLAS O WAGMAN · JOHN W WRIGHT · BO
· VALLANCE G ARKIE · ROBERT E BROWNING · DAVID CAR
ASKALOU · LEWIS C GILDER · FRANCIS B AMOROSO · KA
ERN · JIMMY GENE MAYFIELD · HERBERT W MOORE Jr · WIL
D · JAMES THOMPSON · GAIL F WILSON · ALFRED F ALVAR
OUR · JACK A BERRY · JACKLIN M BOATWRIGHT · WILLIAM
SE · EARL R COBB · HAROLD C COOK · STEVEN T CORNELL
VEN · FRANKLIN D ENDICOTT · MICHAEL D DE CAMP · JOH
NCAN · SAMUEL L DASH Jr · CLIVE L EVANS · CHARLES FINK
SHER · FERNANDO V FOOTE · TONY E GABALDON · JAMES
BBS · SAMUEL D GIBBS · ANDREW M GIORDANO · EDWAR
RRERO Jr · CAREY HAMMOND Jr · TIMOTHY J HARTMAN ·
ORTO   HURLEBA   IULIO A IGLESIAS III · WILLIA
LEY   Jr · R   KEMPKES · BOBBY
TTLE · DOV   KHART   IAM B MA
O · FOS E   R   MICHA L R MINER · O
ONEY · ROB   ORGAN   E A MORT   N · DON
SHAWAT   O'REILL   DENNIS   AN · JAM
Z · LAWR   ACL   RS · H   R PHEL   LES W
RIEST · JACKI   OWA   RT SO
OTT · DOU   L F   MM
STEWART   E TEL   N CK
NER · ERIC   LL   WO   EN
ENNAN   ETER   ER   YR   D   CAI

The Vietnam War Memorial in Washington D.C.

The Women March

In January 1962 as the U.S. and the U.S.S.R. escalated nuclear testing, as U.S politicians and journalists solemnly declared, "Better Dead than Red," and as our President and Governor advised us to build fall-out shelters and buy guns to keep our neighbors out of them...women marched on Washington in the first mass demonstration since the beginning of the cold war and the repressions of the McCarthy period. Carrying banners and balloons that read "Pure Air: Not Poison," "End the Arms Race Not the Human Race," and "Peace is the Only Shelter," the WSP [Women Strike for Peace] women confidently declared that they were marching to raise the conscience of the nation regarding the use of science, technology and the nation's resources for death instead of life. Confronting a Congress that had abdicated the right to make foreign policy, WSP women educated their legislators on the dangers of Strontium 90 and Iodine 131 and showered them with literature regarding methods for monitoring a test ban treaty. Years later President John F. Kennedy's science advisor, Jerome Weisner, stated in an article in *Science* (May 1970) that it was not the nuclear arms specialists within the government, nor the members of Congress who moved the President to sign the first nuclear test ban treaty, but rather the action of Women Strike for Peace and similar groups.

Amy Swerdlow

Turn Toward Peace

Turn Toward Peace is a rather complex affair. It seems to be more in the nature of a miracle than an organization. It is a kind of combination coalition and campaign, at the core of which are the traditional American pacifist and peace-oriented groups such as the American Friends Service Committee, the Fellowship of Reconciliation, the War Resisters League and the Women's International League for Peace and Freedom, together with such associated organizations as SANE, the American Association for the United Nations and the Committee for World Development and World Disarmament. But Turn Toward Peace has reached out beyond this core and now includes as "communicating" organizations the American Veterans Committee, the United Auto Workers, Brotherhood of Sleeping Car Porters and the National Association of Social Workers. A whole conglomeration of additional organizations have been invited to associate themselves in this venture....

[An] advertisement in the *Register-Guard* put it this way:

> We believe the best defense against communism is to strengthen our commitment to freedom and democracy. Freedom and democracy cannot survive nuclear war, but they can flourish in peace. To preserve our way of life and safeguard our future we must:
> — turn toward peace
> — support the President's appeal for total and complete disarmament
> — strengthen the United Nations
> — accept and develop world law
> — establish non-military solutions to international conflicts and take new initiatives toward peace.

Robert Martinson, 1961

BREAKING THE CHAINS

How to Eat an Elephant

Sometimes you get the notion that people try to inject the notion into your heart that what you do is insignificant; it cannot make a difference. Let me disabuse you of that notion. When people see a colossal problem, they wonder whether they could do anything to make a difference. They need to keep remembering what they are told about how you eat an elephant—one piece at a time. What you do, where you are, counts and makes a difference, if only to those who have their noses rubbed daily in the dust, to know that the world cares.

*　　　*　　　*

I stand here appealing to people of conscience. Help us. Please help us. Our country is burning. Our children are dying. An 11-year-old was kept in jail for five months in solitary confinement because he had thrown a stone in protest against being treated as less than what God intended for him. It is a country that some have said is a last bastion of Cain's community.

If people are concerned for the fate of white South Africans, the best way of ensuring that white South Africans survive is to be part of the process of dismantling apartheid.

I speak with a heavy heart. I love that country and its people passionately and I do not like to see it destroyed. I speak on behalf of people among the white community, which has some tremendous people, who by right ought to be saying, "We cannot oppose a system that provides us with such substantial privileges," and yet they are not. However, South African whites are not demons. They are ordinary people, many of them scared people.

The best way of ensuring they survive is to be part of a process that will ensure the destruction of this monster that dehumanizes both the victim and the perpetrator and perhaps, dehumanizes the perpetrator even more.

Bishop Desmond Tutu

Bishop Desmond Tutu addresses Arts Against Apartheid rally in Toronto, 1986.

The Effect of Amnesty

Since it was founded in 1961, Amnesty International has worked on behalf of more than 25,000 prisoners around the world. Last year 150 of the prisoners of conscience adopted by groups in the United States were released. These aren't just numbers. Amnesty members give direct and effective assistance to people who become more than a number and more than a name. A released prisoner from Malaysia wrote to a group member, "Today I took out all the letters and cards you sent me in the past, reread them, looked at them again, and it is hard to describe the feelings in my heart...these things I regard as precious jewels."

A released prisoner from Pakistan wrote, "A woman in San Antonio had written some kind and comforting words that proved to be a bombshell for the prison authorities and significantly changed the prisoners' conditions for the better....Suddenly I felt as if the sweat drops all over my body were drops from a cool, comforting shower."

Amnesty International

A Bleak Projection

In the last 20 years, Africa has seen a drop in its total food production. Today, 24 countries have serious food deficits. The population of the continent will grow to 800 million in the next 15 years.

In the Sahel region which borders on the Sahara, already half of the land has become desert which is growing by 10,000 square kilometres a year. Seven million people are Nomads who are on the move in constant search of grazing lands. 20 million peasants cultivate the dry lands, which are dependent on rainfalls.

There is no indication of immediate improvement in this situation. The ecology does not hold much promise for the near future; rainfall may decrease; salt content is increasing in underground water supplies; sand dunes are building up in irrigated areas. There is also increased deforestation for fuel needs and overgrazing.

However, despite these causes of drought, the most important cause is human. This began in the colonial period and continues today. Europe turned Africa into its own agricultural supplier (coffee, peanuts, cotton) not allowing Africans to grow crops for themselves (corn, sorghum, cassava). This agricultural imbalance is still characteristic of Africa today. The land is used for export crops rather than meeting the food needs of the African peoples.

Today the world food system still privileges the rich countries to the detriment of Africa.

The emergency in the Sahel demands an immediate response to save lives. However, there is another urgent problem, which, though less visible, equally demands our attention: changing the present situation which favours export agriculture over food production to feed the local people. Africa is now at a decisive turning point on this issue. The food crisis is either going to be resolved in favour of the growing agribusiness trend on the continent, or in favour of agriculture controlled by the people to meet local needs. Development and Peace only support projects which favour this latter option.

Development and Peace is the partner of the African Office for Development and Cooperation, a local non-governmental development agency.

To stave off these natural disasters, people have to take active control of the development process themselves. Communities must determine their needs, and be allowed to control the process and use their resources to fulfill these needs. This is what OFADEC is working to bring about.

Development and Peace

Aid to the World

OXFAM-Canada has chosen to concentrate its work in those areas of the world where it has expertise and knowledge of local conditions. Current OXFAM-Canada projects are in Africa, Latin America and the Caribbean.

OXFAM supports projects of trade unions, slum associations, peasant cooperatives and other organizations which group together disadvantaged people to work for change and to improve their lives. Projects must be locally initiated and managed, and lead toward self-sufficiency. Many OXFAM projects receive matching funds from the Canadian government and provincial governments.

The following are a sample of projects:
Rural Women's Health and Nutrition Program, Bolivia
Health Campaign in Slum Areas, Santiago, Chile
Women's Centre, Chimbote, Peru
Emergency Supplies for Displaced People, Angola
Water Supply Systems, Mozambique
Irrigation, Eritrea
Pesticide Health and Safety Project, Nicaragua
Community Health Clinics, El Salvador
Literacy, St. Vincent

Inside OXFAM newsletter

Universal Rights

All human beings are born free and equal in dignity and rights. They are endowed with reason and conscience and should act towards one another in a spirit of brotherhood.

Everyone is entitled to all the rights and freedoms set forth in this Declaration, without distinction of any kind, such as race, colour, sex, language, religion, political or other opinion, national or social origin, property, birth or other status. Furthermore, no distinction shall be made on the basis of the political, jurisdictional or international status of the country or territory to which a person belongs, whether it be independent, trust, non-self-governing or under any other...sovereignty.

No one shall be subjected to torture or cruel, inhuman or degrading treatment or punishment. . . .

All are equal before the law and are entitled without any discrimination to equal protection of the law. All are entitled to equal protection against any discrimination in violation of this Declaration and against any incitement to such discrimination. . . .

Everyone charged with a penal offence has the right to be presumed innocent until proved guilty according to law in a public trial at which he has had all the guarantees necessary for his defense. . . .

Everyone has the right to freedom of movement and residence within the borders of each state.

Everyone has the right to leave any country, including his own, and return to his country.

Everyone has the right to seek and to enjoy in other countries asylum from persecution. . . .

Everyone has the right to a nationality. No one shall be arbitrarily deprived of his nationality or denied the right to change his nationality.

Men and women of full age, without any limitation due to race, nationality or religion, have the right to marry and to found a family. They are entitled to equal rights as to marriage, during marriage and at its dissolution.

Marriage shall be entered into only with the free and full consent of the intending spouses.

From the United Nations Universal Declaration of Human Rights, 1948

Live Aid

Live Aid, the first global rock concert and telethon to raise money for famine victims in Africa, attracted 90,000 people to John F. Kennedy Stadium in Philadelphia and 72,000 to Wembley Stadium in London, July 15, 1985. Dozens of the foremost names in popular music performed at the two concerts beamed by satellite to approximately 152 countries and a record 1.5 billion potential viewers and listeners. The 16-hour super-concert, part live and part taped, was organized by Irish-born Bob Geldof, lead singer with the Boomtown Rats. He spent about four months lining up performers such as Madonna, Mick Jagger, Tina Turner, Duran Duran, Bob Dylan, David Bowie, Paul McCartney and the Soviet rock group Autograph.

Band Aid Foundation, run by Bob Geldof, distributed the astounding $70 million (Canadian) pledged world-wide for both immediate and long-term relief measures for the famine regions.

Janis Alton

Live Aid, Wembley Stadium, 1985

Human Rights

In struggling to protect human rights we must, I am convinced, first and foremost act as protectors of the innocent victims of regimes installed in various countries, without demanding the destruction or total condemnation of these regimes. We need reform, not revolution. We need a pliant, pluralist, tolerant community, which selectively and tentatively can bring about a free, undogmatic use of the experiences of all social systems. What is *détente*? What is rapprochement? We are concerned not with words, but with a willingness to create a better and more friendly society, a better world order.

Andrei Sakharov

Machine. Gun. Nest.

The blood goes through your neck veins with a noise they call singing.
Time shatters like bad glass; you are this pinpoint of it.

Your feet rotting inside your boots, the skin of your chest
festering under the zippers, the waterproof armour,

you sit here, on the hill, a vantage point, at this X or scuffling
in the earth, which they call a nest. Who chose that word?

Whatever you are you are not an egg, or a bird either.
Vipers perhaps is what was meant. Who cares now?

That is the main question: who cares. Not these pieces of paper
from somewhere known as *home* you fold, unread, in your pocket.

Each landscape is a state of mind, he once told me:
mountains for awe and remoteness, meadows for calm and the steam

of the lulled senses. But some views are slippery.
This place is both beautiful as the sun and full of menace:

dark green, with now and then a red splotch, like a punctured
vein, white like a flare; stench of the half-eaten.
Look at it carefully, see what it hides, or it will burst in your head.

If you lose your nerve you may die, if you don't lose it
you may die anyway, the joke goes. What is your nerve?

It is turning the world flat, the moon to a disc you could aim at,
popping the birds off the fence wire. Delight in accuracy,

no attention paid to results, dead singing, the smear of feathers.
You know you were more than that, but best to forget it.

There's no slack time for memory here; when you can, you plunge
into some inert woman as into a warm bath; for a moment
comforting, and of no consequence, like sucking your thumb.

No woman can imagine this. What you do to them
is therefore incidental, and also your just reward,

though sometimes, in a gap in the action, there's a space
for the concepts of *sister*, *mother*. Like folded laundry. They come and go.

But stick your hand up a woman, alive or freshly-
dead, it is much like a gutted chicken:
giblets, a body cavity. Killing can be

merely a kind of impatience, at the refusal
of this to mean anything to you. He told me that.

You wanted to go in sharp and clean like a sword,
do what they once called battle. Now you just want your life.

There's not much limit to what you would do to get it.
Justice and mercy are words that happen in cool rooms, elsewhere.

Are you your brother's keeper? Yes or no, depending
what clothes he has on, what hair. There is more than one brother.

What you need to contend with now is the hard Easter-
eggshell blue of the sky, that shows you too clearly

the mass of deep green trees leaning slowly towards you
as if on the verge of speech, or annunciation.

More likely some break in the fabric of sight, or a sad mistake
you will hear about in the moment you make it. Some glint of reflected light.

That whir in the space where your left hand was is not singing.
Death is the bird that hatches, is fed, comes flying.

Margaret Atwood

A History of CARE

Since its founding in 1945, CARE has provided aid valued at approximately $4 billion in over 80 countries:

1945...CARE begins as the work of many hands – a cooperative effort among 22 major American organizations to form a voluntary, nonprofit, nonpolitical, nonsectarian, nongovernmental organization to help the survivors of World War II in Europe.

1946 The first CARE packages land at Le Havre, France, on May 11th, and soon packages are being distributed in 11 other European countries. President Truman, former President Hoover, and General Eisenhower ask Americans to support CARE. CARE Canada opens.

1948 CARE airlifts food to people in Berlin throughout the Russian blockade. CARE begins services outside Europe.

1950 Delivering farm tools becomes the forerunner of today's self-help programs.

1954 The U.S. Government's Public Law 480 (The Food for Peace Program) becomes effective in June, making large quantities of surplus American farm produce available to help the hungry overseas. CARE begins large shared-cost feeding programs, mostly for undernourished children.

1962 MEDICO affiliates with CARE, adding medical training and services to CARE's repertoire.

1966 Phasing out of CARE packages begins. CARE signs the first shared-cost, self-help partnership agreement with the government of Honduras for a school construction program.

1974 CARE initiates a long-range planning system in its development programs.

1976 The goodwill of Europeans who remember CARE packages after World War II leads to the opening of CARE Europe. In the next few years, CARE Deutschland and CARE Norge open, joining CARE Canada, in a further move toward internationalization to broaden the base of CARE's support.

Good Over Evil

Until the philosophy which holds one race superior and another inferior is finally and permanently discredited and abandoned –
That until there are no longer first-class and second-class citizens of any nation –
Until the colour of a man's skin is of no more significance than the colour of his eyes –
That until the basic human rights are equally guaranteed to all, without regard to race –
That until that day, the dream of lasting peace, world citizenship and the rule of international morality will remain but a fleeting illusion to be pursued, but never attained –
But we know we shall win as we are confident in the victory of good over evil, of good over evil. . . .

Bob Marley

Interrogation 1 *by Golub, 1981.*

1979 CARE begins emergency operations in Thailand to aid Kampuchean refugees.

1981 CARE celebrates its 35th anniversary, begins a temporary food package program in Poland during that country's harvest emergency, and enters Somalia at the request of the United Nations High Commission for Refugees to manage and monitor the delivery of relief supplies to the nation's 35 camps for Ethiopian refugees. The CARE for the Earth Campaign begins.

1982 CARE International becomes a reality when CARE Canada, CARE Deutschland, and CARE USA adopt articles of incorporation.

1984 CARE enters Mozambique in response to the drought emergency. CARE enters the Comoros Islands. CARE develops a food aid policy to promote the most appropriate use of food resources.

CARE Canada

PRESERVING THE EARTH

In Defence of Nature

1971 The ships *Greenpeace I* (the *Phyllis Cormack*) and the *Greenpeace Too* (the *Edgewater Fortune*) sail toward Amchitka Island in the Alaskan Aleutian Chain to focus attention on U.S. nuclear tests there. After one 5-megaton underground explosion, publicity stops the tests.

1972 The ship *Greenpeace III* (the *Vega*) sails to the Mururoa Atoll in French Polynesia to stop French atmospheric nuclear tests. After 3 years of protests with massive support from other anti-nuclear groups, the French government ceases atmospheric blasting, but moves its testing program underground.

1975 Greenpeace confronts a Russian whaling fleet off the California coast. Within 48 hours, through media exposure, millions of people know that whales are endangered, and a huge public outcry against the slaughter begins.

1976 **Canada** Greenpeace confronts seal hunters off the East Coast, bringing worldwide attention to the slaughter of baby harp seals.

1977 **Canada** Three Toronto Greenpeacers invade, by canoe, the unguarded Bruce Nuclear Power Station Lake Huron, to expose the reactor's vulnerability to attack.

1979 **Canada** Greenpeacers parachute into the world's largest nuclear power plant construction site at Darlington, Ontario, as part of a mass occupation with other anti-nuclear groups.

1980 **Japan** Greenpeace ecologists free several hundred dolphins being held for slaughter at Iki Island. One Greenpeacer is arrested, jailed, and eventually deported. Massive publicity highlights the issue to the Japanese public.

1980 **Spain** The *Rainbow Warrior* is seized and held for several months by the Spanish government for interfering with illegal Spanish whaling operations. Five months later, the ship's crew makes a daring nighttime escape, pursued by the Spanish Navy. An admiral is fired for allowing the escape.

1982 **U.S.S.R.** The Greenpeace ship *Sirius* sails to the Soviet Union to protest Soviet arms buildup. The crew meets with Soviet government representatives and the official Soviet Peace Committee, but the *Sirius* is expelled from Leningrad after Greenpeace releases 2,000 balloons bearing the message "Stop Nuclear Testing."

1983 **Europe** Seven years of protests result in the European Economic Community (EEC) recommending a two-year total ban on the importation of harp seal pelts, effectively ending Canada's commercial seal pup slaughter.

1983 **Germany** The Greenpeace hot air balloon *Trinity*, carrying a banner reading "Peace—Stop Nuclear Tests," is piloted from West Berlin into East Germany. The *Trinity* is impounded and two Greenpeacers are fined.

1983 **Canada** Simultaneous demonstrations are staged against the proposed testing of U.S. cruise missiles in Canadian airspace.

1983 **Antarctica** Photographic evidence of penguin habitat destruction convinces French authorities to halt construction of an airstrip in Antarctica.

1983 **Canada** Greenpeace continues to fight acid rain by purchasing shares in International Nickel Company (INCO) of Sudbury, and mounting a shareholder proposal to force the company to reduce acid-rain-causing emissions.

1984 **Europe** The French freighter *Mont Louis* sinks off the coast of Belgium. Despite French claims that the ship is carrying "medical supplies," Greenpeace reveals the cargo is actually uranium hexafluoride and plutonium waste. At the request of the salvage company, the Greenpeace ship *Sirius* stands by at the recovery site.

1984 **U.S.A.** Campaigners highlight major sources of toxic pollution in Washington, California, Illinois and Massachusetts, plugging waste water discharge pipes and chaining pipe valves shut.

1984 **Canada/U.S.A.** Greenpeace offices in both countries assist the members of the International Association of Atomic Veterans (IAAV), in their public attempt to have the U.S. government recognize their claims that the domestic atmospheric testing program caused severe health problems. The U.S. government is later held responsible by a U.S. District Court in Utah.

1984 **Europe** Banners are simultaneously hung in eight countries—Denmark, Netherlands, France, Czechoslovakia, West Germany, Belgium, Austria and the U.K.—highlighting the need to reduce acid-rain-causing emissions in Europe.

1984 **England** A "Time to Stop Nuclear Testing" banner is draped from the south face of Big Ben in London.

1984 **U.S.A.** Four Greenpeacers are arrested for hanging a banner from the Statue of Liberty reading "Give Me Liberty from Nuclear Weapons—Stop Testing."

1984 **Worldwide** Greenpeace announces a boycott of Japan Air Lines, in an attempt to halt commercial whaling by Japan, which has threatened to ignore the 1986 worldwide commercial whaling moratorium voted by the IWC. Twenty-six environmental groups join the boycott.

1985 **U.S.A.** Judge Richey rules in Greenpeace's favour forcing the U.S. government to apply fishing sanctions against Japan for violation of the zero sperm whale quota. The U.S. Department of Commerce and the Japanese government appeal, but the decision is upheld.

1985 **Canada** Greenpeace pinpoints the exact flight path of the U.S. cruise missile. Later, Greenpeace erects its 'cruise catcher,' a fishing net held aloft by balloons, in the missile's flight path, causing it to fly above its operational altitude, and demonstrating the system's vulnerability.

1985 **Canada** Greenpeace Vancouver banners the uranium transport route through the city, warning people of the dangers of moving radioactive cargoes through populated areas.

1985 **South Pacific** The *Rainbow Warrior* undertakes a three month, anti-nuclear tour of the South Pacific. Among its activities is the full-scale move of 306 Rongelap Atoll people with animals, equipment and buildings to a new home at Majeto Island, 100 kms away. The move was conducted at the request of the Rongelap people, who have suffered heightened incidents of cancer and related illnesses since the U.S. 1950s atmospheric testing program.

1985 New Zealand During a rest stop in July, prior to its next major stop in the Pacific Peace Tour, the Greenpeace flagship *Rainbow Warrior* is bombed and sunk in Auckland harbor. Portuguese photographer Fernando Pereira is killed. The French government admits responsibility for the blast, as an effort to prevent the *Rainbow Warrior* from reaching Mururoa Atoll, the site of the French nuclear testing program.

1985 Canada The population of Beluga whales is declining rapidly in the St. Lawrence and Saguenay rivers. Levels of the pesticide Mirex as well as other contaminants are showing up in amounts as high as 1,700 ppm in the whales' breast milk. Greenpeace targets Alcan Aluminium in Chicoutimi on the Saguenay River as one of the major emitters of toxics (PAHs) into the river.

1985 Canada Greenpeace occupies Diachem Industries' pentachlorophenol plant in Richmond, B.C., shutting down plant operations for a day. City officials take water samples and discover them to be ten times more toxic than the earlier samples obtained by Greenpeace. Diachem is put on an unprecedented outfall monitoring system by local authorities.

1985 Canada/U.S.A. Crew from the *Alycon* sneak aboard a barge carrying 1,000,000 lbs of PCB waste from Alaska to the lower 48 states. Greenpeace hangs a banner on the back of the barge reading "Kick Me Off the Water—I've Got PCBs."

Greenpeace

Toxic Rain

The Canadian Environmental Law Research Foundation...together with the U.S. Environmental Law Institute, has released a 257-page study on toxic rain....

Solutions are bound to be elusive. As the study showed, toxic rain is to be found virtually everywhere, but its sources are not always easy to pinpoint. Like acid rain, it comes from the sky. The term "rain" really isn't adequate to describe either problem.

Both are caused by industrial and vehicle emissions, which mix with water vapor to form polluted clouds. Such material can then condense into rain or snow, or reach the ground as "dry deposition" – a term scientists use to describe microscopic particles mixed with air.

But acid rain can be traced to a few large sources, and consists mostly of two components, sulphur dioxide and nitrogen oxides.

Toxic rain is made up of virtually every chemical spewed out of every smokestack and tailpipe. As the foundation said, this poses "potentially greater threats to the environment and human health," than acid rain ever did.

The toxic rain...can itself be divided into two types of pollution – toxic air pollutants and photochemical oxidants.

Toxic air pollutants are the chemicals that spew into the air, where they can travel, react with each other and make their way into soil, water and food. Photochemical oxidants are familiar to city-dwellers as smog. They are produced when nitrogen oxides, produced by burning fuel, mix with vaporized petroleum and petrochemical products.

Think about the Way of Survival for the Earth *by Tamadi Yamada.*

They travel long distances, and even though they come mainly from cities they can blow into rural areas and pollute them. These two forms of toxic fallout have turned the air over North America into a chemical soup.

The report said, among other things:
- That toxic rain could be responsible for up to 2,000 cancer deaths a year in the United States;
- That "there appears to be some risk of mutations, cancer or neurological problems associated with chemicals in the environment." Respiratory and behavioral problems also appear to be linked;
- That toxic rain is suspected of causing up to $200 million a year in crop damage in Ontario alone, and may be the No. 1 cause of damage to forestry, Canada's largest industry;
- That this pollution contributes significant amounts to the Great Lakes of deadly chemicals such as dioxin, pesticides and PCBs (polychlorinated biphenyls), now banned world-wide.

The message is not new. Late last year [1985], an Environment Canada publication, *Storm Warning*, called such pollution "a distinct threat to human health." The pamphlet was hastily banned.

"PCBs and DDT have been found in mothers' milk and passed along to nursing babies. Toxic chemicals are found in the body tissue of individuals who eat little or no fish from the Great Lakes," it said....

The prestigious Royal Society of Canada and the U.S. National Research Council said much the same in a report released shortly after the Environment Canada booklet was banned.

David Israelson

Dunes #7 by Jonas Kalvelis, 1974.

Declaration of Interdependence

We have arrived at a place in history where decisive action must be taken to avoid a general environmental disaster. With nuclear reactors proliferating and over 900 species on the endangered list, there can be no further delay or our children will be denied their future.

The Greenpeace Foundation hopes to stimulate practical, intelligent, non-violent actions to stem the tide of planetary destruction. We are "rainbow people" representing every race, every species, every living creature. We are patriots, not of any one nation, state or military alliance, but of the entire earth. . . .

Ecology teaches us that mankind is not the center of life on this planet. Each species has its function in the scheme of life. Each has a role, however obscure that role may be.

Ecology has taught us that the entire earth is part of our "body" and that we must learn to respect it as much as we respect ourselves. As we love ourselves, we must also love all forms of life in the planetary system – the whales, the seals, the forests and the seas. The tremendous beauty of ecological thought is that it shows us a pathway back to an understanding of the natural world – an understanding that is imperative if we are to avoid a total collapse of the global ecosystem. . . .

If we ignore the logical implications of ecology we will continue to be guilty of crimes against the earth. We will not be judged by people for these crimes, but with a justice meted out by the earth itself. The destruction of the earth will lead, inevitably, to the destruction of ourselves.

So let us work together to put an end to the destruction of the earth by the forces of human greed and ignorance. Through an understanding of the principles of ecology we must find new directions for the evolution of human values and human institutions. Short-term economics must be replaced with actions based on the need for conservation and preservation of the entire global ecosystem. We must learn to live in harmony, not only with our fellow humans, but with all the beautiful creatures on this planet.

Greenpeace

Pax Antarctica

A look at the far southern part of the globe, the one-fifteenth of the Earth's surface that lies below 60 degrees south latitude, sheds light on the urgent, sometimes sharp, arms control debate between Washington and Moscow.

This region – which includes the Southern (or Antarctic) Ocean, holding one-fifth of Earth's ocean water, and Antarctica, the seventh continent – has an arms control treaty as its form of government. The Antarctic Treaty was signed by 12 nations in December 1959 and entered into force in June 1961.

Drawn up in the full flower of President Dwight D. Eisenhower's hopes for regional arms control and denuclearization, the six-page Treaty has grown into a robust system of administration. Although many other arms control accords have eroded with time, there have been no charges of violations of the Antarctic Treaty, and it seems likely to survive a statutory review due in 1991.

A widespread misperception holds that the Treaty internationalized Antarctica by erasing national claims. It did not. Rather, it allowed the seven nations with announced claims to keep their viewpoints, while the basis for U.S. and Soviet claims could remain also. With the Treaty, all these nations run less risk of conflict in the region than without it. And their operating costs there are less because the Treaty prohibits militarization. Thus the Treaty

City Dwellers en Route to Paradise *by Carolyn Gowdy.*

has worked because it suits the individual national interests of those countries with stakes in Antarctica – not because it asks them, in effect, to join hands and sing.

The original 12 parties negotiated the Treaty while their scientists were cooperating in the Antarctic during the 1957-1958 International Geophysical Year (IGY). For the IGY, they had agreed informally that stations could be built wherever scientists wished and that expeditions could go anywhere without political complications such as passports or sovereignty disputes.

By cooperating on research, the traditionally rivalrous nations discovered a means of peaceful coexistence, as well as a healthy outlet for their energies there. Accordingly,

their representatives met in the board room of the National Academy of Sciences in Washington to formalize this understanding before the IGY ended and trouble broke out again.

The Treaty demilitarizes the region by saying, "Antarctica shall continue forever to be used exclusively for peaceful purposes and shall not become the scene or object of international discord." No military maneuvers are allowed, but military personnel and logistics can be used to support scientific activities. Nuclear explosions and disposal of radioactive wastes are banned. Each party has the right to unilateral inspections of all stations, ports and cargoes in order to enforce these terms.

Deborah Shapley

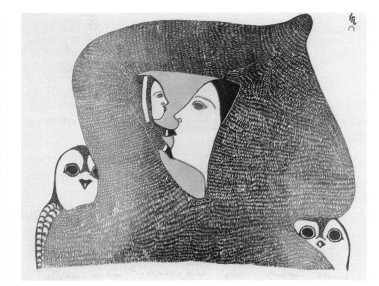
Arctic Madonna *by Pitaloosie Saila.*

Untitled Poem

And then all that has divided us will merge
And then compassion will be wedded to power
And then softness will come to a world that is harsh and unkind
And then both men and women will be gentle
And then both women and men will be strong
And then no person will be subject to another's will
And then all will be rich and free and varied
And then the greed of some will give way to the needs of many
And then all will share equally in the Earth's abundance
And then all will care for the sick and the weak and the old
And then all will nourish the young
And then all will cherish life's creatures
And then all will live in harmony with each other and the Earth
And then everywhere will be called Eden once again

Judy Chicago

The Chinese Model

China has largely succeeded in eliminating malnutrition – no mean feat in a country that supports one in five of humankind. The Chinese not only produce massive amounts of food, but – equally to be acclaimed – they ensure it is fairly shared among all. Furthermore, they are leaders in "ecological agriculture," with emphasis on wasting nothing. They recycle much of their crop residues and by-products, and also their general garbage and waste (not surprising, when we remember that the Chinese have long had to learn how to make do with limited natural resources).

The largest irrigation network in the world, built at a cost of much human sweat, enables China to grow more than one-third of the world's rice, almost as much as the next five together, *viz*. India, Indonesia, Bangladesh, Japan, and Thailand. Farming methods do not rely on heavy machinery, so that hundreds of millions of peasants are usefully employed on the land. Abundant human labour further allows several crops to be grown in one field in alternate rows, with symbiotic benefit all round (*e.g.*, beans, as legumes, supply "free" nitrogen fertilizer to wheat plants).

Amazon Casualties

The Waimiri-Atroari are Carib-speaking Indians who inhabit the forests of the northern Amazon region of Brazil. Since the end of the 19th century, the Waimiri-Atroari have suffered periodic massacres and invasions of their lands. When Brazil launched the Amazon development program in the late 1960s, the government declared that the Indians could not stand in the way of "progress." As a result, dozens of Indian tribes were reduced in population because of the highways, military assaults and massacres, epidemic diseases, and invasions by cattle ranchers. FUNAI (Brazil's equivalent of the Bureau of Indian Affairs) failed to protect the Indians or to demarcate any of their lands.

The lands of the Waimiri-Atroari were in the path of the Manaus-Boa Vista Highway. When construction began on this highway in the early 1970s, the Brazilian Army tried to drive the Indians southward out of the way of the road. Numerous eye-witness accounts verify that the Brazilian Army conducted machine-gun massacres and bombings of the Waimiri-Atroari. As a result, the Indian population declined from 3,000 to 600 between 1968 and 1975.

The highway has been completed and now the Indians are faced with new threats. Mineral companies are seeking authorizations for mining on Indian lands and a large hydro-electric project may flood the Indian reserve. The government has refused to reveal any information on either of these projects.

These actions have now pushed the Waimiri-Atroari Indians into a highly critical situation. Not only is their survival as a group with their own way of life and own culture now in jeopardy, but their very survival as such may, after 300 years of struggle, become virtually impossible.

Association for Endangered Peoples

Labour-intensive pest control permits crop spraying only against particular outbreaks – a strategy that is far more cost-effective than regular broadscale spraying.

From *GAIA: An Atlas of Planet Management*

Green Policies

Along with bloc-free regionalism and the eventual development of weapons-free zones, the [German] Greens' peace policy calls for global coordination in two areas: peace and the ecological balance of the planet. To address these two tasks, the Greens' Federal Program calls for a restructured United Nations, one with minimal centralization that would respect the right of self-determination of all peoples. Its work would include worldwide disarmament treaties; control of the weapons trade; protection of human rights, with special attention to the rights of minorities, women, and children; control over pollution of the world's oceans; and the introduction of renewable-resource technology, as well as birth control assistance, to the developing nations. In addition, the Greens call for an international tribunal that would subpoena the politicians, technologists, and military strategists who plan, build, operate, or support weapons systems or technologies leading to mass destruction and genocide. . . .

Partnership with the peoples of the Third World is an integral part of the Greens' peace policy. In the United States, the crushing problems of developing nations have been ignored by nearly everyone except the radical left. . . .In West Germany, in contrast, there is a broad-based Third World movement that includes church groups, student groups, and community groups, as well as the left. Almost every city has a Third World store, which sells coffee and other products from cooperatives.

Fritjof Capra and Charlene Spretnak

Stillness

The wood is riddled through with sun
Which pours down in dust-pillared rays,
And here, they say, the elk comes out
Into the forking of the ways.

Within the wood is silence, peace:
Life in the vale stills to a pause
As though spellbound, not by the sun
But for some other secret cause.

And, sure enough, not far away
A young elk stands where thickets press,
And trees, dumbstruck to look at her,
Fill all the wood with voicelessness.

She chews the tender forest green
And nibbles where the fresh shoots twine;
An acorn swinging on a twig
Keeps bumping gently on her spine.

Purple cow-wheat, gold Saint John's wort,
Rosebay, thistle, camomile—
As though enchanted by a spell
They gaze on her, and stare, and smile;

While through the forest one lone stream,
Its music filling the ravine,
Sings now in hushed, now ringing tones
Of this which it had never seen,

And drowns out the woodcutters' blows
As through the wood it peals its way:
In human, almost human, words
There's something that it longs to say!

Boris Pasternak

Earth Day 22 April by Robert Rauschenberg, 1970.

IMAGINE THE FUTURE

Turning on the Light

Historically, peace efforts have been aimed at ending or preventing wars. Just as we have defined health in negative terms, as the absence of disease, we have defined peace as non-conflict. But peace is more fundamental than that. Peace is a state of mind, not a state of the nation. Without personal transformation, the people of the world will be forever locked in conflict.

If we limit ourselves to the old-paradigm concept of averting war, we are trying to overpower darkness rather than switching on the light. If we reframe the problem – if we think of fostering community, health, innovation, self-discovery, purpose – we are already engaged in waging peace. In a rich, creative, meaningful environment there is no room for hostility.

War is unthinkable in a society of autonomous people who have discovered the connectedness of all humanity, who are unafraid of alien ideas and alien cultures, who know that all revolutions begin within and that you cannot impose your brand of enlightenment on anyone else.

Marilyn Ferguson

Past and Future

The human condition can almost be summed up in the observation that, whereas all experiences are of the past, all decisions are about the future. It is the great task of human knowledge to bridge this gap and to find those patterns in the past which can be projected into the future as realistic images. The image of the future, therefore, is the key to all choice-oriented behavior. The general character and quality of the images of the future which prevail in a society is therefore the most important clue to its overall dynamics. The individual's image of the future is likewise the most significant determinant of his personal behavior.

Elise Boulding

Untitled painting by Keith Haring, 1985.

Ultimatum

Let us remember that soul *is* joy, the reflection of Spirit which is Bliss. The surest test of our link with the soul. . .lies in the existence within us of an eternal note of joy, sounding steadily throughout all our earthly dilemmas, pains and tortures. Those who have achieved this link can testify that it is so. Joy is what this poor world needs. Its loss has been the greatest tribulation and sacrifice attendant on man's submergence in matter.

So, firstly, let those of us who would rebuild bring joy, the soul radiation, into our environment. This must be the foundation of our edifice.

Secondly, let us bring unity. Let us find each other. Let us link up, and pool our resources of inspiration, wisdom, strength, purpose and conviction. We shall soon discover that we are sounding a note strong enough to rally both the seen and the unseen to endeavour. . . .

Thirdly, let us be practical. We have the blue-print before us. We see that it is planned upon the law of synthesis, the blending of all facets and activities of life, the formation of groups, each representing all-round complete links with human living. There can no longer be purely scientific groups, or occult groups, or political groups or artistic groups. Each group must possess a channel and a link to all of these. The structure for the new civilisation must be planned by such integrated representative groups as these. . . .Potential members of these groups move among us today. They must be recognised and linked together. The "army of the new dispensation" must be mobilised. Remember that war and its propaganda is the "vice" side of an equally strong complementary virtue, the virtue of mobilised faith and light, the propaganda of wisdom, the force of love, and the power of high endeavour, all of which becomes irresistible if allied to the strength of plan, purpose and organisation.

Fourthly, comes organisation. . . .From Deity downwards the whole universe is thoroughly organised, the keynote being always the keeping of balance between all facets of existence, a balance, however, in which one aspect always slightly predominates. . . .

When in this manner the advanced intellectuals of the world come together to meditate in unison, what power and what inspiration will be released, what vision will be experienced, and what work will be achieved! For something new will have happened. The human family as a whole will have achieved an integrated intellect!

The human being depends upon his mind for rational and successful living. The entire human family is also one being – but it is still scatterbrained. Our lunatic world must have a collective mind, sufficiently powerful to influence it, before present madness can end.

The task that lies ahead for those who will embrace it is to Give the World a Mind!

Vera Stanley Alder

Sun gleaming on a peak overlooking a Navaho reservation.

Imagine

Imagination is the ability to create an idea or mental picture in your mind. In creative visualization you use your imagination to create a clear image of something you wish to manifest. Then you continue to focus on the idea or picture regularly, giving it positive energy until it becomes objective reality...in other words, until you actually achieve what you have been visualizing.

Your goal may be on any level – physical, emotional, mental, or spiritual. You might imagine yourself with a new home, or a new job, or having a beautiful relationship, or feeling calm and serene, or perhaps with an improved memory and learning ability. Or you might picture yourself handling a difficult situation effortlessly, or simply see yourself as a radiant being, filled with light and love. You can work on any level, and all will have results...through experience you will find the particular images and techniques which work best for you.

Let us say, for example, that you have difficulty getting along with someone and you would like to create a more harmonious relationship with that person.

After relaxing into a deep, quiet, meditative state of mind, you mentally imagine the two of you relating and communicating in an open, honest, and harmonious way. Try to get a feeling in yourself that your mental image is possible; experience it as if it is already happening.

Repeat this short, simple exercise often, perhaps two or three times a day or whenever you think about it. If you are sincere in your desire and intention, and truly open to change, you will soon find that the relationship is becoming easier and more flowing, and that the other person seems to become more agreeable and easier to communicate with. Eventually you will find that the problem will resolve itself completely, in one way or another, to the benefit of all parties concerned.

It should be noted here that this technique *cannot* be used to "control" the behavior of another or cause them to do something against their will. Its effect is to dissolve our internal barriers to natural harmony and self-realization, allowing everyone to manifest their most positive aspect.

Shakti Gawain

The Mental Climate

One of the most important tasks of the moment is to recognize the great problem of the *mental climate* in which we live. Our minds are filled with images that call for violent and erratic reactions. We can hardly recover our senses long enough to think calmly and make reasoned commitments. We are swept by alternate fears and hopes which have no relation to deep moral truth. A protest which merely compounds these fears and hopes with a new store of images can hardly help us become men of peace.

Thomas Merton (1915-1968)

Na-Mu Myō-Hō-Ren-Ge-Kyō

It is false to talk of peace
while possessing weapons
destined to take life.
When we talk of peace,
we must lay down all
murderous tools.

Nichidatsu Fujii

227

Nave Nave Fenua (Delicious Earth) *by Paul Gauguin, c. 1894.*

Could It Make a Difference?

Fundamental change in societies has always come from vast numbers of people changing their minds just a little. We, the people, give legitimacy to institutions and institutional behaviors. . . .

When you consider the predicament the world is in, almost anything seems worth a try. Almost anything is better than just standing by feeling impotent, or suppressing your knowledge with the soporific that humankind is really too intelligent ever actually to wage a nuclear war.

So, suspending judgment that it could really make a difference, let's examine the following three-part strategy for accomplishing the goal of sustainable peace:

1. Spend a little time each day at *inner work* aimed at three things:
    a) understanding the ways in which your own beliefs may be contributing to personal fear, anxiety, conflict, hostility;
    b) understanding the ways in which collective beliefs that you have unquestioningly accepted may be contributing to the problems of the planet; and
    c) working on the discovery of and identification with the innermost core of your own being.
2. Get (or remain) involved with some kind of *outer work* related to bringing about global peace.
3. Recognize the power of repeatedly and persistently *affirming and imaging a positive goal of sustainable peace*, and commit to doing that regularly.

Willis W. Harman

The Root of Faith

I become what I see in myself. All that thought suggests to me, I can do; all that thought reveals in me, I can become. This should be man's unshakable faith in himself, because God dwells in him.

Sri Aurobindo

The Real Revolution

Be concerned with radical change, with total revolution. The only revolution is the revolution between man and man, between human beings. That is our only concern. In this revolution there are no blueprints, no ideologies, no conceptual utopias. We must take the fact of the actual relationship between men and change that radically. That is the real thing. And this revolution must be immediate, it must not take time. It is not achieved through evolution, which is time. . . .

Conflict is our main concern. All the social maladies you mentioned are the projection of this conflict in the heart of each human being. The only possible change is a radical transformation of yourself in all your relationships, not in some vague future, but now. . . .

If you really see this contradiction passionately, then that very perception is the revolution. If you see in yourself this division between the mind and the heart, actually see it, not conceive of it theoretically, but see it, then the problem comes to an end. A man who is passionate about the world and the necessity for change, must be free from political activity, religious conformity and tradition – which means, free from the weight of time, free from the burden of the past, free from all the action of will: this is the new human being. This only is the social, psychological, and even the political revolution.

Krishnamurti (1895-1985)

Cause and Effect

He thought before the war
Of conflicts, heroism, enemies
Who had to be crushed;
Causes that had to be fought for.

He had no time before the war
For bright skies, fields, the warm
Sun, his woman – only
Causes that had to be fought for.

I see him now after the war
In my lifetime. I notice his love
Of the sun, bright skies, fields, his
    woman:
Causes that have to be fought for.

Alan Bold

From Many Minds

Today the atomic bomb has altered profoundly the nature of the world as we know it. . . . Our defense is not in armaments, nor in science, nor in going underground. . . . Future thinking must prevent wars.

Albert Einstein

People ask me whether I think a nuclear war will actually occur, whether we have a chance of averting such a catastrophe. My answer is always that the issue is undecided. It depends on what we human beings do. The odds are probably against us. But the weapons are a product of the human imagination, and human imagination is capable of getting rid of them.

Robert Lifton

It is the mind and brain which has been responsible for social evolution. A thousand years from now biological evolution will not have significantly changed. But now how man uses his mind and the computer in his brain is just as important as biological evolution once was for the species.

Wilder Penfield

Whatever you can do or dream you can do, begin it. Boldness has genius, power, and magic in it.

Goethe

The starting point for a better world is the belief that it is possible. Civilization begins in the imagination. The wild dream is the first step to reality. It is the direction-finder by which people locate higher goals and discern their highest selves.

Norman Cousins

Nuclear Madness

The nuclear threat brings with it both nightmares, in the form of holocaust visions, and dreams, in the form of utopian possibilities. For centuries scholars have engaged in lofty discussions about the lush, idyllic, peaceful world mankind could create while mankind generally has focused on improving his capacity to kill and to destroy. Now the world is, as Buckminster Fuller recently noted, "too dangerous for anything less than utopia." To face the prospect of nuclear war is to face the reality we are creating. It is to find oneself suddenly recognizing underlying dichotomies such as life/death and health/illness. It is to realize that we can consciously choose to shift from one pole to the other. . . .

Nuclear Madness is *a way of thinking* characterized by nightmare images, paranoid thinking, and helpless circularity. Those holocaust images which in the daylight are so often denied are more persistent and tangible than we realize. Mental images which become vivid tend to transform themselves readily from thought to physical form. Expectations of attack can cause someone to mistake a flock of geese for missiles on a radar screen and to reject even the possibility of verifiable arms reduction. Our way of thinking which Albert Einstein has termed "outmoded" and Charles Osgood has called "neanderthal" keeps hostile and fearful thoughts circling in our heads. . . .

A first step is, perhaps, to look at our world in terms of basic human needs. To do so is to begin to form an image of people everywhere feeling relaxed, enjoying sunshine and fresh air, talking rather than fighting, and using their minds to solve problems like pollution, overpopulation, and food shortage. To move ourselves in the direction of that vision is to move ourselves toward planetary mental health. Nuclear weapons are unlikely to appear in the image and when it becomes reality they will have vanished from the planet.

Tana Dineen

STRENGTH OF SPIRIT

One panel from the Peace Ribbon.

A New Vision

In the new vision of peace, there is no place for self-centredness and antagonism. We are all involved; we carry the responsibility for our own conversion to thoughts and actions of peace.

One person alone cannot change the world, but all of us together, strong in the conviction and determination that peace begins in our own hearts, will be able to create a peaceful and peace-loving society.

Pope John Paul II

One Spirit—One Voice

We who have signed this letter have done so out of a deep personal conviction that the time has come for us to express our growing concern about the threat to human survival consequent upon the development of weapons of ever greater destructive power. Undergirding our concern are theological and ethical principles rooted in Biblical truth: our stewardship of God's creation; our vocation as Christians to respect and nourish life and to strive for peace and justice; and our hope in a sovereign God.

Our letter is an expression of hope, not despair. We have been encouraged by the obvious desire of our leaders of political parties and other parliamentarians to work for peace and justice. We are encouraged too by the prayerful concern of many of our clergy and people. Above all, because we are Christians we place our hope in God, who is the First and the Last, the Beginning and the End of all things.

A letter of disarmament from church leaders in Canada, 1983

Working for Peace

The Fellowship of Reconciliation (FOR) was founded in Cambridge, England, in 1914 when Henry Hodgkin, an English Quaker, and Friedrich Sigmund-Schultz, a German Lutheran pastor, pledged to remain friends and continue to work for peace, even though their countries were at war. The following year the FOR was established in the United States. FOR groups have subsequently been organized in 27 countries, with an international secretariat in Holland. Highlights in FOR's history include:

1916 Organizes the National Civil Liberties Bureau, now the ACLU

1917 Supports World War I conscientious objectors and contributes to eventual legal recognition of CO rights

1918 Helps found Brookwood Labor College

1923 Helps organize the National Conference of Christians and Jews

1931 Provides leadership for Pennsylvania textile strike

1936-40 Sponsors Ambassadors of Reconciliation to visit world leaders, including Leon Blum, Adolf Hitler, Benito Mussolini and Franklin Roosevelt

1940-45 Encourages members to participate in nonviolent resistance to war; European FOR members help rescue Jews and other political refugees from Nazism

1943 Backs first interracial sit-in; Leads national protest against internment of Japanese Americans;

1947 Sponsors an interracial team on the first "freedom ride" to test court decision outlawing discrimination in interstate travel

1953 Organizes the American Committee on Africa to support movements for African independence

1954 Begins six-year Food for China Program in response to Chinese famines

1955 Sends first interracial teams to train Southern civil rights groups in nonviolent action

1957 Sends FOR staff to join Martin Luther King, Jr., in leading the Montgomery bus boycott

1961 Launches Shelters for the Shelterless – a FOR campaign responding to fallout shelter fad – build real shelters for homeless people

1976 Launches national disarmament petition campaign, presenting 30,000 signatures to the White House and Congress; Co-sponsors Continental Walk for Peace and Justice; Organizes and provides leadership for United Farmworkers work camp

1977 Joins ACLU in concerted campaign opposing death penalty; With AFSC launches national effort to close Rocky Flats National Weapons Plant in Colorado

1978 Sponsors Plowshare Coffee House and Discussion Center during UN Special Session on Disarmament; Joins with Mobilization for Survival to intensify work on disarmament

1979 Begins all-out campaign against draft registration; Co-sponsors Plowshare II at MIT at World Council of Churches Conference on Faith, Science and the Future; Sponsors second work project at Red Wind Native American School in California

The Fellowship for Reconciliation

A Modest Proposal to the Court

I would like to open with a supposition whose point will shortly become clear.

Suppose that in a small German town, in 1942, there was brought before a judge a group of accused troublemakers. They had been rounded up by the police at a rather seedy, smoke-ridden, heavily guarded camp near the town. There, went the complaint, they had paraded in death masks, leafletted, shouted sentences about "genocide," refused to move when so ordered. They had even poured over the gates of the camp a "red substance which they declared was their own blood."

The defendants were undoubtedly fractious; they annoyed the court exceedingly. On that hushed air their intemperate voices rose. The camp, they declared, was a vast extermination mill, where children, women, the aged and ill were routinely slaughtered like cattle in an abattoir, their flesh processed into soap, their bones into buttons, their hair into upholstery, their teeth into pendant ornaments. A use had been found at last for "human life devoid of value." So went their accusation.

The camp commandant took the stand. He was, he declared, all but speechless: such garbled idiocies! The camp, one among many such instruments of the fatherland, was, in fact, performing certain tasks under the immediate supervision of the department of defense. Tasks intimately connected with the security of the people. These dissenters must be mad. He spread his hands.

Thereupon he was questioned by defense counsel. He answered, stern, impeccably polite. He was permitted to reveal exactly – nothing. No detail of the work, production, numbers of workers, wages. No information relative to the camp. Security demanded secrecy in a time of grave national crisis.

Would he comment on this fact? The fallout of peculiarly filthy, acrid smoke, drifting on the town when winds were southwardly.

He would not. National security.

Daniel Berrigan

The Last Judgement *by William Blake.*

Building a Violence-Free Society

The process of building a violence-free society is already well underway. There is a new wave of awareness sweeping the earth. People in every corner of the world are re-evaluating their systems of belief, their notions of the nature of man, their understanding of the purpose of life, their family relationships and their participation in the life of their communities. An integral part of this process, throughout the world, is the rise of the Bahá'í community in some 340 countries and major territories. It is a community united in its purpose, co-ordinated in the efforts of its members, undaunted in its determination, confident of its direction and filled with joy and hope. Its existence demonstrates that mankind can build a world characterized by unity in diversity and freedom from prejudice, war and violence. In this sense the Bahá'í community is important both as a symbol of hope and as a model for mankind's future. By recognizing the nobility of man and the spiritual nature of his creation, and by regarding the family as a "fortress for well-being" and the main foundation of human society, each individual Bahá'í serves directly and actively in the building of a violence-free society.

Such is the opportunity of every person who is willing to dedicate himself to this noble task. The inevitable arrival of mankind's age of maturity may be ushered in by a prolonged adolescence marked by continuing violence, or by an increasingly peaceful and creative stage in mankind's history. The choice is ours.

Hossain Danesh

231

Love Is the Key

In the current world atmosphere, some people may think that religion is for those who remain in remote places and is not much needed in the areas of business or politics. My answer to this is "No!" For, as I have just said, in my simple religion, love is the key motivation. . . . Thus motivation is very important, and thus my simple religion is love, respect for others, honesty: teachings that cover not only religion but also the fields of politics, economics, business, science, law, medicine – everywhere. With proper motivation these can help humanity; without it they go the other way. Without good motivation, science and technology, instead of helping, bring more fear and threaten global destruction. Compassionate thought is very important for humankind. . . .

Deep down we must have real affection for each other, a clear realization or recognition of our shared human status. At the same time, we must openly accept all ideologies and systems as means of solving humanity's problems. One country, one nation, one ideology, one system is not sufficient. It is helpful to have a variety of different approaches on the basis of a deep feeling of the basic sameness of humanity. We can then make joint effort to solve the problems of the whole of humankind. The problems human society is facing in terms of economic development, the crisis of energy, the tension between the poor and rich nations, and many geopolitical problems can be solved if we understand each other's fundamental humanity, respect each other's rights, share each other's problems and sufferings, and then make joint effort. . . .

Everybody loves to talk about calm and peace whether in a family, national, or international context, but without *inner* peace how can we make real peace? World peace through hatred and force is impossible. Even in the case of individuals, there is no possibility to feel happiness through anger. If in a difficult situation one becomes disturbed internally, overwhelmed by mental discomfort, then external things will not help at all. However, if despite external difficulties or problems, internally one's attitude is of love, warmth, and kindheartedness, then problems can be faced and accepted easily. . . .

Without love, human society is in a very difficult state; without love, in the future we will face tremendous problems. Love is the center of human life.

His Holiness Tenzin Gyatso. The 14th Dalai Lama.

Children light candles at the Bodh Gaya temple, during three-day-long sermon by the Dalai Lama, 1974.

World Peace Prayer

Lead me from death to life
From falsehood to truth
Lead me from despair to hope From
fear to trust
Lead me from hate to love
From war to peace
Let peace fill our hearts,
    our world, our universe.

Project Ploughshares

The $400 Tax Resister

On Monday, November 7, on the new moon of Kislev, myself and sixteen friends held a ritual/demonstration to kindle the lights during dark times, to gather our power, and to re-dedicate ourselves to our work of bringing light into the world.

Outside the Minneapolis Federal Building, we cast a Rainbow Circle (our "Rainbow Sign" Banner). We sang "Lo Yisa Goy." Calling all our inner souls to do Torah, to witness, we chanted everyone's name in unison. Lynn Rosen then told a wonderful story about the Exodus from Egypt, and the Israelite people's struggles with slave consciousness, hard times in the desert, and desires for security and the familiar. She told how in fear they made a golden calf, and how out of necessity, it and the visible "laws" had to be broken.

In the center of the circle were bags with 40,000 pennies – my taxes – the pieces of the calf. We decided to give it back to Pharaoh – we didn't need it anymore. We built a mishkan, and each put into it a message of hope.

Lifting the bags, we carried them into the building, and our voices rang out in song – filling the old hallways. The feeling was tremendous – together – with just our voices, we were taking back our power to follow the laws of life. No one tried to stop us as we walked right in to the IRS [Internal Revenue Service] collections division – still singing. Some workers were amused – some were very scared by our singing and called security guards.

We gave our broken calf pieces back to Pharaoh, and left singing.

Stephen Booth

Our Mission

The mission group at the center of World Peacemakers, Inc., has focused our call as follows:

To confess Jesus Christ as Lord and to live out Christ's call to peacemaking in both personal and public domain by:
• Seeking to be converted ourselves by Christ's call to peacemaking even as we seek to be instruments of this conversion in our churches and in the world.
• Saying "no" to the idolatry of the national security state and its values represented in the present U.S. foreign and military policies, and "yes" to the gospel values for justice and peace and "yes" to our belief that God's grace is sufficient to enable the nation to change toward these values and new policies.
• Envisioning alternative security structures and systems consistent with the gospel of Jesus Christ and taking concrete actions to help the nation move in this direction of change.
• Nurturing and encouraging small groups of persons who are also seeking to follow Christ's call to peacemaking.
• Joining with the vanguard of the U.S. Confessing Church – the network of small groups and many others in the churches throughout the nation witnessing by lives and actions to God's grace moving us all toward true security.

*　　　*　　　*

A World Peacemaker Group is a small gathering of people (two to perhaps twelve) who, conscious of the action of the Holy Spirit in their lives, offer the gift of their corporate life for the world's healing and unity through peacemaking. The Group has both an "inward" and an "outward" journey. The inward journey enables the Group members to nurture their prayer and contemplative life...and give their lives in peacemaking activities. . . . The outward journey, empowered by the inward, takes shape in specific peacemaking activities selected by each particular group. Groups engage in activities which express their inner centeredness in their approach to global issues of peace and justice. . . .

World Peacemakers

On the Great Plains near Winner, South Dakota; photo by Dororthea Lange.

Mennonite Witness

Therefore be it resolved that the Mennonite Central Committee call its supporting churches to reflect on what it means to be people of the Kingdom, sharing the good news of the gospel and its full implications in a broken world. Specific initiatives by MCC and the supporting churches are suggested as follows:

To answer the Mennonite World Conference call to "witness against powers and principalities who trust in bombs and move toward nuclear holocaust":
• We call upon the supporting churches to work for a moratorium on all military exports and for redirection of resources from production of military weapons to the service of human need.
• We call upon all people and nations to renounce the research, development, testing, production, deployment and use of nuclear weapons. We call for the conversion of jobs in science and industry from warmaking to peacemaking purposes. Individuals are encouraged to review their industrial employment and investments to make sure they are not contributing unknowingly to the arms race.

Mennonite Central Committee

Taking Up the Cross

As followers of Christ, we need to take up our cross in the nuclear age. I believe that one obvious meaning of the cross is unilateral disarmament. Jesus' acceptance of the cross rather than the sword raised in his defense is the Gospel's statement of unilateral disarmament. We are called to follow. . . .

I am told by some that unilateral disarmament in the face of atheistic communism is insane. I find myself observing that nuclear armament by anyone is itself atheistic, and anything but sane. I am also told that the choice of unilateral disarmament is a political impossibility in this country. If so, perhaps the reason is that we have forgotten what it would be like to act out of faith. But I speak here of that choice not as a political platform – it might not win elections – but as a moral imperative for followers of Christ. A choice has been put before us; anyone who wants to save one's own life by nuclear arms will lose it; but anyone who loses one's life by giving up those arms for Jesus' sake, and for the sake of the Gospel of love, will save it.

Most Rev. Raymond Hunthausen
Archbishop of Seattle

A Healing Presence

Although we speak with the many voices of the world's diverse religious traditions, we are one in our belief in the sacredness of life and the holiness of the earth. It is from this common faith that we wish to speak out in the name of the present and future generations. Today [1982], as never before, the survival of humanity is threatened by the possibility of nuclear extermination. Even if those fearsome weapons are not actually used, they attack the poor through an unchecked arms race that consumes the very resources – $500 billion annually – which should feed, clothe, house and heal the world's people. In the name of the Spirit of Life may the work of those within the United Nations and outside of it during the Special Session on Disarmament be blessed with the vision and courage to turn the nuclear tide while there is still time. Together let us choose life so that we and our children will live.

Statement of the Reverence for Life Conference

Covet Not Riches

When that spirit works which loves riches. . .it desires to defend the treasures thus gotten. . . .Wealth is attended with power. . .and hence oppression, carried on with worldly policy and order, clothes itself with the name of justice and becomes like a seed of discord in the soul. And as a spirit which wanders from the pure habitation prevails, so the seeds of war swell and sprout. . . .May we look upon our treasures, the furniture of our houses and our garments and try whether the seeds of war have nourishment in these our possessions.

John Woolman, English Quaker

Buddhist monks lead the culmination of the World Peace March; New York, 1982.

The Prayer of St. Francis

Lord, make me a channel of your peace,
Where there is hatred, let me sow love,
Where there is injury, pardon Lord,
Where there is doubt, let me sow your faith.
Where there is despair, let me bring hope,
Where there is darkness, light, where there is sadness, joy.
Master, may I never seek so much to be consoled as to console,
To be understood as to understand,
To be loved as to love.
For it is in pardoning that we are forgiven,
It is in giving that we receive,
It is in dying that we are born to eternal life.

St. Francis of Assisi (1182?-1226)

Religious of all faiths have participated in pro-peace actions; above, at the New York Peace March; below, at the Ribbon Round the Pentagon demonstration.

A Pastoral Letter

An influential panel of bishops of the United Methodist Church, the third largest church body in the United States, has drafted a pastoral letter denouncing the use of nuclear weapons and the doctrine of nuclear deterrence.

"We have said a clear and unconditional 'no' to nuclear war," the letter says, "and to any use of nuclear weapons."

The letter and an accompanying 100-page foundation document were prepared under the authority of the United Methodists' influential Committee on Episcopal Initiatives for Ministry and Mission. . . .

The pastoral letter and foundation document reject the concept of nuclear deterrence as unacceptable. The foundation document also says the concept of an ethically justifiable war, which originated with Saint Ambrose and Saint Augustine in the fourth and fifth centuries, is inapplicable to nuclear warfare. It also affirms that the nuclear arms race adds to social injustice in the world.

[Bishop] White said the position on nuclear deterrence differed from the stance taken by America's Roman Catholic Bishops in a pastoral letter that stirred considerable attention in 1983. The Catholic document, White said, employed "an interim ethic to say that nuclear deterrence is ethically justified while arms negotiations are continuing, and only under those circumstances. . . ."

"We hope that the documents will be influential not only among our own people but throughout the Christian world," White said.

Eric Pace

The Illusions of Peace

To some men peace merely means the liberty to exploit other people without fear of retaliation or interference. To others peace means the freedom to rob others without interruption. To still others it means the leisure to devour the goods of the earth without being compelled to interrupt their pleasures to feed those whom their greed is starving. And to practically everybody peace simply means the absence of any physical violence that might cast a shadow over lives devoted to the satisfaction of their animal appetites for comfort and pleasure.

Many men like these have asked God for what they thought was 'peace' and wondered why their prayer was not answered. They could not understand that it actually *was* answered. God left them with what they desired, for their idea of peace was only another form of war. The 'cold war' is simply the normal consequence of our corrupt idea of a peace based on a policy of "every man for himself" in ethics, economics and political life. It is absurd to hope for a solid peace based on fictions and illusions!

So instead of loving what you think is peace, love other men and love God above all. And instead of hating the people you think are warmakers, hate the appetites and the disorder in your own soul, which are the causes of war. If you love peace, then hate injustice, hate tyranny, hate greed – but hate these things *in yourself*, not in another.

Thomas Merton (1915-1968)

PEACEABLE STUDIES

Russian veteran E.N. Krutchkov takes part in peace lesson which is conducted in every USSR school on the first day of the new school year.

Teachers in a Changing World

Teachers and students all over [the U.S.] are responding to the need to think about our world in new ways and to reform their curriculum accordingly, not only because they believe it is their professional responsibility to inform and educate, but also because it is their ethical commitment to young people. Much to their credit, many teachers have realized that their role goes beyond the mere transferral of information. It must also entail preparing young people to live in this world and make thoughtful value choices.

Born and raised in the nuclear age, high school and college students have lived under the shadow of the bomb all their lives. Inevitably, they have questions about the meaning of security and the nature of peace. From the hostage crisis in Iran to the oil crisis at home, from the debacle of Vietnam to the furor over the nuclear freeze, international crises touch the lives of young Americans every day. Our youth is perhaps more resilient than we think, and more willing to confront these troubling questions than we know.

For example, a core group of professors at West Chester State College in Pennsylvania polled the student body on their rural campus of 6,000 undergraduates in the spring of 1981, and found that over a third of the students were

interested in taking courses on conflict and the arms race. With the result of this poll in hand, the professors were able to demonstrate to the college administration the need for a program of study in peace and war issues.

Many such examples can be found throughout the country in junior colleges, at public and private universities and high schools. The following is a brief sampling of the major trends and curriculum innovations taking place today:

• The University of California system has established a new statewide Institute of Global Conflict and Cooperation (IGCC), involving all nine campuses – Los Angeles, Fullerton, San Diego, Berkeley, Santa Barbara, Davis, Santa Cruz, Long Branch, and Irvine. IGCC, with its main office at UC San Diego, is the central vehicle to help faculty develop research and teaching in global security, arms control and world problems. IGCC sponsors projects, provides small grants, conducts summer teaching seminars, and publishes a newsletter on developments at each campus.

• Augsburg College in Minnesota, Monroe and Berkshire community colleges in upstate New York, and Warren Wilson College in the Blue Ridge Mountains of North Carolina are among the hundreds of smaller schools now offering degree programs in the areas of peace, alternative lifestyles, self-reliance, economic justice and sustainable societies.

• The University of Illinois, the University of Wisconsin at Madison, Ohio State University and six other colleges have established special academic/research centers focusing on national security and increased citizen participation in foreign policy questions.

• Universities in the northeast United States, such as Tufts and Brandeis, have recently launched minor studies on the effects of militarism and the arms race on the economy and civil liberties, conflict from the local to the global level, and justice in world society.

• Some campuses are taking an innovative approach which goes beyond the curriculum in order to have an impact on the college as a whole. Beginning in 1981, Baldwin-Wallace College in Ohio made peace and social justice a central organizing theme on the campus for two years. Artistic performances, public lectures, film festivals, faculty seminars and many new peace studies courses were part of the campus-wide programming on peace.

• Divinity schools and seminaries have intensified their efforts to connect religious education with war and peace. Particular impetus was provided by the Catholic Bishops' Pastoral letter. Yale Divinity School offers courses on the nuclear arms race and religious teachings. Earlham College has a well-established Master of Ministry degree that examines poverty and the philosophies of nonviolence. Two seminaries in Elkart, Indiana, and Chicago offer peace studies curricula.

• Pooling expertise and resources, institutions of higher learning and high schools are creating joint activities. Many colleges with nuclear war education courses are aiding area high schools to grapple with this very large and hot issue. Discussion questions, materials, guest lecturers, films and other resources are being developed and shared across academic settings.

• The University of Massachusetts, and Amherst, Hampshire, Mt. Holyoke, and Smith colleges have established the Five College Project on Peace and Disarmament. With each institution offering peace and world order courses, a rich and varied curriculum is now available to their student bodies.

• Single academic departments and professors can make a difference. The physics department at the University of Illinois, Urbana-Champaign, has a course called "The Bomb" which includes physical, medical, and political dimensions of the invention of nuclear weapons. At the University of Minnesota, "Nuclear Weapons, Nuclear War," an independent study course, was offered in conjunction with the special television broadcast of *The Day After.* A package of course materials, study guide and audio cassette tapes were made available to institutions and individuals. At Hofstra University, an economist and historian combined their talents to create several new world order courses.

• The Center for Peaceful Change at Kent State University offers both an Integrative Change major and a peace studies minor. The Center was also the host of the Consortium for Peace Research, Education, and Development (COPRED) for

six years. COPRED is a national network of educators, practitioners, researchers and activists who are developing classroom materials on the environment, social justice and peace.

• Major educational publications from national teachers' associations have devoted articles and entire issues to peace and nuclear war education as a tremendous area of growth in the field of education. To name several – *The Chronicle of Higher Education*, *The Forum for Liberal Education* of the Association of American Colleges, *Teachers College Record* of Columbia University Teachers College, *Social Education* of the National Council of the Social Studies, and *The Radcliffe Quarterly*.

• Peace and world order studies serve as a common ground for collaborative efforts across academic departments. Frequently, a teacher may feel that he or she does not have enough expertise to conduct a world order course single-handedly. An interdisciplinary approach is used in the peace studies programs at Manchester College in Indiana, Manhattan College in New York City and scores of other schools.

These case studies are only a handful of the approximately 120 programs now in existence in the U.S. Teachers who have led the efforts, as well as those who have only recently become involved, have been gratified by their role in this crucial educational movement. On this movement depends not only the education of the young, but perhaps the survival of us all.

World Policy Institute

A Message to Our Parents:

On November 18, 1985, WBZ-TV4 in the New England Area broadcast a special program entitled *A Message to Our Parents*. Hosted by Christopher Reeve, the show examines children's views and concerns about growing up in a nuclear world, and features a 20-minute segment created by a group of fifth-, sixth-, seventh-and eighth-graders from the Boston area. These students interview Hiroshima survivors and a number of specialists about war, peace, arms control, Soviet and U.S. positions and the human considerations within the nuclear dilemma. The list of experts participating with the students in this project is extensive: Dr. Kosta Tsipis from M.I.T., John Chancellor of NBC News, Frank Miller of the Pentagon, Drs. William and Helen Caldicott of [WAND], Dr. Eric Chivian of Harvard International Children's Project, [ESR] National President Roberta Snow and others.

Shown in the New England area the week of the U.S.-Soviet Summit Talks, the program's aims were to show adults that kids do have questions and to encourage parents to talk to their children about these questions. The show is part of WBZ-TV's public service series, "For Kid's Sake." WBZ's national affiliate, Westinghouse, is in the process of syndicating this series so it can be shown in cities around the country.

Susan Jones, of Boston ESR, has written a booklet for WBZ for parents and teachers responding to children's questions and concerns. WBZ plans to distribute it widely, and has stocked a first printing of 10,000 copies.

Gene Thompson

Festival Lights by Mark Côté, 13 years old, Canada.

A New Peace Corps

• The primary function of Nuclear Age Peace Corps volunteers will be to educate others on the urgent need to reverse the nuclear arms race, using the results of recent reports issued by scientists.

Scene from the Children's Peace Walk, New York, June 1982.

• The Nuclear Age Peace Corps will spread knowledge of the techniques of peaceful conflict resolution showing how violent conflicts can be averted.

• The Nuclear Age Peace Corps will be composed primarily of young leaders (clergy, educators, civic leaders, etc.) who will return to their communities to teach others.

• Training will be accomplished in a series of seminars, and the ordinary work of the Nuclear Age Peace Corps volunteers will go on in addition to their volunteer work.

The Nuclear Age Peace Corps will be built upon these propositions:

• That the likelihood of climatic change and environmental destruction found in "Nuclear Winter" studies make the destruction levels of a nuclear war unacceptably high;

• That the increasing likelihood of nuclear war occurring by accident or inadvertance makes the risk of nuclear war unacceptably high;

• That there are feasible alternatives to the present course of action, including the expansion of trade, cultural and scientific exchanges between nations; and

• That citizens in a democracy have the right and responsibility to create a better and safer world.

Frank K. Kelly

Training Peacemakers

The International Peace Academy (IPA) began its work in 1970 on the premise that it is essential for those who are most responsible for peace to have *professional* training. Its mandate then and now is to serve the cause of peace through practical, educational means.

The Academy was established as a non-profit, non-governmental, academic training institute to teach the skills of peacekeeping, peacemaking and peacebuilding to mid-career diplomats and military officials on a global basis – an innovative and untried concept. Though the original Academy agenda has remained unchanged, the scope of its training programs, workshops and research has continued to enlarge each year. Experience has shown that all three skills – peacekeeping, peacemaking, peacebuilding – are inextricably related and are essential requisites for the peaceful resolution of conflicts.

The Academy is a distinctive blend of pragmatism and theory combined with a transnational perspective. Its primary objectives are reflected in its major activities:

• design and organization of international training seminars in peacekeeping and peacemaking to prepare professionals in crisis management

• initiation and administration of off-the-record meetings between disputing parties to facilitate their discussions

• publication of reports and books related both to practical experience and to scholarly research to identify options for resolving conflicts

All of these activities are aimed at mobilizing the resources of scientific, scholarly and professional knowledge for the peaceful resolution of conflicts.

Since its founding in 1970, over 2,250 diplomats, military officers, policy-makers and scholars from 129 nations, representing the diverse regions and ideologies of the world, have attended Academy programs held in Africa, Asia, Europe, Latin America and North America.

International Peace Academy

Balance and Hope

The immediate claim of peace education is urgent. The young must be given the facts, the perspective and the analytical tools to deal positively with the daily accounts of threat and doom that can dominate their lives. For this reason teachers and community groups who are now working in the field must be supported so they can produce effective materials for the classroom and also lobby for change within the system.

At the heart of the peace education movement is a recognition by parents and teachers of the potential for despair among the young. Faced with a future filled with conflict or sabre-rattling, they can "turn off," suffer, or they can learn to interpret and act on the information they receive. Most concerned adults in the movement are educating themselves about the arms race so their responses to the young will offer balance and reliability and hope. By acting on such information, young people can assume confidence and responsibility over their lives – instead of despair.

Peace education is not confined to the arms race. It encompasses values education for the very young, and sophisticated studies of the future for senior high school students. It must include the means to build a peaceful world as well as the means to prevent war. The pursuit of global economic justice, the state of human rights in the world, respect and care for the environment, and co-operative decision-making are all aspects of peace education.

Penny Sanger

Angolan child's painting

Watermelon, not war.

Not Material but Moral Weapons

Education today is still confined by the limits of a social order that is now past. Education today not only is contrary to the dictates of science; it also runs counter to the social needs of our time. Education cannot be dismissed as an insignificant factor in people's lives, as a means of furnishing a few rudiments of culture to young people. It must be viewed first of all from the perspective of the development of human values in the individual, in particular his moral values, and second from the point of view of organizing the individuals possessed of these enhanced values into a society consciously aware of its destiny. A new form of morality must accompany this new form of civilization. Order and discipline must be aimed at the attainment of human harmony, and any act that hinders the establishment of a genuine community of all mankind must be regarded as immoral and a threat to the life of society. . . .

The special province of morality is the relation between individuals, and it is the very basis of social life. Morality must be regarded as the science of organizing a society of men whose highest value is their selfhood and not the efficiency of their machines. Men must learn how to participate consciously in the social discipline that orders all their functions within society and how to help keep these functions in balance.

The crux of the question of peace and war thus no longer lies in the need to give men the material weapons to defend the geographical frontiers separating nation from nation, for the real first line of defense against war is man himself, and where man is socially disorganized and devalued, the universal enemy will enter the breach.

Maria Montessori (1870-1952)

HONOURED ARE THE PEACEMAKERS

Lester B. Pearson, shown here before a dinner in his honour, 1966.

Pearson Peace Medal

Any Canadian may nominate a fellow citizen for this prestigious award presented each year by the United Nations Association in Canada for outstanding achievement in the field of international service.

The Pearson Peace Medal is awarded annually to that Canadian who "through voluntary and other efforts, has personally most contributed to those causes for which Lester Pearson stood: aid to the developing world, mediation between those confronting one another with arms, succor to refugees and others in need, and peaceful change through world law and world organization."

A jury of eminent Canadians meets each year to choose the recipient. The medal is presented by the Governor-General of Canada around United Nations Day, 24 October. Recipients to date have been: Paul-Émile Cardinal Léger (1979), J. King Gordon (1980), General E.L.M. Burns (1981), Hugh Llewellyn Keenleyside (1982), Most Reverend Georges-Henri Lévesque (1983), George Ignatieff (1984) and Lois Wilson (1985).

United Nations Association in Canada Bulletin

Nobel Laureates Praise Peace

1947

We believe that war is a habit, a curious habit, a somewhat accidental habit that men have adopted, although in other areas they have found different means for pursuing similar ends. . . . We recognize that there are times when resistance appears at first to be a real virtue, and then only those most deeply rooted in religious pacifism can resist by other than physical means. We have learned that in the end only the spirit can conquer evil and we believe that in many recent situations those who have unwillingly employed force have learned this lesson at the last. . . .

Henry J. Cadbury AFSC

1949

The new powers which science has let loose cannot be bottled up again. They must be used for constructive ends or they will break loose in another world war which will destroy our European civilization. . . . For Europe at least, peace is inevitable. It can either be the peace of the grave, the peace of the dead empires of the past, which lost their creative spirit and failed to adjust themselves to new conditions, or a new dynamic peace applying science in a great leap forward in the evolution of human society to a new age in which hunger, poverty and preventable diseases will be eliminated from the earth – an age in which the people in every country will rise to a far higher level of intellectual and cultural well-being, an age in which 'iron curtains' will disappear and people, though intensely patriotic for their own country, will be able to travel freely as world citizens. That is the hope science sets before us.

John Boyd Orr, MD, FAO

1957

In all the long story of mankind, arms alone, however powerful, have never been sufficient to guarantee security for any length of time. Your strength for defense becomes the weakness of those against whom you feel you must be ready to defend yourself. Your security becomes their insecurity; so they in turn seek safety in increased arms. A vicious circle commences which in the past has cost untold misery and destruction and might now, if we cannot cut through it, cause mankind's extinction. Even adequate collective defense, then, is no final solution. It is merely a means to an end – peace based on something more enduring than force. Today, less than ever, can we defend ourselves by force, for there is no effective defense against the all-destroying effect of nuclear missile weapons. Indeed, their very power has made their use intolerable, ever unthinkable, because of the annihilative retaliation in kind that such use would invoke. So peace remains. . . balanced uneasily on terror, and the use of maximum force is frustrated by the certainty that it will be used in reply with devastating effect. Peace. . .must surely be more than this trembling rejection of universal suicide.

Lester B. Pearson

1975

In struggling to protect human rights we must, I am convinced, first and foremost act as protectors of the innocent victims of regimes installed in various countries, without demanding the destruction or total condemnation of these regimes. We need reform, not revolution. We need a pliant, pluralist, tolerant community, which selectively and tentatively can bring about a free, undogmatic use of the experiences of all social systems. What is détente? What is rapproachment? We are concerned not with words, but with a willingness to create a better and more friendly society, a better world order. . . .

Andrei Sakharov

1984

The peace prize is to show that God is in charge here in this world and that justice, goodness, peace, love and compassion will prevail, that God cares, the world cares and we are winning.

Bishop Desmond Tutu

1985

Perhaps the signal accomplishment of IPPNW [International Physicians for Prevention of Nuclear War] has been the broad-based, free-flowing dialogue between physicians in the two contending power blocs. We heed Einstein's words: "Peace cannot be kept by force. It can only be achieved by understanding." In a world riven with confrontation and strife, the IPPNW has become a model for cooperation among physicians from East and West, from North and South. Paranoid fantasies of a dehumanized adversary cannot withstand the common pursuit of healing and preventing illness. Our success in forging such cooperation derives largely from an insistent avoidance of linkage with problems that have embittered relations between the great powers. We have resisted being sidetracked to other issues, no matter how morally lofty. Combating the nuclear threat has been our exclusive preoccupation, since we are dedicated to the proposition that to ensure the conditions of life, we must prevent the conditions of death. Ultimately, we believe people must come to terms with the fact that the struggle is not between different national destinies – between opposing ideologies – but between catastrophe and survival. All nations share a linked destiny; nuclear weapons are their shared enemy.

Dr. Bernard Lown

Dr. Bernard Lown (left) and Dr. Evgueni Chazov, founders of IPPNW.

Nobel Peace Prize Winners

Year	Winner	Year	Winner	Year	Winner
1901	Jean H. Durant and Frédéric Passy		and Ludwig Quidde	1960	Albert Luthuli
1902	Elie Ducommun and Charles Gobat	1928	Prize not awarded	1961	Dag Hammarskjöld
1903	Sir William Cremer	1929	Frank Kellogg	1962	Linus Pauling
1904	Institute of International Law	1930	Nathan Söderblom	1963	International Committee of the Red Cross and League of Red Cross Societies
1905	Baroness Bertha von Suttner	1931	Jane Addams and Nicholas Butler		
1906	Theodore Roosevelt	1932	Prize not awarded	1964	Martin Luther King, Jr.
1907	Ernesto Moneta and Louis Renault	1933	Sir Norman Angell	1965	United Nations Children's Fund (UNICEF)
1908	Klas Arnoldson and Fredrik Bajer	1934	Arthur Henderson		
		1935	Carl von Ossietzky	1966-67	Prizes not awarded
1909	Auguste Beernaert and Paul d'Estournelles de Constant	1936	Carlos Saavedra Lamas	1968	René-Samuel Cassin
		1937	Viscount Cecil of Chelwood	1969	International Labor Organization
1910	International Peace Bureau	1938	Nansen International Office for Refugees		
1911	Tobias Asser and Albert Fried	1939-43	Prizes not awarded	1970	Norman E. Borlaug
		1944	International Committee of the Red Cross	1971	Willy Brandt
1912	Elihu Root			1972	Prize not awarded
1913	Henri La Fontaine	1945	Cordell Hull	1973	Henry Kissinger and [declined by] Le Duc Tho
1914-16	Prizes not awarded	1946	Emily Balch and John Mott		
1917	International Committee of the Red Cross	1947	Friends Service Council and American Friends Service Committee	1974	Eisaku Sato and Sean MacBride
				1975	Andrei Sakharov
1918	Prize not awarded	1948	Prize not awarded	1976	Mairead Corrigan and Betty Williams
1919	Woodrow Wilson	1949	Lord John Boyd Orr of Brechin		
1920	Léon Bourgeois	1950	Ralph Bunche	1977	Amnesty International
1921	Karl Branting and Christian Lange	1951	Léon Jouhaux	1978	Anwar Sadat and Menachem Begin
		1952	Albert Schweitzer		
1922	Fridtjof Nansen	1953	George Marshall	1979	Mother Teresa of Calcutta
1923-24	Prizes not awarded	1954	Office of the United Nations High Commissioner for Refugees	1980	Adolfo Perez Esquivel
1925	Sir J. Asten Chamberlain and Charles Dawes			1981	Office of U.N. High Commissioner for Refugees
		1955-56	Prizes not awarded	1982	Alva Myrdal and Alfonso Garcia Robles
1926	Aristide Briand and Gustav Stresemann	1957	Lester Pearson		
		1958	Georges Pire	1983	Lech Walesa
1927	Ferdinand Buisson	1959	Philip Noel-Baker	1984	Bishop Desmond Tutu
				1985	Bernard Lown, M.D. and Evgueni Chazov, M.D. (IPPNW)

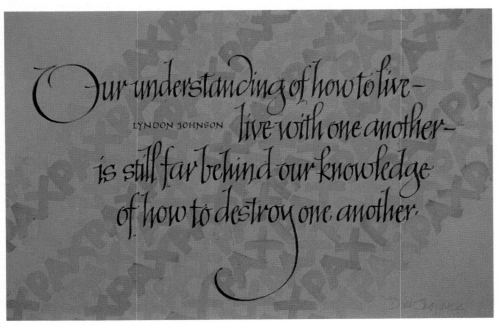

LYNDON JOHNSON

Our understanding of how to live— live with one another— is still far behind our knowledge of how to destroy one another.

Calligraphy by Dini Chynick.

Swackhamer Prizes

The Swackhamer Prizes are awarded annually for the outstanding essays by high school students on a theme related to peace in the nuclear age. The contest seeks to encourage young people to consider and make suggestions for constructive approaches to the problems of war and peace.

The Swackhamer Prizes were established by Gladys Swackhamer in honor of her parents, Austin H. and Florence Anderson Swackhamer. They are to be awarded annually.

The Nuclear Age Peace Foundation is responsible for choosing the theme of each year's essay contest, publicizing the contest, selecting the winners, awarding the prizes, and publishing and distributing the winning essays.

Founded on Love

No one is perfect. Yet, as a perfectionist, I hope that many people will try to make the world more perfect by making themselves more perfect. Through exposure to other countries and ideas, we can cultivate compassion and understanding, losing the need to destroy the beliefs of others. Instead, we can appreciate the value of other cultures. It is not so difficult to enjoy caviar from Russia or the cuisine of China. Certainly it cannot be impossible to respect their political ideologies as well. If we can accept others, this acceptance moves toward peace. The greatest sign of strength is humility, which indicates a satisfaction with oneself that leaves no need to appear powerful. We must create a society founded on love. George Orwell writes in *1984* of the futuristic world that "The old civilizations claimed that they were founded on love or justice. Ours is founded upon hatred." We must eradicate the possibility of such a world ever existing.

Janet Aileen Mercer
(Swackhamer Award Winner, 1985)
Santa Barbara High School

The UNESCO Prize

In an international dispute, the peacemaker's function is not to expound to those involved an indivisible immutable Truth, but to help them create a new truth about their relationship by finding firm ground for agreements that will benefit both parties and bring their vital interests into closer harmony.

The creation of *new* political and social truths, *new* sympathies and relationships, is always the goal of great peacebuilders.

Peacemaking, peacekeeping, and peacebuilding require a high degree of consistency in the conduct of those who seriously profess them.

Awarded annually, the UNESCO Prize was established in 1980 with a trust fund created by the Japan Shipbuilding Industry Foundation "to promote all forms of action designed to. . .mobilize the conscience of mankind in the cause of peace." As the organization's constitution states: "Since wars begin in the minds of men, it is in the minds of men that the defenses of peace must be constructed." Laureates are selected by the Director-General of UNESCO on the basis of proposals submitted by an international jury.

Major General (Ret.) Indar Jit Rikhye, President, International Peace Academy

Olive Branch Book Award

On August 6, [1985] the fortieth anniversary of the Hiroshima bombing, the WPA [Writers' and Publishers' Assoc.] announced the first Olive Branch Book Award, to be given annually for the outstanding adult and juvenile books on the arms race, nuclear weapons, and world peace.

Along with the Editors' Organizing Committee, the WPA has cosponsored the Olive Branch Magazine Awards for the past two years. Now the WPA and EOC have been joined by New York University's Center for War, Peace and the News Media, which will help us conduct an expanded series of awards and other activities. The first book award will be given in February 1986 for the outstanding books published in 1985. In 1987 the Olive Branch Awards will be further expanded to recognize outstanding newspaper and television journalism on the arms race.

Unique to the Olive Branch Book Award will be the participation of a group of independent booksellers, currently being formed, who will choose the shortlist of finalists from among nominees submitted by publishers. The winners will be chosen from this shortlist by a panel of WPA member judges.

WPA Newsletter

Beyond War

The Beyond War Award is presented annually to the individual, group, organization or nation who, in the opinion of the Selection Committee, makes a significant contribution toward building a world beyond war. The Award was presented in 1983 to the National Conference of Catholic Bishops, in 1984 to the International Physicians for the Prevention of Nuclear War, and in 1985 to the signatories of the Five Continent Peace Initiative.

1985 Selection Committee: Gro Harlem Brundtland, *former Prime Minister of Norway;*
Betty Bumpers, *Founder and President of Peace Links;*
Helen Caldicott, *President Emeritus, Physicians for Social Responsibility;*
Rodrigo Carazo, *President, United Nations University for Peace, and former President of Costa Rica;*
Yevgeni I. Chazon, *Director-General, National Cardiological Research Center, USSR, and co-founder, International Physicians for the Prevention of Nuclear War;*
Marvin Goldberger, *President, California Institute of Technology;*
Theodore Hesburgh, *President, University of Notre Dame;*
Matina S. Horner, *President, Radcliffe College;*
James A. Joseph, *President, Council on Foundations;*
Richard Leakey, *Director, National Museums of Kenya;*
Bernard Lown, *Professor of Cardiology, Harvard University, and co-founder, International Physicians for the Prevention of Nuclear War;*
Hiroji Mukasa, *Former chairman, International Congress of Social Psychiatry, and founder, Mukasa Hospital, Japan;*
Esther Peterson, *former White House advisor to three U.S. Presidents;*
John R. Quinn, *Archbishop of San Francisco;*
Richard L. Rathbun, *President, Creative Initiative Foundation;*
Carl Sagan; *Director, Laboratory for Planetary Studies, Cornell University;*
Jonas Salk, *Founder, Salk Institute for Biological Studies;*
Jacqueline G. Wexler, *President, National Conference of Christians and Jews;*
Andrew Young, *Mayor of Atlanta, Georgia, and former U.S. Ambassador to the United Nations.*

Beyond War

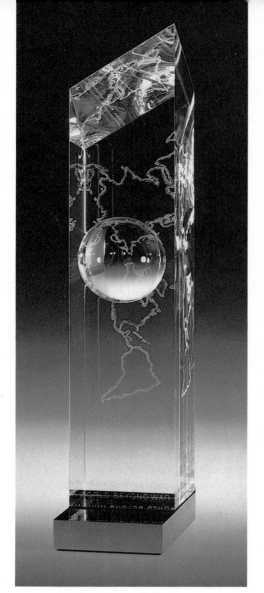

The "Beyond War" Award, designed by Steuben Glass.

Einstein Peace Prize Winners

To my mind, the nuclear bomb is the most useless weapon ever invented. It can be employed to no constructive purpose....It is only something with which, in a moment of petulance or panic, you perpetrate upon the helpless people of another country such fearful acts of destruction as no sane person would ever wish to have upon his conscience.

George F. Kennan

I am directing a first call for a public opinion resistance movement to the peace organizations. "Peace" may have become too much of a pious cliché. We must make it into a vigorous movement, anti-war and anti-militarism, by getting public opinion mobilized in all kinds of local groups. People must be made "propaganda-proof."

Alva Myrdal (1902-1985)

The Right to Life

We have lost the right to life.

Nobody demanded that we surrender it. We never renounced it voluntarily. But almost without us realizing it, the nuclear arms race took that right away from us....

All rights and freedoms, as well as all material goods and spiritual wealth, have a common foundation: the right to life....However, today we have lost it: in a few minutes a small group of people can destroy everything that each human being has....

Raúl Alfonsin, President of Argentina

What makes this nuclear age unique is that we have reached a stage where we are able to destroy not only ourselves but also everyone and everything which would come after us. All of the human civilization, so rich and so fantastic, developed over thousands of years of human effort, with its fine arts, its literature, its architecture and traditions, all of our life – all this might quite simply come to an end because of the folly of man....

We share the same world. We share the same future. The madness of the nuclear arms race is the common threat to this one future. Let us therefore work together. Let us join our efforts with people and nations all over the world. Now is the time to turn the course. Let us make 1985 the turning point.

Olof Palme (1927-1986), Prime Minister of Sweden

Edwin T. Dahlberg Peace Award

Awarded every two years to a Baptist church or individual that has made a significant effort for peace over a period of time. Under the terms of this award the word "peace" includes international peace, racial peace, community peace, peace between labor and management and other types of peace that bring reconciliation between persons, groups and nations.

The Edwin T. Dahlberg Peace Award

CITIZENS OF THE WORLD

What Shall We Do Without Us? *by Kenneth Patchen.*

No Other Way

There is no alternative in the nuclear age to finding a *modus vivendi* between conflicting systems through diplomacy, through co-operation, instead of through outright unbridled competition. This is the imperative of the interdependent world in which we live.

George Ignatieff

We Must Be Citizens of the World

The peace movement has been focusing so far on stopping the next round of the arms race – and not without good reason. Freezing the arms race is the least we can do to keep things from getting even worse.

And yet, it's clear that for the peace movement to succeed, we must do much more than just oppose weapons. Governments everywhere are resisting disarmament. The reasons are unmistakable: war remains a fearful possibility and armed force is still a useful tool in diplomacy. If we are ever to make progress toward disarmament, we will do it only by first eliminating the practice of war itself.

While keeping up the opposition to new weapons, we must add a second set of strategies to prevent war by building peace. The peace movement must start demanding of governments specific measures to lessen the likelihood of war, and eventually to replace it altogether with a peaceful means of settling disputes, as well as an alternative global security system which does not rely on national militaries.

Strategies for building peace will recognize that wars are the product of our international system. Very simply, there is nothing in the international system to prevent them. Indeed, the international system actually encourages them by keeping people divided in isolated camps called nations and giving them little opportunity to work together except through their governments, which are in perpetual competition.

Strategies for building peace would therefore emphasize cross-cultural communication, East-West people exchanges, city-twinning and global education.

Other strategies would aim directly at changes in the international system. As a first step we could examine our own attitudes. To what extent do they reinforce the present system in the very things that cause wars? Do we see ourselves as citizens of the world as well as nationals of a country? Which should take precedence, the interests of humanity, or the interests of our country?

We can challenge systematically the ethic that nations are accountable only to themselves. In its place we can promote the principle that all decision-makers, be they ours or those of other governments, should be accountable to the people whom their decisions affect. To make other governments more accountable to us we can insist that on matters which seriously affect us, like war, they must answer to world bodies, like the United Nations, in which we have some say as Canadians. By demanding a stronger role for world institutions, we can build up a tradition of due process at the global level.

World Federalists of Canada

The Harmony of Nations

The Purposes of the United Nations are:
• To maintain international peace and security, and to that end: to take effective collective measures for the prevention and removal of threats to the peace, and for the suppression of acts of aggression or other breaches of the peace, and to bring about by peaceful means, and in conformity with the principles of justice and international law, adjustment or settlement of international disputes or situations which might lead to a breach of the peace;
• To develop friendly relations among nations based on respect for the principle of equal rights and self-determination of peoples, and to take other appropriate measures to strengthen universal peace;
• To achieve international co-operation in solving international problems of an economic, social, cultural, or humanitarian character, and in promoting and encouraging respect for human rights and for fundamental freedoms for all without distinction as to race, sex, language or religion; and
• To be a centre for harmonizing the actions of nations in the attainment of these common ends.

From the Charter of the United Nations

Dag Hammarskjöld listens to a speech at the U.N., 1960.

Crimes Against Peace

Art. 6. The following acts or any of them are crimes coming within the jurisdiction of the Tribunal for which there shall be individual responsibility:

(a) Crimes against peace: Namely, planning, preparation, initiation or waging of a war of aggression or a war in violation of international treaties, agreements or assurances of participation in a common plan or conspiracy for the accomplishment of any of the foregoing:

(b) War Crimes: Namely violations of the laws or customs of war. Such violations shall include, but not be limited to, murder, ill-treatment or deportation to slave labour or for any other purpose of civilian population of or in occupied territory; murder or ill-treatment of prisoners of war or persons on the seas, killing of hostages, plunder of public or private property, wanton destruction of cities, towns or villages or devastation not justified by military necessity;

(c) Crimes against Humanity: Namely, murder, extermination, enslavement, deportation and other inhumane acts committed against any civilian population before or during war, or persecutions on political, racial or religious grounds in execution of or in connection with any crime within the jurisdiction of the Tribunal, whether or not in violation of the domestic law of the country where perpetrated. The leaders, organizers, instigators and accomplices participating in the formulation or execution of a common plan or conspiracy to commit any of the foregoing crimes are responsible for all acts performed by any persons in execution of such plan.

Reflections on Peace and Security.

"I will tell you right away that I am deeply troubled: by an intellectual climate of acrimony and uncertainty; by the parlous state of East-West relations; by a superpower relationship which is dangerously confrontational; and by a widening gap between military strategy and political purpose. All these reveal most profoundly the urgent need to assert the pre-eminence of the mind of man over machines of war..."

Pierre Elliot Trudeau, 1983

Art. 7. The official position of defendants, whether as Heads of State, as responsible officials in government departments shall not be considered as freeing them from responsibility or mitigating punishment.

From the Charter of
the Nuremberg Tribunal, 1945

World Without Countries *by Edward Ruscha, 1980.*

One World

We must all, including the diplomats
and national leaders, change our point
of view. We must recognize that
extreme nationalism is a thing of the
past. The idea that it is just as important
to do harm to other nations as to do
good for your own nation must be
given up. We must all begin to work for
the world as a whole, for humanity. . . .

   The time has now come for morality
to take its proper place in the conduct
of world affairs; the time has now come
for the nations of the world to submit
to the just regulation of their conduct
by international law.

Linus Pauling

A Shaman's Helping Spirits *by Jessie Oonark, 1971.*

Peace in a Beethoven Symphony

When the Ninth Symphony opens we enter a drama full of harsh conflict and dark
threats. But the composer leads us on, and in the beginning of the last movement
we hear again the various themes repeated, now as a bridge toward a final
synthesis. A moment of silence and a new theme is introduced, the theme of
reconciliation and joy in reconciliation. A human voice is raised in rejection of all
that has preceded and we enter the dreamt kingdom of peace. New voices join the
first and mix in a jubilant assertion of life and all that it gives us when we meet it,
joined in faith and human solidarity.

   On his road from conflict and emotion to reconciliation in this final hymn of
praise, Beethoven has given us a confession and a credo which we, who work
within and for this Organization [U.N.], may well make our own. We take part in
the continuous fight between conflicting interests and ideologies which so far has
marked the history of mankind, but we may never lose our faith that the first
movements one day will be followed by the fourth movement. In that faith we try
to bring order and purity into chaos and anarchy. Inspired by that faith we try
to impose the laws of the human mind and of the integrity of the human will on the
dramatic evolution in which we are all engaged and in which we all carry our
responsibility.

   The road of Beethoven in his Ninth Symphony is also the road followed by the
authors of the Preamble of the Charter. It begins with the recognition of the threat
under which we all live, speaking as it does of the need to save succeeding
generations from the scourge of war which has brought untold sorrow to mankind.
It moves on to a reaffirmation of faith in the dignity and worth of the human
person. And it ends with the promise to practice tolerance and live together in peace
with one another as good neighbors and to unite our strength to maintain peace.

   This year [1960], the fifteenth in the life of the Organization, is putting it to new
tests. Experience has shown how far we are from the end which inspired the
Charter. We are indeed still in the first movements. But no matter how deep the
shadows may be, how sharp the conflicts, how tense the mistrust reflected in what
is said and done in our world of today as reflected in this hall and in this house, we
are not permitted to forget that we have too much in common, too great a sharing of
interests and too much that we might lose together, for ourselves and for succeeding
generations, ever to weaken in our efforts to surmount the difficulties and not to
turn the simple human values, which are our common heritage, into the firm
foundation on which we may unite our strength and live together in peace.

Dag Hammarskjöld (1905-1961)

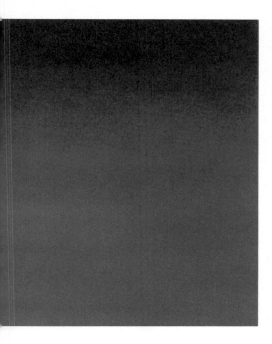

A Blueprint for Co-operation

The Governments of the States Parties to this Constitution on behalf of their peoples declare:

That since wars begin in the minds of men, it is in the minds of men that the defenses of peace must be constructed;

That ignorance of each other's ways and lives has been a common cause, throughout the history of mankind, of that suspicion and mistrust between the peoples of the world through which their differences have all too often broken into war;

That the great and terrible war which has now ended was a war made possible by the denial of the democratic principles of the dignity, equality and mutual respect of men, and by the propagation, in their place, through ignorance and prejudice, of the doctrine of the inequality of men and races;

That the wide diffusion of culture, and the education of humanity for justice and liberty and peace are indispensable to the dignity of man and constitute a sacred duty which all the nations must fulfil in a spirit of mutual assistance and concern;

That a peace based exclusively upon the political and economic arrangements of governments would not be a peace which could secure the unanimous, lasting and sincere support of the peoples of the world, and that the peace must therefore be founded, if it is not to fail, upon the intellectual and moral solidarity of mankind.

For these reasons, the States Parties to this Constitution, believing in full and equal opportunities for education for all, in the unrestricted pursuit of objective truth, and in the free exchange of ideas and knowledge, are agreed and determined to develop and to increase the means of communication between their peoples and to employ these means for the purposes of mutual understanding and a truer and more perfect knowledge of each other's lives....

In consequence whereof they do hereby create the United Nations Educational, Scientific and Cultural Organization for the purpose of advancing, through the educational and scientific and cultural relations of the peoples of the world, the objectives of international peace and of the common welfare of mankind for which the United Nations Organization was established and which its Charter proclaims.

UNESCO Constitution (1945)

Ode to Joy

Joy, bright spark of Divinity,
Daughter of Elysium,
Fire-inspired
We tread thy sanctuary.
Thy magic power re-unites
All that custom has divided,
All men become brothers
Under the sway of thy gentle wings.

Ludwig van Beethoven (1770-1827)

Stained glass window erected at the United Nations in memory of Dag Hammarskjold, designed by Marc Chagall.

Peace Is Law

Analyzing all the wars of history, I think it is possible to define the one and only condition in human society that produces war. This is the non-integrated coexistence of sovereign powers. Peace is law. Peace between warring sovereign units can be achieved only by the integration of these conflicting units into a higher sovereignty...by the creation of a world government.

Albert Einstein

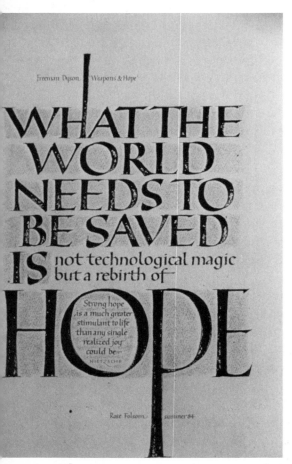

Calligraphy by Rose Folsom.

The Delhi Declaration

Today, THE SURVIVAL OF HUMANKIND IS IN JEOPARDY. The escalating arms race, the rise in international tensions and the lack of constructive dialogue among the nuclear weapons states has increased the risk of nuclear war. Such a war, even using part of the present stockpiles, would bring death and destruction to all peoples.

As leaders of nations, member states of the United Nations, we have a commitment to take constructive action towards halting and reversing the nuclear arms race. The people we represent are no less threatened by nuclear war than the citizens of the nuclear weapons states. It is primarily the responsibility of the nuclear weapons states to prevent a nuclear catastrophe, but this problem is too important to be left to those states alone.

We come from different parts of the globe, with differences in religion, culture and political systems. But we are united in the conviction that there must not be another world war. On this, the most crucial of all issues, we have resolved to make a common effort in the interests of peace.

Agreements which merely regulate an arms build-up are clearly insufficient. The probability of nuclear holocaust increases as warning time decreases and the weapons become swifter, more accurate and more deadly. The rush towards global suicide must be stopped and then reversed. We urge, as a necessary first step, the United States and the Soviet Union, as well the United Kingdom, France and China, to halt all testing, production and deployment of nuclear weapons and their delivery systems, to be immediately followed by substantial reductions in nuclear forces. We are convinced that it is possible to work out the details of an arrangement along these lines that takes into account the interests and concerns of all, and contains adequate measures for verification. This first step must be followed by a continuing programme of arms reductions leading to general and complete disarmament, accompanied by measures to strengthen the United Nations system and to ensure an urgently needed transfer of substantial resources from the arms race into social and economic development. The essential goal must be to reduce and then eliminate the risk of war between nations.

We will do everything in our power to facilitate agreement among the nuclear weapons states. We will continue to keep in touch with one another about the best ways and means of achieving this objective. We will be consulting with the leaders of the nuclear weapons states and with other world leaders as well as pursuing discussions through United Nations channels. . . .

All people have an overriding interest in common security and the avoidance of a nuclear war which threatens human survival. Citizens throughout the world are expressing, as never before, their concern for the future; this public discussion of peace and disarmament must continue and increase. The support and encouragement of an informed public will greatly strengthen governmental action to reverse the nuclear arms race.

We have faith in the capacity of human beings to rise above the current divisions and create a world free from the shadow of nuclear war. The power and ingenuity of the human race must be used, not to perfect weapons of annihilation, but to harness the resources of the earth so that all people may enjoy a life of security and dignity in an international system free of war and based on peace and justice.

Today, the world hangs in the balance between war and peace. We hope that our combined efforts will help to influence the outcome.

H.E. Mr. Raúl Alfonsín, *President of Argentina*
H.E. Mrs. Indira Gandhi, *Prime Minister of India*
H.E. Mr. Miguel de la Madrid, *President of Mexico*
H.E. Mr. Julius Nyerere, *President of the United Republic of Tanzania*
H.E. Mr. Olof Palme, *Prime Minister of Sweden*
H.E. Mr. Andreas Papandreou, *Prime Minister of Greece*

Athens, Buenos Aires, Dar es Salaam, Mexico City, New Delhi, and Stockholm, 22 May 1984

Embarking on a Journey

The age-old skepticism about system change is being challenged by a new awareness of planetary limits, interdependency, and the need for global policy coordination. The potential for mobilizing a broadly based popular movement is increasing because of the growth of planetary consciousness, instant global communication, and the formation of political coalitions among people impressed with the interlocking relationship between militarism, unemployment, poverty, resource shortages, denial of human rights, and ecological decay.

Throughout the world there are literally millions of people who now hold the values that are necessary for building a global community in which the serving of human needs takes highest priority—not for the benefit of any national group at the expense of the rest, but for the benefit of all people riding on the planet together. There are probably millions more ready to join a movement for change when it looks like it might have a chance of succeeding.

More and more people are aware that rationality is on the side of a secure global community, not national armaments. The question is: who will pioneer the belief that social transformation is possible? Will it be you and I, or, lacking courage and conviction, will we wait for another generation to take up this challenge, perhaps after entire continents have been despoiled with radioactive fallout or after large segments of humanity have suffered premature death from malnutrition, ignorance, or political repression? Once a sufficient number of people are committed, enough pressure can be brought to bear on governing elites and their supporters to convince them that their political careers will depend on reducing the share of taxpayers' money going into war equipment. Then officials will take seriously the need to build a more just and peaceful world order in which military power will have no role....

Many skeptics, who refuse to join a movement for change because of uncertainty about how to proceed every step of the way, overlook the uncertainties in their own position.

They are themselves embarked on a journey, riding in an overarmed and unstable system, without the slightest idea of how they will safely enter the twenty-first century. It is no fairer to expect the advocate of an appropriate security system to be able to predict exactly the future of human affairs than to expect the advocate of military security to prove that humanity will be secure with nuclear proliferation, the wasting of scarce resources, and continued military rivalry. To be sure, both paths are risky and fraught with danger. Yet, the risks for global community and genuine security are not unattractive when compared to the risks of perpetuating a system based on the threat of mass destruction.

*   *   *

The Challenge:
—the continued expansion of military arsenals, coupled with their obvious inability to serve human and environmental needs, make us less secure with each passing month;
—present governmental approaches to control armaments have failed—not because of any official's bad intentions but because current policies do not aim at replacing the war system with a peace system;
—the advocates of keeping the United States militarily number one in the arms buildup are in reality advocates of unilateral initiatives that will, in the long run, leave the people of the United States and the world insecure and susceptible to nuclear destruction;
—a more secure, less violent global system can be created;
—this preferred system can provide not only peace but far greater social justice, economic well-being, and ecological security than the present, highly militarized international system;
—the most important *missing* ingredient for creating an appropriate security system is the willingness of ordinary people to work with determination and tireless dedication to abolish war and to build a better system.

That system can be built if enough people believe in its feasibility and act for its realization. Many persons are inactive because they genuinely doubt

that major arms reductions are possible. These people need to consider what they can do to weaken the link between arms and security and to forge a new link between disarmament and security. Other people, pursuing an illusory security through military power or their own financial gain from large military expenditures, will vigorously oppose the policy recommendations, if not the positive vision, offered here. They are entitled to their view, but they are not

Flag of the United Nations, the symbol of the union of all peoples in search of a permanent, durable peace.

entitled to an undisputed right to lay waste this planet and its people. Their view and their vested interests must be challenged.

They *will* be challenged, by planetary citizens acting with reasoned determination. There will be a movement, transcending race, nation, class, and sex, working to create a peace system designed to serve human needs first. Just as legalized slavery among people gave birth to the abolitionist movement against the slave system, so legalized violence among nationalities will produce new abolitionists against the war system. It is now unclear whether the anti-abolitionists, advocating more arms, or the abolitionists, favoring global community, will gain the most adherents. For those who share the positive vision of a world without war, of a world with local communities of people seeking lives of dignity, participation, mutual cooperation, and genuine freedom, now is the time to join the effort for a new peace system.

Robert C. Johansen

WHY NOAH CHOSE THE DOVE

BY ISAAC BASHEVIS SINGER

When the people sinned and God decided to punish them by sending the flood, all the animals gathered around Noah's ark. Noah was a righteous man, and God had told him how to save himself and his family by building an ark that would float and shelter them when the waters rose.

The animals had heard a rumor that Noah was to take with him on the ark only the best of all the living creatures. So the animals came and vied with one another, each boasting about its own virtues and whenever possible belittling the merits of others.

The lion roared: "I am the strongest of all the beasts, and I surely must be saved."

The elephant blared: "I am the largest. I have the longest trunk, the biggest ears, and the heaviest feet."

"To be big and heavy is not so important," yapped the fox. "I, the fox, am the cleverest of all."

"What about me?" brayed the donkey. "I thought I was the cleverest."

"It seems anyone can be clever," yipped the skunk. "I smell the best of all the animals. My perfume is famous."

"All of you scramble over the earth, but I'm the only one that can climb trees," shrieked the monkey.

"The only one!" growled the bear. "What do you think I do?"

"And how about me?" chattered the squirrel indignantly.

"I belong to the tiger family," purred the cat.

"I'm a cousin of the elephant," squeaked the mouse.

"I'm just as strong as the lion," snarled the tiger. "And I have the most beautiful fur."

"My spots are more admired than your stripes," the leopard spat back.

"I am man's closest friend," yelped the dog.

"You're no friend. You're just a fawning flatterer," bayed the wolf. "I am proud. I am a lone wolf and flatter no one."

"Baa!" blatted the sheep. "That's why you're always hungry. Give nothing, get nothing. I give man my wool, and he takes care of me."

"You give man wool, but I give him sweet honey," droned the bee. "Besides, I have venom to protect me from my enemies."

"What is your venom compared with mine?" rattled the snake. "And I am closer to Mother Earth than any of you."

"Not as close as I am," protested the earthworm, sticking its head out of the ground.

"I lay eggs," clucked the hen.

"I give milk," mooed the cow.

"I help man plow the earth," bellowed the ox.

"I carry man," neighed the horse. "And I have the largest eyes of all of you."

"You have the largest eyes, but you have only two, while I have many," the house fly buzzed right into the horse's ear.

"Compared with me, you're all midgets." The giraffe's words came from a distance as he nibbled the leaves off the top of a tree.

"I'm almost as tall as you are," chortled the camel. "And I can travel in the desert for days without food or water."

"You two are tall, but I'm fat," snorted the hippopotamus. "And I'm pretty sure that my mouth is bigger than anybody's."

"Don't be so sure," snapped the crocodile, and yawned.

"I can speak like a human," squawked the parrot.

"You don't really speak. You just imitate," the rooster crowed. "I know only one word, 'cock-a-doodle-doo,' but it is my own."

"I see with my ears; I fly by hearing," piped the bat.

"I sing with my wing," chirped the cricket.

There were many more creatures who were eager to praise themselves. But Noah had noticed that the dove was perched alone on a branch and did not try to speak and compete with the other animals.

"Why are you silent?" Noah asked the dove. "Don't you have anything to boast about?"

"I don't think of myself as better or wiser or more attractive than the other animals," cooed the dove. "Each one of us has something the other doesn't have, given us by God who created us all."

"The dove is right," Noah said. "There is no need to boast and compete with one another. God has ordered me to take creatures of all kinds into the ark, cattle and beast, bird and insect."

The animals were overjoyed when they heard these words, and all their grudges were forgotten.

Before Noah opened the door of the ark, he said: "I love all of you, but because the dove remained modest and silent while the rest of you bragged and argued, I choose it to be my messenger."

Noah kept his word. When the rains stopped, he sent the dove to fly over the world and bring back news of how things were. At last she returned with an olive leaf in her beak, and Noah knew that the waters had receded. When the land finally became dry, Noah and his family and all the animals left the ark.

After the flood God promised that never again would he destroy the earth because of man's sins, and that seed time and harvest, cold and heat, summer and winter, day and night would never cease.

The truth is that there are in the world more doves than there are tigers, leopards, wolves, vultures, and other ferocious beasts. The dove lives happily without fighting. It is the bird of peace.

translated by Elizabeth Shub

Opposite: Dove by Doug Workman.

INDEX

CREDITS

Photos

The producers of this book would like to thank the following artists, photographers, institutions and copyright holders for permission to reproduce material used herein. Every reasonable effort has been made to ensure that the correct permission to reproduce was obtained. Should there be any errors in copyright information, please inform the publisher of same, and a correction will be made in subsequent editions. Numbers in boldface are page references.

2 © 1984 James Marsh; **8** Courtesy of Rafal Olbinski; **16** The Fogg Art Museum, Bequest of Grenville L. Winthrop; **18-19** Courtesy of National Aeronautics and Space Administration, Washington, D.C.; **20** Top: Museum für Völkerkunde, Vienna Austria. Bottom: Hirshhorn Museum and Sculpture Garden, Smithsonian Institution; **21** Courtesy of the Germanisches National Museum: **22** Frontispiece from "The Ancient of Days," 1794. Courtesy of the Lessing J. Rosenwald Collection, Rare Books and Special Collections, Library of Congress: **23** © 1971 by Georgia O'Keefe/HKL Limited; **24** Universidad Autonoma de Chapingo Chapel/Dirk Bakke. Courtesy of the Detroit Institute of Arts; **25** Top: Courtesy of Graphische Sammlung Albertina, Vienna. Bottom: Courtesy of the Library of Congress; **26** Gallery of Modern Art. Courtesy of SCALA/Art Resource, New York; **27** Courtesy of the Pennsylvania Academy of the Fine Arts; **28** Courtesy of the Auckland Institute and Museum, New Zealand; **29** Top and bottom: Courtesy of the Ledel Gallery, New York; **30** Courtesy of the Sanavik Co-operative, Baker Lake, N.W.T.: **31** Courtesy of the Art Gallery of Ontario, Toronto. Bequest of Charles S. Band, 1970; **32** © 1972 Terry E. Eiler/The National Geographic Society; **33** Courtesy of the Ledel Gallery, New York; **34** © 1984 Jerzy Kolacz. Courtesy of Reactor Art and Design, Toronto; **35** Courtesy of the Kunsthistorisches Museum, Vienna; **37** Courtesy of SEF/Art Resource; **38** Courtesy of Borromeo/Art Resource, India: Ajanta; **39** Courtesy of the Nelson-Alkins Museum of Art, Kansas City, Missouri (Nelson Fund); **40** Courtesy of SEF/Art Resource; **41** Courtesy of SCALA/Art Resource; **42** Courtesy of the National Gallery of Art, Washington, D.C. Gift of Edgar William and Bernice Chrysler Garbish; **43** Top and bottom: © 1983 John Launois/Black Star; **44** Top: © Nir Bareket; Bottom: Courtesy of Hancock Shaker Village Inc., Pitts. MA; **45** From the collection of Sam Moskowitz; **46** © Costa Manos/Art Resource; **47** Courtesy of the Saint Louis Art Museum; **48** © Cliché Bulloz, Paris; **50** Courtesy of SCALA/Art Resource; **51** Venezia, Accademia. Courtesy of SCALA/Art Resource; **52** Courtesy of the Bettmann Archive; **53** Courtesy of Shelburne Museum, Shelburne, V.T.; **54** Appeared in *The Satirical Etchings of James Gillray*, Dover Publications Inc, 1976. Courtesy of Draper Hill; **55** Left: Courtesy of the Bettmann Archive. Right: Courtesy o f the Bettmann Archive. **56** Top: © 1984 Blair Drawson. Bottom: Courtesy of Topkapi Sary Museum, Istanbul, Turkey; **57** Courtesy of Communica/Art Resource; **58-59** Prado, Madrid. Courtesy of SCALA/ART Resource; **60** From Plate 14, *The Book of Job*. Courtesy of the Library of Congress, Washington, D.C.; **61** From the collection of State Museum Kroller-Muller, Otterlo, The Netherlands; **62** Courtesy of the Bettmann Archive; **63** Left: © 1986 Bernice Eisenstein. Right: Courtesy of the Bettmann Archive; **64** Photograph by Nir Bareket. Courtesy of the Metropolitan Toronto Library and Mrs. Bernarda Shahn; **65** From *What Shall We Do Without Us?* by Kenneth Patchen. Reprinted by permission of Sierra Club Books, 1984. Courtesy of Miriam Patchen; **66** Top: Courtesy of the New York Public Library. Middle: Studtbibliothek, VLM. Bottom: Courtesy of the Galerie St. Etienne, New York; **67** Courtesy of SCALA/Art Resource; **68** Photograph by Nir Bareket. Courtesy of the Metropolitan Toronto Library; **69** Courtesy of the Bettmann Archive; **70-71** From the Louvre, Paris. Courtesy of SCALA, New York/Florence; **72** Courtesy of SCALA, New York/Florence; **75** Illustration by Jan Lenica first appeared in *Swiat* magazine, from *Graphic Designs: Visual Comparison* by Allan Fletcher, Colin Forbes, and Bob Gill. Studio Books, London © 1963 Jan Lenica. **76** Courtesy of Rafal Olbinski; **78** Courtesy of the Allen Frumkin Gallery, 50 West 57th Street, New York; **79** © 1983 Akira Yokoyama and Yusako Kamekura; **80** Courtesy of UPI/Bettmann Newsphotos; **83** © 1982 Fred Ward-Owen/Black Star; **84** Top: Courtesy of Sygma. Middle: © Rene Burr/Magnum. Bottom: Courtesy of Sygma; **85** Top: Courtesy of Life Picture Service. Bottom: Courtesy of UPI/Bettmann Newsphotos; **86** Top: Courtesy of the Bettmann Archive; Middle: © 1985 Jim Allen; **87** Top: *From Unforgettable Fire*. Reprinted by permission of Pantheon Books, New York, 1981. Bottom right: Courtesy of the Hiroshima-Nagasaki Publishing Committee; **88** Top: From *Unforgettable Fire*. Reprinted by permission of Pantheon Books, New York, 1981. Bottom: Courtesy of International News Photos/Bettmann Archive; **89** Courtesy of the Hiroshima-Nagasaki Publishing Committee; **90** Fritz Loro/*Life* magazine: © 1939 Time Inc.; **91** ©Gero/Black Star; **92** Fritz Loro/*Life* magazine: © 1945 Time Inc.; **93** Alfred Eisenstaedt/*Life* Magazine: © Time Inc.; **94** Courtesy of the Fuller Goldeen Gallery, San Francisco, California; **95** Courtesy of United Press Photo: © United Press Photo; **96** Courtesy of the Smithsonian Institution, Washington, D.C.; **97** Top and middle: © Jim Lerager; **98** Top: © by Brown Brothers, Sterling, PA; Bottom: Walter Sanders/*Life* Magazine. © 1960 Time Inc.; **99** From *When the Wind Blows*. Reprinted by permission of Hamish Hamilton, London. © 1982 Raymond Briggs; **100** Top: © Charles Michael Helmkin, The Shosin Society. Bottom: © 1983 Robert Giusti; **102** Courtesy of Black Star; **104** © Henri Cartier-Bresson/Magnum Photos, Inc.; **105** From a private collection; **107** Courtesy of Sygma; **109** Photograph by Larry Clark. © 1971 Larry Clark; **110** Bush Hollyhead/N.T.A. Studios, London; **111** © 1983 Danny Inwards; **112** Courtesy of the Peace Museum, Chicago, Illinois; **113** Top: Courtesy of Tri-Star Pictures. Bottom: © 1986 Greg Mathieson/Sygma; **114** Top: © 1964 Seymour Chwast. Bottom: © 1985 Anthony Suau/Black Star; **116** © Michael O'Brien/Archive Pictures Inc.; **117** © Michael O'Brien/Archive Pictures Inc.; **118** Courtesy of the Allen Frumkin Gallery, 50 West 57th Street, New York; **119** © 1983 Christopher Morris/Black Star; **121** Courtesy of AP/Wide World; **122** © 1985 Anita Kunz; **123** Top: © Geoffrey Moss/The Washington Post Writers Group. Middle: © 1983 Dennis Brack/Black Star; **125** © Geoffrey Moss/The Washington Post Writers Group; **127** © 1985 Rene Zamic, Courtesy of Reactor Art and Design, Toronto; **131** © 1985 Jon Lomberg. **138** Top: © A. Nogues/Sygma. Bottom: © P.J. Griffiths/Magnum; **139** © Epifanio/Outline Press; **140** © Erich Hartmann/Magnum; **141** © Guichard/Sygma; **142** Regis Bossu/Sygma; **143** Top: Photograph by E. Fornaciari. © Gamma: Paris. Bottom: © Ellen Shub; **144** Courtesy of the Bettmann Archive; **145** © Charles Harbutt/Archive Pictures. Inc.; **146** Photograph by Nir Baraket. Courtesy of the Metropolitan Toronto Library; **148** © UPI Photos; **151** © Bruce Davidson/Magnum; **153** Photograph by E. Fornaciari. Gamma: Paris. **154** Top and bottom: © Stuart Franklin/Sygma; **155** Top: © Chris Steele-Perkins/Magnum. Bottom: © Stuart Franklin/Sygma; **156** Photograph by K. Kurita. © Gamma: Paris; **157** © 1985 Francesc Torres; **159** Top and bottom: © 1985 John Roper; **160** top: Photograph by K. Kurita. © Gamma: Paris. Bottom: © 1985 Dave Mazierski; **161** © James Keyser/*Time* magazine; **162** © Rene Buvic/Magnum; **163** Photograph by Phillip J. Griffiths. © Magnum; **166** © Caye Huss. Courtesy of Save Life on Earth, Cambridge, MA.; **169** © 1981 UPI Photo; **171** Top: Courtesy of Betsy Bell/Target Seattle. Bottom: © 1983 The Soviet Peace Movement; **172** © Bernice Eisenstein; **173** Top: © Sygma. Bottom: Courtesy of Sygma. © 1986 Greg Mathieson; **174** © Zahm/Hurwitz Productions; **176** © 1982 Zahm/Hurwitz Productions; **177** © 1946 W. Eugene Smith. Courtesy of Black Star; **178** Top and bottom: © 1982 Zahm/Hurwitz Productions; **179** Right: Painting by an anonymous child from the Soviet Union; Left: © 1982 Zahm/Hurwitz Productions; **180** © Arthur Tess; **181** © 1986 Francesc Torres; **182** © 1982 Zahm/Hurwitz Productions; **183** © Peace Museum, Chicago, Illinois; **184** © 1983 Ellen Shub; **185** Courtesy of the Peace Museum, Chicago, Illinois; **186** © 1981 W. Buchanan; **187** Poster by Takashi Ishida, Toho Gakuen Junior College Thirteenth Graphic Design Course Graduation Work. 1981; **188** © 1980 Yoji Yamamoto; **189** Photograph by Herbert Josse. Courtesy of Universités de Paris; **190** © R. Gwynn/Liaison; **191** © 1963 Columbia Pictures Corporation; **192** © Bob Gruen/Star File; **194** Courtesy of the Peace Museum, Chicago, Illinois; **195** From the collection of Alan Parker and with his kind permission; **196-197** © Geoffrey Moss/The Washington Post Writers Group; **198** © Rene Burr/Magnum; **199** © 1982 Don Carr; **200** First appeared as winner of *Avant Garde* magazine's "No More War" peace poster contest, November, 1968. © 1968 James Grashow; **201** © the Bettman Archive; **202-03** Used by permission of Kim McConnel and the Holly Solomon Gallery, New York; **204** © Randy Taylor/Sygma; **205** © Barbara Pfeffer; **207** © 1984 Cathie Felstead; **208** Used by permission of Shigeo Fukuda; **209** © 1982 Carrion/Sygma; **210** Used by permission of Heather Cooper; **211** Used by permission of Timothy Botts; **213** © 1983 The Soviet Peace Movement; **215** © Judy Sloane/Gamma Liaison; **216** © 1986 Nir Bareket; **218** Photographs by De Keere. © 1985 Gamma-Liaison; **219** Courtesy of the Ledel Gallery, New York; **221** Used by permission of Tadami Yamada; **222** Courtesy of Jonas Kavelis and the Photo Art Society of Lithuania; Top: Courtesy of Carolyn Gowdy. Bottom: Courtesy of the Eskimo Arts Council; **225** Photograph by Photo Shunk-Kender. Published by Castelli Graphics, New York; **226** © 1985 Keith Haring; **227** © 1978 John Running/Black Star; **228** Courtesy of the Philadelphia Museum of Art: W.P. Wilstach Collection; **230** Courtesy of the Peace Museum, Chicago, Illinois; **231** The National Trust, Petworth House. Courtesy of Bridgeman Art Library/Art Resource; **232** Courtesy of UPI/Bettmann; **233** From the Collection of the Oakland Museum; **234** Photograph by Andrew Sacks. Courtesy of Art Resource; **235** Top and middle: © 1982 Ellen Shub; **236** © 1983 The Soviet Peace Movement; **238** Top: Courtesy of Mark Côté. Bottom: © Tannenbaum/Sygma; **239** © Michael D. Ruttan; **241** Courtesy of Beyond War, Palo Alto, CA.; **242** © Dini Chynick; **243** Photograph by Willem Diepraam. Courtesy of the International Physicians for the Prevention of Nuclear War, Boston, Ma.; **244** From *What Shall We Do Without Us?* Reprinted by permission of the Sierra Club Books, 1984. Courtesy of Miriam Patchen; **245** © 1960 Wemer Wolff/Black Star; **246** Top: © 1980 Edward Ruscha. Bottom: Courtesy of Jessie Oonark; **247** Stained glass window by Marc Chagall. Erected at the United Nations in memory of Dag Hammerskjold. U.N. photograph 167114/Lois Conner; **248** Bottom: © 1984 Rose Folsom; **249** Courtesy of the Bettman Archive. © The United Nations; **251** Photograph by Doug Workman, Futura Photographic. Used with his permission

Text

The producers of this book would like to thank the following authors, publishers and copyright holders for permission to reprint material used herein. Every reasonable effort has been made to ensure that the correct permission to reprint was obtained. Should there be any errors in copyright information, please inform the publisher of same, and a correction will be made in any subsequent editions. Numbers in boldface are page references.

18 Lewis Thomas from *The Cold and the Dark: The World After Nuclear War*. Reprinted by permission of W.W. Norton & Co., Inc., New York; Russell Schweickart from a Beyond War booklet. Reprinted by permission of Beyond War, Palo Alto, CA.; Louise B. Young from *The Blue Planet* 1983. Reprinted by permission of Little, Brown and Company, Boston; **20** Helen Caldicott from *Missle Envy*, 1984. Reprinted by permission of William Morrow and Company, New York; Lao Tzu from *The Tao Te Ching*, translated by D.C. Lau, 1963. Reprinted by permission of Penguin Books, Harmondsworth; **21** Pierre Teilhard de Chardin from *Building the Earth*, 1965. Reprinted by permission of Dimension Books, New York; **22** Marilyn Ferguson from *The Aquarian Conspiracy*. Reprinted by permission of Jeremy P. Tarcher, Inc., Los Angeles. © 1980 Marilyn Ferguson; Jonathan Schell from *The Abolition*. Reprinted by permission of Alfred A. Knopf, Inc., New York. © 1984 Jonathan Schell; **23** Carl Sagan from *To Preserve a World Graced by Life*, by Carl Sagan. Reprinted by permission of Carl Sagan. © 1984 Carl Sagan; Albert Einstein from a Beyond War booklet. Reprinted by permission of Beyond War, Palo Alto, CA.; **24** Desiderius Erasmus from *The Complaint of Peace*, 1974. Reprinted by permission of Open Court. La Salle; W.B. Yeats from "The Lake Isle of Innistree" in *Collected Poems*, 1956. Reprinted by permission of MacMillan, New York; **25** Dr. Lyall Watson from *Supernature*, 1973. Reprinted by permission of Hodder and Stoughton Ltd., London; Barbara Ward and René Dubos from *Only One Earth*, 1972. Reprinted by permission of W.W. Norton and Company, New York; **26** Margaret Mead from *World Enough*, 1975. Reprinted by permission of Little, Brown and Company, Boston; **27** John A. Livingston from *One Cosmic Instant*, 1973. Reprinted by permission of McClelland and Stewart. Toronto; **28** George Copway from *First People, First Voices*, 1984. Reprinted by permission of University of Toronto Press; Prince Modupe from *I Was a Savage*, 1958. Reprinted by permission of Museum Press. London; **29** Chief Lololomai from *Poems of War Resistance*, 1969. Reprinted by permission of Grossman Publishers, New York; Reprinted by permission of James Mooney; Reprinted by permission of Alice C. Fletcher; **30** Chief Seattle from *Indian Oratory: Famous Speeches by Noted Indian Chieftains*, edited by W.C. Vanderwerth, 1971. Reprinted by permission of the University of Oklahoma Press, Norman, Oklahoma; **31** Excerpt from *I Have Spoken*, compiled by Virginia Irving Armstrong. Reprinted by permission of Gage/The Swallow Press; Chief Luther Standing Bear, from *Touch the Earth*, edited by T.C. McLuhan, 1971.Reprinted by permission of New Press, Toronto; **32** From "Song in Favor of Peace" from *Extracts from Dr. Wyatt Gill's Papers* as quoted in *Legends of the South Seas* by Anthony Alpers, 1970. Reprinted by permission of Thomas Y. Crowell Co., New York; **34** Margaret Mead from *My Country Is the Whole World*. Reprinted by permission of Routledge and Kegan Paul, Inc.; Aldous Huxley from *What Are You Going To Do About It?* Reprinted by permission of Harper and Row Publishers, Inc., New York; **36** Peter Farb from *Man's Rise to Civilization as Shown by the Indians of North America from Primeval Times to the Coming of the Industrial State*, 1969. Reprinted by permission of Secker and Warburg, London; Arthur Koestler from *Janus: A Summing Up* 1978. Reprinted by permission of A.D. Peters & Co. Ltd., London; Henry Reed from *A Map of Verona and Other Poems*. Reprinted by permission of Jonathan Cape, Ltd.; **37** Sue Mansfield as quoted by Sam Keen in *Psychology Today* magazine. Reprinted by permission of *Psychology Today* magazine. © 1985 APA; John Newlove from *Canadian Poetry/The Modern Era*. Reprinted by permission of McClelland and Stewart, Ltd., Toronto. © 1977 John Newlove; **38** From *The I Ching; The Richard Wilhelm Translation* by Cary F. Baynes, 1950. Reprinted by permission of Bollingen Foundation, Inc., New York; From *The Dhammapada. The Gospel of Buddha*, edited by Paul Caros, 1915; **39** Motse from *The Wisdom of China and India* , as translated by Y.P. Mei and edited by Lin Yutang, 1942. Reprinted by permission of Modern Library; From *The Bhagavad Gita* as translated by Juan Mascara. Reprinted by permission of Penguin, Harmondsworth. © 1962 Juan Mascara; **40** From Psalm 85:8-10 as quoted in *War and Peace in the World's Religions*, by John Ferguson, 1977. Reprinted by permission of Sheldon Press; From the Book of Isaiah 2:4 as quoted in *War and Peace in the World's Religions* by John Ferguson. Reprinted by permission of Sheldon Press, 1977; Nahum N. Galtzer from *The Judaic Tradition*. Reprinted by permission of Breacon Press, Boston. © Nahum N. Glatzer; **41** From *The New English Bible*, 1961. Reprinted by permission of Oxford University Press; Lucretius from *War and Peace in the World's Religions* by John Ferguson, 1977. Reprinted by permission of Sheldon Press; **42** Robert Owen from *Robert Owen in the United States* by Oakley C. Johnson, 1970. Reprinted by permission of Humanities Press; **43** From the Oneida *Circular* (January 6, 1896). Reprinted by permission of The Oneida Community Historical Committee, Kenwood, Oneida, New York; **44** From *The Nauvoo Neighbour*. Reprinted by permission of Mormons of Utah Nauvoo, 1967; Martin Buber from *Paths in Utopia* 1967. Reprinted by permission of Beacon Press, Boston; **45** H.G. Wells from *The Quest for Utopia, Anthology*. Edited by Glenn Negley, 1952. Reprinted by permission of H. Schuman; Alice Constance Austin from *Seven American Utopias*. Reprinted by permission of The MIT Press. Cambridge; **46** Pericles from *Thucydides: History of the Peloponnesian Wars* translated by Rex Warner. Reprinted by permission of Penguin. Harmondsworth. ©1954 Rex Warner; From *The Human Rights Reader* 1979. Reprinted by permission of Temple University Press; **47** Denis Diderot from *Peace on Earth* 1980. Reprinted by permission of UNESCO; **48** Alexis de Tocqueville from *Democracy in America*, 1956. Reprinted by permission of New American Library; Walt Whitman from *Leaves of Grass* 1956. Reprinted by permission of Penguin Books, Harmondsworth; **49** Bertrand Russell from *The Spokesman*, 1972. Reprinted by permission of The Partisan Press. © The Partisan Press; **50** Emeric Crucé from *The Pacifist Conscience* by Peter Meyer, 1967. Reprinted by permission of Holt Rinehart and Winston, Inc.; **51** Hugo Grotius from *The Rights of War and Peace* 1901. Reprinted by permission of Mr. Walter Dunne, Publisher; **52** From a letter by William Penn contained in *Annals of Pennsylvania from the Discovery of the Delaware 1609 - 1682* Published by Hazard and Mitchell. 1850; **53** Johann Gottfried von Herder from *Briefe zur Befarderundan der Humanitat.* William Blake from *Blake: Complete Writings*. Reprinted by permission of Oxford University Press; Claude Henri de Saint-Simon from "A Golden Age of Posterity" from *Henri Compte de Saint Simon Selected Writings*, 1952. Reprinted by permission of Oxford University Press; **54** Victor Hugo from *The Pacifist Conscience* edited by Peter Meyer, 1967. Reprinted by permission of Holt Rinehart and Winston. Inc.; **55** From *The German Treaty*, 1920. Reprinted by permission of Oxford University Press, London; **56** Lester B. Pearson from his Nobel Peace Prize Acceptance Speech. Reprinted by permission of the Nobel Foundation. Stockholm; Sigmund Freud from *Why War*, 1933. Reprinted by permission of the International Institute of Intellectual Cooperation; **57** Christine de Pizan from *Lament on the Evils of the Civil War*, 1984. Reprinted by permission of Garland Publishing Inc.; **58** Desiderius Erasmus from *The Complaint of Peace*. Published by Headley Brothers. Publishers, Limited. London, 1917; Ralph Waldo Emerson from "Essay on War" in *Aesthetic Papers*. © 1849 Elizabeth Peabody; W.E. Channing from "Remarks on the Character and Writings of Fenelon," in *Works* (London, 1884); **60** From *The Peace Testimony: The Soul of Quakerism* (London: The All Friends Conference, August, 1920) in *The Quakers: Their Story and Message*, 1982. Reprinted by permission of A. Neave Brayshaw/The Ebor Press; **61** J. Krishnamurti from the *First and Last Freedom: A Quest Book*. Reprinted by

Shurek from *My Shalom, My Peace*, published by McGraw-Hill Books, 1975. Reprinted by permission of Sabra Books, Tel Aviv; Joan G., Cynthia K., and Cynthia G., from *Please Save My World: Children Speak Out Against Nuclear War*, edited by Bill Adler. Reprinted by permission of Arbor House, New York. © 1984 Bill Adler; **179** Tanya Birenbaum as quoted in "Out of the Mouths of Babes," by Marcia Yudkin, in *Village Voice* (June 15, 1982). Reprinted by permission of *Village Voice*; From a composition. "The World of the Twenty-First Century." Reprinted by permission by Vetchininov, Form IV "B" School 397, Leningrad (Children Aged 10); **180** Dr. Benjamin Spock from "Killers in Your Toybox." Reprinted by permission of New England War Resisters League, Box 1093, Norwich, CT. 06360; Shel Silverstein from "Hug O'War." Reprinted by permission of Shel Silverstein; From "War Toys." Reprinted by the permission of the Peace Pledge Union, London; **182** Ariel Dorfman from "Evil Otto and Other Nuclear Disasters" from *Village Voice* (June 15, 1982). Reprinted by permission of Ariel Dorfman and *Village Voice*; **183** Terry Orlick from *The Cooperative Sports and Games Book*. Reprinted by permission of Pantheon Books. © 1982 Terry Orlick; **184** William. E. Colby from "No. A Nuclear Freeze is Essential to Western Security" in *The Washington Post* (April 19, 1983). Reprinted by permission of *The Washington Post*; From "Call to Halt the Nuclear Arms Race." Reprinted by Nuclear Weapons Freeze Campaign, St. Louis, MO.; **185** George H. Crowell from *The Freeze Strategy*, 1984. Reprinted by permission of George H. Crowell; Excerpt from "The Nuclear Freeze." Reprinted by permission of Project Ploughshares; Excerpt reprinted by permission of The Norwich Peace Center, Norwich, CT.; **186** Dorothy Livesay from "A Poem for Now," published in *Women's Peace Write*. Reprinted by permission of Dorothy Livesay/Women's Peace Write, c/o Women & Words, 210-640 West Broadway, Vancouver, B.C. V5Z 1GR; Margaret Laurence from "My Final Hour" in *Canadian Literature* (Spring, 1984). Reprinted by permission of Margaret Laurence; Judith Neissen from "Giving Peace a Chance" in *Chicago* magazine (June 1983). Reprinted by permission of *Chicago* Magazine. © 1983 WEMT, Inc.; Hunter Drohojowska from "Festival of Anti-Nuke Artists" in *The Los Angeles Herald Examiner* (July 10, 1985). Reprinted by permission of *The Los Angeles Herald Examiner*; **188** Kate Lushington from "Griefkit," published in *Women's Peace Write*. Reprinted by permission of Kate Lushington/Women's Peace Write, c/o Women & Words, 210-640 West Broadway, Vancouver, B.C. V5Z 1GR; Greta Hofman Nemiroff from *Women's Peace Write*. Reprinted by permission of Greta Hofmann Nemiroff/Women's Peace Write, c/o Women & Words, 210-640 West Broadway, Vancouver, B.C. V5Z 1GR; **189** Irene Mock from "Neopolitan," published in *Women's Peace Write*. Reprinted by permission of Irene Mock/Women's Peace Write, c/o Women & Words, 210-640 West Broadway, Vancouver, B.C. V5Z 1GR; **190** Carrie Rickey from "Do You Think the End of The World Will Come at Night or at Dawn?" in *Village Voice* (June 15, 1982). Reprinted by permission of *Village Voice*; **191** Courtesy of Peter Ustinov; Joanne Woodward as quoted by Katherine Banett and Lesley Hazalton from *Ladies Home Journal* (September, 1984). Reprinted by permission of Katherine Banett/*Ladies Home Journal*. © 1984 Meredith Publications, Inc. **192** From "The Peace Anthem," in *Newsweek* (December 1, 1969). Reprinted by permission of *Newsweek*; Rado & Ragni from "The Age of Aquarius in *Hair*, 1966. Reprinted by permission of James Rado and Jerome Ragni and United Artists Music Corp. Inc.; From a Soviet Children's Peace Song, "May There Always Be Sunshine!" from *Singalong Songs for Peacemongers*, compiled by Project Ploughshares. Reprinted by permission of Phyllis Sanders and W.I.L. © 1984 by CRS, Inc., Delaware, O., USA; John Lennon from "Imagine" (1971). Reprinted by permission of Northern Songs Limited; **193** Stevie Wonder from "I Am Singing," (1976). Reprinted by permission of Jobete Music Co., Inc. and Black Bull Inc.; Gordon Sumner ("Sting") from "Russians" from *The Dream of the Blue Turtles*. Reprinted by permission of A&M Records. © 1985 Magnetic Publishing, Inc.; Pete Seeger from "Andorra" from *Singalong Songs for Peacemongers*, compiled by Project Ploughshares; Ed McCurdy from "Last Night I Had the Strangest Dream." Reprinted by permission of Almanac Music, Inc. © 1950, 1951, and 1955 Almanac Music, Inc.; **194** From a pamphlet distributed by the Professionals's Coalition for Nuclear Arms Control, Washington, D.C. Reprinted with their permission; Peter Matson and Bob Bender from an advertisement in *Publishers Weekly*. Reprinted by permission of the Writers Alliance for Nuclear Disarmament, New York; Anne Simon from "The Lawyers' Committee on Nuclear Policy Newsletter." Reprinted by permission of The Lawyers' Committee on Nuclear Policy Inc., New York; **195** John Robertson from "Walk now or else pay later" in the *Winnepeg Free Press* (June 8, 1982). Reprinted by permission of John Robertson; **196** From a pamphlet distributed by The Union of Concerned Scientists, 26 Church Street, Cambridge, M.A. 02238. Reprinted with their permission; From a pamphlet distributed by Physicians for Social Responsibility, Toronto. Reprinted with their permission; From *American Women Confront the Arms Race: A Statement Submitted to Delegates Attending the Second United Nations Special Session on Disarmament, June 7, 1982*. Reprinted by permission of The American Association of University Women, Washington, D.C.; **197** Gary Chapman from a pamphlet distributed by the Computer Professionals for Social Responsibility, Inc., Palo Alto, CA. Reprinted by permission of Gary Chapman; **198** From a statement from conference participants of the June 18, 1983, Annual Meeting at Murikka, Finland; From "Military Recruiting in the High Schools: Creating a Dialogue" from *Educators for Social Responsibility Newsletter*. Cambridge, MA. Reprinted by permission of E.S.R.; Paula Baron from *Forum* (Winter, 1985). Reprinted from *Educators for Social Responsibility Newsletter*, Cambridge, MA. Reprinted by permission of E.S.R.; From "Statement of Purpose" in *News* (Fall, 1985) Reprinted by permission of Architects, Designers, and Planners for Social Responsibility; **199** From "Social Scientists Can Help Prevent Nuclear War." Reprinted by permission of The World Constitution and Parliament Association, USA. 1614 19th St., N.W. Washington, D.C. 20009; From "Psychologists for Social Responsibility" newsletter. (Summer, 1982). Reprinted by permission of Psychologists for Social Responsibility, Suite 216, 1841 Columbia Road, N.W., Washington, D.C. 20009; **200** Captain Sir Basil Liddell Hart from *Strategy*. Reprinted by permission of Praeger Publishers, New York; General Omar Bradley from an address delivered at the "Report From the World" meeting on January 10, 1947, jointly sponsored by *Time* magazine and the Cleveland Council on World Affairs. Reprinted by permission of *The Bulletin of the Atomic Scientists*, a magazine of science and world affairs. © 1947 Educational Foundation for Nuclear Science, Chicago, Ill.; **201** Dwight D. Eisenhower from "Dwight Eisenhower Was Prophetic in his Military-Industrial Complex Warning," by Norman Cousins (*Los Angeles Times*) in *The Toronto Star* (January 16, 1986); From a statement by Retired NATO Generals for Peace and Disarmament in *Peace* magazine (September, 1985); **202** General Douglas MacArthur and Lord Louis Mountbatten, from *The Role of the Military in the Nuclear Age* (Booklet 6, Waging Peace Series) by Admiral Gene R. La Rocque, 1985. Reprinted by permission of Nuclear Age Peace Foundation, Santa Barbara, C.A.; General David Jones from the article "Is Arms Control Obsolete?" in *Harper's* (July, 1985). Reprinted by permission of *Harper's*; **203** Admiral Gene R. La Rocque from *The Role of the Military in the Nuclear Age* (Booklet 6, Waging Peace Series), 1985. Reprinted by permission of the Nuclear Age Peace Foundation, Santa Barbara, CA; **204** Reprinted by permission of Common Security; **205** Seymour Melman from the proceedings of a Project Ploughshares workshop, 1984. Reprinted by permission of Project Ploughshares, Waterloo, Ontario; From "Balancing the Budget on the Backs of Women." Reprinted by permission of Women's International League for Peace and Freedom/Council for a Livable World; **206** Ruth Leger Sivard from *World Military and Social Expenditures, 1985*. World Priorities. Reprinted by permission of Ruth Leger Sivard; **207** Excerpt reprinted by permission of Peace Pledge Union; From *Win* magazine. Reprinted by permission of the Council on Economic Priorities, 84 Fifth Avenue, New York, NY 10011; **208** From a pamphlet published by the War Resisters League, 339 Lafayette St., New York, NY 10012. Reprinted with their permission; From "101 Ideas for Preventing the Last Epidemic," 1982. Reprinted by permission of The Nuclear War Study Group, Harvard Medical School; **209** Excerpt reprinted by permission of the Center for Defense Information, Washington, D.C.; **210** Excerpts from "Peace Links Peace Kit." Reprinted by permission of Peace Links, 747 8th Street, S.E. Washington, D.C. 20003. **211** From *A Handbook for Women on Nuclear Mentality*. Reprinted by permission of Acorn Press, Chelsea, VT.; **212** From "An Open Letter to the Canadian Government" in *The Globe and Mail*. Reprinted by permission of Project Ploughshares, Ottawa; From "A Statement: Emergency Committee of Atomic Scientists," in *Bulletin of Atomic Scientists*, 1947. Reprinted by permission of Emergency Committee of Atomic Scientists, Chicago, IL; From *Bulletin of Atomic Scientists*, 1957. Reprinted by permission of Emergency Committee of Atomic Scientists, Chicago, IL; **213** From *Listen Real Loud*, 1985. Reprinted by permission of Fraven für Frieden, West Germany; From "Appeal by American Scientists to Ban Space Weapons," Reprinted by permission of the Union of Concerned Scientists, Cambridge, MA; **214** Adolfo Perez Esquivel in *National Network for Direct Action*, Spring, 1985. Reprinted by permission of The National Network for Direct Action For Disarmament, Box 271, New York, NY. 10960; Robert Cooney from *The Power of the People: Active Nonviolence in the United States*. Reprinted by permission of Peace Press, Culver City, CA. © 1977 Robert Cooney; Martin Luther King, Jr., from *Essay Series #1*. Reprinted by permission of the A.J. Muste Memorial Institute; **215** Robert Martinson from "A City Chooses Peace..." in *The Nation* (February 10, 1962). Reprinted by permission of *The Nation*. © 1961 Robert Martinson; Amy Swerdlow from *Women Strike for Peace Journal 1961-1979*. Reprinted by permission of Women Strike for Peace; **216** From an Amnesty International pamphlet. Reprinted by permission of Amnesty International USA, 322 Eighth Ave., New York, NY 10019; Bishop Desmond Tutu from a speech delivered at Queen's Park, Toronto, 1986; **217** From "Who Feeds Whom?" Reprinted by permission of Development and Peace, 3028 Danforth Ave. Toronto, Ont. M4C 1N2; From "Inside Oxfam: the 1985 Annual Report." Reprinted by permission of Oxfam-Canada, 251 Laurier Avenue West, Suite #301, Ottawa, Ont. K1P 5J6; From "United Nations Declaration of Human Rights" in *Human Rights:*

Meaning and History by Michael Palumbo, 1982. Reprinted by permission of Robert E. Krieger Publishing Co., Malabar, Florida; **218** Reprinted by permission of Janis Alton; Andrei Sakharov, from his Nobel Peace Prize lecture in *Champions of Peace*, 1976. Reprinted by permission of Elsevier Science Publishers, Amsterdam and Les Prix Nobel 1975. Reprinted by permission of Margaret Atwood; **219** From "The What and Where of CARE." Reprinted by permission of CARE Canada, 1312 Bank Street, Ottawa, Ont. K1S 5H7; Song by Bob Marley entitled *War* (1968). Lyrics reprinted by permission of Island Records, Inc.; **220-2** From "Greenpeace: Capsule History." Reprinted by permission of Greenpeace, 427 Bloor Street West, Toronto, Ont. M5S 1X7; **221** David Israelson from the article, "Adding Toxic Rain To The Chemical Soup," in *Toronto Star* (May 3, 1986). Reprinted by permission of David Israelson; **222** From "Greenpeace: Declaration of Interdependence." Reprinted by permission of Greenpeace International; **223** Deborah Shapley from *Bulletin of Atomic Scientists*; Reprinted by permission of Judy Chicago; **224** From *The GAIA Atlas of Planet Management*, 1984. Norman Myers, general editor. Reprinted by permission of Doubleday and Company, New York; Fritjof Capra and Charlene Spretnak from *Green Politics*. Reprinted by permission of E.P. Dutton, Inc., New York. © 1984 Fritjof Capra and Charlene Spretnak; From "Emergency Response International Network—Bulletin #18," 1982. Reprinted by permission of Emergency Response International Network; Poem by Boris Pasternak, "In the Interlude." from *Poems 1945-1960*, translated by Henry Kramer, 1962. Reprinted by permission of Oxford University Press; **226** Marilyn Ferguson from *The Aquarian Conspiracy*. Reprinted by permission of Jeremy P. Tarcher, Inc. © 1980 by Marilyn Ferguson; Elise Boulding from *The Image of the Future* by Fred Polak, 1983. Reprinted by permission of Elsevier Scientific Publishing Co., New York; Vera Stanley Alder from *The Fifth Dimension*, 1970. Reprinted by permission of Rider and Co., London; **227** Shakti Gawain from *Creative Visualization*, 1978. Reprinted by permission of Whatever Publishing; Thomas Merton from *New Seeds of Contemplation*, 1961. Reprinted by permission of New Directions Publishing Corp., New York, 1961; **228** Willis W. Harman from "The President's Letter," 1985. Reprinted by permission of the Institute of Noetic Sciences, 475 Gate Fire Road, Suite 300, Sausalito, CA. 94965; Sri Aurobindo from *Sri Aurobindo or the Adventure of Consciousness* by Satprem. © 1968 Sri Aurobindo Ashram, Pondicherry, India; **229** Krishnamurti from *The Second Penguin Krishnamurti Reader*, 1984. Reprinted by permission of Penguin books, New York; Poem by Alan Bold, "Cause and Effect," from *Penguin Book of Socialist Verse*, 1970. Reprinted permission of Penguin Books, New York; Albert Einstein, Robert Lifton, Wilder Penfield, Goethe, and Norman Cousins, from "Using Your Brain to Save the Planet," a pamphlet compiled by Tana Dineen and Eli Bay; Tana Dineen from "A Vision of Planetary Mental Health," 1984. Draft of a paper prepared for discussion with the Primary Prevention Committee of CMHA; **230** Pope John Paul II in a message for the celebration of Peace Day, January 1, 1983; Church Leaders in Canada, from "A Letter on Disarmament," February 1, 1983; From "Statement of Purpose." Reprinted by the permission of the Fellowship of Reconciliation, Nyack, NY; **231** Daniel Berrigan from "A Modest Proposal to the Court—An Excerpt from Daniel Berrigan January 31, 1977, Alexandria Va." in *Catholic New Times*; Hossain Danesh from *The Violence-Free Society: A Gift For Our Children*. © 1970 by Association for Baha'i Studies (formerly the Canadian Association for Studies on the Baha'i Faith); **232** His Holiness Tenzin Gyatso from *Kindness Clarity and Insight*. Reprinted by permission of Snow Lion Publications, Box 6483, Ithaca, N.Y. 14851; Poem courtesy of Project Ploughshares; Stephen Booth from "Rainbow: Breaking the Golden Calf." Reprinted by permission of the Reconstructionist Rabbinical College; **233** From "World Peacemakers: Our Call and Program." Reprinted by permission of World Peacemakers, Washington, D.C.; From "An Agenda on Militarism and Development," January 27, 1979. Reprinted by permission of the Mennonite Central Committee, Akron, PA.; Most Rev. Raymond Hunthausen from *Peace Education Supplement No. 4*. Reprinted by permission of The Catholic Peace Fellowship, New York; **234** From a flyer calling for an assembly for the United Nations Special Session on Disarmament, June 8, 9, 10 1982. Reprinted by permission of Reverence for Life; John Woolman from *The Peace Testimony of the Society of Friends* by Howard H. Brinton. Reprinted by permission of American Friends Service Committee; "The Prayer of St. Francis," from "Peace Worship Resource Kit," 1983. Reprinted by permission of Project Ploughshares; **235** Eric Pace from the article "Methodist bishops assail Nuclear Arms," in *The News and Observer*. Raleigh, N.C., April 27 1986; Excerpt by Thomas Merton, from *New Seeds of Contemplation*, 1981. Reprinted by permission of New Directions Publishing Corp., New York; **236-37** From an advertisement for *Peace and World Order Studies: A Curriculum Guide*. Reprinted by permission of World Policy Institute, New York; **237** Gene Thompson from an E.S.R. newsletter. Reprinted by permission of Educators for Social Responsibility, Cambridge, MA; **238** Frank K. Kelly, from "Needed: A Nuclear Age Peace Corps—An Alternative to Annihilation". (Booklet 5, Waging Peace Series), 1985. Reprinted by permission of the Nuclear Age Peace Foundation; Excerpt from a pamphlet published by the International Peace Academy. Reprinted by permission of the International Peace Academy, 777 U.N. Plaza, New York, NY, 10017; **239** Penny Sanger from "The Group of '78" in *Disarmament* magazine (1985); Maria Montessori from *Education and Peace*. Reprinted by permission of Contemporary Books, Chicago, IL.; **240** From an advertisement that appeared in the United Nations Association of Canada Bulletin. Reprinted by permission of the United Nations Association of Canada, 63 Sparks Street, Suite #808, Ottawa, Ont. K1P 5A6; **240** Henry J. Cadbury, John Boyd Orr, Lester B. Pearson, and Andrei Sakharov, Reprinted by permission of Paddington Press © 1976, London; **241** Bishop Desmond Tutu from his Nobel Peace Prize lecture delivered in Oslo, Norway. Reprinted by permission of the author and the Nobel Foundation, Stockholm; Bernard Lown, M.D., from his Nobel Peace Prize lecture delivered in Oslo, Norway, December 11, 1985. Reprinted by permission of the author and the Nobel Foundation, Stockholm; **242** Janet Aileen Mercer from "Steps Than Can Change Our Thinking in the Nuclear Age." Reprinted by permission of the Nuclear Age Peace Foundation, Santa Barbara, CA; Major General (Ret) Indar Jit Rikhye, from "Coping With Conflict." Reprinted by permission of the International Peace Academy; From WPA newsletter. Reprinted by permission of the World Peace Association; **243** From a Beyond War Booklet. Reprinted by permission of Beyond War, Palo Alto, CA; Excerpt by George F. Kennan (1981) and Alva Myrdal (1980), reprinted by permission of Albert Einstein Peace Prize Foundation, Chicago; Raul Alfonsin and Olaf Palme, from speeches at the 1985 Beyond War Award presentation, December 14, 1985, for the Five Continent Peace Initiative. Courtesy of Beyond War, Palo Alto, CA; From "Criteria and Procedures for the Edwin T. Dahlberg Peace Award." Statement courtesy of the Edwin T. Dahlberg Peace Award, **244** George Ignatieff from symposium proceedings of the United Nations World Federalists of Canada. Reprinted by permission of George Ignatieff; From the Charter of the United Nations. Reprinted by permission of the Nobel Foundation, Stockholm; **245** Excerpt by Willy Brandt. Reprinted by permission of the Albert Einstein Peace Prize Foundation; Nuremberg Tribunal from *Bulletin of Atomic Scientists*, 1945. Reprinted by permission of Bulletin of Atomic Scientists, 1945; **246** Linus Pauling from *No More War!* Reprinted by permission of Dodd, Mead and Co., Inc., New York; **247** UNESCO Constitution. Reprinted by permission of UNESCO, New York; **248** Courtesy of The Five Continent Peace Initiative; **249** Robert C. Johansen from "World Policy Paper #8: Toward a Dependable Peace." Reprinted by permission of the World Policy Institute, New York; **252** Isaac Bashevis Singer from *Why Noah Chose the Dove*. Reprinted with the permission of Farrar, Straus and Giroux, New York.